AF594631

INTERNET_ART

Omar Kholeif

INTERNET

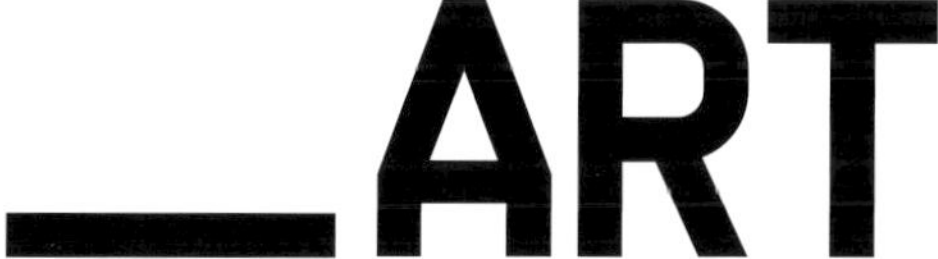

From the Birth of the Web to the Rise of NFTs

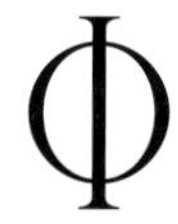

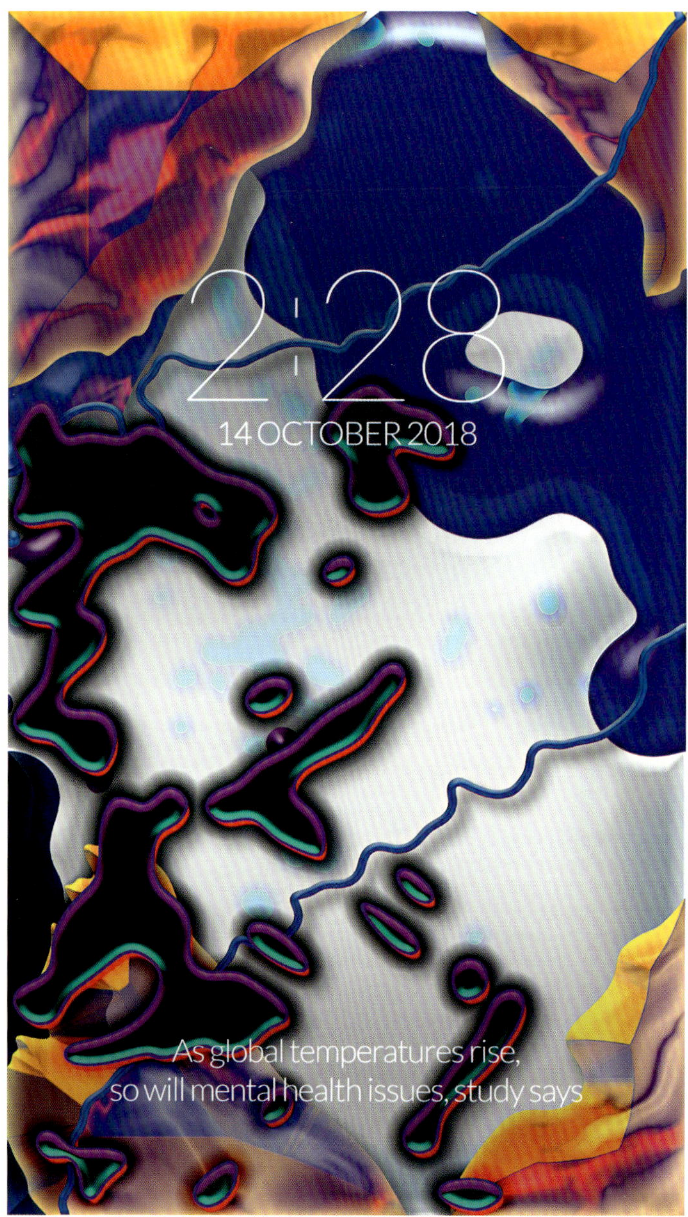

Tabor Robak, *Drinking Bird Universe*, 2018
__Digital video with live data, 30 min. (looped),
72 3/8 × 41 7/16 × 2 3/8 in. (183.9 × 105.2 × 6.1 cm)

— For the misfits, departed and booming, never lost or forgotten.
— For my three younger siblings, Yousef, Ali, and Shereif.
— For my unwavering partner, Frank Gallacher.
— For our son B. K. M., you are exceptional in ways that are impossible to put into words.
— For Mike, whose hypnosis sessions made the words come back to me.
— For the beloved Zoomers, my godchildren: Ariel, Ayk, and Anouk—ruffle a feather or two. You might just change the world.
— To the readers who continue to read, thank you for picking this up. It is because of you that I still dare to dream.

___ Prelude:
Time Is Just a Memory

Hello, World! The Future Is Now.

Internet_Art: From the Birth of the Web to the Rise of NFTs maps out a shift in history—the flashing decades when a pioneering constellation of artists and curators, in tandem with programmers, engineers, and investors, altered contemporary culture forever.

Traversing a time span from 1989 to the present, it chronicles shifts in generations—from the booming babies that we have come to know as Gen X (born 1965–80), to the social consciousness of the millennials, also known as Gen Y (born 1981–96), the hypersociality of the Zoomers—Gen Z (born 1997–2012), and the speculative futurism that is being attributed to Generation Alpha (Gen A, born post-2012).

As with many nascent and underrepresented histories, it felt imperative to grapple with this freewheeling subject through lived experience. This is the story of how a contemporary culture was formed through the lens of the author, interspersed with firsthand accounts from a motley crew of artists, curators, and techies—collectively highlighting a dissonant world in constant motion.

Every story gleaned from memory is susceptible to certain slippages, or a looseness that mirrors life itself—remembering things as they were "felt," as this book argues, is part of the very nature of the hyperlinked mind. Some of the artists in *Internet_Art* broke ground prior to 1989 but took precedence after this pivotal year; others are coming into view only at the time of writing, and their influence will continue to shape how we look at and experience art for generations. The issues, context, and debates herein stretch across expanses of time—inching forward as much as they pulse backward. These are markers that offer us a way to think about how internet-related technologies will carry us forth in lifetimes to come.

I chose this juncture in history not only because I felt I could confidently narrate this time span, but also because it marks an entry into a new age, sometimes referred to as the digital revolution—from the birth of the World Wide Web to the augmented and virtual metaverse. Traversing generations of artists and their experiences, this story, like the internet itself, although intended to be chronological, may leap back and forth, in the same way as digital consciousness itself. It reflects what Colombian author Gabriel García Márquez implied to be the "fluidity of time" in 1967,[1] which was, incidentally, the same year that the concept of the internet was born.

This is a book for the present, as much as it is of and for the future.

_ Scroll forward!

What's in a Name?

The genres of art taught to me in the British curriculum of my English-language junior school—twentieth-century painting, sculpture, literature, architecture, cinema, and music—seem to have more to do with material and technique than the nature of the artwork itself.

Many people have heard of art practices, such as Minimalism, which today may be more recognizable as a lifestyle organization approach that can be watched in a reality TV series on Netflix, or kinetic art, which now may conjure thoughts of wind turbines that transform wind energy into electricity. Likewise, forms of artistic imagemaking, from portraiture to landscape and beyond, can be produced in limitless ways because of networked technologies: Photoshop, social-media apps, or with a whole range of purchasable high-speed and/or wide-angle lens cameras.

The seismic promise that was enabled by the internet—the network of all networks—crisscrosses the globe, fashioning a way of making art that straddles the two-dimensional web browser, as well as the augmented screen, and beyond. The internet has enabled a more porous attitude toward definition in all its forms, making the concept of change the only constant. In the late 1990s, when "connected art" gained relevance in art museums, internet art was often defined as art that was "made on" and "for the internet." But the internet is more than a space that we visit. It is formed of a multiplicity of sites that we carry in our pockets to augment everyday activities and to self-archive our legacies; it is a means to work and play, from meal planning to producing sounds that aid in sleeping.

The internet is the mass medium of our time—a time that began before I was born but has proliferated globally and mutated in form during my lifetime. Writing this book, it felt urgent to present an expansive and personal field guide of the internet's relationship to art as experienced through the eyes of an early breed of millennial. Broadly speaking, Internet Art, or internet art, is defined as a subset of postwar and contemporary art that is inclusive of specific antecedents in its history, including, but not limited to, computer art, browser art, and telematic art, as well as certain seemingly analogous fields, such as new media art or media art, among others. Conversely, what I have sought to elucidate are the possibilities of a democratic sphere of art that is neither a singular genre, style, or movement, nor confined to members of a certain academic art school or generational club. Instead, here, art is underscored (_) by the internet and its attendant aftereffects. *Internet_Art* proposes a distinct method of looking at artists' work; it considers the detailed processes that have helped multiple publics forge new ways of seeing how creativity is sparked, how artistry has developed, and how audience experiences have felt across the changing arena of our freewheeling present as well as for our inevitable future.

Beginnings: From Here to There to Everywhere

A Kind of Overture

"There's just no time to die," sings Billie Eilish in the hookiest part of her contribution to the arsenal of James Bond theme songs. Her voice booms out of my television, my phone, the wireless speaker on my desk, my two laptops: a mantra, a swirling cacophony, consuming the entire space where I live and breathe. My hands tremble as my large thumbs try and untether Billie from all of my devices. Bluetooth is switched off, but her pop-alto is still omnipresent. I am ridden with a sense of anxiety. I am writing a book about technology, but I cannot maintain control of my own devices. Thoughts of fraudulence circle. I measure my heartbeat on an application using my smartphone: abnormal. I am soothed by this datum. Diagnosis of one's malfunctions in the age of the internet means that treatment is possible. In today's today, everything can be cured at warp speed with a pill, an inoculation, another pill, interspersed with a virtual meditation session or tele-videoed art therapy or streaming a how-to yoga session from YouTube. Breathe, pause, and out. The internet is full of autodidacts who write books about the so-called internet, I tell myself, still quivering. WebMD tells me to understand that you, me, and everyone we know has generalized anxiety disorder (GAD) and that every problem will meet its end. Now try again. Begin.

The book that you hold in your hands is intended for any sentient being who has an interest in the internet and its potential effects on art and culture over the thirty-plus years since the concept of the World Wide Web (WWW)—a mass-connective tool that connects us to the internet—first emerged. With it, I seek to untangle divergent pathways for and of the internet. It has indubitably come to dominate our lives, not only in practical terms but specifically in relation to its aesthetic systems and possibilities. It is true that humans engineered and designed the computer and connected them through something we know as the internet. But what does it mean to consider how artists have used this thing, this space, these tools to create art? Does it offer up new possibilities, or does it withhold certain opportunities and experiences from ever taking place again?

It can seem impossible to imagine how life and its attendant pleasures existed outside the universe of hyperlinked web pages and endless scrolling. Do you feel like your existence has become little more than a series of chat boxes waiting for a robot to reply to your inquiry? Is every screen before you sullied by the pressure of interminable open tabs and windows, accumulating to-do lists of other to-do lists, and web applications that help you manage your to-do lists? The muted Zoom call: it's all just noise. A silent but deafening din. But I can hear myself breathe in and out as I acknowledge the need to heal from technology before reengaging with technology.

The internet is as much a thing as it is a space. Cables and wires are funneled underground and underwater, connected to data points and centers across the globe—in the rural countryside and deserts, to name but a couple of examples—where large pieces of hardware consume all forms of energy, making an almighty series of sonic blurts, burps, and beeps. The Zoom conversation has moved to the subject of race, to white privilege, or is it white guilt? Your organization must make a statement. This is your chance to stop the old guard from banging on about inclusivity and to be really heard. It is time to make some impact. This is because in the digital era, or what is commonly referred to as the postdigital age, everyone needs to make an impact in order to be seen, if even for a split second. To do so, amidst the sea of endless on-demand content, is a feat that makes those who succeed the greatest of commodities. But has what Andy Warhol once predicted would be our fifteen minutes of fame now been diluted to fifteen seconds?

Speaking of commodities, it is time for my break. I am perusing color swatches for paint on Farrow & Ball's website for an aspirational new kitchen, then I intend to attend to my psoriasis. Flaking skin is an apt metaphor for a life fragmented through constant digital interruption and access, at least for the more than four billion people who have the means to make it online. Time to make dinner for my godchildren. Their mother won't allow frozen foods. Deliveroo. More than five bucks for a cucumber seems worth it in pandemic times—a sphere where logic collapses in favor of the ease of the instantaneous potential offered by the digital. Netflix for children is on. They won't go for *Power Rangers*, my favorite kids' TV show, so I let them choose. Choice is an operative word for Gen Z. I need to return to my mood board of colors so that I can place an order for swatches before the clock hits whatever o'clock. The day is bookended by delivery windows.

In actuality, I cannot tell you what time it is, although there are clocks everywhere, embedded into the smart home that I temporarily occupy. I do not believe in the order of time and space, only that which takes place on the computer screen. I am informed that my screen time is "up" again. My psychologist warned me of this. It is sliding to 60 percent above last week's average. Eleven hours on a screen, almost half of my life on a laptop, tablet, or smartphone. Narrative programming, such as broadcast television or movies, does not count: they are for my meditation. I have acquired an analog projector to ensure that those hours cannot be tracked or logged. Is all this bad? Or good? And what of these virtual corridors and amphitheaters: should we take a moment to discuss their aesthetics? Should a screen, an internet connection, or a browser be used for art? Or are they purely functional nonspaces that we have to simply live with to

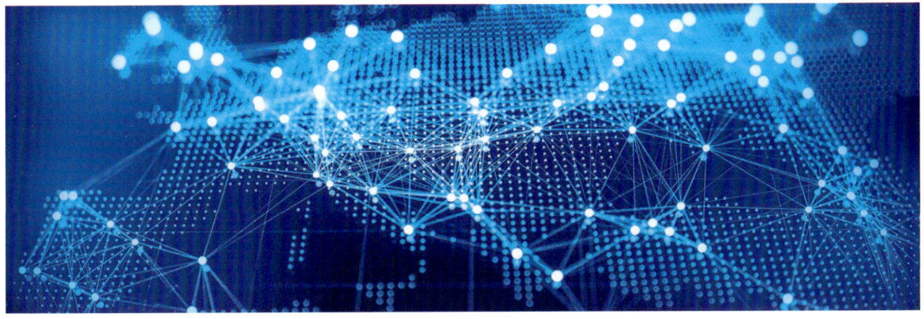

The world connected

get by? Perhaps we have a choice. What would it mean to argue for autonomy from them in 2022 and onward?

As a historian by training, I have never approached time through a romantic lens. I am neither a digital utopian nor do I subscribe to the dystopian rhetoric proffered by certain critics who fear that innovations, such as artificially intelligent technologies, could take over our lives. I candidly speak from the position of being an early breed of millennial. The novelist Lev Grossman, a Gen X-er, once declared that his generation would be the last to remember what the world was like before the internet.

It is peculiar perhaps, then, that as a so-called millennial, I do vividly recall a pre-internet world, filled with the sonic and visual hum of radio and television. I remember the day that I encountered my first personal computer (PC). My father lugged an unboxed apparatus into the narrow doorway of our small prefab house, which was set amidst the sprawling Saudi Arabian desert. It was the mid-1990s. Although money did not regularly appear in the family coffers, as children we were encouraged to aspire to a middle-class lifestyle. This meant keeping up with the Joneses. It was a Friday afternoon. Right after prayer time and blazingly hot. My father entered dripping in sweat as he carried aloft a rotund piece of hardware. He clenched it as if it were a decapitated head straight from the guillotine. Was it a screen or a projector? It came in multiple parts. I was instructed to help unload the rest of it from the trunk of his second-hand Chevrolet.

The ceremonial act of switching on the Kholeif family's first computer did not hold my attention for long, nor that of my younger brother. It seemed that we had been bestowed with little more than a glorified typewriter. An ugly typewriter it certainly was. A second-hand cream-colored clamshell that consumed the living room, spewing cranking noises as it slowly flickered on. The only difference between it and its analog forefather was that its word processor checked for spelling mistakes (often making inaccurate suggestions) and we could play Solitaire, which came pre-installed with Microsoft's

Windows platform. It also jacked up the electric bill, we were told. And it often liked to "crash." The invisible cost constituted a new usage time limit, which was fine by me: the television, even with its limited channels, still held possibilities that seemed boundless. It was the primary field for my imagination now that I had graduated from the age-old technology of books.

We could not afford to connect the computer to our landline to access the WWW, the interface that made the internet readily accessible to others, like our wealthy second cousins who used it for business correspondence. It was so near yet forever at bay. Not until my final year of high school did I become "connected." The sense of elation that this first interaction stirred, the energies that it recalibrated within me, were more sensorial, phenomenological, and haunting than any event in my life thus far.

You could hear the muffled telephone numbers being dialed, then there was further clamor, a screech, a throttle. Lift-off! My younger brother and I butted elbows playfully as we wrestled for the seat in front of the family PC. The obsessive impulse now so often associated with compulsive users of the technological sphere quickly reached its apex. He tackled me to the ground and strangled me, the kid brother whom I had not realized had suddenly grown to be twice my size. I may have been the eldest of four siblings, but I was certainly not first in line. The aggression that manifested that Saturday afternoon became a marker in the sand between the two of us. I wanted to use the internet to consider its potential for unifying people. I needed to figure out how to be with people online. The only human whom I had a crush on had moved halfway across the world to Australia. I had fantasized about our romantic, lyrical correspondence by electronic mail. My brother dubbed himself a techno-warrior. His fervor for the internet was fueled by a capitalist desire to purchase video games and to build insular communities or closed chat groups with people who bore similar conservative beliefs to his own. The slow dial-up pace infuriated him. The nights when my father worked his late shift would crescendo with the reverb of my brother smashing the keyboard against the dining table in frustration.

I did not get to experience the internet until six months later, when my father was loaned what I recall to be a Toshiba laptop by his employer. Its function was to keep sensitive and imperative patient data at close hand. Before going to work in the hospital, he would bury the thick black machine among personal mementos in a large analog safe that came with the newly furnished apartment into which we had moved on the East Coast of Saudi. I studied his gestural maneuvers in front of the metal depository with the ingenuity of the sleuthing Catherine Zeta-Jones in the film *Entrapment* (1999). The code was mine. The unlocked world beckoned. Finally, a realm existed outside of the clustered compounds of expats whose social status and pay were dictated by the color of their passports.

I had wanted to be a screenwriter. My father's sister, much more affluent than us, lived a two-hour drive away. Her many TV sets broadcast a channel called Super Movies that played black-and-white films, which I enjoyed far more than the humdrum fare offered in daily life. Now, using the WWW to access the internet, I no longer had to wait for our allotted schedule of cinema viewing. Instead, I found the screenplays for seemingly every film ever produced freely available online. Each would take about five minutes to download. I would skim the first ten pages before making the crucial decision of whether to use the limited ink in our printer. Now, I could craft my own movies, envisaging every detail from the cinematography to the casting. In a matter of weeks, I became fanatical about making my mark on cinema history. I examined the structure of these documents and began my screenplay on the laptop's word processor. Written in a stream-of-consciousness style, the initial result was a cryptic horror film in the manner of an early David Fincher movie, mashed together with Arab melodrama and filled with secret revelations. I wanted Billy Bob Thornton to play the lead. But where could I get my manuscript seen? I did not know of the internet's technical ability to correspond with the outside world.

My brother, therefore, became a necessary ally. In return for training and access to the WWW, I ghostwrote his school essays. The day he showed me Yahoo's now-defunct platform GeoCities would change my understanding of the world. These were websites crafted as architecture, devised as places, each dedicated to a kind of community interest, from Broadway, where I'd never been, to Hollywood, which we had driven past when living in South Los Angeles County. I began posting fragments of my haphazardly constructed script online, hoping to be discovered. The response, in the form of esoteric ramblings from anonymous users whose names were composed of letters and numbers, did little to foster hope, development, or a sense of community.

My unfulfilled belly left me desperate for any form of satiation. I scoured the limits of the web, eventually learning, as every teen did, of the presence of the images of nudes and half-nudes, which I would print out, petrified of being caught as the device ground out each inch of colored image at a snail's pace. The allegiance with my brother dissipated before long. His friends—my classmates and formerly my comrades—had installed a joystick and other gaming equipment on the family computer, transforming it into a portal for their aggression. As the WWW began to roll out in 1991, the philosopher Bruno Latour articulated that we had become a "divided" people.[1] My brother and I could not even sit at the same table and converse anymore. We were at opposing ends of the new world order. His ambitions took him to Silicon Valley in pursuit of nothing more than the security offered by dollar bills. I ended up trotting around the world attempting to decode how the internet was changing human perception, the ways in which, as Walter Benjamin and John Berger had intimated, we *feel* and *see* images, and, therefore, the world.[2]

Writing about the Internet

I began writing about the internet under a pseudonym in my first year as an undergraduate in Glasgow. A new form of writing known as blogging had become popular in the early millennium. It felt nourishing to be afforded the right to speak in the first-person voice; opinion and analysis were crucial components of its form. Blogging was also marked by its instantaneous nature. It was a kind of reportage, which ran the gamut from war reporting (which became greatly influential after the 2003 invasion of Iraq) to finding its perfect context in the pithy sarcasm of bloggers, such as Perez Hilton and Ted Casablanca, who relished celebrity misfortune. The latter was by no means considered a reputable profession, but I, too, had begun to earn a living as a diaristic blogger. It handsomely supplemented the afternoons spent kneeling at the shoe store where I worked after the day's classes. By nineteen years of age, I was reporting from backstage at concerts held in Glasgow's infamous Barrowland Ballroom and live blogging about the newly rebirthed fad of reality television programs, such as MTV and *PopMatters*. I had a following. I regularly received pieces of electronic fan mail. I was connecting, connected, networked, together. Had I finally built a sense of community? Or was I fabricating these characters, calculatingly authoring my words to the demographic profiles I hoped would consume these versions of a truth that were not my own?

This book follows the story of navigating the sphere of opportunities that the internet has offered for visual culture. Like any storytelling, or what poet Kevin Young has called storying,[3] I feel that it is most authentic to narrate it through my own experiences—or at least, how they were felt. The internet, or more precisely, the web, connected me to hackers and tinkerers whom I soon discovered to be artists. It teleported my career from the blogosphere into documentary film and television and into the picture palace of museums, where I spend most of my days as a curator of art. It was my knowledge of networked culture—art that engaged with the internet in some way—that landed me my first full-time job at the Foundation for Art and Creative Technology (FACT), Liverpool, then dubbed the UK's national center for art, film, and "new media." At twenty-three years of age, I was both thrilled and terrified to take up the role. That was until I began butting heads with the established demigod-like figures in the institution. Some disapproved of my compulsion to use the instruments of the internet and its encompassing technologies to parse academic theory, to want to make the field of new media more porous for artists and their audiences.

Filled with the youthful angst of being a queer, disabled person of color, I hastily decided that I would craft an unconventional life and career path. I invited artists into the world of "internet art" who were rarely pre-authorized by my supervisors. My loyalty was to artists as opposed to any single institution. If an opportunity presented itself to work with an artist who fell out of the sanctioned fold, I would grab it, book time off work, and attempt to realize the project without institutional backing. Unburdened by the weight of a singular western art history, I felt that my covert attitude might have mirrored the realities of both the deep and dark web. Conversations about generations, class and division, and race and gender consistently came to the fore in all of my work. I was holding something in my hands, and I did not know what to do with it yet. Initially, I had no mentors, guides, independent grant money, or authorized direction for how a wayward immigrant should operate.

How was I to enact my supposed duty, "the care" of artists, as a curator when I could not find support for my work in the world of art? The artists for whom I lobbied, despite using what was quickly becoming the mass medium of our time, were constantly chastised by senior arts administrators as being too niche or too nascent for the general public. I was asked by a director of documenta, one of the world's largest art exhibitions in the world, "Who wants to see art on a computer?"[4] Perhaps that person was correct.

What Internet Art Is and Isn't

The misunderstanding in the example mentioned above is that internet art isn't necessarily art for the computer or even art about the computer. Instead, it is art that is produced with a knowing awareness of the networked nature of our collective culture. In theory, internet art could be an oil on canvas painting where the artist's inspiration emerged from a cornucopia of visual images found online, or it could be composed of a series of photographs that are physically printed, which take the internet on as subject matter. Likewise, it could be a website that is made to be experienced alone at home or on a smartphone, or a piece of augmented reality software that alters your likeness, adding a layer of animation to the quotidian nature of life. A 3-D-printed sculpture, a drawing sketched on an iPad, and a performance on Instagram are all examples of what could constitute internet art.

I have navigated the variants of this discipline with both nervousness and enthusiasm. At each professional juncture, swinging up and around the hierarchies of art and its institutions, I was informed that my work was concerned with media art, electronic art, net art, digital art, and—the disputed term—*post-internet art*, which we will return to in the "Will This Destroy Us?" chapter. As we move through these pages, I will seek to decode and demystify these terms and demonstrate the reasoning for their existence. Regardless, the fundamental takeaway is not to debate semantics. Instead, my aim is to make evident that every art form has the potential to use the internet in some way, whether discreetly or deliberately, critically or adoringly. Internet art is not merely an art-historical genre or a field of practice, but a catalytic and considered request to invite the viewer to consider how we look at art produced in the twenty-first century.

After all, the internet is a connective tissue that binds and fragments us as humans. To many, it is an abstract formation often referred to through metaphors, such as the bulbous and immaterial *cloud*, when it is in fact as tangible as the object that you hold in your hands. Initially conceived by government military bodies, it went from being a tool for a small elite group to the basis of a new industrial revolution. The internet is a place that has enabled and ennobled the numerous citizens using it to find a voice through its multiple content-sharing platforms. Political activism and human-rights lobbying have found bold and expansive ways of engaging people online, as have authors and politicians who have formed entire careers through social media. But with that interdependence on the internet emerges the opportunity for perpetual exploitation, from data and identity mining to economic co-optation and manipulation by large corporations.

The digital freedom fighters mythologized in films, such as *The Net* (1995) or *Hackers* (1995), have mutated in many spheres into the corporate honchos who hold the majority of the world's wealth. They also govern our privacy, many of our intellectual property rights, and even the gestures that we use to engage with devices every day. Sociologists, anthropologists, and psychologists from across the liberal and conservative spectrum have made it evident that our very consciousness is increasingly shaped by computer programmers and software engineers who work for major for-profit corporations. This is an ironic fact when one is reminded that the web, the first major platform to democratize the internet, was given to the people of the world freely in 1993 by Tim Berners-Lee, a British computer scientist based at CERN (European Organization for Nuclear Research), who first conjured up the idea in 1989.

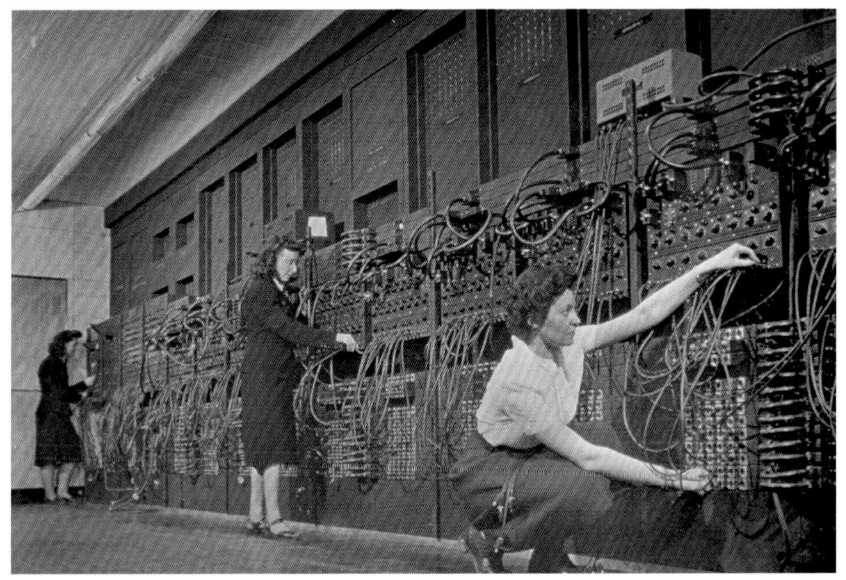

Computer operators program ENIAC, the first electronic digital computer, Philadelphia, c.1946

At the outset, artists used the internet, just as video artists used television, as a means to interrogate the limits of the world around them. Yet somehow, after every talk or discussion that I lead, the conversation around internet art tends to descend into a degradation of the figures who have pioneered the form and function of the internet as a medium. This book is here to redress this, as well as to serve multiple purposes. It is a memoir, a social history, and, like any expansive field, a selective survey. It traces a history of art that is part of everyone's lives—one that is social, economic, and political. It attempts to make visible a few of the individuals who have created the lexicon for how we look at art today, ultimately forming a manifesto for reimagining how we see art through the lens of today's mass medium. It is a step toward balancing out and exploring divergent narratives, shifting the axis to look to the margins as well as the center. I hope that for some (including myself), it will serve as an act of redemption.

1989: The Year That Changed the World

The Propensity to Dream

Slabs of battered concrete are lined up irregularly, forming a seemingly endless barricade. They are spray-painted with incomprehensible graffiti, the stain of years of human interaction, of dissidence against an immutable authority. Human chains form and disperse across the different fragments of the so-called wall: Berlin, 1989, just before the fall. The bodies of a desirous youth, often smoking, occasionally posing, glare at the cameras surrounding this ambiguous fortress that is about to come slowly tumbling down, frame by frame in front of the cameras. As a young child transfixed by the modern-day anarchists on screen, I didn't fully understand the import of the images flickering on the globular television set that consumed half of our living room.[1] Sorting through the pictures today using Google, I recognize them. It was like yesterday. But the revolutionary spirit on screen now looks a little crisper, sharper, and more focused.

My parents, recent émigrés to the UK from Egypt, were not yet familiar with words such as *ideology* in the English language, nor perhaps in their mother tongue of Arabic. But it wasn't their limited vocabulary that prevented them from pronouncing what it was we were witnessing on screen, but the very composition of the images, which were more alien to them than to me. The pixelated images of 1989 bore a different weight for their generation. They were still learning to decode the swiftly evolving image culture. Before arriving at the northern edges of the British isle, my family educated itself on international affairs through Egypt's government-owned and/or sanctioned newspapers and an analog radio—a sonic reverb sandwiched between cooking appliances in a Cairene kitchen. Produced by self-selected ideologues, these channels presented a biased vision of a new social and political conservatism in the country that evolved in the 1970s, reaching its apex in the late 1980s.

Unlike my parents, the same generation in the western world, who have been dubbed the boomers, had lived with the mass-image culture of television since the 1950s and 1960s. With an ever-growing constellation of public-service media outlets in countries such as the USA, Canada, and Great Britain, theirs was a generation that had seen war and revolution broadcast in close-up over supper. The televising of the Vietnam War infamously re-calibrated how conflict was experienced; war now bore new shapes and contours. Simultaneously, media theorists and post-modernist semioticians from Jacques Derrida to Michel Foucault and Jean Baudrillard interrogated the means through which the human gaze was constructed in relation to the newly proliferating image society, or what Situationist writer Guy Debord termed, "The Society of the Spectacle."[2] Debord's was

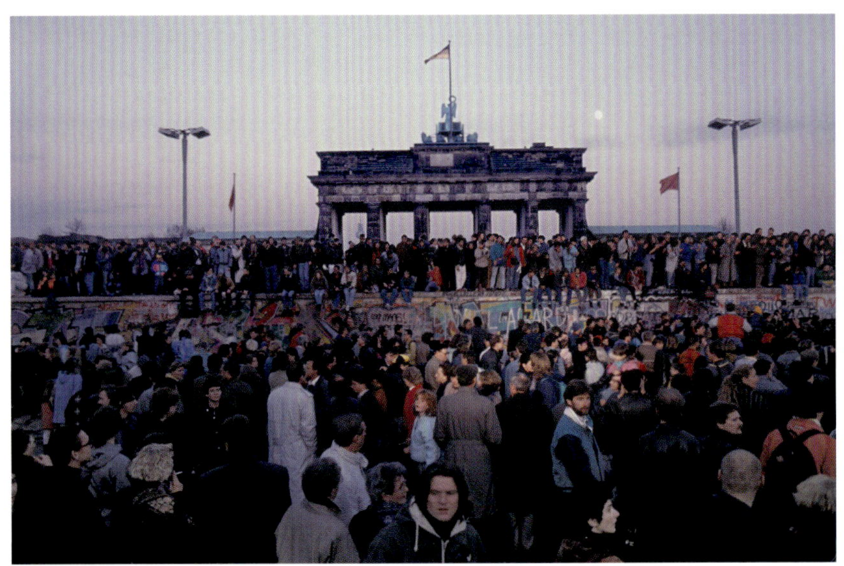

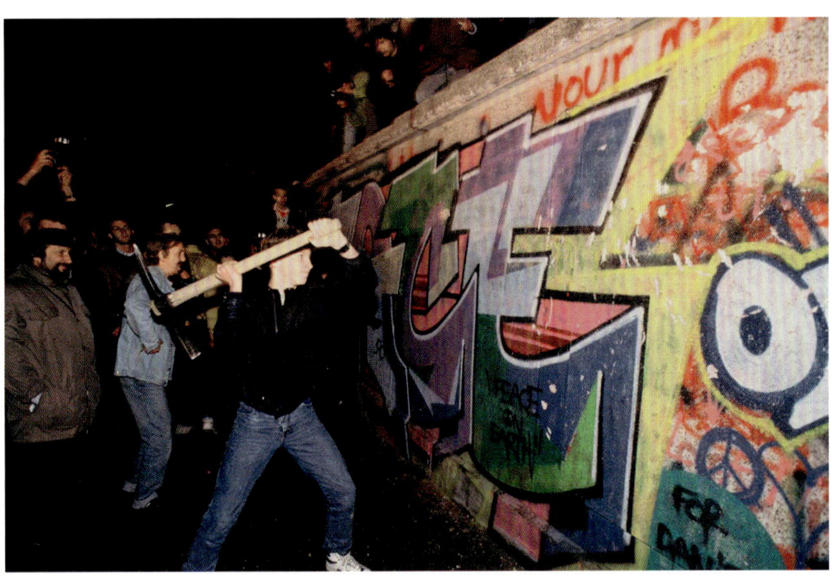

Fall of the Berlin Wall, 1989

a world of performing phantasms where one could no longer differentiate between genuine lived experienced and the (re)presentation of one's self as a performance. This is a theory that in 2009, in the age of the internet, I called the irresistible act of "performing the self"[3]—a simulation of one's identity carefully crafted and contorted to fit the formations of the Web 2.0 era's new social-media platforms such as YouTube and Facebook. Unlike Web 1.0, which offered users tools to publish content, often by a single sanctioned authorial voice, the second generation of the web allowed for a constantly mutable, seemingly democratized sphere, where the audience themselves were as much a part of shaping the content as the propriety website owners.

Back in 1989, as my parents and I sat watching the Wall fall, we did not yet realize that we were approaching the end of an era and that a new dawn was about to commence. The year, according to many historians, and our trusted Wikipedia, has frequently been called a turning point in political history. The crescendo that resulted in the dismantling of the Berlin Wall that had sought to divide "the East" and "the West" also signified an end of a lengthy Cold War era. The year began with revolutions across the Eastern bloc of Europe, initially in Poland and Hungary, as well as in Czechoslovakia. The result has been said to have led to the peaceful end of communism.[4] South of the equator, the seeds were planted to end the apartheid regime in South Africa. In parallel, computer scientist Tim Berners-Lee initiated what would become the world's first web browser, which would become the unprecedented primary free tool for citizens to access the internet.[5]

In 1989, many forms of liberty were also infringed upon. At the Corcoran Gallery of Art in Washington, DC, an exhibition of photographs by Robert Mapplethorpe was canceled because it horrified conservative trustees with its sexually provocative imagery of gay men. Across the pond in Britain, my mother, an author, was debating the damnation of the author Salman Rushdie, who was reported to have a bounty on his head in the millions for writing *The Satanic Verses*, a novel inspired by the life of the Muslim prophet Mohammed. In Lebanon and my birth country, Egypt, on the other hand, there appeared to be resolutions to ongoing conflicts, a temporary truce in the Lebanese Civil War and the return of Taba, a town near the tip of the Gulf of Aqaba, from Israel back to Egypt.

My birthday that year coincided with two triggering political events. The first was the FA Cup semi-final. I was instructed by my family to root for Liverpool Football Club. But I do not recall a kick-off here. After five and a half minutes of gameplay, I am alerted retrospectively, one would bear witness to streams of bodies crushing one another resulting in ninety-seven deaths and hundreds of injuries. It became known as the Hillsborough Disaster, the worst tragedy in British sporting history.[6] On screen, humans were reduced to figurines. Disco Demolition Night,[7] which had taken place a decade before, now comes to mind, as does 2011, when my grandfather and I gathered with other civilians in Tahrir Square in downtown Cairo during the first eighteen days of the Egyptian Revolution. Although the world was in full focus to me, online and on satellite screens, we were mere flattened dots tessellating without a form.

The second triggering event took place in April 1989, after a major official of the Chinese Communist Party, Hu Yaobang died of a heart attack, which many student dissenters believed to be related to his forced resignation. A week later, his funeral acted as a site of student protests in Tiananmen Square, which, despite the ensuing massacre, began the multi-year "cultural revolution" led by the Chinese Democracy Movement.[8]

At the Centre Georges Pompidou in Paris, the world of art museums and its critics responded to an emerging new order. The museum's director Jean-Hubert Martin presented *Magiciens de la Terre* (Magicians of the Earth), the first major contemporary exhibition that sought to readdress historic imbalances in modern and contemporary art history. He presented a show of 50 percent western artists and 50 percent nonwestern artists to demonstrate the breadth of art emerging from the varied corners of the globe. Much debated at the time, reviled by some, and praised as significant by others, *Magiciens de la Terre* was a clear sign that the world was morphing to expanded contours. Citizens, artists, and politicians were increasingly aware that globalization had created a networked culture where difference could become a thing of fashion.[9]

The schematics of political upheaval and renewal have historically been propelled by advances in technology. Developments in the military arsenal are an example: in the twenty-first century, wars are rarely fought by humans in the trenches but by dispensed drones. Those in communication are another. Political figures can now send their messages on social media; lobbying can be fulfilled through Facebook advertisements,[10] seeping into the unconscious in a manner more efficient than the more laborious practice of distributing carefully authored pamphlets, posters, and manifestos, which emerged after the popularization of the printing press. The escalating speed in which technological hardware can develop was articulated in 1965 by Gordon Moore, who went on to cofound the Intel Corporation.[11] In what has been dubbed Moore's Law, he explained how integrated circuits—that is, the circuits that run electronic machines—double in efficiency roughly every two years. The concept is simple: every two years technology will be twice as good, but for the same price or cheaper.

Yet, as fierce revolutions swept around the world at warp speed in 1989, they also signaled another form of evolution.[12] The world would soon enter a new industrial era where the accelerate button is always on.

If history repeats itself, why study it? History is a bore. It's just a series of stories by and about people, mostly men, mostly white, who are no longer alive. Right? Well, that isn't so true anymore. History, the story of events and of people and places at a given moment in time, is now in constant update mode. It is evolving so rapidly with the growth of artificially intelligent (AI) computing that humans soon won't even have a moment to reflect before they are forced to click *update* on all their devices again. Historians of the image, such as W. J. T. Mitchell, Jonathan Crary, and Laura Mulvey, have intimated that the reflective pause may become a thing of the past. Increasingly, it is considered nostalgic to look back on that which came before. It is now thought naive, even incendiary, to hold a critical mirror up to the media. We now live in public, asleep, but awake.

Remember, remember 1989. It set the pace for the things that were soon to come—the effects manifest are neither dream nor delusion.

The Future Is Here: Who Was Nam June Paik?

When I was first appointed as a curator at the Foundation for Art and Creative Technology (FACT) in Liverpool in the first decade of the millennium, I went around like the David Attenborough of internet art, extolling the virtues that connectivity had given to artists. One of my aims was to explain to artists and audiences that many contemporary ideas about the internet were foreshadowed by artists working decades before. In 2009, I began working on an exhibition of the late Korean American artist, Nam June Paik (1932–2006), often referred to as the father of video art. The show, which would open at FACT in December 2010, led by Tate's Sook-Kyung Lee, took me on an archaeological dig into the semantics of the internet as we know it today.

I recall walking behind my CEO, Professor Mike Stubbs, as numerous dignitaries, including an ambassador, arrived to inspect our venue during the exhibition's planning phase in 2010. They were accompanied by a gentleman whom I was informed was the late artist's nephew, Ken Hakuta. He looked familiar, like someone I'd seen on TV, but I assumed I was mistaken. He turned to me and asked, "Are you enjoying your time on the electronic superhighway?" Surprised by the phrase, I was only able to swallow and murmur nonsensically.

Seeing my confusion, Professor Stubbs later took me into his office and asked his assistant to print a document. It was written in a Courier font similar to that used in screenplays and evoked an age long before I was born. “You’ll need this for this afternoon’s exhibition meeting,” said Stubbs. I scurried out with nervous excitement, eager to digest the document, a report authored in 1974 by Paik commissioned by the Rockefeller Foundation entitled, “Media Planning for the Postindustrial Age: Only 26 Years Left Until the 21st Century.” It read like a manifesto, with argumentative directives about the state of the media industry and the need for intervention within it. Paik used the networked connections of the U.S. Highway System as a metaphor for telecommunications infrastructure. He proposed that deepening these connections would alter human connectivity, understanding, and consciousness building. As much as they spoke to technology’s potential, his words also cautioned against the politics of control around telecommunications but, as he did often, he ended his narration on a high note. Envisaging what he called “electronic superhighways,” the artist dreamed of a world where Los Angeles and New York could be connected within seconds via fiber-optic cables; a universe that could be free for everyone to access. His cautionary tale was that “history repeats itself” and that one must “prepare” to avoid “digital divides” between the poor and the wealthy, as well as the healthy and the disabled.

I read the text numerous times, immersed in the detailed foreshadowing of the world today presented by Paik. His unequivocal renderings of the future are testimony to the importance of artists in shaping the collective language around mass cultural forms. It is not politicians who create the lexicon; the superhighway was imagined in the creative sphere. It would be crucial for the exhibition to provide a context that linked Paik’s recent works to his pivotal historical thinking. In the process of my research, I learned that Ken Hakuta was, indeed, a familiar face from television: Dr. Fad, the Japanese American inventor whose popular children’s TV show ran from 1988 to 1994.

Simultaneously to working at FACT, I was pursuing a degree at what was then *the* prestigious MA program in Curating Contemporary Art at the Royal College of Art, London. I asked my mentor and tutor, the artist, writer, and educator Professor Jean Fisher, about Paik, whom I knew was part of her milieu when she lived in New York in the 1980s. In a one-to-one tutorial, she brushed this off and asked if I had given any consideration to how historians had theorized Paik’s Korean identity and whether one of the show’s sponsors, the corporation known as Samsung, would be attempting to take credit for his legacy. I didn’t know. Samsung and Paik’s relationship seemed symbiotic. Fundraising affairs in the art world are often as covert as a nuclear-weapons deal.

Our joint penchant for smoking led us down to Kensington Gardens. Fisher offered a meta-commentary on postcolonialism; she spoke of ducks and swans as mechanized city dwellers that, she intimated, were forced to put on a show for tourists. Something in her tone was always scratching, digging. She would later introduce me to an entire counterculture of feminist artists whose experiments with art and technology would guide my interests in the years to come.

Life Behind the Computer

Since 2002, my life had been largely lived online. I became more sedentary, believing that I could reach everyone and everything through my computer. I enjoyed my virtual coffees, which back then were held in front of chat boxes in my room measuring eighty square feet (7.4 m^2) that I was subletting from a university friend in the Greater Glasgow enclave of Maryhill. A year later came Myspace, where individuals seemed eager to have interactions in person. In the years before, I had put on a hefty thirty pounds (13.6 kg) and was not prepared to do "real life." I crafted a simple profile picture, which was heavily cropped; I can still barely use Photoshop. I anticipated that my curated musical tastes would woo friends and suitors alike, in place of selfies demonstrating bodily aesthetics.

Myspace, once one of the world's highest-ranking social-media sites, was a progenitor of a new form of connectivity. Conversations held in these chat boxes were transformative, designed aspects of a platform that allowed one to perpetually self-broadcast. Performing yourself, or a *versioned* version of yourself for an anonymized public, became de rigueur. "I'm into punk, denim overalls, foreign language tattoos, travel, and lots of coffee. Also: Nietzsche. Hardcore Existentialist." These were the initial notes that I drafted for my profile. The truth was less erudite. I preferred Diet Coke over coffee. I chafed in denim and couldn't afford to travel. Did I mention that I didn't yet have a passport?

Was Myspace Paik's Electronic Superhighway? In "Media Planning for the Postindustrial Age," he had conjured a low-cost means to link Los Angeles with New York. He spoke of an age where the world would progress at rapid speeds that had seemed unfathomable when that lumpen, yellowed device entered our family home less than a decade earlier.

Connecting

Human connection was the bedrock of Paik's career. In 1969, he played a key role in an artwork devised by Allan Kaprow (1927–2006) called *Hello*. The work was staged as part of a public-service TV event, *The Medium is the Medium*. Acting as the director, Kaprow dispatched artists to various locations and ran five video cameras and twenty-seven monitors through a four-channel system. Each of the locations was connected through closed-circuit television (CCTV). The cameras filmed the artists repeating the words "Hello, I see you" as Kaprow switched focus between the different locations and the footage was played back on the monitors. His intention with this project was to illuminate the opportunities for remote connection that networks could engender; we could all be disruptors together, uttering nonsense.

Kaprow, like Paik, was associated with Fluxus, an interconnected but informal constellation of artists, poets, and musicians working in the 1960s and 1970s who created art, such as *Hello* and their famous happenings, that did not necessarily lead to a finished product. Artist and musician John Cage, artist and avant-garde composer George Brecht, dancer and choreographer Simone Forti, artist Alison Knowles, artist Shigeko Kubota, as well as artist and musician Yoko Ono, were leading lights in this movement. Intrinsically, internet art, which is a form of making art that links communities together, finds its genesis in the late 1960s in Fluxus, performance, and video art. Those divergent but interconnected histories laid the basis for what was to come.

Realizing a Vision

In 1994, Paik crafted *Internet Dream*, a psychedelic "video painting" composed of fifty-two television sets. The abundance of images across these multiple screens, mostly digitally generated, at first seem completely fragmented, moving in tangents. Yet look at the screen for a breath or two and the frames start to gradually inch closer, forming ambiguous shapes as well as clear forms, such as an all-encompassing, beating heart. Despite his acknowledgment of the potential for the internet to fragment humans, Paik continued along the path that emerged from his early Fluxus days, dreaming that it could create a networked culture that would bring about a form of solidarity, love, and unity.

The year before, Paik had experimented with ideas of connectivity in the German pavilion at the Venice Biennale with the installation *Electronic*

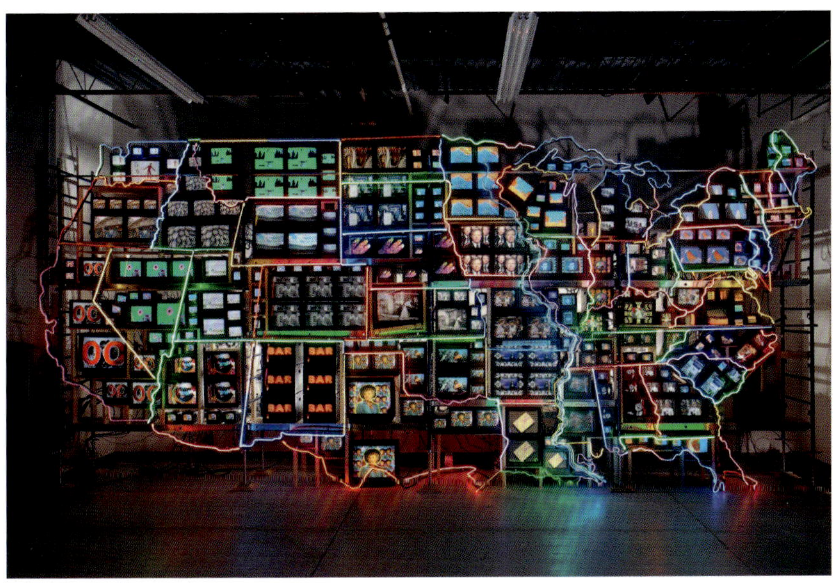

Nam June Paik, ***Electronic Superhighway: Continental U.S., Alaska, Hawaii***, 1995 —(Continental U.S. only) Forty-nine-channel closed-circuit video installation, neon, steel, electronic components, c.15 × 40 × 4 ft. (c.4.6 × 12.2 × 1.2 m)

Super Highway 'Venice → Ulan Bator' (1993). In 1995, he revisited the earlier installation, realizing it with a magisterial grandeur as *Electronic Superhighway: Continental U.S., Alaska, Hawaii.* Here, 336 TV sets wrapped in a multiplicity of colorful electric lights take on the form of the United States. This momentous installation presents evocative preprogrammed footage reflective of each state's culture. For instance, clips from the *Wizard of Oz* (1939) boom out of Kansas's screens, and scenes from *Meet Me in St. Louis* (1944) emanate from Missouri's (Paik was perhaps a Judy Garland fan). Mississippi is portrayed in scenes from the civil rights movement, while Iowa is presented through an assemblage of imagery of politicians campaigning during the Iowa caucuses. Meanwhile, an inbuilt CCTV camera captures the viewer's movements, creating a two-way system suggestive of future surveillance strategies.

Donated by the artist to the Smithsonian American Art Museum in Washington, DC, in 2002, the work has remained largely on continuous display ever since. One of the most iconic works of art produced using networked technology, it exists in the nation's capital as both a nod to the meeker past, as well as a marker of the freewheeling future. In 2016, I opened an exhibition at the Whitechapel Gallery, London, inspired by this work.

Connecting the Dots

The internet used to be attributed a capital I. That was because it was perceived as a monolithic thing, a noun, not yet a forum or a space that could be used in terms of adjectives and verbs. The basis for "the Internet" was a network called Advanced Research Projects Agency Network (ARPANET), which was devised by the Advanced Research Projects Agency (ARPA), an arm of the U.S. Defense Department, in 1967. This proposal came to life in a humble sense in 1969, when the agency was able to connect four university computers together. Unique to this process was a protocol that involved sending packets of information across what is called the Internet protocol suite. That was the beginning of the internet as we know it today. Now, when we speak of the internet, it embodies a great deal more. It encompasses the computer code or text that creates platforms, such as websites, connected software, the World Wide Web (WWW), email, mobile telephony, and satellite networks filled with applications, including social-media platforms from WhatsApp to Instagram, as well as file-sharing and storage spaces such as WeTransfer, Dropbox, iCloud, and Amazon Web Services.[13]

Unlike Paik's superhighway, the internet is a globular system that moves across multiple, transversal routes. The proliferation of this technology began under the auspices of government agencies such as ARPA. In the 1980s, when it became evident that the internet was both a social and political tool, it was renamed and rehoused as the Defense Data Network. In 1989, British computer scientist Tim Berners-Lee invented the concept of the WWW, with the intention that it should be a free tool of access and knowledge sharing for all. The web that he conceived used uniform resource locators (URLs) to help people connect to individual websites that could be hosted anywhere in the world. By 1990, Berners-Lee had produced his first website, and, by 1991, the WWW concept was released to a more general public, becoming part of everyday use among those with computer connectivity about 1993–94.

The utopianism of the early web was intertwined with personal human desires for innovation, growth, and capital gain. As humans inched toward the second millennium, the *dot-com boom* became a term in popular parlance. In retrospect referred to as the *dot-com bubble*, it reflects a period from the mid-1990s through to the initial years of the new millennium. This was a time when for-profit companies yielded excessive stock-market speculation, ultimately leading to their demise, and with that, the loss of innumerable jobs, hopes, and dreams. For my generation, this was the closest thing to a Y2K apocalypse. We realized that the internet would not necessarily narrow the divide. We would not all be solvent enough to decide a free path in life as we had hoped.

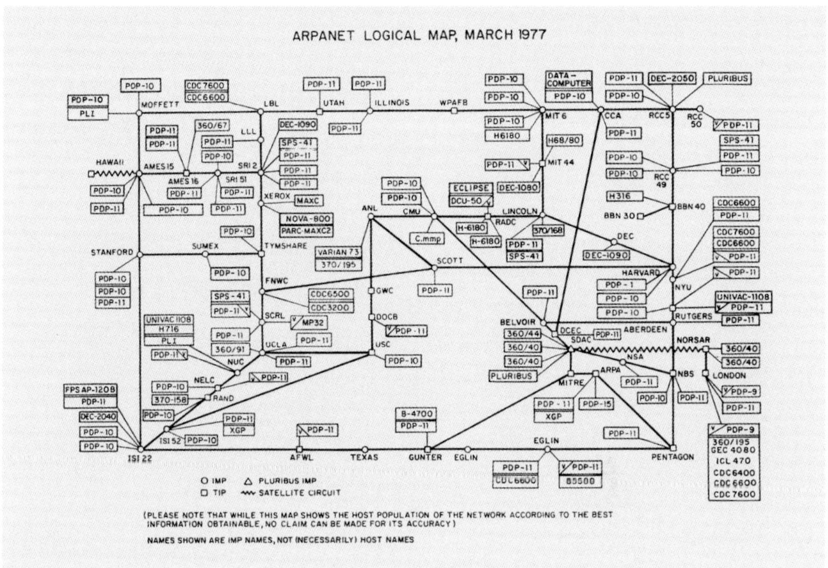

ARPANET logical map, 1977

The exceptionalism intrinsic to this way of thinking rematerialized a decade later with the rise of the social-media influencer. Billionaire Kim Kardashian and her sister Kylie Jenner—at the time of writing, the world's youngest "self-made" billionaire—are famous for supposedly doing nothing, but they have been exploiting a series of virtual assets to build brands and diffusion lines that can be sold for profit. Few people can do this, because it requires careful, constant management.

A Wayward Career Path

I met my first boss in the world of art, a person by the name of Paula, at a concert of the indie rock band the Yeah Yeah Yeahs in April of 2004. I was still writing under a blogging alias for media outlets, including MTV. I had managed to secure the gig a couple of years earlier by claiming that I had worked at *Rolling Stone*. It was a half-baked truth.

The Yeah Yeah Yeahs were promoting their breakthrough album, *Fever to Tell*. I had a free ticket and backstage access but everyone I knew who could accompany me was busy working their restaurant or bar gig. I chugged a couple of pints of cheap beer as the support act played to quell what had become constant anxiety. By the time the concert was full throttle, a mosh pit began to form up front at the Barrows, Glasgow's premier venue for everything "alt." Paula, a lithe, middle-age woman who got caught up in it, flew at me like a bird with a broken wing. Latching onto my forearms, she thanked me for saving her. She joined me backstage for the perfunctory one-word Q&A.

We went back to her place, drinking the dregs of wine from bottles in her fridge. She brought out "The Weary Blues," a poem by Langston Hughes, citing tales of slavery and a life lived on Lenox Avenue as if it were her own: "New York was modeled after Glasgow you know!" Phrases by David Foster Wallace were scrawled on paper that began their lives as table mats. We spoke of Benedict Anderson's concept of imagined communities, of what we would later understand to be disaster capitalism—the corporate sphere taking advantage of collective trauma for financial gain—as well as the undergirding structures of power online.

An activist and an anarchist, Paula volunteered her time helping asylum seekers assimilate into the city. It was an experience that I had not been offered when my family arrived in Great Britain in the 1980s. In 2003, she was part of a team that codirected Document, an international documentary human-rights film festival that focused on experimental film at the Centre for Contemporary Arts (CCA) in Glasgow. Within weeks, I was working in the document office at the CCA, which at the time was just a little larger than a broom cupboard. I watched hundreds of hours of films without any sense of day or night. It was in these corridors that I came to learn the history of video and performance art. The CCA had played host to some of the world's luminaries, showcasing the work of Black British artists, such as Sonia Boyce and Victoria Ryan in 1987 (when it was known as the Third Eye Centre). It was a seat of what was once called a counterculture. Allen Ginsberg had spoken here, as had queer feminist poet Kathy Acker. Exhibitions were held by legendary video artists, such as Tamara Krikorian, the Ghanaian-Scottish author and artist Maud Sulter, and many of the artists with whom I would soon come to work. Experimental video and internet art were shown in a modest space called the Intermedia Gallery, which exists to this day. As I ventured in and out of these rooms, my mind was a motherboard upgraded with a new video card. The possibilities of art felt limitless.

A New Horizon

In my first few months at the CCA, a film starring the acclaimed Scottish actress Tilda Swinton was screened. *Teknolust* (2002) by the artist Lynn Hershman Leeson was a science-fiction film, in which Swinton's character continually self-replicated. The notion of fashioning multiple versions of one's self seemed to resonate deeply with the concept of identity performance that I saw translated into the newly launched online platform, Facebook. My college friends had assumed polished identities; they were self-fulfilling commentators in dialogue with themselves. This was before Facebook had reached the multibillion user reach that it holds today.

I dug into Hershman Leeson's exhibition history to discover another captivating feature film starring Swinton, *Conceiving Ada* (1997). The picture told the life story of the mathematician, Ada Lovelace, who was one of the first people to draw up a proposal for the mechanical computer but who had for a long time been left at the margins of computing and internet histories. Hershman Leeson's time-traveling science-fiction adventure seeks to reclaim Lovelace's "genius," enshrining it in collective history. The artist's interest in feminism and technology, it transpired, had been a lifelong pursuit that had occupied her since early childhood.

Lorna

Since the early 2010s, I had exhibited fragments of Hershman Leeson's films and installations in cinemas and galleries, and occasionally communicated with her online, though we didn't meet in the flesh, or as some would say, IRL (in real life) until November 2016, when Eva Respini, the chief curator at Boston's Institute of Contemporary Art, invited her to respond to a paper that I was to present about art and the internet. The event was one of those cozy affairs, by invitation only, sometimes referred to as a think tank. I charged through my PowerPoint presentation, impatient to get to the point when Hershman Leeson would respond with her thoughts and questions. I looked across the table: "Hello Lynn, nice to see you." "We haven't met before," she responded, correcting me. A flush of heat spiraled up my spine, stretching across my head, reddening my face, bursting out of my nose, and releasing a spontaneous load of snot. We had nearly ten years of correspondence between us, but she was, indeed, correct; this was our first encounter. But surely, she understood of the concept of digital dualism?

I had prepared for a series of questions based on what I understood of Hershman Leeson's art, and on my experience of the riveting interlocutor to whom I had spoken online. But instead, she was questioning me with a restrained teacherly air about curatorial responsibility. She was eager to understand how my generation considered issues, such as archiving, and any number of technical questions. As I picked up my coffee cup, it swerved out of my hand and splattered across my keyboard. A subconscious act: I was demanding a time out.

I had spent years pursuing Hershman Leeson to make sense of her art. This is the privilege, after all, of working with living artists. In the first decade of the millennium, her work was in major museum collections but rarely exhibited. Long before the numerous cultural movements, such as #MeToo and #TimesUp, many female artists were concealed from view in this way. She is known for her pioneering interactive art, such as the video installation *Lorna* (1979–84), one of the first interactive installations. Like much of her work, it was concerned with explorations of the human psyche. Narrated in thirty-six chapters, *Lorna* is the story of a young woman who has become so consumed by the world of television that she can no longer leave her tiny flat. The installation, staged in a makeshift rendering of the apartment, invites the viewer to make decisions on Lorna's behalf by answering a series of questions on a remote control. As the minutes turn to hours, one grows increasingly aware that the audience, just like the artist's protagonist, is stuck in a *forever loop*—a term that was introduced to me by the artist Eddie Peake.

I first experienced *Lorna* in a museum on a blistering winter day in Germany in or about 2004. It was the only artwork that I remembered from that trip. I encountered it again years later at Modern Art Oxford in 2015, and then at the Whitechapel Gallery, London, where I presented it in 2016, and in San Francisco at the Yerba Buena Arts Center in 2017. Each time, I sat on the floor with Lorna's remote control, trying to help her overcome her agoraphobia. I, too, would begin to feel the walls caving in on me. These pivoted in different directions in each installation, but the affective qualities of the work remained similar each time.

Getting to Know You

After that meeting at ICA Boston, I left behind my sweat patches and embarrassment. I became close enough to Hershman Leeson to ask more personal questions over email. I was surprised when she informed me that my generation was "the only ones to get her work."[14] I was honored to hear that millennials could be attributed to some form of positivity, instead of the term being used as a passive-aggressive insult.

To make sense of the artist's work, I interviewed her over the years about her life, details of which she volunteered. When I ask her about the genesis of *Lorna*, for instance, she returns to her childhood, issues of class, rural versus urban communities, as well as the personal, situated fear of growing up with anxiety and depression.

She was born in 1941 in Cleveland, Ohio, in what she had described to me as a lower-middle-class Jewish neighborhood. Her family—two parents, two elder brothers, and her grandmother—was insular. There were no aunts or uncles; they had been left behind in the brutal gas chambers of the Holocaust. That tight household unit was ruptured by domestic violence; Hershman Leeson was unable to speak until she was six years old. Solace was found in the local Cleveland Museum of Art and its library, where she was fascinated by a work by Jean Tinguely (1925–1991), *Homage to New York* (1960), a self-destructing assemblage the artist described as a suicide machine. By the seventh grade, she proclaimed that she was also attending classes at Case Western Reserve University, hanging around with freaks, as she called them. But the abrupt double-suicide of her friends Micky and Jo, followed by her grandmother's death, slung her into a "slow, long depression."[15]

It was in this state that she became fixated on the concept of the cyborg, the notion of a hybrid of human and machine that emerged in 1960. The artist began experimenting with drawing, sculpture, and performance, creating alter egos—what we would come to refer to today as avatars—as digital stand-ins for the body and as a form of liberation.

Cyborgs

In 1989, Hershman Leeson released several groundbreaking artworks that she had spent years developing. The most haunting was the third installment in her *Electronic Diaries* (1984–2019) series, entitled *First-Person Plural.* She addresses her audience in the same manner a celebrity YouTuber would reveal their most intimate obsessions and secrets. She begins, "Sometimes I would pretend I was other people that I had read about." Her voice is hushed against the clamorous audio backdrop of impending doom reminiscent of a David Cronenberg film. Aspects of her autobiography come to the fore. She speaks of the possibilities of new technologies to enable her to take on multiple personae, to contort oneself through media to confront or eschew the violence of her own lived experience. The sense of foreshadowing is uncanny. This is social media before such a term had ever been uttered.

Simultaneously, she released her *Phantom Limb* (1986–89) series of photographs. Posed female bodies disappear and reappear through technological appendages—a face encased in a television screen or a camera, acting as a counter to the dominance of the male gaze articulated by the film theorist Laura Mulvey.[16] These cyborglike creations would form the genesis for a project that started in 1989 and took until 1996 to realize. The artist's iconic work, *CybeRoberta* (1994), part of her *Dollie Clone* (1995–98) series, instantly drew attention from historians of the technological arts. Here, dolls have cameras for eyes, which reflect the contents of a mirror placed in front of them. Hershman Leeson describes this as an act of transference, where person and machine become one. The viewer embodies the world of the seemingly inanimate doll, surveilling their surroundings through its eyes. “The audience becomes cyborgs by using the doll’s gaze,” she told me.[17]

It is no surprise that these works were dovetailed with the publication of the feminist theoretician Donna Haraway’s “A Cyborg Manifesto” in 1985 in *Socialist Review.* The imaginative paper argues against traditional notions of western patriarchy toward women and for hybrid ways, not only of looking but also of being. It seeks to consider the relationship between humans and machines, specifically in relation to female identity, arguing for new forms of collective imagination by means of a “coalition through affinity.”

Shadow Stalking

I was eager to know where Hershman Leeson was in 1989 when the net was born, but instead our correspondence veered me to her new work in development *Shadow Stalker* (2018–21), commissioned and first presented at the Shed in New York in 2019. *Shadow Stalker* is an immersive installation, film, and website (designed by researcher Francis Tseng) that looks at how algorithms—sets of rules or code that are traditionally fed into computers—were used in a governmental tactic called algorithmic policing or predictive policing. This approach, which came to public attention about 2011,[18] has been used by law-enforcement agencies to predict which zip codes are more likely to be hot spots for crime. The results revealed a world of racial bias and resulted in ongoing police bullying and brutality. She makes the viewer complicit within the drama of her unfolding narrative by capturing their image and displaying their personal information in the gallery. The viewer is exposed but also aware of their safety, because they remain enclosed in the gallery’s controlled spaces. I showed a part of this installation in the exhibition I curated at the Sharjah Art Foundation in the United Arab Emirates, *Art in the Age of Anxiety*, which was set to open in 2020 on the eve of the global pandemic that would be COVID-19. The gallery doors opened and closed as regulations continued to adjust. As 2020 unfolded and visibility grew around the Black Lives Matter movement, and the intentionality of police brutality, her artwork took on new agency. It was a microscope on a global problem, but also an affirmation of what many of us had known all along.

I am writing on Hershman Leeson’s birthday. I hurriedly send her an email in lieu of a gift or a card. The artist responded, jubilant: at eighty years

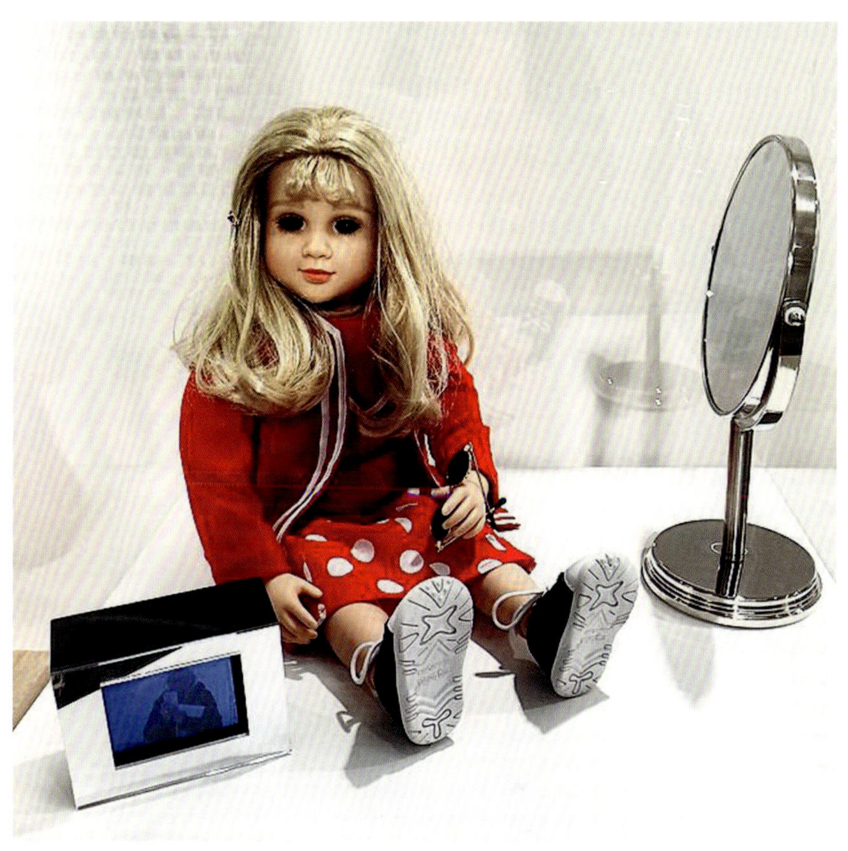

Lynn Hershman Leeson, *CybeRoberta*, 1994 — Telerobotic/surveillance webcam, custom-made doll with custom-made wig and dress, two webcam eyes, mirror, monitor programmed by Colin Klingman/Palle Henckel, c.17¾ × 17¾ × 7⅞ in. (c.45.1 × 45.1 × 20 cm), edition of 3 + 1 AP

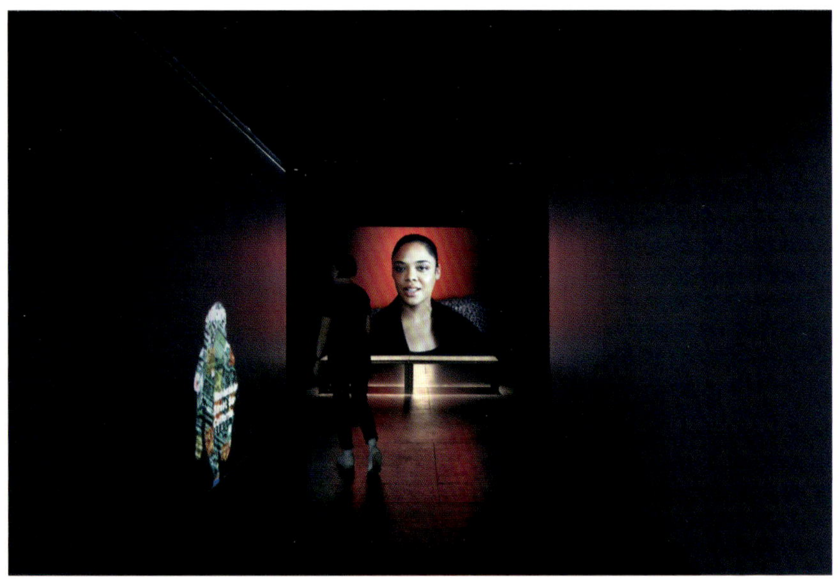

Lynn Hershman Leeson, *Shadow Stalker*, 2019 —HD 4K video installation with interactive programming, 11 min., edition of 3 + 1 AP

of age, she was installing *Twisted,* her first major museum solo show in New York, at the New Museum. Despite the length of time it had taken for such recognition to emerge, there was not a hint of lament in her tone. Jori Finkel published a laudatory review and interview with the artist in the *New York Times* emphasizing her landmark works, such as *CybeRoberta.*[19]

Cyborgs Come to Life

Multimedia French artist Mireille Porte, who adopted the name ORLAN at the age of fifteen, became a global phenomenon in the 1990s with her technologically inflected body art. Pushing the limits of what was then perceived as publicly allowable, ORLAN continually refashioned her identity using her own body as a site for extensive plastic surgery, body modification technology, and the corporeal implantation of accentuating materials that would make her resemble a real-life cyborg—a living and breathing amalgamation of the possibilities of evolutions in medical technology, alongside her genetically birthed physical characteristics. Her most famous persona, that of Saint-ORLAN, would emerge and reappear over the years. These hybrid identities spoke to the mechanisms through which the media in all its forms demands an impossible performance of unattainable formal identity. Today, with easy access to augmented reality (AR), almost anyone can now perform such transformations through illusions. In 2018, ORLAN first presented the ORLANOÏDE, a robotic version of herself equipped with the possibility to produce responsive personae generated by artist interactions.[20]

ORLAN laid the groundwork for a field of artists who explored the limits of the human body. In 2004, the artist Neil Harbisson had an antenna implanted permanently into his head and is now considered the world's first legally recognized cyborg. The artist worked with computer scientist Adam Montandon to develop technology that would provide Harbisson, who is color blind, with a new sensory experience wherein a webcam translates color into sound waves perceptible to Harbisson through headphones. Over time, the apparatus has expanded to send other signals to their brain, which Harbisson reports includes various forms of data received via a Wi-Fi network installed in their body. Harbisson is and has become an activist for trans-species rights and cofounded the Cyborg Foundation, which has the mission to support cyborgs and defend cyborg rights, with artist Moon Ribas in 2010.

Meeting a Specter From the Future?

In 2010, I believed I had encountered my first cyborg IRL in the form of Wafaa Bilal, an Iraqi-born artist who spent two years in refugee camps after fleeing Iraq during the first Gulf War and was now teaching photography at New York University (NYU). I was on a research trip in the United States in pursuit of diasporic Arab artists whose work engaged with technology. I was preparing an exhibition at Cornerhouse in Manchester, England, where I was senior curator at large alongside my position at FACT. On campus to attend a lecture, I caught sight of Bilal and followed him apprehensively. I could see a bulbous lens poking out of the back of his head. I wondered if it would be against professional norms to corner someone whom I knew only by virtue of a search-engine image result. I was introduced to him on that trip at a reception, perhaps through curator Anne Barlow, who was then director of Art in General. Upon meeting, I muttered a few hurriedly put-together words in Arabic, incoherent gibberish. Bilal smiled at me with a glorious Cheshire-cat grin. "You want to know what is in my head?" he teased in a lilting polyglot accent. We struck up a conversation and exchanged details. I texted him while I was in New York, but I did not get to know what was in his head at this time.

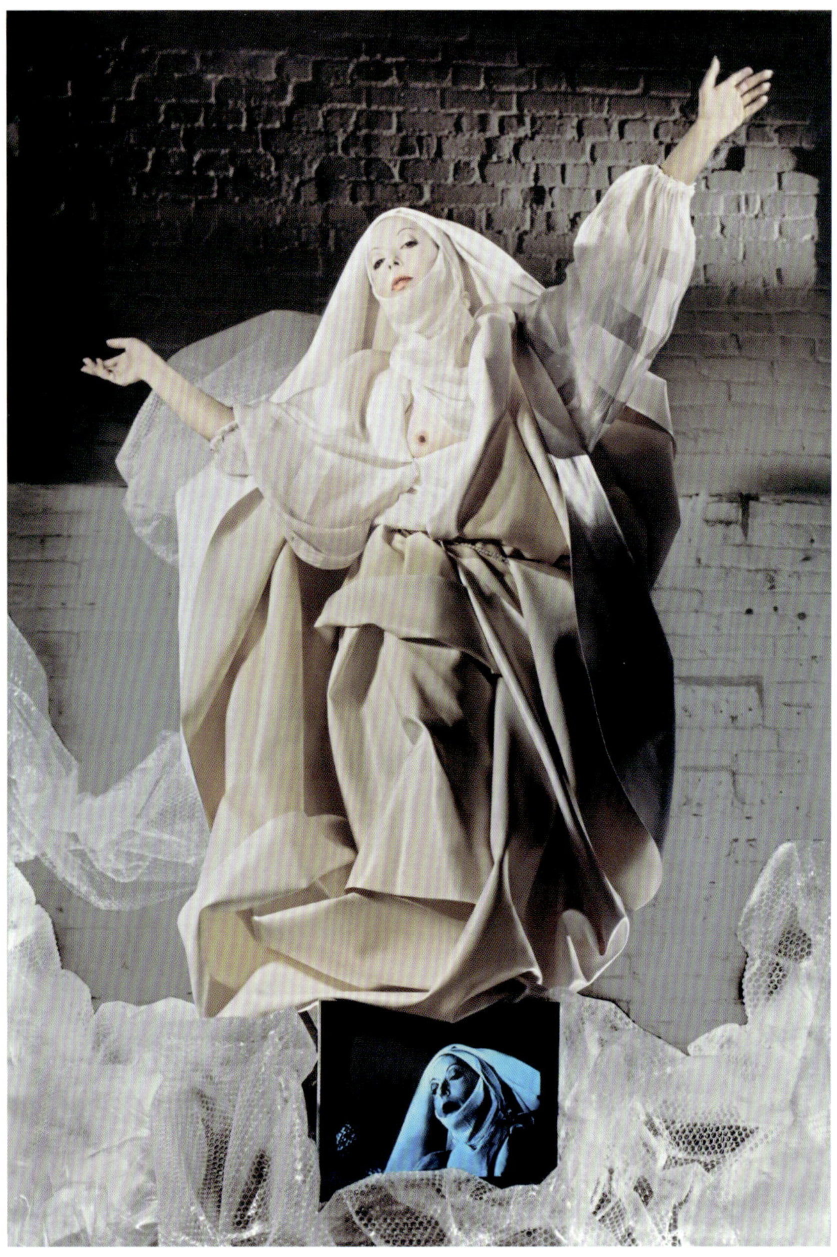

ORLAN, *Whites virgins with plastic bubbles clouds,* 1983
__Color photograph, 63 × 47¼ in. (160 × 120 cm)

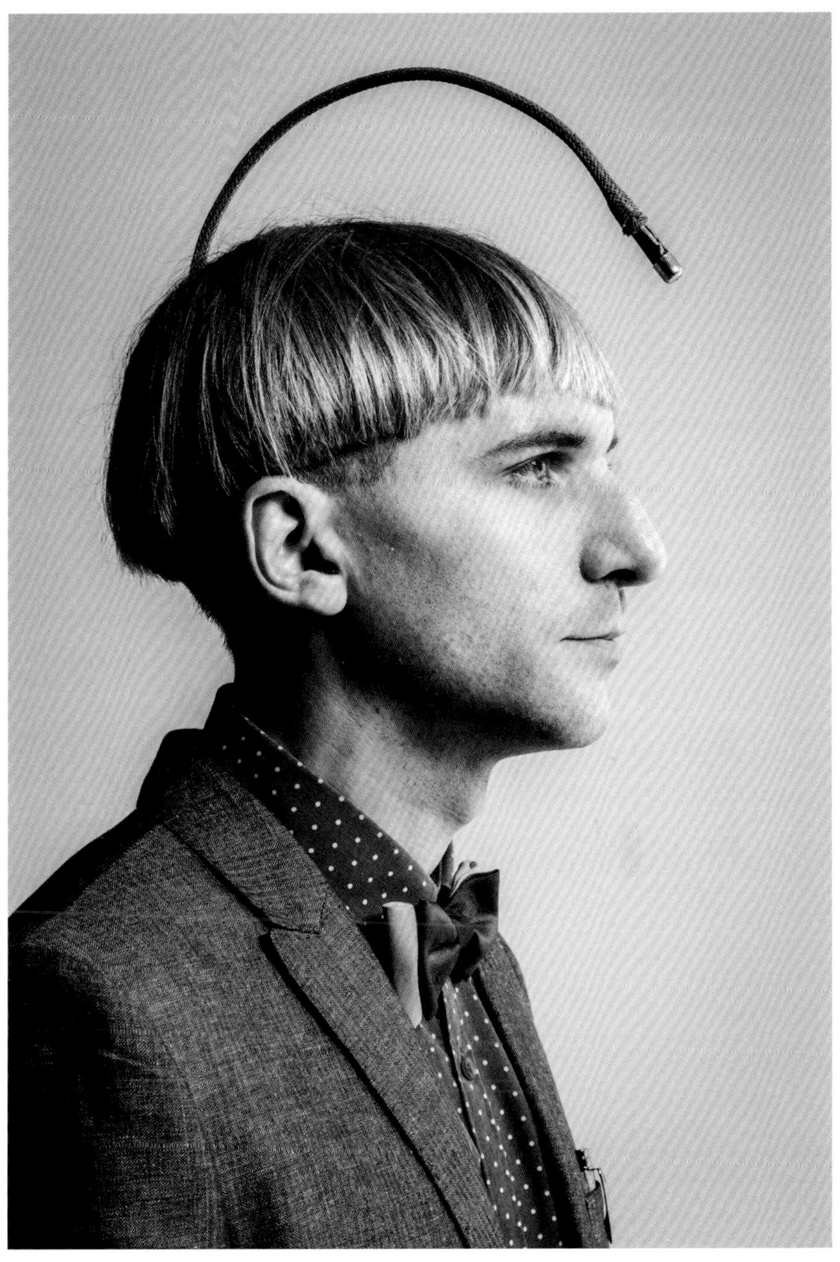

Cyborg—Neil Harbisson, 2015

In the two-way process between artist and curator, earning their trust is pivotal.

In the airport on my way to Dallas at the end of the week, I researched the artist further on one of the airport's pay-as-you-go desktop computer stations. I took copious notes on my smartphone, as well as compiled audio recordings, which I then transcribed into text in little notebooks that I lined up on my bedroom floor and against the wall. The news online revealed sensationalist stories about a university professor installing a camera into his head. The camera took one photograph every minute over the course of a year and the results of Bilal's project, *3rdi* (2010–11), were broadcast onto a livestream station held by the artist, first privately and subsequently online. His intention or purpose was not examined in these articles. More attention seemed to be given to the fear that something or someone caught on his camera might be accidentally exposed to the world.

Most of the footage he had captured was quotidian at best. The point of it all, as I gathered from subsequent in-person conversations with Bilal over the years, was perhaps to understand what it meant to hold a camera back at a structure of power. But in this case, the censorial potential of the institution to stop the artist was not possible. If the camera was a part of who he was, then it would surely be discrimination to ask him to remove it or punish him by halting his classes or denying him tenure. Bilal was no stranger to controversy. His previous artwork *Domestic Tension: Shoot an Iraqi* (2007) was a month-long interactive performance during which the artist lived in isolation in a gallery accessible to viewers via webcam. Those watching were able to remotely shoot the artist with a paintball gun, revealing the propensity of art to elicit subconscious human desires for violence and discrimination. The work was triggered by the death of the artist's brother via an unmanned aerial drone; the result also explored the automated violence associated with the culture of first-person shooter video games.[21] His exhibitions have been the subject of censorship, closure, and widespread threat.

Over the years, Bilal and I became friendly, bound by a shared sense of dissonance, speaking in multiple accents in western cultural institutions while sticking by our principled personal and political beliefs. After a year of his performance *3rdi*, he had the camera removed. He described the agony it caused in worrying detail. He suffered numerous recurrent infections, his life almost stripped out of him.[22]

Years later I asked him, "Do you need to have a machine in your body to be a cyborg?" He shook his head and pointed to the foggy air in the dingy Lower East Side coffee shop where we sat against a radiator, squeezed up against a window in the winter. "Machines are everywhere. We have already become them."[23]

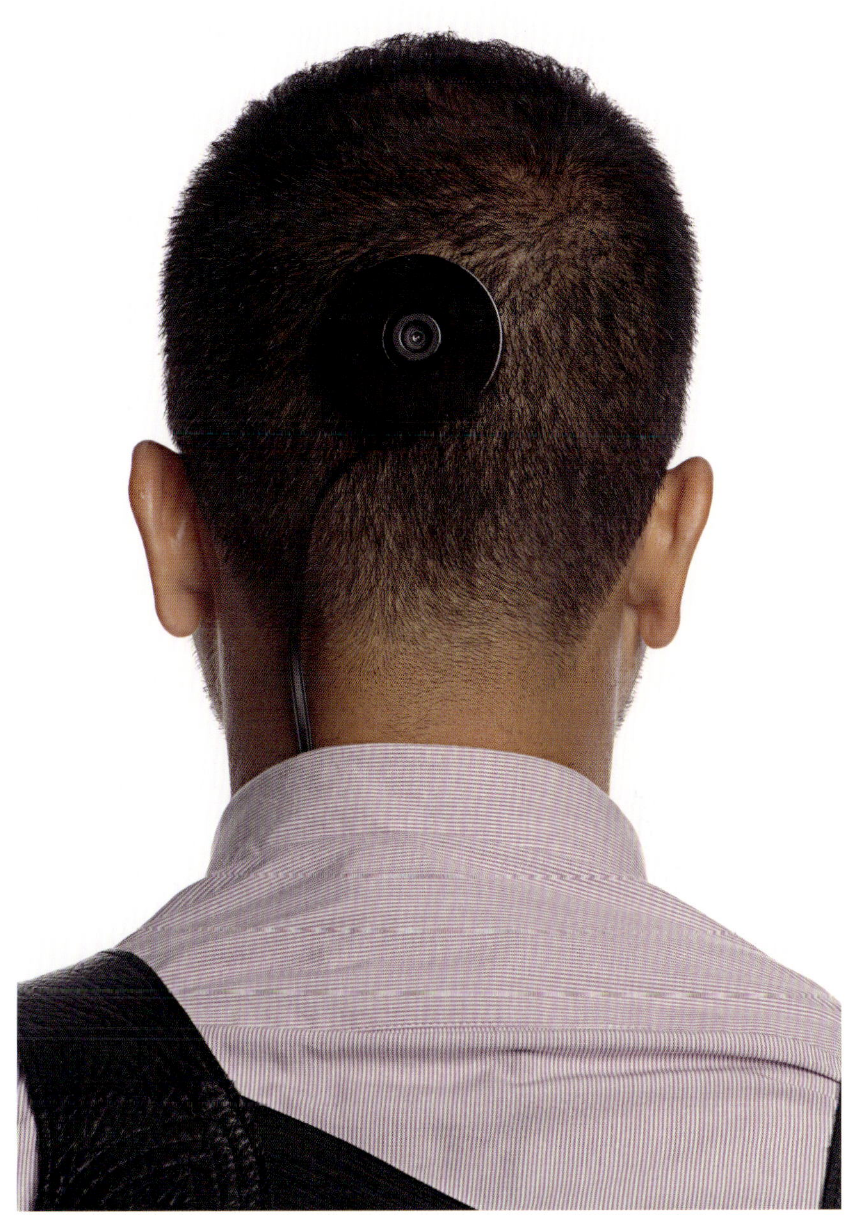

Wafaa Bilal, *3rdi*, 2010–11

Will This Destroy Us?

Nervous Technology

The neural pathways in my brain feel as if they're short-circuiting. I'm staring at an anonymous painting of rugged waves, practicing mindfulness on an app that's intended to suffuse me with calm. I play sea sounds from another application called Insight Timer; low tide sounds from a BBC podcast; ocean sounds from Spotify. It takes me twenty minutes to settle on which aural landscape to descend into. After repeat viewing of the 2020 Netflix documentary *The Social Dilemma*, I've been keeping notifications at bay. Now, I'm making extra time for relaxation. Two decades into the twenty-first century, relaxation is often conflated with the popularized concept of mindfulness—a state of conscious awareness that has become the vogue, as well as the subject of criticism. If attempting to soothe one's anxiety actually engenders more stress, perhaps things aren't adding up.

The heightened state of nervous consciousness associated with everyday life became the inspiration for one of the most popular group exhibitions I curated on the subject of the internet—*Art in the Age of Anxiety*, presented at the Sharjah Art Foundation in 2020. As mentioned in the previous chapter, the exhibition was scheduled to open just as the world entered a lockdown triggered by COVID-19. It was an apt beginning for the project's public launch.

The inspiration emerged while scrolling through Twitter one evening in my London apartment. In 2017, pop star Olly Murs had broadcast a message from Selfridges, one of London's most beloved department stores, that gunshots were being fired on Oxford Street. News spread like wildfire across RSS feeds. I conjured images of armed terrorists barricaded outside, as adjacent streets were closed off by police. I prayed to a cream-painted ceiling that the shooters bore no resemblance to my kind—people of color with Arabic or Islamic names. The policies enacted after September 11, 2001, and London's 7/7 Attacks in 2005 had become tools to strip many individuals of their rights; random stop and search by police had become pervasive—subjects that I would become more deeply attuned to through the art of Lawrence Abu Hamdan, whose juridical investigations through sound revealed how governments had used the ambiguity of language to separate families and strip individuals of their citizenship.[1]

The cavalcade of panic quickly came to a halt. The event was revealed to be fake news, propagated by unwitting agents. I immediately deleted my Twitter account after considering the potency that smartphones now held—these connective devices were now acting as super-spreaders, agents of contagion and unrelenting surveillance concealed beneath an amiable, corporate-designed facade.

I began writing a manifesto for a new age. My entire career had been anchored by a language for looking at art that was not my own. It was constructed by a generation of curators who emphasized the technical aspects of production when referring to art that engaged with technology, such as media arts or electronic art. I wondered if we could define art and its aesthetics through the concept of feelings. Feelings such as anxiety.

I picked up my landline phone for the first time since it had been installed and called the artist Trevor Paglen. A dozen WhatsApp messages and a couple of emails later, we were in conversation between Berlin and London about the potential for technological anxiety to shift human consciousness. Paglen, who trained as a geographer as well as a visual artist, often produces life-size photographs and feats of engineering that deploy programmed machines in their making. His photographs of clouds, dead historians, and deceased criminals, rendered through the lens of what he calls machine vision, formed the basis for the selection of artists whom I wanted to speak to for the new project that was taking shape in my head. What does it mean to look at a picture made by a machine and for it to resemble all the formal and aesthetic features of an image taken by a person with a camera held in their hands? If pictures, whether in museums or on social media, are representative mediators of some form of truth, one should interrogate the criteria that a machine uses to narrate history. That is if we are to believe that computers are devoid of the complexities of human subjectivity. I hung up the phone and continued to ruminate on my conversation with Paglen long after disconnecting.

Much has been authored, speculated, and hyperbolized about the algorithms that engineers use to program machines. Algorithmic culture finds its genesis in the everyday tools of commerce. Amazon.com uses algorithms to suggest further purchases to its customers built on buying and search history; Instagram sells lustful desire, influencer accounts based on the likes that you might have flippantly made while also watching TV; OnlyFans presents you with accounts to subscribe to based on your previous subscriptions; airline companies and tour operators anticipate your next holiday destination based on your online searches; Tinder and Hinge match potential romantic connections based on keywords and aesthetic profiles; Spotify and YouTube auto-play music selections that feel as if they've been gleaned from your unconscious. How? Most of these examples are functions devised by corporations that collect and mobilize your consumerist tendencies and make assumptions regarding your potential online activity. Everyone wants your money and, of course, your cultural capital—your tastes fit into demographic profiles that can be sold to develop further business opportunities, but many of you already know that.

We are all, by now, aware that without a targeted audience base and the potential for mass appeal, these forums can disappear without a hiss like so many of their predecessors and rival companies. MySpace anyone?

But what happens when we begin to consider the training of new artificial intelligence (AI) machines that in the not-too-distant future might act in place of border agents, security guards, or mortgage brokers? There is speculation that we cannot trust that programmers are truly able to fashion technological aids that are free of the bias of the person coding a given program or machine. In a project that has now come to be known as *ImageNet Roulette* (2019–ongoing), Paglen and AI researcher Kate Crawford worked together to trace six hundred thousand images found in ImageNet, a largely crowd-sourced photograph archive of more than fourteen million images. Through their research, the duo examined the indexical characteristics attached to certain pictures that have been used by AI developers as training images for machines. The first such experiment using ImageNet's archive was believed to have been carried out by researchers working at Stanford University in 2009.

I commissioned the first iteration of the project with the V-A-C Foundation for an exhibition I curated titled, *Time, Forward!*, which was timed to coincide with the 58th Venice Biennale. Paglen, incidentally, proposed the name of this group exhibition, which was a reference to a well-known Soviet slogan and popular film that had seemed to have lost its meaning in the contemporary era that was being defined by acceleration. The exhibition was anchored around what internally as organizers we were referring to as techno-futurism.

In the ornate central room on the first floor of the Venetian Palazzo del Zattere, thousands of carefully pinned thumbnails of pictures revealed the systemic racism and imperial violence inherent within these images and their indexical groupings. Attributions, which Paglen called person categories, classified gallery visitors with certain features as, crazy, bad person, convict, drug addict, kleptomaniac, fundamentalist, and terrorist, to name but a few examples.

Surrealist artist René Magritte (1898–1967) inspired Paglen's installation layout, which was intended to resemble the shape and contour of Magritte's *This is Not an Apple* (1964). I expected hushed nervousness or a sense of unease among viewers. Yet, as is the case in many an exhibition or large art festival, I witnessed visitors keeping their heads burrowed in their smartphones. Occasionally, they looked up, perhaps appreciating the artwork's formal composition, and posed for a selfie before marching on between the narrow corridors of the exhibition. The endless skip and trot of the art lover at the world's largest public festival of visual art, is itself a

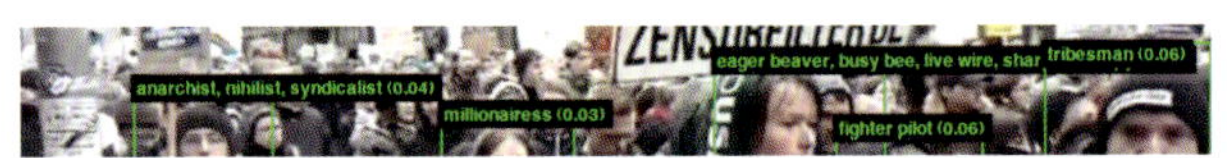

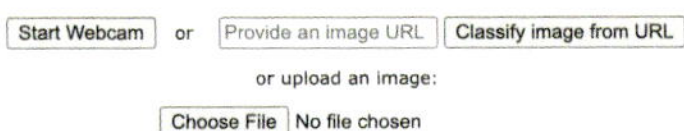

ImageNet Roulette is a provocation designed to help us see into the ways that humans are classified in machine learning systems. It uses a neural network trained on the "Person" categories from the ImageNet dataset which has over 2,500 labels used to classify images of people.

Warning: ImageNet Roulette regularly returns racist, misogynistic and cruel results.
That is because of the underlying data set it is drawing on, which is ImageNet's 'Person' categories. ImageNet is one of the most influential training sets in AI. This is a tool designed to show some of the underlying problems with how AI is classifying people.

Start Webcam or Provide an image URL Classify image from URL

or upload an image:

Choose File No file chosen

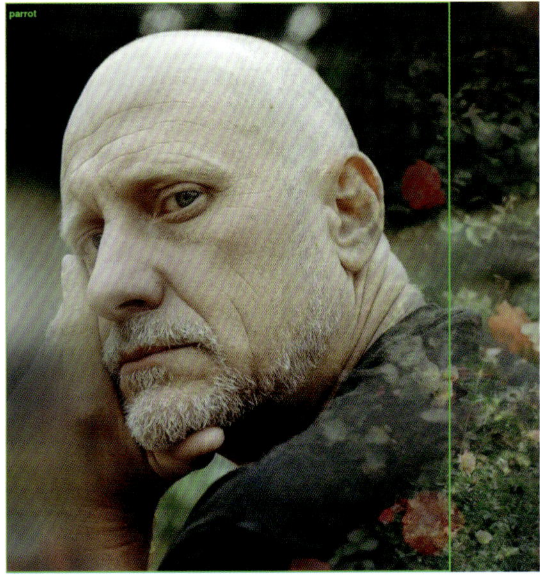

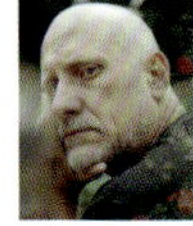

parrot: *a copycat who does not understand the words or acts being imitated*

- person, individual, someone, somebody, mortal, soul > copycat, imitator, emulator, ape, aper > parrot

Trevor Paglen, *ImageNet Roulette*, 2019

form of anxiety, as the visitor attempts to take in the hundreds of exhibitions on display.

A few months later, an expanded constellation of the images was presented at the Fondazione Prada in Milan, before another version was opened to public view in the Curve gallery at the Barbican Art Centre, London. At this point, the singular lens of the mass media brought the project into focus, calling ImageNet a "racist technology."[2] Within days of this maelstrom, which spread from broadcast to print media, ImageNet decided to dump all six hundred thousand of the categorical pictures identified by Crawford and Paglen from its publicly accessible system.

What is one to make of this response? One could interpret it as evidence of success—social justice that proved technological bias. Alternatively, the immediate erasure of these pictures can also been seen as a signal of failure. Withdrawing them from view allowed a reprieve from public criticism and the accusation of bias. Did the project just reveal that ImageNet can have its datasets critiqued and dumped without a single individual being held accountable? In such an instance, it is unclear how one can interrogate the taxonomy of an image, especially when the structural powers that create it are relying on selective crowd-sourced information without the editorial will to protect certain technologies from misuse.

From online bullying to cyberstalking and identity theft, exploitation has been rife on internet platforms—namely, Web 2.0 technologies, such as Facebook and Twitter—ever since these spaces came into existence. In 2016, the talk of the virtual town was the Facebook-Cambridge Analytica Scandal. The scoop: British consulting firm Cambridge Analytica harvested what is now assumed to be eighty-seven million Facebook user accounts by incorporating discrete personality tests into Facebook that would allow Cambridge Analytica to craft targeted political advertising. The result was intended to aid in the political campaigns of former U.S. President Donald Trump and Senator Ted Cruz. Unconfirmed allegations subsequently materialized that the data compiled was also co-opted to influence the result of the UK's Brexit Referendum.

A 2019 Netflix documentary *The Great Hack* was released to critique the culprits, and Facebook agreed to pay a £500,000 ($643,000) fine to the UK's Information Commissioner's Office—the maximum possible at the time, but a mere fraction of its total annual profit, which is forecast to be between nineteen and twenty-one billion U.S. dollars per annum, if one is to consider the company's publicly traded stocks as a reference. Facebook, now called Meta, continues to be one of the largest conglomerates in the world and is one of the "Big Five" tech companies, which also include Apple, Amazon, Microsoft, and Google's parent company, Alphabet.

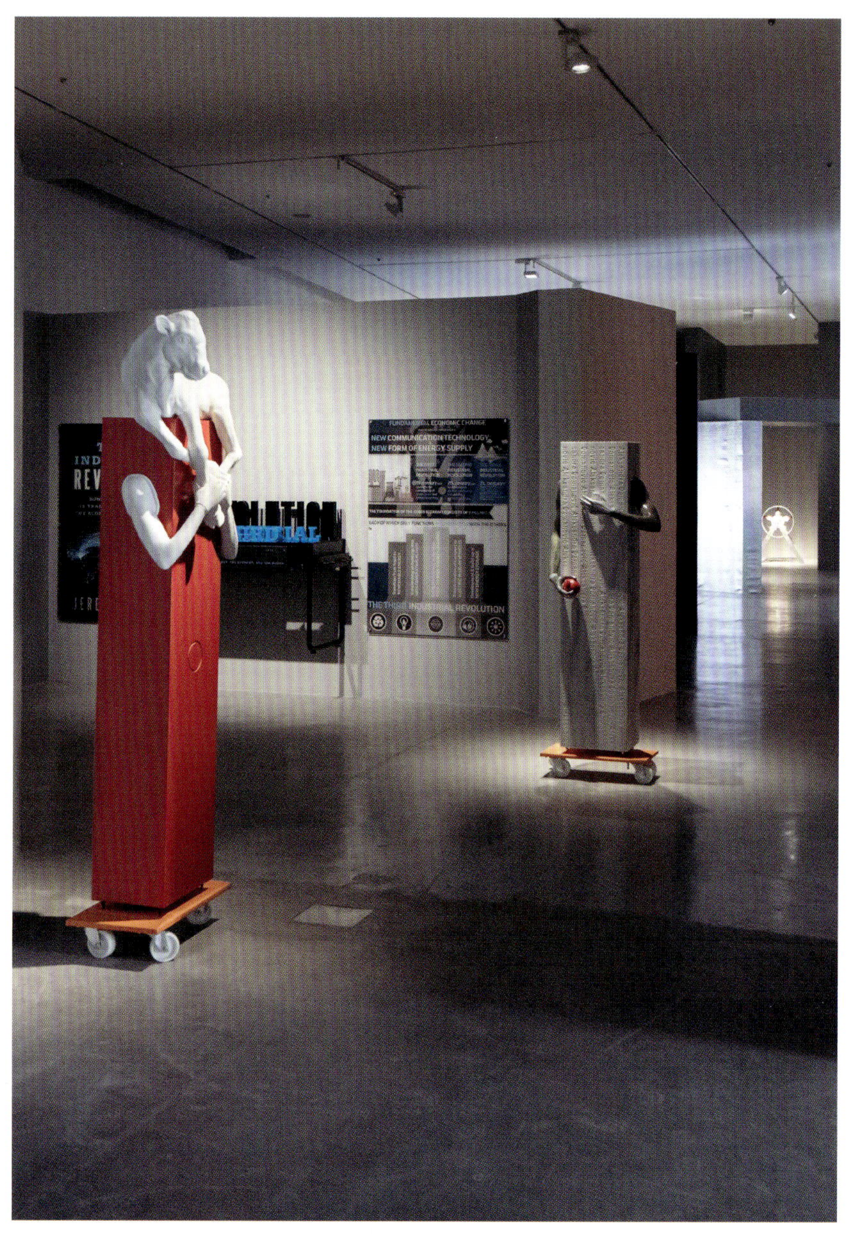

Art in the Age of Anxiety, 2020 —Installation view: Gallery 1, Al Mureijah Art Spaces, Sharjah Art Foundation, UAE

According to a 2019 article from the BBC, the four most downloaded applications from 2010–19 were Meta's digital programs: Facebook, Facebook Messenger, Instagram, and WhatsApp. All of these are reported in some capacity to boast in the orbit of one billion users each.[3] The company's investment portfolio has continued to grow, including leading virtual reality (VR) provider Oculus (which emerged through a Kickstarter campaign), as well as companies such as LiveRail and Threadsy.

Market intelligence aside, the context and existence of the internet—from its endless newsfeeds filled with woe to the countless circular email chains it spawns to the fear provoked by web surveillance and censorship—all have the potential, if not managed carefully, to induce a sense of perpetual anxiety. With nearly half the world's population online, the internet—the system of networks that connects us through numerous guises including the World Wide Web and mobile telephony applications—has irrevocably ushered in the greatest technological revolution known to humanity. If society is to aspire to be democratic, these spaces must somehow be claimed as our own. Cultural and technological innovations, both rapid and slow, create schisms. One way that these fractured moments have taken shape has been through the pursuit of online forms of activism—a practice that has sought to decolonize certain aspects of the virtual world. A major example is the bringing of the Black Lives Matter movement to global visibility. With this foundation in place, we cannot deny our complicity if we continue to allow ourselves to be controlled by the players who own daily technological tools that we use. Instead, we have the potential to strip the infrastructure and technologies apart, and perhaps even find ways to shift the spotlight.

Art in the Age of Anxiety

When the president of the Sharjah Art Foundation invited me to conceive of an exhibition that reflected the internet's future potential, I was compelled to formalize the concept that had been taking shape in my head: *Art in the Age of Anxiety*. I hid the title from the organizers at first, wary that they might find it alienating to the local public. At the same time, I was cocurating the 14th edition of the Sharjah Biennial (2019), the international contemporary art and cultural programming platform for modern and contemporary art from the Global South and beyond. During the planning of the Sharjah Biennial, I brought luminaries from the field of internet art, such as Cory Arcangel and Ian Cheng, to the United Arab Emirates to conceive new projects. During the biennial, they took over the walls of heritage houses and public squares with their animated critiques of narrative and mass-produced culture. In the lead-up to the event's opening, I was also to become the Sharjah Art Foundation's first director of collections and senior curator. As a new recruit, I didn't want to provoke feelings of anxiety in the team; I volunteered to push back the exhibition when the opportunity arose to do so.

Although no longer actively planning for that exhibition, I continued thinking about the artists whose interests dovetailed with my own. As well as Paglen, there was Lawrence Abu Hamdan, whose investigative pursuits have led him to unfurl the technological forms that governments use to categorize human identity, and Cao Fei, whose experiments in the online virtual world, Second Life, have led her to interrogate how millennials, in particular, construct and perform their sense of self. As I looked into this field of vision, the question emerged: how do we define an age? If one is to conform to historical precedent, it is essentially a span of years when one event began and ended. Examining this largely European concept, one notices that the Middle Ages, the Stone Age, and the Iron Age are all constructed around technological evolution, but equally, the proliferation of capitalist ideas. Ages are also defined by conflict and rule, from the Persian Empire (559–331 BCE) to the Victorian era (1837–1901), World War I (1914–18), and World War II (1939–45), and the trauma of the Great Depression (1929–33) in the United States. While attempting to put a label on the work of a group of artists who emerged largely after the new millennium, it became increasingly difficult not to take into consideration their concerns and preoccupations. The artists working today were not merely interested in the formal potential of their technologies; I couldn't classify them as subjects of the Age of Big Data, the Counterculture, or of a specific revolution. These three artists, like the many others I had visited in preparation for the now-postponed exhibition of internet art, were all consumed with and by a certain kind of chaos.

Abu Hamdan, who goes by the alter ego or avatar, Private Ear (akin to a private investigator or PI), is largely preoccupied by the disorder of governance that occurs when governments misuse or misrepresent technologies, especially when deployed as tools to make decisions around immigration or purported narratives of the truth. Paglen is arguably anxious that the software and hardware of the internet disguise invisible obstructions of power, thus making it easier for states to co-opt citizens into decisions, experiences, or lives that are not of their own choosing. Cao has consistently produced propositional works that illustrate the interior desires of youth in her native China to argue for a new visual sphere, where the users are also authors and makers, not merely corporations under the thumb of state censorship or control. Pooling these ideas together returns us to the notion of instability, of political incoherence—the fragmentation of a linked-up public sphere, whereby there is a single means to negotiate solidarity—a unified concept of togetherness in support of a cause, aim, or set of beliefs.

Not knowing what to believe was a theme explored by the artistic duo, Joana Hadjithomas and Khalil Joreige. Their 2016 exhibition, *I Must First Apologize . . .*, which I co-organized at various venues, among them, in 2016 at the MIT List Visual Arts Center, Cambridge, Massachusetts, focused on the social, economic, and political limits of email spamming and scamming. Presenting narratives from spam and scams collected for more than fifteen years, the pair animated this information as data. For example, a globular sculpture made from oxidized steel titled *The Geometry of Space* (2014) sought to reveal the geographic movement of networked communication. At the heart of the show was *The Trophy Room* (2014). Through sculptural displays invoking the architecture of Lina Bo Bardi, the artists presented lengthy scrolls of correspondence between scammers and scambaiters—individuals who seem to take pleasure in trying to scam the scammers, often by promising them financial rewards while in return requiring certain, sometimes heinous, acts. One of the documented examples included being tattooed with a racial slur.

Through these artworks, along with the accompanying video installations, documentaries, and investigative work, Hadjithomas and Joreige demonstrate how the power dynamic of who scams and who is being scammed replicates a hierarchy of global power struggle. The exhibition maps resource scarcity and how this contributes to social and economic inequity. Still, the artists articulate that their proposition constellates around a shared human desire for belief. The will to be scammed helps foster a space for active and engaged storytelling—a defining feature in the age of the internet.[4]

Slippages in conscious terminology are rampant in the hypersaturated world of social-media overflow. Instead of attempting to return to a neat definition of how to present art's recent history, the aggregation of conversations and encounters with artists insisted on a return to my original premise: *Art in the Age of Anxiety* was to be. Instead of defining an age through the concept of the event, I would build up an exhibition anchored around the concept of emotion. I wanted to consider how technologies had affected our subconscious minds—the anxiety provoked, for example, by the spread of fake news on social media.

Art in the Age of Anxiety finally opened in the public squares and galleries of Sharjah Art Foundation's Al Mureijah Art Spaces on June 26, 2020.

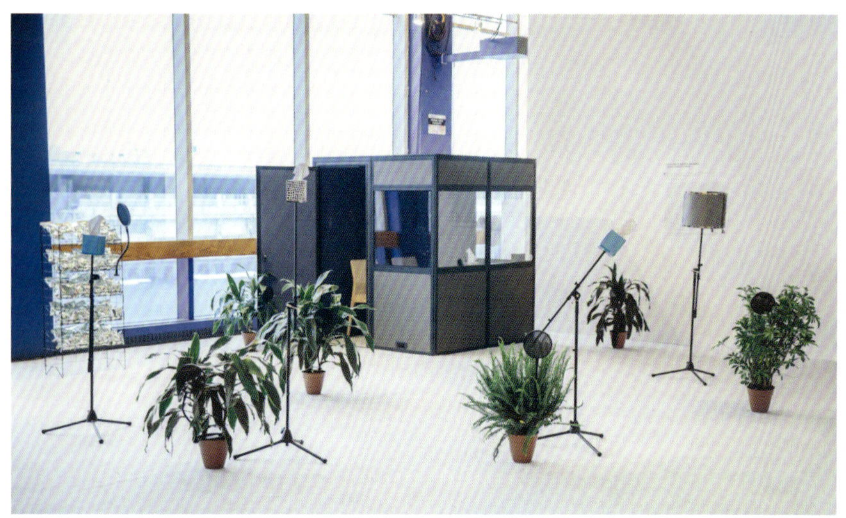

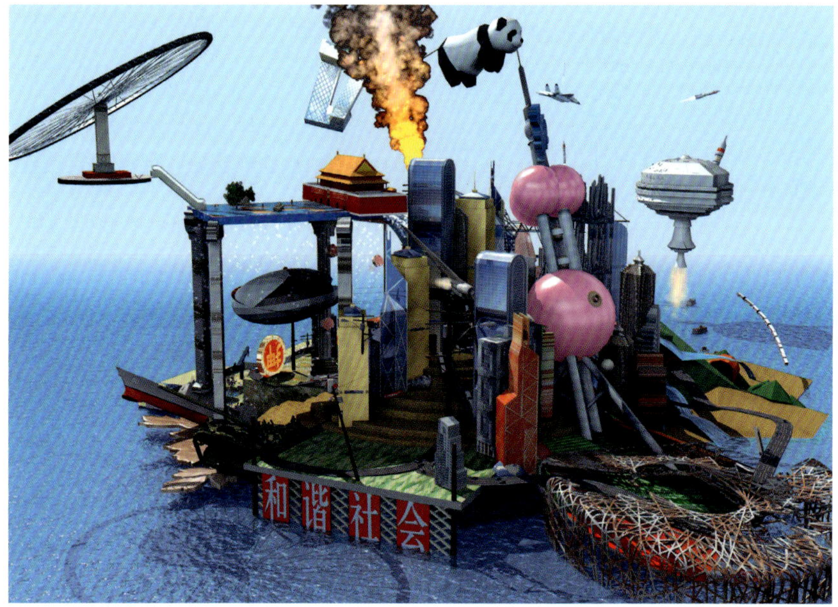

Lawrence Abu Hamdan, *A Convention of Tiny Movements*, 2015
—Mixed-media installation. Installation view: Armory Show, New York, 2015

Cao Fei, *RMB City: A Second Life City Planning*, 2007
—Video, color, sound, 5 min. 57 sec.

My last memory of visiting the show was watching visitors, cross sections of age, gender, and ethnicity, congregating in Fen Café, awaiting their prebooked ticket entry slot—a practice put into place to ensure social distancing after the start of the pandemic.

The exhibition experience began before the visitor could even see the gallery. Hushed sounds were audible on the approach to the Foundation's venues. Depending on the time of day, they would crescendo from the sound of someone singing "Baa, Baa, Black Sheep" to the deafening noise of a chopper overhead at the entrance to the first gallery. This was a project that I began working on with Abu Hamdan in 2014, *A Convention of Tiny Movements* (2015–ongoing), commissioned by the Armory Show in New York. It emerged after the artist learned of an object called the visual microphone, which was being developed, trialed, and tested at the Massachusetts Institute of Technology (MIT). Scientists had discovered that with this high-speed camera, they could recover the latent sounds from everyday objects, from potato-chip bags to mugs, through the vibrations made against the surfaces of each vessel. Words spoken between two people can forever remain embedded in a nearby object—everyday containers of surveillance.

In the first iteration of *A Convention of Tiny Movements*, thousands of silver, shimmering potato-chip bags lined the spaces of Pier 92 in New York at the VIP preview of one of the city's most popular art fairs, the Armory Show. The chips were devoured by patrons and the bags tossed onto tables, becoming an apparatus that shadowed and followed them. Upstairs, an installation consisting of a garden of microphoned plants and a private booth demonstrated the covert technology, playing back sounds from the most unexpected of places.

In Sharjah, the courtyards surrounding the venue held Abu Hamdan's speakers, hidden among plants and trees, spitting back experiences of private life. The sense of foreboding created by this artwork was mirrored in the exhibition's design. For the first time in my curatorial career, I enlisted an architect, Todd Reisz—author and former researcher and architect at Office for Metropolitan Architecture (OMA)—for the job. I gave him one directive: I want everyone who walks into these spaces to feel as though they're being funneled down a fiber-optic cable. Reisz responded by creating slanted walls in fifteen shades of gray; reflective surfaces to create spectral shadows that would disorientate the viewers; and mazelike structures invoking queer bathhouses and the German Expressionist film, *The Cabinet of Dr. Caligari* (1920). Reisz also incorporated interactive sonic landscapes by artist Aura Satz and a cat peeping from a metallic ceiling. Was it alive, a meme, or a taxidermized animal?

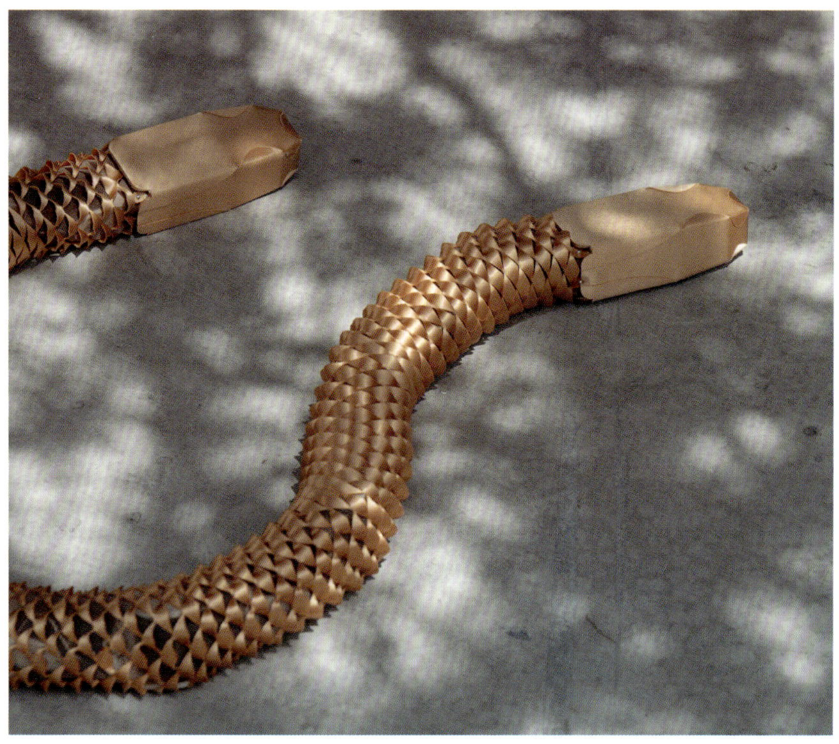

Pamela Rosenkranz, *Healer (Sands)*, 2019 —Robot snake, 47¹⁄₁₄ in. (120 cm). Installation view: Art in the Age of Anxiety, Sharjah Art Foundation, UAE, 2020

We began to refer to the first gallery as the digital silkscreen, a site that blurred the boundaries between what is real and virtual. The visitor proceeded to the finale of Abu Hamdan's work, a voice from behind summoned you. An airport chatbot? An AI bot? In fact, it was *Homo Sacer* (2014), an artwork by James Bridle, in which a virtual assistant read out legal statements about citizenship and death. In between these two spaces one could bear witness to reflections—scenes from Cao Fei's *RMB City* (2007–ongoing), a virtual city designed by the artist in Second Life. In *People's Limbo in RMB City* (2009), a group of characters takes over the artist's cityscape, including avatars of figures, such as Karl Marx and Mao Zedong, as well as a character named Lehman Brothers. In a comedic interplay, these figures dance around the issues of the global economic crisis of 2008. Whether their conversations are real, fictive, or staged are for the viewer to decipher. One of the pivotal questions that arises is whether credibility is developed through language. During the exhibition's run, many visitors questioned me about the concept of making art in the Second Life world. If one can exist behind the anonymity of an avatar, is it then all right to enact heinous behavior, or is this just a temporary site of escape from a world decaying through ecological and political disaster, one where behaving badly is acceptable? In the exhibition's publication, I explored the concept of digital dualism. Separating one's virtual self from their perceived real identity is a dangerous binary that requires interrogation.

In between the gallery buildings, an algorithmically programmed snake commissioned for the 14th Sharjah Biennial called *Healer (Sands),* created by Pamela Rosenkranz in 2019, hid and contorted in the sunlight, It offered an eerie distraction as one wandered through the labyrinthine halls, where one could witness Douglas Coupland's silkscreens of soldiers with redacted faces and Bogosi Sekhukhuni's reenactment of his first meeting with his father on Facebook Messenger—his paternal figure here animated as a preprogrammed robotic avatar. Streaks of red light beamed out into the street, ushering visitors into a makeshift karaoke venue by Thomson & Craighead (Jon Thomson and Alison Craighead), where visitors could sing along to lyrics gleaned from spam email, before entering a vast expanse where Antoine Catala's animated robot emojis hovered in motion. Paglen's *Houghton Cloud #865* (2019) sat at one end of the exhibition—a metaphor visualized through machine vision, while Tabor Robak's oversize iPhone drew alarming headlines from the news media, spurting out pandemic-era terror. As one exited, a word poem by an artist who chose to remain anonymous beamed in shimmering gold. It begged the question, "Is Your Centre Inside of an Email Chain?" A specter of what was to come perhaps: a life lived in a never-ending email chain.

We had originally planned to open our doors the second week of March 2020. But as we prepped the final details for the show—the meticulously designed metallic vinyl panels and the contrasting lights—the team started to panic, because of the daily news media alerts regarding what they referred to as coronavirus. A number of our consultants scurried off on planes, having heard rumors that Dubai International Airport—the busiest long-haul airport in the world—was to close.

Anxiety levels soared, from RSS feeds to everyday life. One after another, exhibiting artists canceled their trips to the opening—more than thirty artists and collectives representing nearly eighty works. I was sent "home," to an empty apartment into which I had just moved, sleeping on an air mattress, my belongings in the two suitcases. The airports—all of them—did, indeed, close that evening. A curfew was instated. Permissions became required for everything. Had my hallucinations become real? Was the only life left to be lived through a telephone screen? Collecting hygienic supplies became a new obsession.

Thinking New

The early renderings of internet art occupied several institutional spaces, anchored by the specific media that artists were using at the time. Internet art that utilized video, such as the work of Judith Barry or Lynn Hershman Leeson, was often consigned to the black box—every western museum's newly constructed video-art gallery in the 1970s and 1980s. As technological forms progressed, institutional focus gave birth to venues, festivals, labs, and museums focused solely on what was most often referred to as new media art. These developments found their genesis in the late 1970s and became completely formed by the late 1990s. In 1978, MonteVideo, one of the first organizations to focus on the emerging field of media art, was founded in Amsterdam. It was later renamed the Netherlands Media Art Institute (NIMk). A year later, in Linz, Austria, Ars Electronica began as a premier festival of experimentation with media technologies. It has since grown into a center with a research and development lab and galleries that also houses the Museum of the Future within its space.

In 1981, the V2 Institute for the Unstable Media opened its doors in Rotterdam, the Netherlands, welcoming artists and theorists who are now of global renown, from performance artist Stelarc to the pioneer of carnal art ORLAN, and architects, such as the Pritzker Prize–winning resident, Rem Koolhaas. It has also played into festival culture, hosting the Dutch Electronic Art Festival since 1987. The emphasis on these events was conceived as a mechanism to showcase the year-round, intangible work of these organizations. Encouraging conversation across disciplines, the theory was that these labs could operate as discursive spaces free from the hermetic fold of the burgeoning tech industry in Silicon Valley and elsewhere. In 1988, the Dutch art scene introduced Impakt, a festival of media art in Utrecht, which aimed to broaden the discussion around new media, linking it with art-house and independent cinema. These are two fields of practice that have become increasingly interlinked through the mainstream success of visual artists and film directors, such as Sam Taylor-Johnson, Steve McQueen, Chris Moukarbel, Pipilotti Rist, David Salle, Amalia Ulman, and Martine Syms, to name but a few examples.

Perhaps the most prestigious venue to come onto the scene was ZKM Centre for Art and Media in Karlsruhe, Germany, which was founded in the pivotal year of 1989, and since 1999 it has been under the artistic direction of artist and theorist Peter Weibel. ZKM, set in a city known for promoting open access to the internet, served a catalytic purpose. It enshrined the art form that was always expected to be new in a museological context. Its institutional mission argued for the necessity to archive the art of our time, despite the fears expressed by many of the world's megamuseums of the potential obsolescence of new media. In 1993 in Werkleitz, Germany, the influential Werkleitz Society was formed. Now based in Halle, Germany, it is responsible for launching a major international festival of commissions and an attendant institute for education.

The Third Eye Centre in Glasgow, Scotland, had played host to many of these experimental forms until Liverpool's Moviola was cofounded by Eddie Berg in 1988. Moviola's biannual festival, entitled Video Positive, became a pioneering seat for all things that blurred the boundaries between technology and the moving image. In 2003, with Berg as the inaugural CEO, Moviola was transformed into the Foundation for Art and Creative Technology (FACT), the UK's national center for artists' film, video, and new media. While these histories might be known among an insular community of DIY artists and curators, the public record gives little space to them, or to the influence that they have had in shaping the context of what we understand as internet art today.

When I began my fully fledged curatorial career as a curator at FACT, I spent my afternoon cooped up in an archive filled with Betacam, VHS, and the early form of U-matic tapes, which were sandwiched among archival posters, notebooks, brochures, and visitor feedback from the Moviola days. What struck me most from the 1991 festival was that it showcased Palestinian-British artist Mona Hatoum's early video work, *So Much I Want to Say* (1983). Here, still images alternate every eight seconds: the artist's face in close-up, while a pair of male hands try to gag her attempts to speak. The soundtrack repeats the title in Hatoum's voice. Watching this on a degenerating VHS tape, after having spent a year working for a magazine, living between Egypt, Lebanon, and the West Bank, made all too painfully clear that the silencing of dispossessed voices was as suffocating today as it had been more than two decades before.

In my early days at FACT, I was sent off to understand the festival circuit for new media art. One of my first destinations was a Berlin-based festival known as transmediale. Founded as VideoFilmFest in 1988 as a festival for art and digital culture, the 2009 edition was being held primarily at the Haus der Kulturen der Welt (HKW) in Berlin. I asked for directions as I left my hotel. I was informed by the concierge (a figure that has all but disappeared in the era of self-check-in) that it looked like a spaceship that had crashed into Earth. It was in a park of some description; there was a fountain. I scurried on my way, on a train and off a train, my trousers covered in congealed black smudges from badly planned puddle hopping.

The HKW was dimly lit. Animations of a kind were being projected. The music was techno. An attempt to decipher a program guide led me nowhere. I felt alienated by the attendees with dyed blue and orange hair, who looked as if they'd been pulled from a poster of the 1995 film *Hackers*. It was my first time in Berlin, and I had no sense of orientation beyond my hotel room and little social clout to help me. I was the newbie. My fellow curators in the new media sphere (some of whom are now retired from art), spoke of this event as if it were some transcendent rite of passage. I stuck to the conference rooms, listening to a curator named Bronac Ferran as she introduced the web poet Lamis Saidi, from Algeria.

The theme that year celebrated an anniversary that has become emblematic for many of my generation—1989. Under the umbrella concept of the Deep North, the organizers sought to consider the impending effects of social, environmental, and economic catastrophes—discussions that are collectively still being debated, and largely not acted upon, in the public consciousness. A panel discussion on the problems of technology in Africa included political scientists, technologists, and writers, but no actual artists from the continent. I listened to innumerable people who spoke of design and architecture; nothing was ever discussed about the power or potency of art.

Thus began my circuitous dance around these spaces, whose directors and curators quickly became partners. With Bandit-Mages in Bourges, France; Ars Electronica; LABoral in Gijón, Spain; the Impakt Festival; the Werkleitz Institute; and others, I co-organized the European Media Art Residence in Exchange (EMARE) network. Artists were chosen by a committee from hundreds of commissions, most often based on each organizer's agenda and what they envisaged their publics would best respond to. I recall the desire for artists who could code. When I explained that artists could make new media art without knowing how to code, or even how to use a computer, I was laughed at by the men in the decision room.

I transposed some of my frustration into a pitch for Professor Stubbs, suggesting we partner on commissions and residencies with organizations in Brazil and Mexico instead of the weathered industrial towns of western Europe. Back then, such countries were eligible for so-called diversity points. We put in a funding bid, and as we waited, I was invited to join Stubbs to speak at ISEA International 2011. Founded in the Netherlands in 1990, ISEA International is the organizer of the International Symposium on Electronic Art (ISEA). It aims to contribute to the academic discourse around art, design, science, technology, and society, including new media and electronic art, and to work with, as its organizing body describes it, "culturally diverse organizations and individuals."

The fall 2011 edition, ISEA2011, was to take place in Istanbul, to coincide with the prestigious Istanbul Biennial of contemporary art. But after the initial keynotes, I felt drained. ISEA2011 gave me my first taste of the word *meta.* This seemed to be a site where people paid to speak to themselves in a language no one else could understand. But there was a high point that came whooshing toward me on that first afternoon: a robotic sculpture that went by the name of *Diamandini* (2011–13). It resembled a classical statue who had fled the museum and found herself stuck in the dry, subaltern cave of ISEA. The work was produced by the artist Mari Velonaki. It was exhibited at FACT a couple of years later.

I salvaged my trip with an excursion to two giant warehouses near the Istanbul Museum of Modern Art. There was an epic exhibition curated as an homage to the late artist Félix González-Torres (1957–1996). There was little discussion of computer or internet technology in these spaces, but the homage to González-Torres was more rhizomatic to me because of the way it linked artworks by living artists together using the oeuvre of a deceased artist as a curatorial lens through which to consider and understand their relevance historically and from a contemporary perspective. New, I was reminded, was not a simple matter of a technical apparatus, but instead the potential to put dissonant ideas into conversation with one another—curating itself could be made new!

Is This Art?

When I began navigating the terse terrain of internet art, of which I was a representative, I found myself perpetually perplexed by the terminology that was in use. I was called a curator of new media art, but this dovetailed with other fragments of a vocabulary that was constantly remaking itself. The art world in which I operated was responsible for representing *net art*, sometimes styled, *net.art.* It was also dubbed *electronic art,* as I've noted, as well as *digital art.* In other arenas, subfields have been referred to as, *interactive art*, *robotic art*, *cyborg art*, *telematic art*, and *systems art.* The binding quality of many of these subdisciplinary fields is that these practices are networked, whether through analog or digital protocols, and, today, are most often influenced by the network of all networks—the internet.

With the burgeoning of festivals, centers, and museums dedicated to emerging technologies, a warped aesthetic tendency began to emerge—technological spectacle. In 2011, the colossal *Translife* exhibition of fifty-three artworks by more than eighty artists from the field was staged at the National Art Museum of China in Beijing. The exhibition proposed to explore the post-human era but was representative of a form of kitsch kinetic ostentation, from Edwin van der Heide's *Evolving Spark Network* (2010–11) displaying a vast set of sparkling electric circuits situated in an overhead grid, to Diane Landry's *Knight of Infinite Resignation* (2009), which presented a flurry of bicycle wheels with luminescent plastic bottles attached that became animated like windmills. One of the most photographed works was a light sculpture that was thirteen feet (3.9 m) wide, supposedly the most authentic replica of the moon to have been produced at the time, by Wang Yuyang. It was aptly titled *Artificial Moon* (2011).

Translife was widely reviewed internationally, including in the *New York Times*. The local government had produced the event as a sequel to its arts festival to coincide with the 2008 Beijing Olympic Games. The government leveraged its funds to fly in journalists and major players in the technosphere of new media art. The woeful outcome was the result of the exhibition's objective of demonstrating artists' innovations with technology, and the gatekeepers of this field promoted figures who were not necessarily artists but designers and engineers experimenting with creative technology and co-opting the space of artists to display their feats of ingenuity. Search for the exhibition online today and there is barely a trace of it; the original website that hosted the show is all but a dead link.

Debates oscillate across the spectrum around this perspective, but the artists I was interested in were producing something altogether more daring. They created alternative landscapes that subverted the mechanisms of our newly adopted mainstream media. Through myriad interactions, they proposed tools for the co-option of social media to the omnipresent powers of branding and product placement. In 2004, Marisa Olson intervened in the reality television format, auditioning for the talent competition *American Idol*—a big no-no in the sacred sphere of art—while maintaining a training blog that followed her year-long journey. Petra Cortright warped our sense of the selfie by counterintuitively applying digital effects to her face. Amalia Ulman invoked a performative alter ego on Instagram that exposed how belief is constructed online, and Jayson Musson, aka Hennessy Youngman, melded African American vernacular with the alienating semantics of art theory and practice.

Youngman's vlog, ART THOUGHTZ, which has been viewed hundreds of thousands of times, was presented online over two years. Nonchalantly delivering his comments in hip-hop style, the artist, who acted as presenter, revealed the inherent contradictions of art's infrastructure—from the absurdity of paying for art school to the obtuse language that

Marisa's American Idol Audition Training Blog

The diary of my training to audition for American Idol. Auditions were 10/5/04 (in SF) & being there didn't guarantee me an audition, so I went on a mission to set myself apart from the crowd...

ABOUT

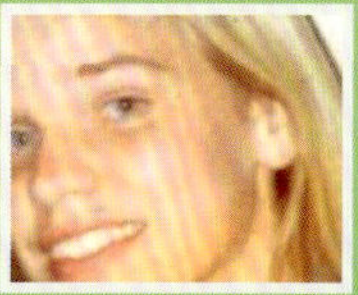

Email Me

ARCHIVES

May 2005
February 2005
January 2005
November 2004
October 2004
September 2004
August 2004
July 2004

CATEGORIES

Music (68)
Musicology (25)
Physique Training (18)
Show-womanship Training (33)
Song Selection (19)
Technology Rehearsal (13)
Television (66)
Training Diet (10)
Voice Training (18)
Wardrobe Training (18)

BROUGHT TO YOU BY...

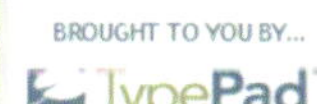

It's Over!!!

I'm surprised how many people are surprised that I'm not still blogging about American Idol. Like all endurance projects, this one had an end in mind, and like this season of the show, this project has come to an end. Of course, now that the season's over, some of my contractual obligations have loosened, and **in three months I'll be eligible to sign a record contract.** So, please, *keep those offers coming!* Like most blogs, this one is organized with the most recent posts at the top. If you want to read the entire three-month diary of my American Idol Audition training, scroll to the bottom and work your way up. If you just want to peruse the greatest hits, check out some of my fondest training memories, like the time I went high heel training, the time I toasted myself at the tanning salon, the time I campaigned in front of Fox HQ, my practice interview with Tabitha Soren, my solid gold weight training, and of course, the behind the scenes pix I took until they stopped me... Meanwhile, this is my *absolute final post* (sniffle), so I'll bid you a fond farewell and thank you for reading. It amazes me how many people I connected with over this silly site--even if my family thought I was crazy! Big ups to those who came to my show at 667 Shotwell (especially Chris Sollars, who helped me shoot a fictional re-enactment video of my audition)! Be sure to check out this blog and its iPod translation in the Rhizome Artbase 101 show, at New York's New Museum of Contemporary Art, June 23-Sept 10. {Update: Here is the NY Times review of the show.} Hugs and kisses in the key of E, marisa.

May 26, 2005 at 01:35 | Permalink | Comments (48) | TrackBack (0)

No More American Idol Secrets

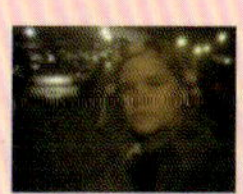
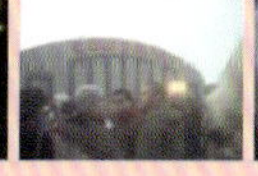
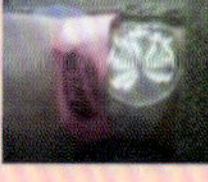

By now the cat's out of the bag: *I got rejected!!!*
I made it all the way to the Executive Producers, only to be turned down. After eating, sleeping, and breathing American

Marisa Olson, *Marisa's American Idol Audition Training Blog*, 2004–5

curators and writers use, such as the oft-deployed term, *relational aesthetics*. Episodes bear titles such as, "ART THOUGHTZ: How to Be a Successful Black Artist," "ART THOUGHTZ: How to Make an Art," and "ART THOUGHTZ: Poetic Waxin'." Here are a few introductory snippets for your pleasure:

> WHAT UP INTERNET. THIS YA BOY HENNESSY YOUNGMAN, AND TODAY I WANTED TO MOVE BACK INTO THEORY A LITTLE BIT AND INTRODUCE AND EXPLAIN THIS THING CALLED RELATIONAL AESTHETICS TO YA'LL. U KNOW I LOVE YOU INTERNET, AND AM JUST TRYING TO ENWISEN YOU TO THESE IMPORTANT CONCEPTS THAT BE SCULPTING THE INTELLECTUAL FRAMEWORK OF YOUR WORLD. LET'S GO![5]

> GYEAH! HELLO ONCE AGAIN INTERNET, TODAY I WANTED TO TALK ABOUT SOMETHING THAT IS VERY ESSENTIAL TO ART AND THAT THING IS BEAUTY. IS BEAUTY STILL RELEVANT IN OUR FUTURE AGE WHERE INFORMATION IS MADE VALUABLE AND NEOLIBERALISM IS THE NUMBER ONE POP TUNE THAT SEEMS LIKE IT WILL ALWAYS BE PLAYING EVERY TIME YOU TURN ON THE RADIO FOREVER INTO INFINITY? WELL I DON'T GOT ANSWERS TO THESE QUESTIONS, BUT THAT DON'T STOP ME FROM ENWISENING YA'LL TO THIS SHIT! LET'S GO![6]

> NOW I PRESENT TO YOU THE FIRST ART THOUGHTZ OF 2012, STARRING DAMIEN HIRST, BONO OF THE ART WORLD.[7]

Who Runs the World?

The cliché of the Anglo-European male bedroom geek turned computer nerd slash college dropout transforming into a young billionaire figure is as brittle a reality as any. The geniuses of start-up culture have often checked certain boxes (but not the "diversity" ones) perpetuated in mainstream media, whether the personification of Facebook's founder Mark Zuckerberg and the Winklevoss twins in David Fincher's award-winning feature film *The Social Network* (2010) or the more than dozen screen depictions of Steve Jobs's life, portraying him as an acerbic and cutthroat innovator-genius. Perhaps most notorious is Aaron Sorkin and Danny Boyle's 2015 screen adaptation of Walter Isaacson's biography, played out with over-the-top OCD by Michael Fassbender.

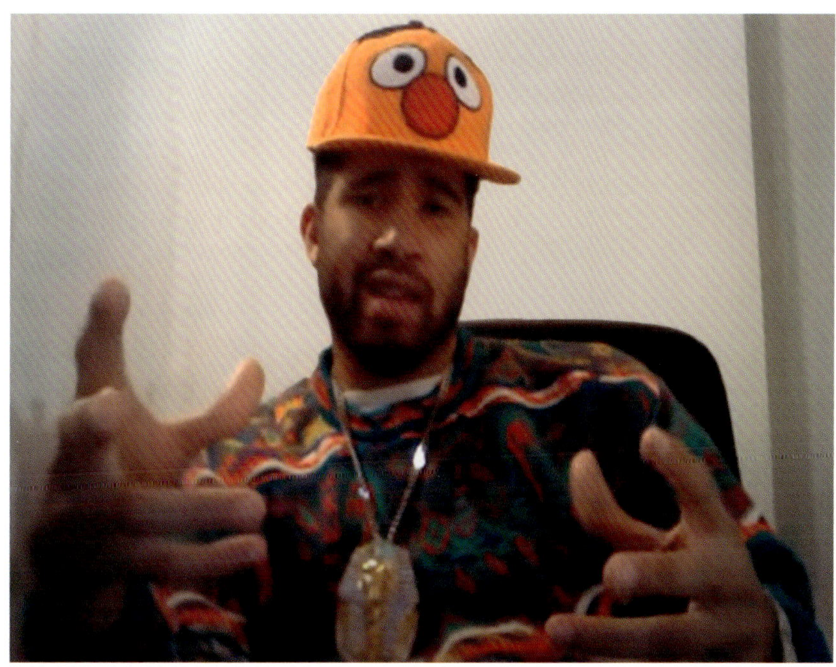

Jayson Musson, *ART THOUGHTZ: How To Make an Art*, 2011 __Webcam

The field of mainstream new media art—the artists and thinkers who circulated the European art new media art festivals and centers—was only marginally different in its makeup. I came to the realization of this when I was asked to organize Rewire, the fourth international conference on the "Histories of Media Art, Science and Technology" in the autumn of 2011 at Liverpool John Moores University. The entire steering committee was composed of white academics who seemed eager to relegate the one person of color in the room to the position of administrator. For the actual event, hundreds of papers and parallel sessions were sandwiched together in a haphazardly constructed layer cake that induced great frustration among delegates. In a moment of identification, I recall seeing two Black women on the final day, binders and folios held to their chests. I scampered after them, terrifying them into mute stillness. Conferences are different from festivals and museums, but here the gatekeepers who were present evinced a structural hierarchy that reflected the tech industry, even if these academics and curators believed themselves to be renegades for researching and teaching in a new field.

When the millennials began conquering the digital sphere, a kind of cancel culture began. Audiences were less obsessed with brick-and-mortar institutions than with the possibilities of experiencing art on and through myriad platforms. It became evident that the constellation of new media venues was creating a self-fulfilling silo for artists and those who worked with them. The broader art establishment—that is, national museums of modern and contemporary art—considered artists who engaged with technology to be uncritical, indeterminable, and unsettled in their identity, or, in other words, newly unfashionable.[8]

Everything that is out of vogue gives birth to another movement. This one was dubbed *post-internet art*. After two years at FACT, I developed a rapport with my colleagues Kate Taylor, a film curator, and Heather Corcoran, now a director at the crowdfunding platform, Kickstarter. Kate and Heather would regularly send me articles, most often video listicles from a website, rhizome.org. Rhizome had been set up in 1996 by the artist Mark Tribe as an email list for the discussion of what was then called *new media art*. By 1999, Rhizome had implemented an online platform called Artbase, with the intention of indexing and archiving website-produced artwork. The early days of Artbase relied heavily on crowdsourcing from a community that Tribe and his fellow employees had developed—of artists, writers, curators, and anyone with a genuine interest in the form. It was a democratically driven project that brought the genre of net art under one roof.

In 2003, the organization became an affiliate tenant of the New Museum, a pioneering space in New York that was founded by Marcia Tucker. Tucker had worked to champion the art of emerging artists from diverse backgrounds and perspectives. She stepped down in 1999, but there was an affinity between her trailblazing spirit and Rhizome's programs, which expanded within the museum to include major public programs and a now-famous commissioning program. From across the Atlantic, Rhizome's blog fueled my desire to make sense of the newly burgeoning field of post-internet art. The term *post-internet art* is broadly thought to have been coined by artist, curator, and writer, Marisa Olson (herself a former Rhizome editor and curator), in 2006, as a means to describe her practice. This laid the foundation for a flurry of debates, including the legendary blog by author Gene McHugh, *Post Internet*.

Many pundits and outsiders were puzzled by the use of the word *post*, which to some suggested an art "after the end of the internet." Yet what Olson, McHugh, and Rhizome's artistic director Michael Connor have argued is that *post-internet* is a condition that is symbiotic with the existence of the internet. It is not necessarily art that is technically connected to, or operated by the internet, but art that emerges from and through an awareness of the internet and its various characteristic tropes, aesthetics, and conditions. In 2014, Stedelijk Museum Amsterdam curator Karen Archey cocurated *Art Post-Internet* at the Ullens Center for Contemporary Art (UCCA) in Beijing with art scribe Robin Peckham, the first exhibition to consider the subject thematically at the time. The curators posited that this was a world where artists were working from an "internet state of mind," fluidly moving between genre and physical form due to the mobility, access, and information provided by and through the internet.

In Search of a Community

In summer 2010, I booked a plane ticket and an Airbnb studio and headed to New York. Before departing, I visited the Whitechapel Gallery in London to see screenings programmed by Ian White (1971–2013), where I was introduced to the work of dancer-filmmaker, Yvonne Rainer, the unusual social subjects of Sharon Lockhart, and the future doyenne of all things internet, Hito Steyerl. Clustered around White and his events were the members of Lux, an agency for artists' film, which grew out of the London Film-makers Co-op (LFMC); a smattering of queer folk including Sam Ashby, founding editor of *Little Joe*, a queer film and art magazine; Chris McCormack of *Art Monthly* magazine; and the drag queen Dr. Sharon Husbands, who ran the intimate literary salon Naked Boys Reading. White always spoke of New York as a home for dissident creative existence and encouraged me to connect when there with his friends, including Lauren Cornell, then the executive director of Rhizome and a curator at the New Museum, and Ed Halter of Light Industry, a space for film and electronic media.

When I arrived in the Bedford-Stuyvesant area of Brooklyn, which still felt like a center for African American culture and music, every corner seemed to be hosting a house party. As the weeks went on, I felt like a regular, scooting back from Manhattan's Bowery neighborhood on the F train to the C train for a spruce, spray, and out again. I quickly found solidarity in New York that I could not locate in Great Britain. Everyone I met seemed much more able to engage with their difference in a manner that, up to that point, I had been too uptight to do. New York became a training ground—a residency that linked me to perspectives around digital culture that still felt alien in Europe. This was ironic considering the sheer volume of European institutions supposedly geared to art and the internet.

On this, my first trip, I became acquainted with a group of intellectual misfits, such as filmmaker Matt Wolf; Halter and Cornell; and the outgoing CEO of Eyebeam Art + Technology Center, Amanda McDonald Crowley, as well as its executive director, the artist Roddy Schrock. Eyebeam is a lab, or atelier, cofounded and initially directed by Johnson & Johnson heir Jack S. Johnson in 1998. Unlike the minute lab space at FACT, with its two out-of-date computers, here was an organization that occupied prime Chelsea real estate. It was the kind of warehouse that every developer wants to tear down or convert into loft apartments. Here, artists worked, for a few weeks and up to a year, on thematic projects around technology, legislation, race, and social justice.

Schrock spoke in a rapid-fire delivery, interchanging between technical phrases and the political histories of internet art. Our first conversation, scheduled for an hour, carried on until the end of the working day. We discussed the singer Grimes's appropriation of the term *post-internet art* and the musical movement vaporwave—associated with lounge music and meme culture, and its affiliation to internet art as a genre. Catching the remaining minutes before the shutters screeched down on the art bookstore Printed Matter, I scoured for books by and on net artists— figures such as Heath Bunting, JODI, and Olia Lialina—but came up empty.

Net art, which is for some synonymous with hacker culture, found its genesis in 1994. Using websites as their primary medium, the artists—from Alexei Shulgin to the duo Eva & Franco Mattes—were deemed to have been making art that was critical of the art world's limits. Interactive websites, such as Olia Lialina's iconic *My Boyfriend Came Back from the War* (1996), held up a mirror to society—interrogating the insufferable struggles faced by everyday citizens who remained marginalized by the mainstream media. It is within this orbit that internet art finds its true genesis. Internet art is an amalgamation and an accumulation, a clustering of divergent forms. As we have seen, it was heralded by the performative gestures of the Fluxus movement (also known as intermedia art) through figures such as John Cage, Alison Knowles, and Yoko Ono. It was later transposed through video art with the works of Vito Acconci, Judith Barry, Nam June Paik, Shu Lea Cheang, and Lynn Hershman Leeson before it sedimented into the virtual sphere with net art, a space crafted to resist hegemony.

With the proliferation of digital technologies as the mass medium of our time, millennials pulled and stretched the limits of these forms. One of the critical drawbacks of this is that it overshadowed the visibility of many of their predecessors. But the seeds were sown. By the late 2000s, internet art was not simply a thing; it was *the* genre that inflected the work of a large swathe of artists who were eager to interrogate structures of power and to create a counter-visuality in an unbridled, epic fashion. In 2002, Jon Ippolito, then assistant curator of media art at the Guggenheim Museum, foreshadowed some of the stereotypes often associated with the field in his now celebrated text “Ten Myths of Internet Art”: internet art is a diminutive mechanism for the display of other media; internet art is only perceived and appreciated as an arcane subculture; internet art requires expensive equipment to make; internet art is a form of web design; and so forth. These might sound like strange perceptions today, but Ippolito’s ironic treatise reflected a reality that at the time was in desperate need of being overturned.

Critical Tactics

I am in London. Reunited with my husband after an extensive period in lockdown in separate countries. It is fall 2020 and we are uprooted once again. The pair of us are working from home, navigating one of the results of one of Great Britain’s worst economic crises, or so we are informed. Amazon’s Alexa seemingly has BBC Radio 4 on auto-play in the mornings. She informs us that we are amidst the greatest decline in the economy since the Great Frost of 1709. We both roll our eyes, sipping lukewarm coffee as we prepare for Zoom conference calls where we must methodically navigate our use of the mute button.

The life of a curator is too often mythologized as glamorous. Famous friends don't pay the bills—not the rent nor the hospital bills. Here we were again. Nearly a decade prior, working as a curator at one of the UK’s most esteemed public institutions—the Whitechapel Gallery—I had to hold down three other jobs to make ends meet. Among these was a stint going back to selling shoes. At least now me and the boo lived in a more spacious apartment, and the obsession with presenteeism 24/7 was not all the rage.

The time to trim fat has arrived, yet again. I log in to cancel my Hulu account. Hulu knows I am not at home in the United States. I fire up my virtual private network (VPN), to which I subscribe to pretend to Hulu that I’m *still at home* in Los Angeles. Canceled. The act of cutting my online subscriptions continues. Goodbye Now TV. No, I do not want to take advantage of your special offer. Sayonara Spotify. Good riddance *New York Times* subscription. Hear you later, Audible! I perform a balance transfer from my credit card to my checking account. All set. Listlessly, I attempt to navigate the *Financial Times* paywall before giving up and resorting to the newly accentuated virtual galleries on Art Basel’s website, and the Metropolitan Museum of Art’s 360-degree video of the Great Hall. Google pings me an advertisement for its most affordable viewing experience yet—Google Cardboard. I am perplexed.

I check and recheck my social-media feeds. I only indulge in 'gram and the book, oh and LinkedIn—there won't be anything of interest on there. My husband and friends joke that I should consider the Web 2.0 Suicide Machine—a project developed by the Dutch art organization Worm. It cleanses your digital presence. I chastise them for being out of date, referencing a pseudo-artwork from more than ten years earlier. I then proceed to a rant about my distaste for the frivolous use of the word *suicide.*

Looking for a messiah who can remind me of the utopian aspects of the world of tech, I peruse video archives on YouTube, Vimeo, and UbuWeb—the eccentric poet Kenneth Goldsmith's public archive of video art, concrete music, and poetry. As the number of tabs balloons, I begin to home in on a video from rhizome.org's Seven on Seven conference in 2012. Also styled as 7x7, the annual event, which began in 2010, takes as its inspiration the 1966 happening *9 Evenings: Theatre and Engineering*—the first in a series of projects that went on to become Experiments in Art and Technology (E.A.T.)—that paired prominent artists with engineers from Bell Laboratories. Conceived by Robert Rauschenberg (1925–2008) and Bell Laboratories engineer Billy Klüver, they explored the cross-disciplinary possibilities of art and science. Incidentally, the inaugural event was produced the same year that the concept of the internet was developed through the ARPA papers.

Seven on Seven similarly brings seven technologists and seven engineers to collaborate on a new project over the course of a day. The results are unveiled the next day at the conference in a public showing that is as thrilling as it is nerve-racking. I can attest to this, having been the moderator of the 2013 conference held at the Barbican, where the pairing of Ryder Ripps and Haroon Mirza resulted in an #EpicFail, with Mirza deciding to spend time with his children rather than showing up to the public day of the conference. I commended him.

Watching: on my video screen is a conversation from the 2012 summit between artist Taryn Simon and the technologist Aaron Swartz (1986–2013). I had known of the result of their collaboration, *Image Atlas* (2012) and exhibited it, but I had never seen their dialogue about the work. Swartz wasn't any old tech geek; he was a bonafide wunderkind. In his late teens and early twenties, he developed the RSS feed; was a cofounder of the news aggregation site, Reddit; and was an architect of Creative Commons. He spent his life as an activist fighting for access to information online.

When I first discovered Swartz, I believed him to be the messiah that I had been looking for—a figure who hailed from the hall of fame and held the tech-industry pedigree, but who was also willing to collaborate and openly share information. Swartz was the opposite of the aspirational

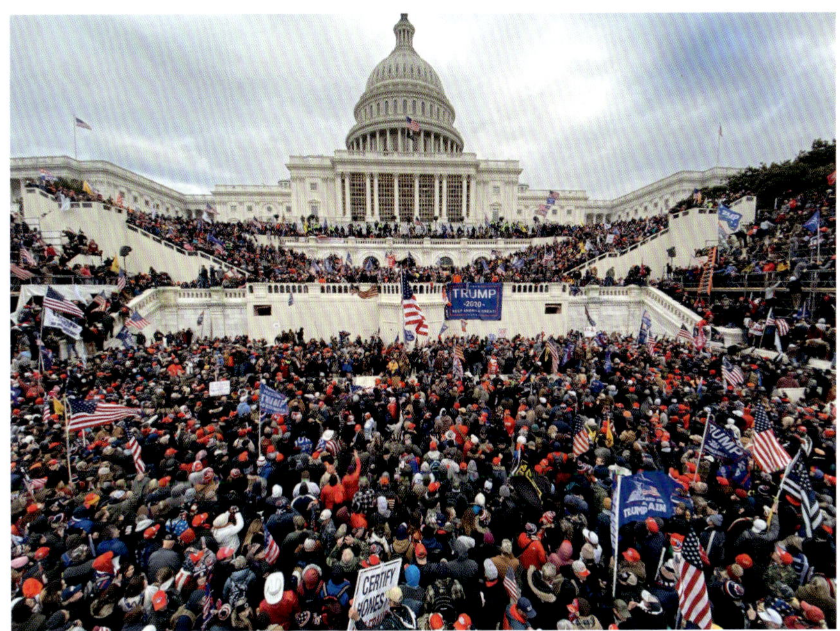

Supporters of Donald Trump outside the United States Capitol Building, Washington, DC, January 6, 2021

blockchain billionaires, gaining astronomical wealth in their twenties, without care or caution for the side effects that their technologies imposed on the world. Blockchain has become a scarily unstable commodity, fizzing with alt-right donors sending bitcoin to groups involved in the January 2021 United States Capitol attack through to endless forms of speculation governed by the aesthetic economy of nonfungible tokens (NFTs), which we will return to in the "The Shape of the Future" chapter.

As a result of Seven on Seven, Swartz and Simon created *Image Atlas*, which operates primarily as a search engine. The visitor enters a keyword, and the *Image Atlas* displays the different search outcomes from fifty-seven countries, organized visually by GDP. Within seconds of inputting distinctive words, what becomes evident to the viewer is the inherent biases imposed upon certain nation-states by local governing bodies. Here, the schematics of control and power are laid bare, as are the vast cultural differences that exist among nations.

Image Atlas brings to mind an early work by the duo Mendi + Keith Obadike, to whom I was introduced by Michael Connor when we were visiting curators at Cornerhouse, then Manchester's international art center in

Great Britain. The *Black Net.Art Auctions* (2001–13) series began with a work as an eBay listing called *Blackness for Sale* (2001). Was it a hoax or a genuine attempt at e-commerce? Critiquing the consumerist nature of the newly minted click-happy culture, the listing sought to sell Keith Obadike's Blackness—an heirloom that had been in the artist's possession for twenty-eight years—to the highest bidder. The archived page listed the highest bid being at $152.50 with six days remaining to bid.

I was introduced to this form of racial critique when I began writing my doctoral thesis. Professor Jean Fisher encouraged me to follow the work of the Nigerian curator Okwui Enwezor. His exhibition, *The Rise and Fall of Apartheid: Photography and the Bureaucracy of Everyday Life* (2012), curated with Rory Bester at the International Center of Photography (ICP), New York, reminded me that the internet granted artists a resuscitating tool for history. It became clear that the internet, and by proxy internet art, was part of a broader image culture that was allowed to access the past and reanimate it for the present. This sphere could be a celebratory space for countless identarian forms but, equally, it is a site of pain and trauma; a vortex into a world of pictures filled with a darkness that is beyond knowing. Choosing how to use and deploy it is an imperative responsibility for artists and curators.

While in New York in fall 2013, I was invited to attend British artist Eddie Peake's first major public performance in the United States as part of the Performa Biennial, a festival of performance art at venues across the city. *Endymion* (2013) featured seven dancers, painted head to toe in glitter, performing to a soundtrack of crescendos that would slowly rise only to dissipate. The ghostly figures moved to the thunderous electronica by musicians Gwilym Gold, Alexis Nuñez, and Tim Goalen. Named both after a moon goddess and a street in Finsbury Park, the neighborhood in London where he was raised, this work beautifully explored the relationship between sound, proximity, and distance. Naked bodies, genderless, amorphous, choreographed by Peake, navigated the prickly intimacies inherent within the body: how one navigates intimacy, loss, comfort, and consent. Staged in the Swiss Institute's former site on Wooster Street, the bustling event explored the tense experience of looking at nude bodies while one's self was simultaneously on view. I felt as if I were in a fishbowl under CCTV surveillance.

I had developed a friendship with Peake and was curious about his seeming obsession with the nude body. He invited me to author the catalog essay to accompany a major solo exhibit at the Barbican's Curve gallery. *The Forever Loop* (2015) explored the rhythmic nature of embodied action in a cellular space that Peake inferred was reflective of the internet itself. Like *Endymion*, the exhibition featured performers clothed in sheer outfits moving around the gallery, coming in and out of view.

One of Peake's preoccupations, he informed me as we spoke in front of a full house at London's Arts Club in October 2015, was how nude imagery in the digital sphere—advertising, magazine culture, dating applications, and pornography—had assumed a sense of uniformity that was a tidy distance from reality. The bodies in his works, such as *The Forever Loop* and *Endymion*, all seek to poke through the standardized views of sexual representation. Instead, they present distinguishing details, the perfections and imperfections. Looking at these features up close, while also being looked at and examined by others, serves as a critical interrogation of the voyeuristic tendencies that have only deepened with human obsessions related to "the performance of the self" engendered by the internet's thickening social technologies.[9]

The day after *Endymion* was my last in New York. A Facebook message from artist and writer Malik Gaines popped up. "We're doing a couple of Performa things, including a twenty-four-hour performance . . . come . . . text me." Early evening, I ventured alone to Recess Activities, Inc. in SoHo. The performance was by the duo Courtesy the Artists (Malik Gaines and Alexandro Segade). When I entered, Gaines was with a mic at a piano, and I immediately felt bashful. I took a seat and kept my face to the ground. My lifelong social anxiety wasn't particularly helpful. Curators were somehow expected to be outgoing, hyperconfident, and even gregarious.

The dimly lit room presented *Trad.* (2013), a muted cabaret where guests were invited to present their interpretations of the song "Black is the Color (of My True Love's Hair)." Some renditions were performed at pianos or with guitars, bookended by personal reflections on love and desire lost. A forlorn heart and a broken home were laid bare for us to see. I always assumed that the song was originally recorded by Nina Simone. Little did I know that it was an Appalachian folk song that emerged from Scotland, where I spent my early childhood. For *Trad.*, which grew from Recess's flagship residency program, the artists explored the histories of traditional musical forms and songs commonly believed to exist without a known or single author. Researching the various and sometimes contested histories of these songs, and allowing for myriad versions within this public gathering, was representative of a distinctly contemporary concept of citation and interpretation. Like the open, growing archive presented to us through the internet, Courtesy the Artists' collective convening—and the propensity to quote, borrow, and remix known historical records through a multiplicity of voices—exemplifies a kind of utopic potential, which we can only aspire to see continue and thrive.

Time Machine: Pioneering Anarchists

Crash and Burn

It's 7:00 a.m. and my migraine is back with a vengeance, following sixteen hours of screen time. My vision is skewed by nausea. Is that 7 actually a 9? Kickoff is late today. Fire up the engines, posterior to chair, coffee in hand, as the Apple beach ball of death, also referred to as the spinning pinwheel, rotates. The *Guardian*'s homepage will not load. I try Amazon to track today's package. Zero. The *Financial Times*, the *New York Times*—all the seats of so-called liberal media will not come online. A 503 Service Unavailable error. Even the UK's government portal is offline. As the day drills on, it transpires that the reason is a power outage on a U.S. cloud computing company, Fastly.

It is an apt reminder, a message of which artists James Bridle, Simon Denny, and Trevor Paglen have always sought to remind me: the *cloud* is a poor metaphor. Data, whether personal or belonging to a giant corporation, are not magically uploaded into bulbous forms where they sediment for eternity. Instead, they are hosted on servers—in desert landscapes, in rural areas, in megacities, in parts of the developed and developing world—where they are subject to failure. The belief that Apple's iCloud or Amazon Web Services can hold your archive in perpetuity, without the necessity for you to watch over it, can only be a myth. It is a misconception supported by corporations to gather user information and archives, and above all, to engender trust.

When digital platforms first became available in the 1980s and 1990s, trust was not a concept that permeated the mainstream public consciousness, especially in the western world. An anarchic fervor spread through the streets with immense demonstrations by organizations, such as AIDS Coalition to Unleash Power (ACT UP), a grassroots HIV/AIDS political group, which on October 11, 1988, occupied the U.S. Food and Drug Administration (FDA) headquarters in Rockville, Maryland, in protest against its ignorance about the AIDS pandemic. The pink triangle, now a symbol for various LGBTQ+ identities, came into public view with the collective Silence=Death Project. It cohered with tensions in Great Britain around race in Toxteth, Liverpool, in 1981 and the infamous Handsworth riots in Birmingham in 1985. Taking cues from 1960s counterculture, the early 1990s became rife with antiestablishment politics across Western Europe and parts of the United States. Riots in the UK, such as the Freedom to Party rally, which saw ten thousand people occupy London's Trafalgar Square in 1990, escalated into a mega-rave between May and October 1994.

This spirit of anarchy dovetailed with the emergence of internet art as a field and forum, with many artists operating in the form of collective webs to create forms of culture-jamming and anticonsumerist protest using the aesthetics and language of consumerism. Examples are the eToy. CORPORATION, who came to prominence in 1994, and the duo known as the Yes Men, who act as "corporate shields" for society, speaking back to "The Man" in the same lingua franca used to sell goods to customers. The modes and tactics of these progenitors remain just as relevant today in a world where businesses are conceivably harvesting our subconscious minds, tastes, and purchasing power to such an extent that we no longer know who is speaking to whom.

Anarchist Pioneers Setting the Stage: Andy Warhol

Some might find this surprising, but perhaps the biggest influence on art that relates to the internet was the artist Andy Warhol (1928–1987). The subject of legend and myth, Warhol bequeathed to society the blurring of high- and low-brow culture. His world was one of constant citation, reproduction, and repetition of imagery and objects from popular culture and everyday use. My obsession with the artist began with the pages of *Interview* magazine, which he had set up to present free-flowing content with key cultural figures, much akin to the manner in which blogs functioned in the early days. The content was often raw, unedited, and straight from the gut. I got my hands on a copy in the late 1990s. I was in my aunt's living room in Saudi Arabia. By this point, the magazine was under the secure ownership of the powerhouse Brant publications. It was glossier than I imagined, featured greater celebrities, and had a more striking focus on fashion under the editorship of the mythological figure that was Ingrid Sischy. Sischy was a quirky doyenne for the fashion world with oversize glasses and a style that could be described as bricolage.

When I was first appointed curator at Whitechapel Gallery, I was asked to visit New York and Pittsburgh to research the possibility of borrowing certain archival materials for a potential Pop art-inspired show. The exhibition did not take place in its envisaged form, but the fire it lit in my imagination fueled my pursuits in my new role.

I had happened upon a walking tour of former artists' studios in New York, from Jackson Pollock and Lee Krasner's Greenwich Village studio to Donald Judd's SoHo home and workspace, now the Judd Foundation. The tour's crown jewel was the former site of Warhol's studio, known as the Factory, in the Decker Building at 33 Union Square. Looking at its majestic but restrained exterior, with terra-cotta details that fused European influences with elements of the Islamic architecture that I had grown to know so well from living in various parts of Africa and West Asia, I felt the ghosts of the past come alive. In the interstices behind its windows, I conjured the figure of Valerie Solanas, who shot Warhol in the belief that he had both scorned her work and was stealing her ideas.

With the Factory, Warhol had not only transformed the laborious task of conceptualizing, producing, and exhibiting art into an industrial process, but he also brought the raw, unbridled aspects of his diverse community of friends, colleagues, and superstars out of the murky shadows. The concept of collecting friends as Warhol did at the Factory reminded me of the social-media time bomb ticking away in my pocket. Before my trip, I had been encouraged by the Whitechapel's communications team and subsequently implored by my friend and colleague, the curator Hans Ulrich Obrist (often known as HUO), to join Instagram. "All the curators are doing it!" they said. Obrist saw Instagram as a site for exploratory archiving, using it as another way to archive his innumerable encounters with artists. Communications teams wanted first-hand, live, behind-the-scenes art experiences from my new acquaintances, and just as important, the followers who would validate my existence in the digital sphere. The turn of the curator into a member of a celebrity asset class was surprising to me at the time.

The notion of an asset class is deeply embedded in Warhol's mythological presence at the Factory, as well in the photographs of him with celebrities at venues such as Studio 54. He once noted, "The key of the success of Studio 54 is that it's a dictatorship at the door and a democracy on the dance floor."[1] Outside of the social sphere, Warhol authored many books, often with assistance from other people, who could capture his precise syntax, which would perhaps be more suited to the digital sphere today. These range from *The Philosophy of Andy Warhol* to *The Andy Warhol Diaries* and his famous posthumous stand alone essay, "Fame," now a Penguin Modern classic. In 2022, *The Andy Warhol Diaries* were to become the framework for a Netflix series, where the artist's words were simulated using artificial intelligence (AI) to replicate the timbre and tone of his voice.[2]

Warhol's ghost continues to reign in the public arena. His celebrated proclamation that "in the future, everyone will be world-famous for fifteen minutes" is potentially misattributed to the artist, but fame is a characteristic so closely tethered to the artist's persona it almost doesn't matter if he originated it or not. The phrase became a cultural phenomenon, which was believed to have seeded (and certainly prefigured) the culture of tabloid journalism, as well as the context for motion pictures, such as *To Die For* (1995), directed by Gus Van Sant, and Sofia Coppola's *The Bling Ring* (2013). We can also attribute the cult of fame to the attention given to a whole slew of public figures, from Paris Hilton to Donald Trump. The day when a real-estate tycoon and casino-owner-turned-reality-TV star could become the president of the free world represents a form of speculative realism that only an artist could have dreamed of. Likewise, the Kardashians owe much to the late artist. Their reality television program *Keeping Up with the Kardashians* (2007–21), which had launched a multibillion-dollar empire, began as a platform to craft a lifestyle aspired to by both millennials and Zoomers. Revealing the ability of social media to build a brand around individual identity, the show went on to produce the world's highest-paid model (Kendall), the youngest "self-made" billionaire (Kylie), numerous makeup and clothing lines (Kim, Khloe, and Kourtney), a fitness conglomerate (Khloe), and more.

A sex tape springs to life. Leaked or not. Most often unseen by the public, these tapes entered public awareness from the likes of Pamela Anderson, Paris Hilton, and Kim Kardashian, piquing interest and fostering a sensuous aura and a sense that everything is public, even if this is not the case. Warhol, who was also often suggestive of the erotic, deployed his friends in movies that opened a window where voyeurism was both allowed and encouraged. *Blow Job* from 1964 was a masterful feat of facial expression, oscillating between boredom and thrill. Although we only see a face, the suggestion that one's most intimate acts can be made public is inherent. His 1969 *Blue Movie*, which received a theatrical release, was a meditation on love and war, interspersing dialogue about the Vietnam War with quotidian actions by its leads Viva and Louis Waldon. Here, unsimulated sex occurs between the stars on what was dubbed a "blissful afternoon." The artist's ability to present these ventures as cultural artifacts worthy of both critical discussion and, indeed, audience obsession created some context for major erotic feature films, such as Bernardo Bertolucci's *Last Tango in Paris* (1972) and Adrian Lyne's *9½ Weeks* (1986), but also legitimates sexual candor—the meaningful examination of pleasure and equally sex as a form of work. Geosocial platforms, such as OnlyFans, Grindr, and Tinder, among others digital assets, are examples of how these forms of desire can manifest through myriad internet technologies.

Computer Art

Fundamentally, computer art is any art that uses a computer in some form or fashion. Once an experimental field of aesthetic trial and error, it is now most often referred to as *art generated by a computer*, as opposed to humans experimenting with one. Dive into the archives and collections of London's

Victoria & Albert Museum (V&A) and you will find a treasure trove of early artworks from the 1950s that set the stage for internet art as we understand it today. One of the first such examples from 1952 was *Oscillon 40*, a piece by Ben Laposky (1914–2000), where the mathematician and artist used an oscilloscope—a device that reveals the movements on an analog screen produced by the tube that produces the lit image (a cathode ray tube). Manipulating the ways the electrical lights moved, Laposky produced ethereal, architectural images that look like proposals for architecture from the future. Also in the V&A collections are a number of plotter drawings by Frieder Nake, geometric forms from the 1960s that resemble the algorithmically generated machine vision produced by accelerated versions of these machines in the twenty-first century. Artists Jean Tinguely and Nam June Paik equally sought to use computers to enhance human function, animating their practices by demonstrating the visual possibilities that machines could be programmed to perform.

Yet, no computer art perhaps gained as much public attention as Andy Warhol's digital drawings from 1985, made on a Commodore Amiga 100. Most of these works had disappeared from public record until the artist Cory Arcangel's sleuthing uncovered them in 2013–14. Invited to realize an exhibition at the Carnegie Museum of Art (CMOA), Pittsburgh, Arcangel went knocking on the Warhol Museum's doors in search of his 1980s experiments. It transpired that many of Warhol's early works using computers were permanently stuck on disks that were impossible to access due to the now-defunct software. Arcangel enlisted the support of students at Carnegie Mellon University, who tinkered with these devices, unlocking a treasure trove of historical context. Files titled campbells.pic, flower.pic, and marilyn1.pic—produced on the Amiga and reminiscent of some of Warhol's iconic artworks—were among those brought to light by an act of reverse engineering of the material devices that stored them.

Even from beyond the grave, Warhol and his unofficial protégé, Arcangel, were firing us up with questions that might have otherwise gone unasked.[3] If the work of one of the most famous artists who had ever lived, an artist with his own museum who continues to break auction world records, could disappear in plain sight, what does this mean for the rest of us? Think of those hard drives on older computers where you've stored your pictures, essays, and personal stories. Will they work in five years when you upgrade your computer? What about fifteen years from now? One can argue that we are readily allowing our biographies, archives, and histories to be reduced to slices of code that will be incompatible with our soft-wired future. The cloud proffers a multitude of alternative possibilities for the indexing of this data, but if these are simply reduced to ones and zeros on a data server in the middle of a desert, there is no guarantee or trust that they won't be lost.

I did not pay attention to Warhol's images until Gilda Williams, a leading Warhol scholar, sent me a YouTube video of an early demonstration of Warhol creating a portrait of the pop star Debbie Harry in the presence of Amiga computer staff. Harry sits demurely, playfully posing for a painter who may or may not be paying attention to her. We witness Warhol donning pink glasses, and with seeming spontaneity select color options and filters. The host of the program, evidently excited to use Warhol to sell the computer as a tool for making art, is hit back with sarcastic rebuttals from Warhol, who nonchalantly plays down the significance of the computer that would come to define a period of his working life. Like any genuine social-media influencer of today, Warhol knew it was not cool to be instrumentalized by a brand but instead should coyly do his thing and reveal his concocted machinations for portraiture through the terms that he had set. Ostensibly, that was the spirit of early computer art. It was not that machines programmed by engineers were the arbiters of taste, but that we as people would always remain in control of our choices. The world may well have changed since then.

Mass Culture

Arcangel tells me that when he first moved to New York in 2000, after his time at the Oberlin Conservatory of Music in Ohio, studying classical guitar and music technology, he had burned out on classical forms. Eager to mash forms together, he and his friends went to nerd heaven, producing tracks on old Atari and Commodore home computers.[4] A block from where he worked was queer activist and artist Keith Haring's (1958–1990) Pop Shop, an immersive boutique that made the motifs from Haring's art on building sides accessible to the masses via affordable clothing and objects. Around the corner was the flagship store for Supreme, an American clothing and skateboarding company inspired by hip-hop culture, with a red-and-white logo that is considered to be a direct reference to the art of legendary collage and conceptual artist Barbara Kruger.

More than a decade later, Arcangel Surfware, a software and merchandise company, was born. The artist spoke to me about the genesis of the brand's aesthetic as being an amalgamation of the aesthetics and positive meme sloganeering of early social-media influencers crossed with the lifestyle brands that emerged in the 2000s along with references to screen life and the packaging and the price points of music merchandise.

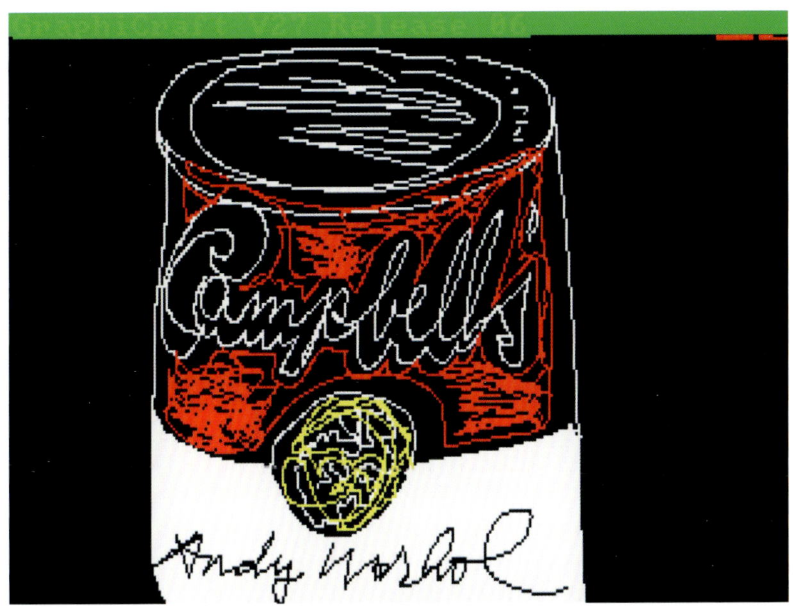

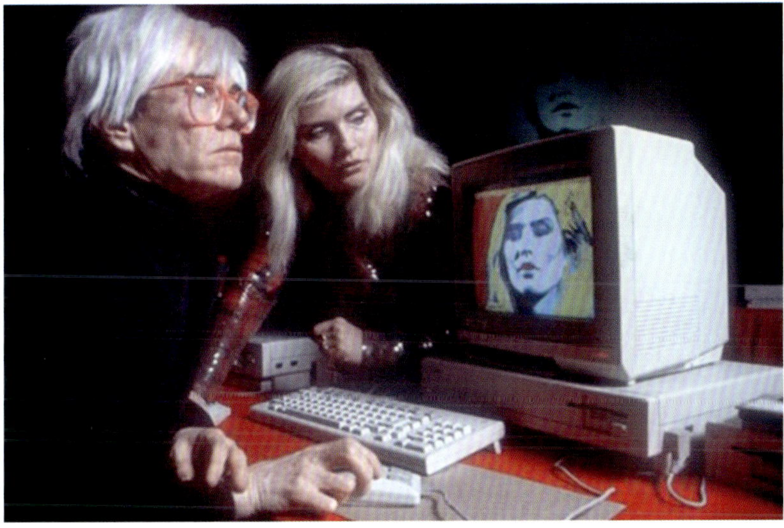

Andy Warhol, ***Campbells,*** **1985** __Digital image, from disk
1998.3.2129.3.22

Andy Warhol creating a portrait of Debbie Harry on an Amiga 1000, 1985

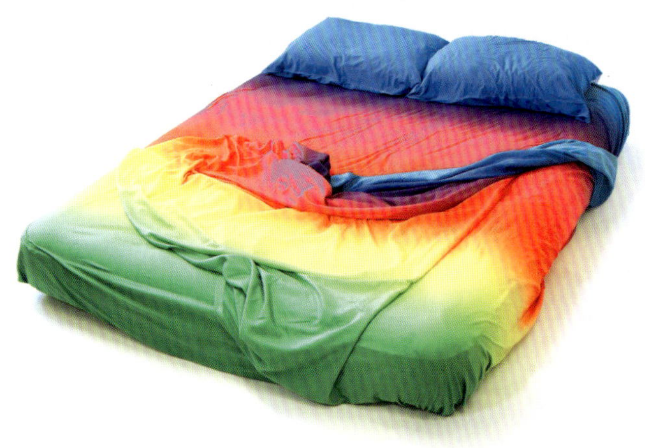

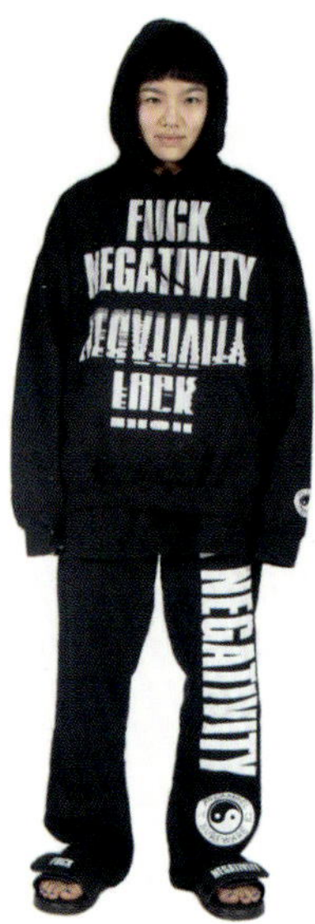

Cory Arcangel x Arcangel Surfware, *Photoshop Gradient Demonstration Bedsheets*, 2014 _Bedsheets in retail packaging

Cory Arcangel x Arcangel Surfware, *Arcangel Surfware S/S/F/W 2015 Fuck Negativity Collection Photoshoot (Tenaya)*, 2016 _Photoshoot

Photoshop gradients on bedsheets were as fun as they were meta.[5] My personal favorite was a pair of soft, cushioned slides emblazoned with the slogan "Fuck Negativity." Both of my pairs were claimed by exes.

Arcangel describes the ambition behind the project as akin to Haring's, but it was also of the specific moment in history when the democratization of art felt urgent. But, after five years—after shuttering the brand's webstore in favor of a brick-and-mortar flagship in Stavanger, Norway, where the artist had opened a European headquarters—the business could no longer sustain itself. Just before the COVID-19 pandemic, in late 2019, Arcangel Surfware announced a closeout sale at its flagship. Now, these objects are almost as collectible as his art, available in online boutiques that often belong to art galleries. I am told that once the economic ramifications of the pandemic resolve themselves, the brand might be in for a reboot.

Artists working with the internet have often been fascinated with brand culture, from the Yes Men to Rafaël Rozendaal's collaboration with men's clothing brand Sidian, Ersatz & Vanes. The defining feature of these collaborations is either that the artists are looking to critique these forums or, in the case of the latter, seeking a tongue-in-cheek means to explore the possibilities of mass distribution.

In 2014, Arcangel released the book *Working on My Novel*, a compilation of Tweets from everyday people writing about working on their novels. Deploying a piece of custom-produced software that captured the keywords, the result is as much a ready-made object as it is a testament to the aspirations of those of us who want to tell our stories, but also the inevitable failure of so many would-be writers, whether distracted by *Fifty Shades of Grey* (2015), Garth Brooks on TV, or dreaming of sitting in Parisian cafés for inspiration. What Arcangel reveals to the reader is how collective imagination manifests in the social sphere. Eight or nine years later and the discussion has evolved to a focus on the possibilities of AI writing our novels and crafting our perfect artworks. The book about working on a novel thus becomes a time capsule of a present that is forever fleeting.

Roy Ascott

When I sat down with Roy Ascott in 2010 to ask him about his practice, the artist clarified the specifics of a field of art and culture known as cybernetics. I was co-organizing a conference called The Future is Now with Tate, Liverpool, to honor the legacy of the late Nam June Paik. It was suggested to me by my boss, Mike Stubbs, that Ascott would be the perfect keynote speaker. In the space of minutes, this kind man jumped from cybernetics to telematics to the artistic movements of Surrealism and Fluxus. He seemed consumed with the state and potential of our consciousness, a subject that he demonstrated to me through videos that ranged from documents of early computer art to African tribal dancing. Despite his carefully pronounced words, his hyperlinked thought processes left me unmoored.

Ascott, a renowned teacher, known today for his research platform the Planetary Collegium, summoned a giant smile and started again, with no less verve and humor. Cybernetics, I understood, was not simply about machines, but just as much an analog concept of how humans communicate and how those methods are controlled. It relates to the notion of embodiment and how individuals develop a sense of autonomy and purpose through networked relationships with machines. The term emerged in the English language in the 1940s to develop an understanding of human coevolution with machines. Telematics, on the other hand, involved telecommunications and computer science—a form of internet art before it existed.

Ascott's obsession with the field of consciousness has come to the surface in popular culture at the same time that we have moved into a world where mindfulness and meditative processes—from the power of psychedelics to the rise of Transcendental Meditation—have come to be considered legitimate means for coping with the pressures of everyday life as well as historical traumas.

Ascott has noted that he sees his practice, which he has spearheaded through research as well as making art, as belonging to the field of technoetics, a neologism that he introduced, merging the fields of making and doing (*techne)* and the branch of the mind concerned with the study of the mind and intellect (*noetic theory*).[6] These experiments can be evidenced in some of his early experiments as a teacher at the Ealing College of Art, London, and later at Ipswich College of Art, where he established the radical two-year program Groundcourse. His students included The Who's Pete Townshend, who was reportedly notorious for smashing his guitar and sitting in a trolley as part of a performance, and later Brian Eno, who re-created a series of absurd and surreal performances by the likes of George Brecht and other Fluxus artists; I recall overhearing conversations of a paper bag on his head. Perhaps this acted as informal inspiration for actor Shia LaBeouf's performance on the Cannes Film Festival red carpet in 2014, where he could be seen with a paper bag on his head bearing the words: "I am not famous anymore." LaBeouf was to have a solo exhibition at the venue where I met Ascott, at FACT, Liverpool, as part of the art collective LaBeouf, Rönkkö & Turner (founded 2014).

Ascott's best-known artwork was a collaboration realized in 1983 called *La plissure du texte*. Here, the artist developed a global fairy tale

```
FROM FRONT TO NEXUS SENT 05.04 12/12/1983
LA PRINCESSE.
                                       *
                                   * ***** *
                                   * ***** *
                                * *********** *
                                * *********** *
                             * ***************** *
                             * ***************** *
                         * ************************* *
                   * ************************************* *
                   * *************   OEIL   ************** *
                   * ************* D'ETAIN  ************** *
                    * ************  DE TON  ************* *
                    * ************ CERCUEIL ************* *
                     * ***********  DIVIN   ************ *
                      * ******************************* *
              * **********PENCHES-TOI  OH  ESPRIT MALIN******** *
              * ************SUR  CE BREUVAGE  ANODIN*********** *
              * **********ET  PAR  TES  ONDES ALCALINES******** *
              * ************RENDS  LA  MAGIE  DIVINE*********** *
                      * ******************************* *
                     * ***********  ASTRE   ************ *
                    * ************    DE    ************* *
                   * ************* L'AURORE ************** *
                  * **************  QUE LA  *************** *
                 * ***************    BOUE   *
                                 * DEVIENNE  *************** *
                 *OR*OR*OR*OR*OR*OR*OR*OR*OR*OR*OR*OR*OR*OR*OR
                     *OR*OR*OR*OR*OR*OR*OR*OR*OR*OR*OR*OR*
                         *OR*OR*OR*OR*OR*OR*OR*OR*OR*
                           ************************
                           ************************
                           ***        **        ***
                           ***  ****  **  ****  ***
                           ***  ****  **  ****  ***
                           ***  ****  **       ****
                           ***  ****  **  ***  ****
                           ***  ****  **  ****  ***
                           ***  ***** **  *****  **
                           ***        **  ******  *
                           ************************
                           ************************
                             ********************
                                **************
                                  **********
                                    ******
                                      **

FROM FRONT TO NEXUS SENT 06.21 12/12/1983
LA PRINCESSE
LE FIL DES JOURS TISSAIT SA TOILE.ET DU ROYAUME DE MENTHE NE SUBSISTAIT
PLUS QUE DESOLATION.LEUR PRINCESSE ETAIT PARTIE ET LA BETE FURIEUSE DE
NE N'AVOIR POINT PAS TROUVER CHLOROPHYLE ET AVAIT DETRUIT LE VERT ROYAUME
VERT DE GRIS SOUVERAIN DU ROYAUME S'ETAIT TOURNE VERT D'ESPOIR VERS SON
```

Roy Ascott, *La plissure du texte*, 1983
—Distributed authorship project

where various participants were encouraged to contribute via an online network that was available over the course of twelve days. Ascott played the role of a magician in Paris. Reflecting on the work today, one sees that it resonates with innumerable avatars and adventures adopted by players in the virtual realm Second Life. It also paralleled the Fluxus artist Allan Kaprow's networked performance *Hello* (1969). It was for this reason that in the 2016 exhibition at the Whitechapel Gallery, *Electronic Superhighway (2016–1966)*, I placed these two artworks side by side.

While researching *La plissure du texte* in 2012, I came across an exhibition at SPACE's East London gallery, where I had just completed a stint as head of art and technology. I was bemused by a body of participatory work that Ascott called *Change Paintings* (1959–61), in which five sliding Plexiglas panes in a wooden frame could be overlaid with oil-painted elements. Of particular interest was a work from 1968 in which each image resembled an alphabet—a language that could be reconfigured to mirror aspects of one's unconscious mind. This concept resurfaced a year later when I encountered Siebren Versteeg's *Daily Times (Performer)* (2012), where a large screen refreshed daily with a scan of the front page of the *New York Times*. Throughout the day, a series of programmed algorithms based on the content of the newspaper's front page would create an abstract composition—a change painting—to emerge on top of the scan. In 2020, I invited Versteeg to re-envisage this work for the United Arab Emirates using the Abu Dhabi–based English-language daily as the cover. The idea came around full circle as I sat in the Magazine, the Zaha Hadid–designed restaurant at the Serpentine North Gallery, London, with my mother in May 2016. She was transfixed by a continuously changing screen that resembled an iPhone and acted as a constant reminder of just how intrusive the digital world can be. "Is this art?" she questioned. I nodded assuredly. "I want one. Can you get me one?" It was Tabor Robak's *Drinking Bird Seasons* (2015), an ongoing digital painting series that creates programmed computer-generated imagery (CGI) while drawing anxiety-inducing headlines from the news, alongside manifestations of fictional holidays. Unfortunately, the price point was a little out of our range.

Artificial Intelligence (AI)

Have you ever wished that you could absorb knowledge at greater speeds? Or that your brain could just operate on autopilot when required? Imagine a microchip that when inserted into the body would constantly learn on your behalf. Consider a model of efficiency that allows for domestic chores

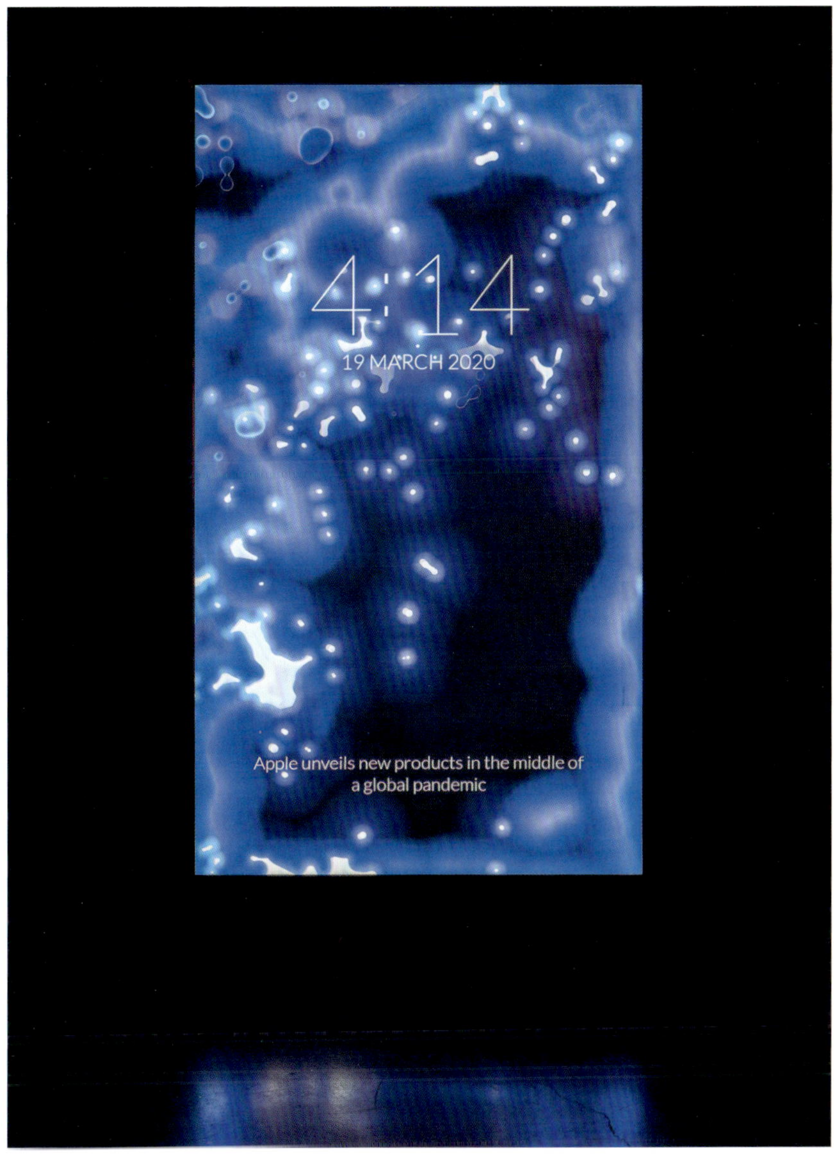

Tabor Robak, ***Drinking Bird Universe***, 2018 __Digital video with live data, 30 min. (looped), 72 3/8 × 41 7/16 × 2 3/8 in. (183.9 × 105.2 × 6.1 cm) Installation view: Art in the Age of Anxiety Sharjah Art Foundation, UAE, 2020

to be performed more swiftly, for books to be read within seconds, thus producing more space and time for thoughtful reflection. The imagination around AI, from self-driving cars to highly functioning robots, which pervaded the boomer generation's fictive cultural sphere, has now become a verifiable reality.

Unlike a human who wants to accelerate to increase leisure time or critical space for thinking, AI machines are programmed in their current form to accrue knowledge, in most cases, purely to fulfill a function. As they exist now, they are not the subjects of a utopic universe where people can exist as cyborgs; nor has the productivity enabled by AI been without its detriments. Fiscal trend forecasters estimate that by 2035, AI could boost profitability rates for certain businesses by up to 38 percent.[7] Simultaneously, AI has also fostered a constant update economy, whereby individuals must recast themselves into new job functions or else risk being marginalized in the workplace, or at worst, erased completely. Global warfare has become increasingly distributed and mediated through the use of drone technology, with unmanned flying devices that use AI in conflict zones, taking lives with enhanced precision—and without the emotional judgment that a human might make. Thus, child and warlord, fleeing mother and dictator may equate to the same target-defenseless subjects.

The genesis for much of AI technology that we see in the world today, from chatbots on Amazon to voice-activated smart-home technology, is in algorithms. Engineers will be eager to differentiate the two. Algorithms are tightly knit pieces of code that encourage a trigger when a certain set of principles or criteria are met, while AI is a confluence of multiple algorithms that are constantly modifying themselves to become more intelligent. Think of it this way. If you are like me and you first began using Google and its platforms about 2000, didn't it all feel different then? Aren't the suggestions of where to shop, what to buy, where to go, how to go there, and when all the more sophisticated now? This intelligence doesn't exist in a vacuum: you and I are fueling it. Every step we take on Google Maps or driving route on the Waze app helps inform the service provider of new road closures and blockages, reveals faster routes and uneven roads. In this regard, the prophecy from the *Terminator* film franchise that we would one day all become subordinate to the machine is, in essence, already true.

When we think of AI's relationship to art today, we often conjure eerie faceless portraits, such as those created in 2017 by Dr. Ahmed Elgammal's AI Creative Adversarial Network (AICAN)—the first machine-generated artist to pass the Turing test. The Turing test (originally called the imitation game) was devised by the computer pioneer Alan Turing in 1950 to see if machines could exhibit intelligent, humanlike behavior. The genesis of AI art was in 1968, when artist Harold Cohen (1928–2016) decided to investigate the potential of a computer to continually generate art. The resulting artwork, called *AARON* (1973–ongoing), pushed toward realism, with paintings of rock formations and plants before it reached the human form. In the 1990s, color was added and, in the 2000s, AARON returned to abstraction. Was this computer program learning to see in the same fashion that a child would learn to see the world in an ontological process of knowledge accumulation?

In the second half of the 2010s, AI art started to develop buzz in the art market. But why would an artwork produced by a piece of code be desirable? If these data sets were not programmed by human beings, why does one not interrogate the artistic credentials of such a maker in the same way one would ask whether a visual artist had graduated from a credible art school? The reason why may be twofold: novelty and acceleration. Young graduates from Goldsmiths College, London, are a dime a dozen, while AI art isn't, not yet anyway. Once the market is saturated with these forms, perhaps no one will care. Although human intelligence is still significantly more advanced than artificial intelligence, media tycoons suggest that this will change by the time we reach 2030. If this is the case, a machine could reinvent its palette, tools, and colors much more efficiently than your up-and-coming da Vinci.[8]

Researchers at the Institute for Human-Centered Artificial Intelligence (HAI) lab at Stanford University, California, caution against a utopian view of AI.[9] AI is an accumulation of what we have come to know as deep learning, a form of intelligence, as well as the biological, physiological, and conditioned human fields of neuroscience and psychology. But the ethos of what constitutes common sense, or in more complex scenarios, the necessity for ethical decision-making, is still very much out of reach for machines.

The ethical impulses, or rather the exclusionary impulses of AI, have been investigated by artist and gaming pioneer Mary Flanagan. Flanagan has argued that the unconscious aspects of gaming software should be interrogated. Perhaps her most infamous work is 2002's *[collection]*. A user is invited to download free software, which scans their various computer hard drives, culling pieces of data and forming a visual display. Looked at two decades later, it seems like an apt indictment of the manner in which tech corporations gather, glean, and sell our data in such a fashion daily.[10] As machine-learning researcher Ian Goodfellow and others have explained, the more assuredly generative AI is an "adversarial network," which allows machines to generate content but also has the capacity to discriminate, i.e., to classify the result into various criteria. These are also known as generative adversarial AIs.[11] In 2019, Flanagan produced *[Grace: AI]*, an artwork that seeks to redress the predominantly white, male figures and outputs that surround the AI conversation. As she describes on her website, using the author Mary Shelley as inspiration, Flanagan sought to create a feminist AI that uses a deep convolutional general adversarial network that is trained to "see" data from thousands of images of female artists. This forms the basis of a teachable program that renders myriad artworks that reference the history of women's art and storytelling.

Some of the greatest female pioneers working in AI and computer-led technology, whether visual artists, programmers, scientists, or theoreticians, often remain in obscurity in comparison to their male peers. One such example is Lillian F. Schwartz, who was a lesser-known figure in the collective event hosted by Experiments in Art and Technology (E.A.T.). Following this, she spent much of her life as a consultant for Bell Laboratories. Her earliest computer-programmed films, rarely shown in museums, such as *Pixillation* (1970), were produced at a time when humans could not manipulate computer pixels. Instead, Schwartz programmed a few lines of code and subsequently hand-painted color into the image using drawn animation. In 1972, she transformed images developed in the radiation from cancer treatments into spectacle in her film *Apotheosis.*

I exhibited Schwartz's work in *Electronic Superhighway (2016–1966)* alongside paintings and computer drawings from the 1960s by Ulla Wiggen. Encouraged to include these in the exhibition by my colleague at the time, Séamus McCormack, I initially knew nothing of the former psychotherapist's life and work beyond that she made paintings of the interiors of iconic computers; I had seen some of these at the Moderna Museet in Stockholm. I was particularly taken by a diagrammatic work entitled *Simultaneous Interpretation* (1965), which resembled an early schematic for the internet. In my research, I was informed that it was a photoscan. I contextualized this work, among numerous others, with videos and ephemera of the nine evenings of performance and engineering that had taken place in the 69th Regiment Armory in New York in 1966, hosted by what would become known as E.A.T. During the opening evening of *Electronic Superhighway*, I gave one of a handful of tours to the museum's patrons. I pointed out *Simultaneous Interpretation* and noted that it was a scan of a computer network. A frail woman with white hair and lively blue eyes squinted at me. It was a painting, she informed me. I stood corrected and hurriedly tried to escape. With the rays of Schwartz's pulsing radiation beaming from behind as I blushed, the woman continued, saying that she knew the artist well. "I was there." Suddenly it dawned on me: it was Wiggen herself. I gave her a hug. We had only corresponded over email up to that point. She was completely unassuming—gentle and kind, despite my public error. I was reminded in that moment that official records, archives, and histories are continually subject to inaccuracy. If this is the case in human hands, we can most certainly anticipate multiple forms of error if we are to leave the world entirely in the hands of AIs.

Judith Barry

In the 1980s, Judith Barry was the best friend of my teacher Jean Fisher when they lived on the East Coast. On a self-directed visited to New York to see curator Okwui Enwezor's *Rise and Fall of Apartheid* at the International Center of Photography (ICP), Barry was tasked with "taking care of me" as I stood behind her in the corners of Chelsea galleries, wearing my only tie. It was a thin, black tie with a pink giraffe sketched on it. I was here to meet "the art world." This was before I realized it should more aptly be dubbed the art industry, and that there was little sense of "belonging" in this fictive "world."

I remember having first met Barry, somewhere between Cairo and Munich. She reminded me of my English teacher at school, who also sported a blonde fringe and shared the artist's distinctive, tickling laugh. We took our seats at a coffee shop, where instant was the deal. Later that afternoon, we would be engaging in a public conversation about her project *Not Reconciled* (1987–ongoing), a body of work that began with a desire to disentangle the American dream. The words flowed from Barry's tongue in musical cadences. Poststructuralist theory had never sounded so fascinating or made so much sense.

Our bond developed around the evolution of *Not Reconciled* into a project titled . . . *Cairo Stories.* Over the course of many years, I stitched together a picture of her prolific oeuvre in exhibitions from New York to Philadelphia to Chicago, Los Angeles, and Lisbon. Her early work was an antecedent to much of the art produced using the internet today. In 1982, her film *Space Invaders* took Warhol's aphorism of everyone's fifteen minutes of fame, revealing a planet of self-obsessed, self-documenting individuals. The globe, metaphorically personified by a disco ball, becomes their singular point of reference. Web 1.0, let alone the Web 2.0 of social media, was yet to be born.

Barry also introduced me to an early sculptural installation, *Ha®dcell* from 1994, in collaboration with Brad Miskell. The work looks like a crate of art that has fallen from the sky; out-of-sync technology spills from it, left on display like debris. As the viewer inches closer, the technical apparatus begins to move and come to life. One could argue that this bore a discerning responsiveness suggestive of an early AI.

Barry and Miskell would reunite again on, among other installations, *Speedflesh* (1998). On a 360-degree screen, a lush painterly panorama of faces and limbs—cyborg creatures that are both human and prosthetic—envelops the viewer. In the middle of the theater, as Barry refers to it, is a joystick, which suggests that the viewer can control the narrative. The five cyborgs—Bladder, Kinetic, Prosthetic, Heads, and Floater—subsume us as they linger in the nude. Newborn flesh hurtling from present to future among virtual worlds, they unfurl their inner neuroses—a nod to Barry's deep-seated interest and study of psychoanalysis, which she undertook as a young artist at the University of California, Berkeley. Dislodged into bodies and states of time that they did not choose, they are caught between different forms of time travel. Kinetic is trapped in a girl's body, while Floater swallows everyone she wants to befriend. Barry's work foreshadows the technical breakdown of a proposed futurity, whether it is through exposing impending technical botch-ups or the potential failure to fuse humans with machines.

In 2003, the artist presented her first interactive website and dynamic game, *The Museum You Want*, at the Institute of Contemporary Art (ICA) in Boston, to acclaim. Before artists, activists, and audiences took to demanding forms of content from art museums, Barry's video game invited users in the gallery to make proposals regarding their desires of and for the museum. As data was fed into the artwork by the audience, progressive details emerged. The result is a collective brain that proposes an integrated dialogue between institutions of power and the public they purport to serve.

In a dimly lit Mary Boone Gallery in New York in 2017, Barry's 1991 video installation, *Imagination, Dead Imagine*, had spectators as enraptured as they were when it was first exhibited at the Renaissance Society in Chicago in 1992. A multisided screen is occupied by a face. Swollen, fragmented, never stable, it swallows and hurls; it is toppled by viscous fluids. As you inch closer, your reflection implicates you within the frame through a mirrored base. Is this abject body a representation of me, what I could be, or who we once were? Drawing its name from Samuel Beckett's short prose text from 1965, which reflected the author's interest in insularity and closed systems, Barry's installation posits the insular body into a form of closed-circuit theater. Produced during the height of the HIV/AIDS crisis, it is also impossible not to draw parallels with this spherical vision, becoming a form of critique of how the media choose to embody minority subjects at the time—and continues to do so. How would the age of social media have negotiated a sexually transmitted pandemic, which was seemingly ascribed to a select group of people, I asked myself then and again after another pandemic had plagued much of our lives. In 2017 the concept of pandemic-crisis social media was but a distant vision. Today, it is a reality as chilly as New York was that night.

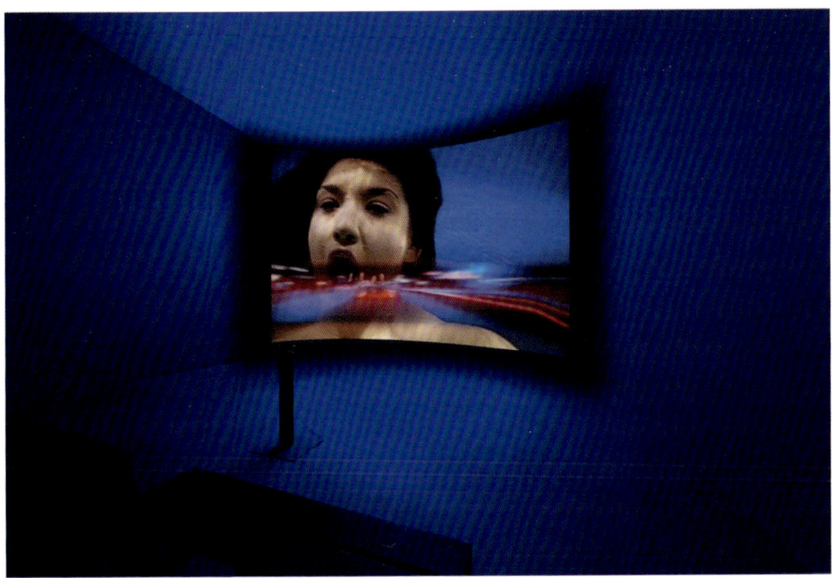

Judith Barry, *Speedflesh*, 1998 —Four-channel 360-degree video installation, edition of 5

Corporate AI

While the first thing that most publishers ask me when we begin a marketing plan, or in some cases, before we even sign a book deal, is "What is your social-media following like?" it is notable that they don't ask about the demographic makeup of those followers, for instance, whether they are art students who frequently buy art books or working-class people of color who might purchase a book on art only once in their lifetime, if at all. Instead, these strategists of Web 2.0 want to only know the figures: how many followers, average likes per post, clicks per link, and so forth. For them, this is a measure of assurance that you can promote your book sales enough to enable them to break even or hopefully make a profit, and it gives them confidence that your persona is liked.

If you are a writer who has never used a computer to interact with the wider world beyond sending the occasional email, unless your fame supersedes Web 2.0 into the realm of evening talk shows, that might no longer be enough to get you a publishing deal. Authors and publishers are enmeshed with Facebook companies and Amazon, to name two of the largest conduits for their existence. Likewise, artists are also expected to manage multiple social-media accounts, uploading articles or arguments of interest or behind-the-scenes pictures of works of art being produced in the physical or virtual studio. In 2020, during the COVID-19 global lockdown, Instagram-led art sales soared. According to numerous articles published in the *Art Newspaper*,[12] Instagram helps shape the tastes of art advisors, enables collectors to identify specific works of art for purchase, and offers a direct window of discovery, which can be examined relatively anonymously by the art-market crowd—institutions, auction houses, consultancy firms, and ultimately, art collectors.

As well as offering a storefront for art, many corporations have continuously developed technologies to help foster bridges to art and culture. Remember the now-defunct Google Glass? In 2014, Google engineer Alexander Mordvintsev developed a platform called Deep Dream. It was a form of computational, artificially intelligent software that lets users add hallucinogenic details to existing artworks. The result is cartoonish, like a picture of the Mona Lisa with a canine nose. As an experiment, I decided to create my own contortion, but I couldn't enter the website without subscribing. Even accessing the "about" page required me to set up an account and log in. For those fearful of security compromise, it seems an odd decision by the webmasters.

DeepMind and OpenAI Gym are other examples of AI-focused giants that link, for example, Google's parent company, Alphabet, Elon Musk, and Microsoft to large-scale visual training grounds, all of which could emerge as prospective sites for artists. Despite what the *Atlantic* has called the "AI goldrush" in art,[13] nobody manages it better than the artists themselves.

Power and Politics

Standing at the base of a foothill in well-trodden grass in 2012, I am waiting for my "roomies" near the documenta Halle in Kassel, Germany. A strand of my carefully flattened hair scoots sideways as wind hits my face. I have convened university professors, curators, and writers from around the globe to share bedrooms in oversubscribed motels for documenta (13), one of the world's most prestigious exhibitions of contemporary art. Another wind gust restores my hair to its morning afro. A hissing sound mutates into a buzzing as a chopper overhead begins to descend. It takes some time for my distracted morning head to understand that this is an artwork. Titled *A Public Misery Message: A Temporary Monument to Global Economic Inequality* (2012), its makers, the collective Critical Art Ensemble (CAE, established 1987), invited participants to be taken up to a height that would let them visualize through a crane-size bar chart the economic distance between the top 1 percent of citizens living on Earth and the bottom 99 percent. When

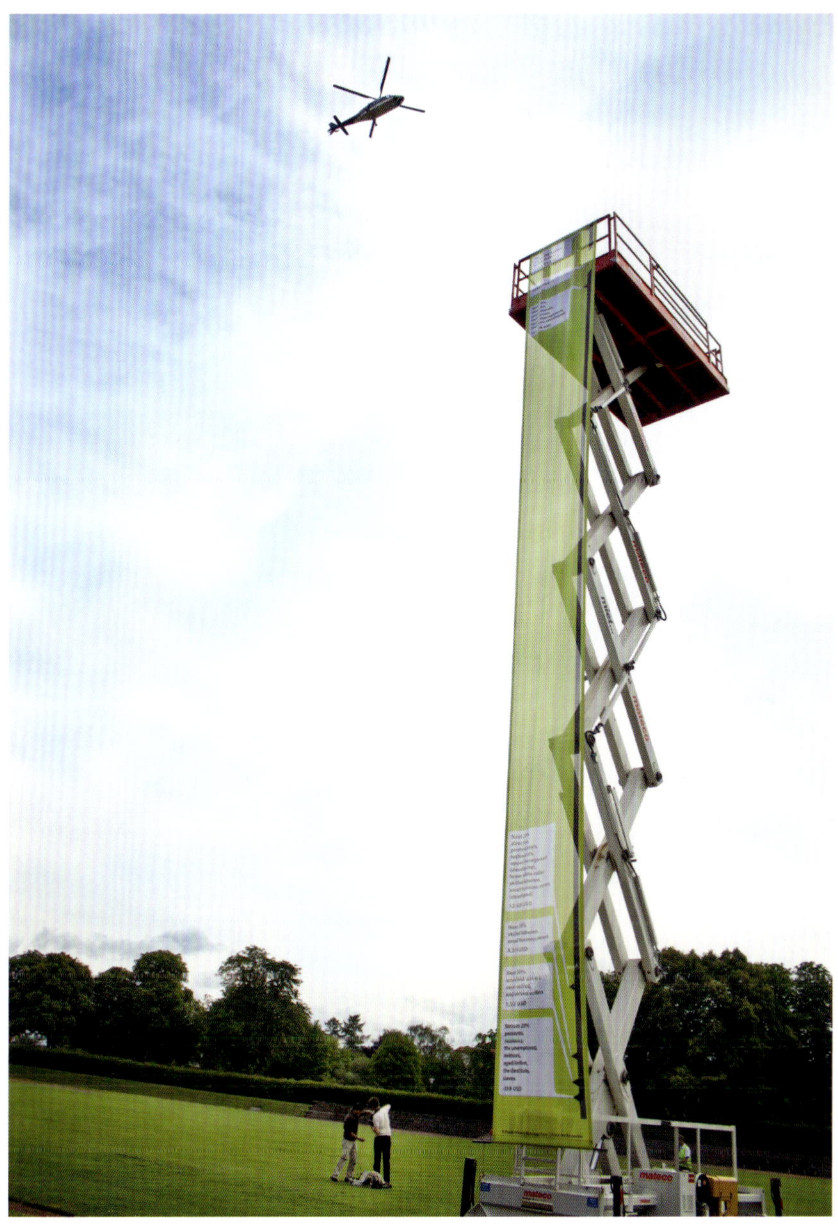

Critical Art Ensemble, *A Public Misery Message: A Temporary Monument to Global Inequality*, 2012 __Installation view: documenta (13), Kassel, Germany, 2012

static, the machine became an aural and sculptural readymade, a found object similar to Marcel Duchamp's *Fountain* (1917) or Nam June Paik's television sets in the 1960s.

CAE, who refer to themselves as "tactical media practitioners," has been deeply influential on a generation of artists, through their interventions and also in their writing, including *The Electronic Disturbance* (1994) and *Electronic Civil Disobedience* (1996). The latter text is often credited as a driving force of the hacktivist movement, which indirectly gave rise to online free speech and human-rights campaigns, as well as free peer-to-peer platforms resistant to censorship, including Anonymous and WikiLeaks. The rhizomatic potential of knowledge to go viral from the small-print publications of university campuses, biolabs, and home design studios was a sign of the confluence of forces that would define a generation not only of artists but of humans.

Electronic Disturbance Theater

One of the original members of CAE, Ricardo Dominguez, an artist and professor at the University of California, San Diego, cofounded the Electronic Disturbance Theater (EDT) collective in 1997, initially focused on virtual sit-ins intended to flood and crash specific websites as a form of nonviolent resistance. In 1998, its members Carmin Karasic, Brett Stalbaum, and Stefan Wray devised *FloodNet*, an applet using the once-popular programming language Java, which would allow users to send requests to a specific target page repeatedly, without a specific reason to do so. It could also send personalized messages to a remote web server in a coordinated manner, constellating with a global activist network. During Web 1.0 and the dot-com boom, when investors were putting their change into websites with the get-rich-quick mentality that we now see in cryptocurrency, this destabilizing act posed a genuine threat to the capitalist fervor that was subsuming what was once envisaged as the entirely free concept of the web. As error logs mounted at the back ends of websites, accumulating protest language and nonsensical terms, the media began to pay attention, propelling downloads of the program. The artists' main targets were the websites of U.S. President Bill Clinton and Mexican President Ernesto Zedillo. Taking inspiration from street theater protests, the group was eager to demonstrate how they could essentially use macronetworks to develop a neural network of like-minded influencers willing to operate a decentralized system against corporate and government hegemony.

EDT's work came into focus in 2007, when the expanding collective released a smartphone application called *Transborder Immigrant Tool*

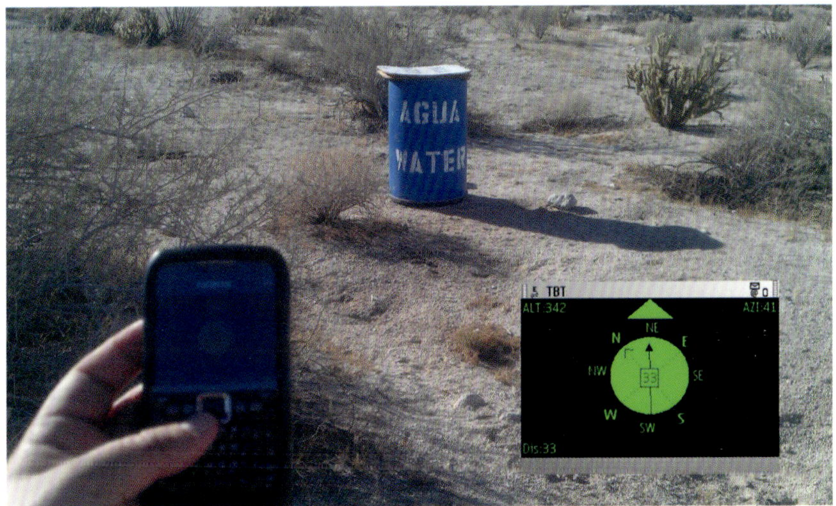

Electronic Disturbance Theater 2.0 and b.a.n.g. lab,
Transborder Immigrant Tool, 2007

(2007–ongoing). In 2006, protests against immigration laws had spread from Chicago to downtown Los Angeles. Carrying placards reading "A Day Without Immigrants," protesting immigrants boycotted work for a day to show the importance of their presence to the economy and country at large. This was a response to proposed changes to the U.S. immigration policy that tightened security across the United States–Mexico border and presaged the hate crimes and violent nationalism that would continue to build and erupt during Trump's time in office.

Back in the UK, the artist Zach Blas showed me a newspaper article about the *Transborder Immigrant Tool* and how it helped individuals traversing the deserts of the United States and Mexico by delivering information on water and food caches. The work was intercepted by the U.S. government and members of the collective were investigated. A friend of EDT member micha cárdenas, Blas popped out his antiquated mobile phone and played back the lyrical output of *Transborder Immigrant Tool.* Poetry narrated to soothe the vulnerable border crosser played alongside a relaxing animation. The work was not so much a get-into-America guide as an intervention into the desperate state of wanting to survive. The emotional and mental health, as well as the physical safety, of the intended audience was thus the paramount takeaway. The app showed how a work of art transposed across a network and onto a telephone can act as a vessel with the potential to heal wounds.

A decade earlier, the Bureau of Inverse Technology (BIT, established 1991), an organization of artist-engineers, began work on *BIT Plane* (1997–99)—a mechanical plane controlled by a remote with a miniature video camera attached. Led by Kate Rich and Natalie Jeremijenko, the project aimed to point the panoptical gaze back at the force that was taking control of collective society. They sent the plane to hover over and map Silicon Valley in California in an attempt to decode the commercial and ideological forces shaping the utopic space of this prosperous basin.

More than a decade later, the visionary artist-duo Thomson & Craighead released *A Short Film about War* (2009–10). My first encounter with this two-channel video was during the research phase for a 2009 exhibition at FACT titled *MyWar: Participation in an Age of Conflict*, which sought to look at how collective identities had been altered by violence in media. The Iraq War had been raging for seven years; distributed warfare was rife, and cameras had become all the more affordable, cross-embedded into every facet of life. Ex-Iraqi President Saddam Hussein's execution in 2006 had become a YouTube spectacle, and citizen journalists were reporting from the trenches, uploading to templated blogs from every corner of the globe. The proliferation of content on the internet is exactly what fuels this narrative documentary, where every single frame is composed of a piece of data found on the web. Using the photo-sharing community Flickr (the Instagram of its time) to mine material, the pair presented images of war zones, some clearly identifiable, others seemingly alien, on one screen and, on the other, a corresponding link to the image's source. This source functions as a stamp of authentication, but equally of transparency and acknowledgment of the original maker. Resembling computer code when presented on screen, these data sets are indicative of a new visual lexicon—one that the artists identify as potentially deceiving. Is one to believe that the images we see are more significant than the source of the image or code of a website? This debate took center stage among certain activist communities, especially after the so-called Arab Spring that began in 2010 and held the global spotlight with the events of the Egyptian Revolution of 2011.

Despite the perceived utopic potential of a Twitter revolution that seemed to consume the global news headlines or the concept of a new dawn that could bring equitable social and political change within and among the nations of the Arab world, the results have left a disenchanted cohort of young people who took to the streets and online. Military dictatorships, covert violence, a culture of secrecy, and, in some cases, civil war, now pervade the imagined and physical borders of these states. One of the unique facets of this cultural revolution was that citizens were using mainstream social-media platforms as rallying cries, information wires, and gathering tools, with Twitter and YouTube being paramount. Yet, when everyday citizens act in an uncoordinated fashion, they seemingly leave themselves defenseless. Everyday people from Egypt to Syria have been hacked, trolled, and targeted. In some cases, they have been arrested, brutally assaulted, or worse. At one point, the Egyptian government managed to shut down all cellular data services in the country, as if believing that it could plunge society in a time machine and back into the past. Although the genesis of much networked culture was funded by government organizations, its development and evolution have been fueled by thinkers, many of whom aspired to a liberated society that is globally connected.

Trevor Paglen

I don't remember where I met the artist and geographer Trevor Paglen. It might be because, as Hans Ulrich Obrist (HUO) constantly reminds me, Google's search engine has become our memory bank. Our minds are "shallower," according to Nicholas Carr, who writes about technology, business, and culture, but that does not mean that our knowledge or awareness is any less vast than it once was. HUO, arguably the world's most famous living curator, regularly invokes historian Eric Hobsbawm's phrase "a protest against forgetting," even using it as the title for his 2013 book of interviews with Hobsbawm. When concerned about the decline in handwriting, HUO converted his Instagram account into a memorial to the form. Each day, an artist, musician, or author would scrawl something onto a Post-it Note that he would photograph and upload online. The result is a shrine to a dying art—one that might encourage us to pick up a pen as opposed to remaining consistently circumscribed by the confines of a QWERTY keyboard.

Paglen unleashed his own protest against forgetting. Collaborating with author and curator Nato Thompson, and the New York–based nonprofit Creative Time, the artist released *The Last Pictures* (2012), a set of one hundred black-and-white photographs that represent life on planet Earth. Satellite pictures sit next to Katsushika Hokusai's (1760–1849) famous *The Great Wave Off Kanagawa* (c.1830–32), images of natural disasters, and aerial studies of military sites. Paglen loaded the images onto an archival disk and attached it to a communications satellite, EchoStar XVI, which launched into geostationary orbit on November 20, 2012. The satellite will continue to circle our planet until it is no more. Will it be found by extraterrestrial life? Or will it disintegrate into plumes of dust before anyone discovers it?

Perhaps I met Paglen in the streets of New York. When Creative Time was hosting a summit on social justice, I do remember hollering down to him, "Hey, are you Trevor Paglen?" Or it could have been on İstiklal Avenue in the Beyoğlu district of Istanbul, where I was organizing a series of talks for an online magazine I used to coedit called *Ibraaz*. Protocinema, an Istanbul-based organization founded by Mari Spirito, had commissioned Paglen to make a nonfunctioning satellite in a feat of engineering crafted and welded as art for art's sake—simply put, an aesthetic form that uses engineering not for function but for its form. As I entered the corridors of my mind, skimming through iPhotos, I found a picture of Paglen's installation at the 2012 Liverpool Biennial, for which I had been a part of the curatorial team. Surely, this is where I met him. "Hey Trev, quick question. Were you at the 2012 Liverpool Biennial?" He mutters something down the crackling WhatsApp line; he isn't certain.

Memory lapses aside, the artist's field of vision is entirely anchored around creating a language for how we see power—indeed, how it can be memorialized. In 2013, using wide-angle camera lenses in helicopters like a human drone, he recorded images of the National Security Agency (NSA) in the United States along with other architectures of mass surveillance. The aerial perspective situates and contextualizes these as forums worth investigation. Akin to the Bureau of Inverse Technology's *BIT Plane*, it is the lens of the people looking back at the apparatus that wiretaps, records, and controls much of citizen users' day-to-day lives. In a kind of performative gesture, Paglen released these images to the world to download and use as they wanted under a free Creative Commons license. When I questioned him on the impetus behind this, he informed me that the root of the project emerged from a "dearth of images" of such structures of control and governance.[14] He wanted to create a kind of mini-encyclopedia, and it felt appropriate to share that with the world. The images were downloaded hundreds of thousands of times in the first week of their release.

Does this gesture function as a form of activism? In 2014, Paglen took me as his plus one to the BFI London Film Festival premiere of *Citizenfour* (2014), a documentary feature by Laura Poitras that revealed the relationship between the filmmaker and ostracized U.S. whistle-blower Edward Snowden. Due to new antiterrorism legislation, Poitras could not attend the premiere due to "fear of arrest" and based on advice from her lawyers. She was projected into the packed main screen of Chelsea's Curzon Cinema over Skype. The connection crashed almost immediately. The host shouted out for Paglen. I didn't get it. Why him? It turned out that he was one of the cinematographers on the film; his haunting images punctured the claustrophobic hotel scenes where we see Snowden being interviewed by former *Guardian* journalist Glenn Greenwald. When the movie won the Academy

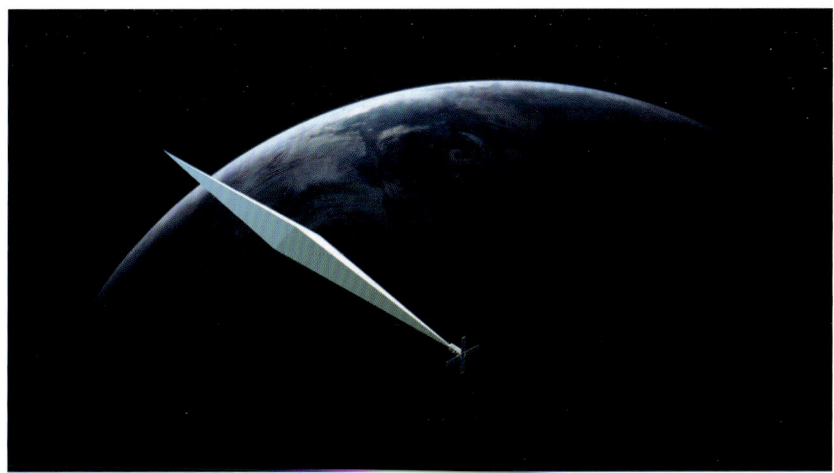

Trevor Paglen, *Orbital Reflector,* 2018 __Digital rendering

Award for Best Documentary Feature the following year, I realized that Paglen was now enshrined in film history, but you might not even realize just how subversively intertwined his work is with culture at large.

Autonomy Cube (2014–18), for example, which Paglen developed with security researchers, is a sculpture that lets you connect to the internet in a museum setting while still being encrypted. Instead of being funneled down the museum's generic Wi-Fi with its requests for approval and personal information, it routes you down the onion router (Tor). You can then browse without surveillance or interception. Your IP address (where you are searching from) is impossible to identify. If you're in London, a surveillance bot might be directed to a randomized location in rural Australia. *Autonomy Cube* is a catalytic call for freedom. The first time I exhibited it in London, journalists and audiences were immersed. The next time, I was a guest curator at a museum in a midsize metropolis; the work had become well-known and, one would expect, trouble-free. However, the questions from administrators, senior staff, and even trustees veered from the mundane to the absurd: "Are we encouraging people to watch porn in the museum?" The ethical question of whether it is acceptable to entertain oneself with pornography in a museum is not the most important one here. But the curiosity that the technology fosters through its proposition of freedom is very much the issue. Paglen is known for making the unseen visible. Therefore, unbuckling the imperceptible opinions and power structures that undergird an institution is part of the artwork's active agency.

Orbital Reflector (2018), a satellite coproduced with the Nevada Museum of Art in Reno has a similar function, albeit perhaps accidentally and in an altogether different fashion. The 1.5 million U.S.-dollar satellite was launched by the artist with the intention of being the first purely artistic object in space, an atmosphere composed of surveillance, telecommunication, and government vessels. The three-month path carved out for the satellite was clipped. Due to the 2018–19 U.S. federal government shutdown, the engineers for the project, who worked at a government-supervised museum, lost contact. The result equals space junk. But does this not reveal yet another aspect of Paglen's art: its potential to expose how divisive politics lead to the loss of certain histories?

Simon Denny

The internet has facilitated numerous mechanisms for artists to visualize the inner realms of digital life. Simon Denny occupies cult status in this area. His intricate installations use key figures in the history of the internet—from the internet entrepreneur and political activist Kim Dotcom to the inventors of the blockchain, which he animates into propositional models for a collective future. My last encounter with Denny involved a desire to evolve his research around patent technology in the UAE. He had transformed this data into his *Document Relief* (2019–ongoing) series, whereby various patents from major corporations were dissected and reformulated using a meticulous process of analog stitching and suturing—an act in opposition to the automated nature that one might expect of today's 3-D technologies. We crisscrossed between multiple Emirates to Masdar City—one of the first zoned areas to rely purely on solar energy—before delving into the details of trash disposal with environmental management companies and major estate agents.

By the time Denny left the UAE, my head was pulsing with puzzles I wanted to understand. I contacted a friend in Brisbane, Australia, who I had anointed as a geo-engineer when I met him at university. I expounded upon the various secret meetings that we had the day before and interrogated the encoded language spurted out to us. Why did it feel like something was being concealed? Is renewable energy not good for us? Won't it save us? Andy, amiable and measured in his responses, began unveiling the contradictions of the various technologies and the impossibility of sustaining them amidst the intricate web of global social, political, and economic relations. He suggested that we really should consider Mars as a serious long-term solution. As his newborn baby began to cry and the Zoom screen flickered off, I sat pondering a boundless set of prospective futures. Isn't that what truly transcendental art can do? Make you think, feel, exist, if even only for a split second?

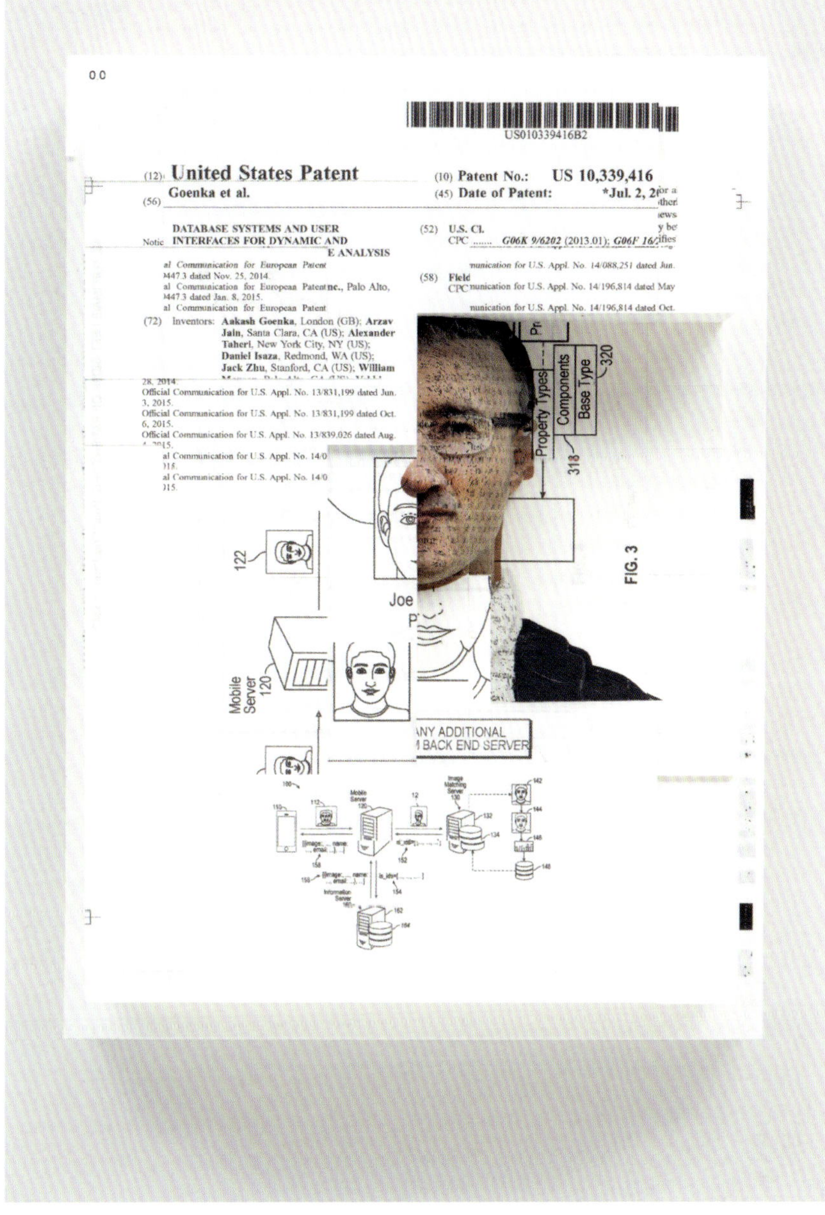

Simon Denny, *Document Relief 31 (Palantir Image Identification patent)*, 2021 __Inkjet print on archival paper, glue, custom metal wall mount, 11¾ × 8¼ × 4⅜ in. (29.7 × 21 × 11 cm)

___ The Rise of the Digital

It is 2009. The dust has settled on the festivities surrounding Liverpool's naming as the European Capital of Culture. I am sitting with a yellow legal pad and pencil in a purple boardroom.

The interest generated in Liverpool after it was picked for the prestigious title in 2008 generated swathes of inward investment into this port city, which was decimated during World War II. New attention was given to the now-former UNESCO World Heritage Site—the Royal Albert Docks. Bars and restaurants appeared at every juncture around the town's center, and adjacent areas were manicured with attractions for a broader public. Residential real-estate projects also emerged around the area. In the cultural realm, widespread programming, including the tenth anniversary of the Liverpool Biennial entitled *MADE UP*, presented ambitious artworks by popular luminaries, such as Yoko Ono and Yayoi Kusama. At FACT, 2008 also marked the year of the organization's most visited exhibition, with the first UK institutional solo exhibition of Pipilotti Rist.

Rist's show formed part of the vision of FACT's new CEO, Mike Stubbs, to consider human futures. Majestic architectural configurations led the viewer into sensuous cinematic spaces, anchored by the UK premiere of *Gravity, Be My Friend*, the title piece created for the artist's exhibition at Magasin III in Stockholm in 2007. (The artist's exploration into concepts of paradise lost had first been shown at the 51st Venice Biennale in 2005.) The exponential growth in audience figures, propelled by art stars and enhanced by marketing budgets from the city and regional development agencies, also encouraged FACT to collaborate with nearby UK art spaces, such as Cornerhouse in Manchester (where I later worked) and Grizedale Arts in Cumbria, to form Abandon Normal Devices (AND)—a festival of art, digital culture, and new cinema. Its inaugural edition in 2009, riding the wave of 2008's success, made FACT a venue teeming with a diverse group of denizens, engrossed in the culture-jamming musings of the Yes Men and the elegiac silence of Apichatpong Weerasethakul's award-winning exhibition, *Primitive* (2009), which went on to tour the world. Much talk surrounded a landmark presentation called *War Veteran Vehicle* (2009) by video artist Krzysztof Wodiczko. In this public installation, a projector situated on top of an ex-military RV cast text and sound into the dark night, telling excruciating tales of post-traumatic stress from Iraq war veterans based in and around Liverpool.

As soon as the inaugural festival wrapped, FACT's curatorial minds had been asked to gather in the boardroom by Stubbs, where we would have to prepare to make a presentation to the board of trustees regarding

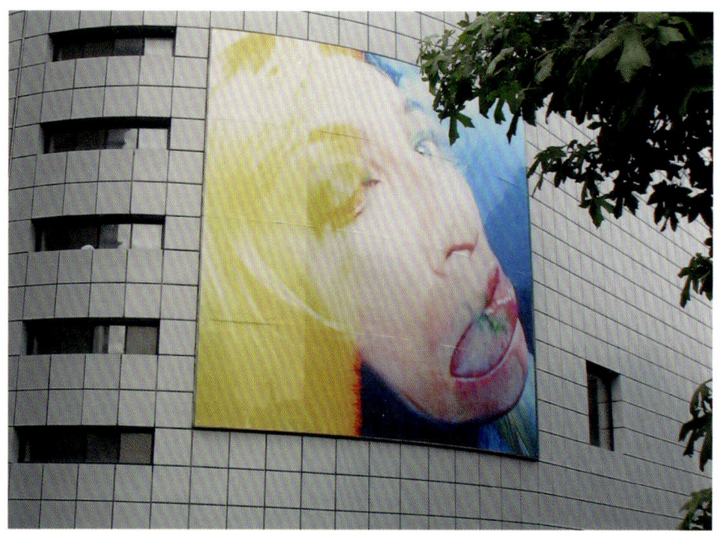

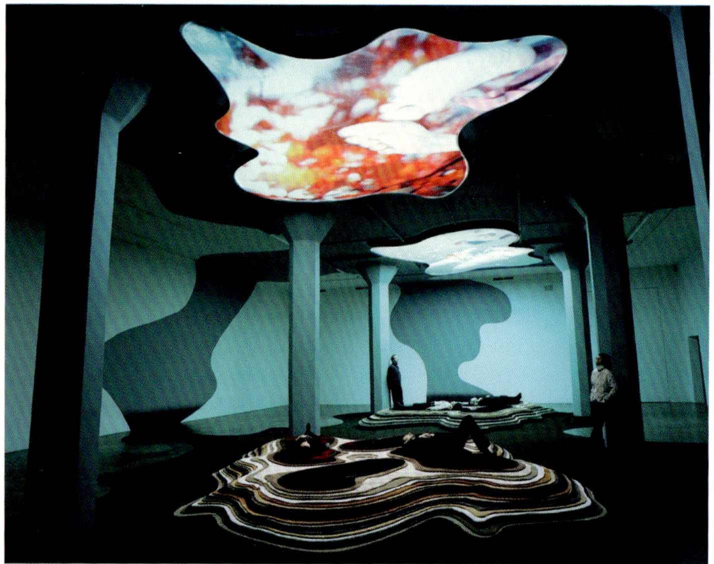

Pipilotti Rist, *Open My Glade (Flatten)*, 2000 __Video installation
Installation view: FACT, Liverpool, UK, 2008

Pipilotti Rist, *Gravity, Be My Friend*, 2007 __Audio video installation, 10 min. 40 sec., edition of 3 + 1 AP. Installation view: Magasin III, Stockholm, 2007 the organization's programmatic future. Though Liverpool and its museums had managed to keep going despite the 2008 financial crisis that had halted much of the newfound influx of funding, the coffers were now relatively empty. It would soon be time to go back to basics. Each member of the curatorial team was asked to define their concept of creative technology. However, the loose nature of the conversation initially ended in murmurs of confusion and even larger aspirations. During the next six months, these meetings ballooned to include consultants who claimed to be specialists in the field of the digital, as well as notable artists, hackers, tinkerers, academics, and board members. "Are we interviewing for our jobs again?" I asked a colleague.

It seemed that we had become unmoored. Creative technology as a concept was equally a product of computing, design, and the broader field of the humanities. It was synonymous with hipsters who could code, musicians who deployed Auto-Tune, and megafunded university projects, such as the MIT Media Lab in Cambridge, Massachusetts. We were most certainly fighting to keep our jobs. One of the recurring concerns was managing the balance and cost of a new tide of sensationalism that was associated with the technical arts and the DIY spirit of early internet art, which was produced in bedrooms using freely available open-source technology. It felt as if a mainstream thirst for the once-marginalized field that put the interdisciplinary creative and tech people together in the same room had come around and swept them all up, subsumed by corporations and branding agencies as opposed to dreaming together of art's possibilities.

The realm of fiction has long generated tools for understanding and imagining the internet's possibilities. The original concept of cyberspace, for example, was coined by novelist William Gibson in the sci-fi classic *Neuromancer* in 1984. The dream of a culture that is globally connected is, in many respects, what led museums to invest in experimenting online. In 1998, the historic Walker Art Center in Minneapolis acquired the online platform *äda 'web* (1995–98), founded by entrepreneur John Borthwick and curator Benjamin Weil. A digital foundry of myriad visual and literary forms, its name paid homage to Ada Lovelace, a writer and mathematician who is now widely believed to be the first computer programmer. In 1998, the Guggenheim Museum commissioned and presented one of the first pieces of internet art to deal explicitly with identarian politics, Shu Lea Cheang's *Brandon* (1998–99). In fragmentary form, the work reveals the heartbreaking story of Brandon Teena, a trans man living in Nebraska who was raped and murdered in 1993. Assuming the splintered, hyperlinked consciousness embodied by the internet itself, the visitor must interact

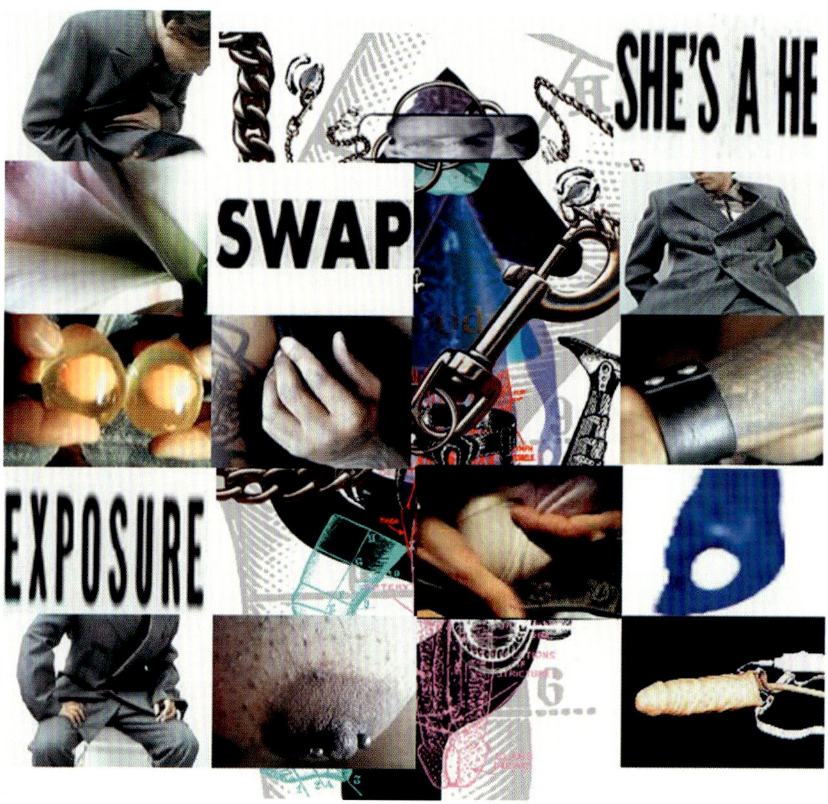

Shu Lea Cheang, *Brandon*, 1998–99 __Interactive networked code (HTML, Java, JavaScript, and server database), dimensions variable

with the artwork, mutating and morphing across genders with the protagonists. Now part of the museum's permanent collection, it predated the feature film *Boys Don't Cry* (1999), which propelled actor Hilary Swank into the spotlight for her Oscar-winning lead role as Teena.

In 2001, at the Whitney Museum of American Art, under the stewardship of adjunct digital art curator Christiane Paul, an online platform for "commissions for net art and new media art" called artport was launched. During this period, creative technologists (i.e., in simplest terms, programmers who could help make interactive projects), momentarily became indispensable to large-scale museums across the western world. Their goal was to produce what curators Michael Connor and Sarah Perks referred to in 2009 as "The Art of With."[1] This was less art for people, but art made with, by, and in conversation with audiences—or at least this has been the constant aspiration ever since.

Audience Equals Data

In 1970, futurist Alvin Toffler released a treatise on rapid evolution, *Future Shock*. The multimillion-dollar, top-selling book argues that "information overload," or too much happening too fast, creates a state of consciousness where one becomes afraid of the future. One can apply this theory to the initial excitement for the internet as a site for art. Yet soon enough, spiraling costs and technical realities led many museums to quickly shift their focus elsewhere; they had brick-and-mortars to maintain. The concept of being online largely assumed that the content would be free and, therefore, the subsistence of such programming became untenable from a business standpoint. *Brandon*, like many other such works, went offline for a number of years. Museum officials were seemingly unable to fund the cost of the work's back-end development. A vacuum emerged, whereby custom-made cultural centers devoted to technology, as well as smaller art ateliers and blogs, bloomed in silos, marginalized from the field of so-called mainstream art, which is arguably why so little has been authored about the story of art and the internet so far. Meanwhile, museums' interest in the digital revolved around their desire to produce slick websites to generate income through ticket sales, memberships, and online retail purchases. Over the years, I have interviewed content producers who have come and gone in the museum field—their positions at first urgent and then suddenly redundant.

One of the exciting figures in this mix, whom I should note I have never met in person, is Jay Mollica, currently director of digital engagement at the Pérez Art Museum in Miami. I came across Mollica's work when he was the creative technologist at the San Francisco Museum of Modern Art (SFMOMA). During his time there, he contributed to the formation of *Open Space*, a blog that quickly became a hybrid space in which a multitude of artists and thinkers could converge. He also made news in the field by lobbying for SFMOMA to become the first museum in the United States to support net neutrality, a principle that all internet service providers and their content should be treated equally, without censure.

In 2017, Mollica's project *Send Me SFMOMA* was launched. It was an SMS-based service that allowed anyone to send the museum a word or emoji that questioned the museum's open website API, and, in return, an image of a work of art from the museum's collection would be delivered to their phone. It was, as Mollica notes, "an attempt to use the appeal of new technology to avoid the [idea that] the museum is an exclusive sphere."[2] If his projects and positions read like those of an artist, it should come as no surprise that he, like many who hold similar positions, identifies as such. After teaching himself HTML and JavaScript programming languages in high school, he went on to study English and spent a stint pursuing medicine, while producing internet art in his bedroom. Mollica found himself working as a web developer at the California Academy of Sciences, San Francisco, where he was emboldened to argue for the web's utility in democratizing various facets of culture.

At the museum, the biggest challenge was how to understand user engagement. "One of the defining characteristics of making anything for the internet is that you have no idea how you'll be meeting your audience: staring at a desktop screen in the dead of night, because they can't sleep; on a layover at a foreign airport; while pursuing research with fifty tabs open at once?"[3] These can be fractious unknowns for organizations anxious to secure attention in a world of freewheeling content. "As soon as someone lands on the web page, they're being asked to buy a ticket, and less incentive is given to lingering on content that does not directly generate revenue," says Mollica. Yet, he does point to *Virtual Cinema* from the Museum of Modern Art (MoMA) in New York, and *On Demand* from the Birmingham Museums in the UK as successful attempts to create subscription-based access to online content.

Levin Haegele, a London-based creative technologist and artist asserts that if these subscriptions do not add up, we will soon see such platforms disappear.[4] He, like everyone I have spoken to, emphasizes that the largest hindrance for museums and galleries, and by proxy, artists, is the technical labor costs of not only making internet art but also its conservation. The latter has been discussed extensively by Christiane Paul, who has argued that to extend the shelf life of digital culture we need to consider the cost of the back-end right at the start;[5] that is, how technology evolves and contorts, demanding new material forms to exist. Because these costs can continue to shift in the marketplace for skilled practitioners, sharing knowledge is key to this process. "I teach artists how to code; how to use software for that very reason," notes Haegele.[6] "I want to be subversive, to encourage artists to eschew the corporatization of their work by relying on large technical firms or engineers. I want them to understand the basics so that they can know how to make their work, but also enable it to subsist."[7]

When I ask him about the most interesting adventures in the digital sphere, he responds without hesitation that he believes that it is emerging in the art market. "Art fairs, auction houses, and commercial galleries are building out virtual set-ups quickly and responsively, because they've understood that, especially recently, not everyone can be everywhere anymore. Traditional economies need to shift." The emphasis on commerce is a clear delineation. The business model of simply sustaining a brand, as is the case with museums and not-for-profit art spaces, makes them move slowly and cautiously, unable to respond to the demand and money grabs one finds in the marketplace.

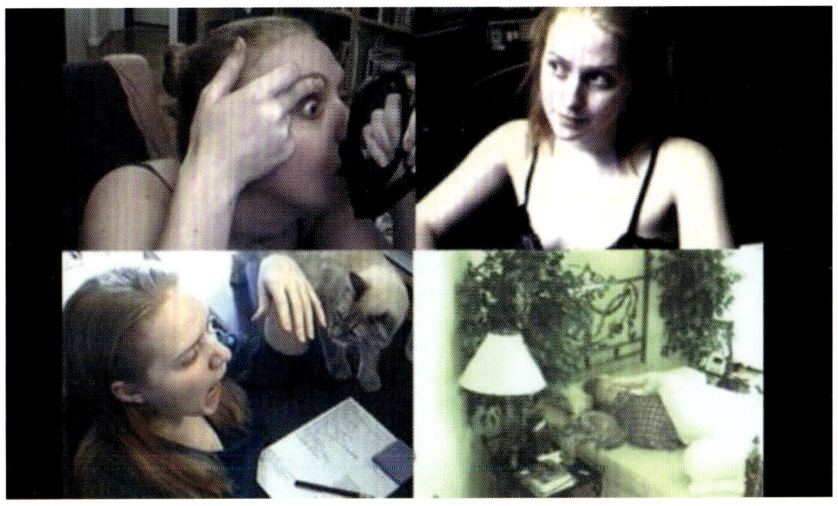

Jennifer Ringley, *JenniCam*, 1996–2003

Haegele and I met at the end of 2011 at SPACE, an organization set up by artists Bridget Riley and Peter Sedgley in London in 1968 to support artists. During our time working together, we discussed our favorite online artworks. I was surprised that Levin's top choice was not a formal artwork per se, but a kind of social-media experiment called *JenniCam* (1996–2003), the now-defunct website by the world's first online female lifecaster. Jennifer Ringley began broadcasting the mundane activities of her daily life before the TV show *Big Brother* hit the airwaves. "I was a student at university, and I found it a profound means to think through anonymous spectatorship," Haegele told me. Like Netflix and the endless video on demand (VOD) services of today, *JenniCam* was consuming huge envelopes of global internet traffic. Unlike Web 1.0 dot-com millionaire Josh Harris, who began webcasting in 1993 through pseudo.com, Ringley wasn't publicly shamed, and nor did she lose all her money in front of a cinema audience in a feature film at the Sundance Film Festival—a revelation shown in Ondi Timoner's documentary feature film *We Live in Public* (2009). Apparently she just quietly disappeared.

It is perplexing to consider that anyone in a hypersurveilled world of public naming and shaming would take such a risk with their identity today, especially if there wasn't monetary recompense involved. The Instagram influencer gets paid to promote products; the music icon reveals their life online as a means to sell a lifestyle that exists beyond the realm of online streaming. It could well be argued that there is a rift between the aspirational desire to generate income through the internet versus the desire to experiment in the virtual sphere with oneself. The original model of online content production relied on a certain kind of novelty. Post-Web 2.0, the public, whether Gen Z or their grandparents, are as much content producers as they are members of a global audience. The use of creative and aesthetic technologies online has shifted. The spectator is eager to become an active agent. They want to deploy the internet's emerging technologies to do something that they could not do before, whether it is meeting new people, developing a different career path, or even seeing and experiencing the world differently. In a searching set of propositions, Haegele suggested that it would be best for museums to use digital tools in ways that are contrary to the ways that corporations might consider. Examples ranged from 3-D modeling artworks so that audiences could literally see aspects of a work not previously evident to them to exposing the backs of flat works, such as paintings. It is not simply about novelty but revealing what is right there but unseen because of traditional museum protocols.

Some of these suggestions fall into the field of interpretative or communicative tools for how we experience art. This takes me down the road of the nineteenth-century German philosopher Walter Benjamin, who noted that the aura, the distinctive quality of an artwork, is lost when it is reproduced through technological means. This thesis has consumed historians and the public for generations, debated beautifully by Erika Balsom, who in 2013 argued against the "novelty of new media."[8]

The question that I have been trying to grapple with as a curator for as long as I have been working is: what do audiences [you] want to see? And how? Art can embody different auras in various spheres. In 2021 an experiential event company took over an industrial site near Spitalfields Market in East London, near where I temporarily lived, staging what was purported to be a Vincent van Gogh exhibition. *Van Gogh: The Immersive Experience* was a world away from the approach of other London venues that have presented the Post-Impressionist painter's work, such as the National Gallery, the Courtauld Gallery, and Tate. Enter the exhibition out of hours and one will find that the canvasses are empty, frames without pictures. Return during hours of operation and the light of projectors fills them with a 360-degree simulacrum, seen through 3-D glasses. One cannot help but wonder if audiences think that this is better than the real thing. My own bias, screams—*yelps*—no! I want to see the precision of the artist's brushstrokes; to encounter an object that the artist has touched, overseen, or lived with, no matter how seemingly fetishistic this proposition may be. Still, putting on an exhibition without loaning hundreds of artworks from institutions located around the world does present a nimble possibility for certain kinds of institutions, especially those without a permanent art collection, and for audiences, who can gain more instant access to content rather than waiting years for an exhibition of tangible objects to move across the world, generating its own carbon footprint. The van Gogh virtual reality show has toured and popped up all over the world. Is it an inevitable result of a culture in pandemic free fall in many respects? If you cannot travel to van Gogh, he can come to you; one could argue this to be techno-fetishism, but it is also a form of democratization. After all, it nurtures and galvanizes interest in an artist all the same.

Can the two forms of exhibition exist simultaneously? Large museums have for years continued to develop the concept of the video wall—interactive screens of artworks. Often featuring artworks from a museum's collection, these forums present "clouds" of hyperlinked artistic content that can help a viewer navigate art history through the museum's offerings. But when presented as contextual, as an addendum to the core activities of the venue, these sites can often become peripheral and quickly stagnate. The more pertinent exploratory point, perhaps, is how to map artistic innovation in the age of the internet. It would be restrictive for creative practitioners to silo themselves within independent platforms where they can control all the contours and tools of dissemination and display. But perhaps there can exist a middle ground that harkens back to the independent spirit of net artists working with the World Wide Web (WWW) in the 1990s or the anarchic spirit of warehouse takeovers by artists in the 1960s and 1970s, alongside the sanctioned forum of the curated museum sphere.

We are currently witnessing a world in a hybrid state whereby a confluence of agents is helping artists assemble a diverse toolbox that they individually must decide how to use. Whatever your position, however, the present has become a virtual one; it is time to dive in headfirst.

Virtual Art

Back in the boardroom at FACT, we began discussing the theories of virtual art proposed by art and technology historian Frank Popper. Popper was a superhero among his peers and held the role of professor emeritus of aesthetics and the science of art at the Sorbonne in Paris. (He lived to an impressive 102 years of age, dying in 2020). Taking note of artist Roy Ascott's early concepts of networking, Popper proposed virtual art as an enhanced, cross-disciplinary experience that created an augmented way of experiencing an art object. Spectacles, stereoscopic screens, and artificially intelligent data were the key identifiers of the virtual in the 1980s and 1990s. It was, therefore, proposed that all artworks made from technical media, or that embodied a techno-aesthetic, were virtual.

From a present vantage point, this poses multiple frames through which to look at and consider internet art. David Hockney's paintings crafted on an iPad and printed to various physical scales, for example, can be considered exemplars of the virtual sphere and, therefore, internet art. A canvas can be virtual so long as its genesis emerged from a technical space. That said, it would perhaps be more apt to argue that the canvas is digitally constructed or imagined through the virtual as opposed to being virtual itself. Another artist who utilizes the iPad in his paintings is Joshua Nathanson. Ebullient colors of California beach scenes and interior renderings of chaotic anxiety from the artist's imagination are first carefully sketched on an iPad. Unlike Hockney, Nathanson then uses traditional paints, such as acrylics and oils, to painstakingly reproduce the digitally native image crafted on his device.

The conversation between physical and virtual forms has led to significant debate among both the tech and art communities regarding the use of the term *IRL*. Arguably, our field of vision and experience are no longer binary: our emotional experience of space and time can be transposed to multiple places at once, engaging and forming a multitude of encounters. I wonder where that leaves our understanding of the virtual. In 2004, historian Oliver Grau published *Virtual Art: From Illusion to Immersion*, which, according to the Archive of Visual Art, has more than two thousand citations internationally, making it the most referenced art history monograph since 2000. In his book, Grau proposes that the virtual is a sphere that encompasses a unique sensuousness, a forum for the creation of new fields of emotion, specifically, a space to let go and reformulate a sense of self. Virtual art bears a unique potential to gradually foster a divergent cognitive mode of being. A significant example of this is the online virtual world Second Life, founded in 2003. With more than sixty-four million active accounts, the user base, which has fluctuated over the years, was reported to have grown by more than 35 percent in 2021.[9] In this virtual world, users craft an avatar of themselves, stand-ins who create imagined worlds, engaging with all manner of activities from banal conversation to intense sexual acts. I first came to understand the dedication of the users in 2013 when I held a panel discussion on Second Life at SPACE, moderated by art historian and magazine editor Victoria Camblin. The panelists were already deeply familiar with each other, having met in the virtual world, yet this was their first encounter in the flesh. They all noted that their face-to-face encounter and presence did not diminish, or alter, the meaningful nature of their engagements or the relationships that they had developed online.

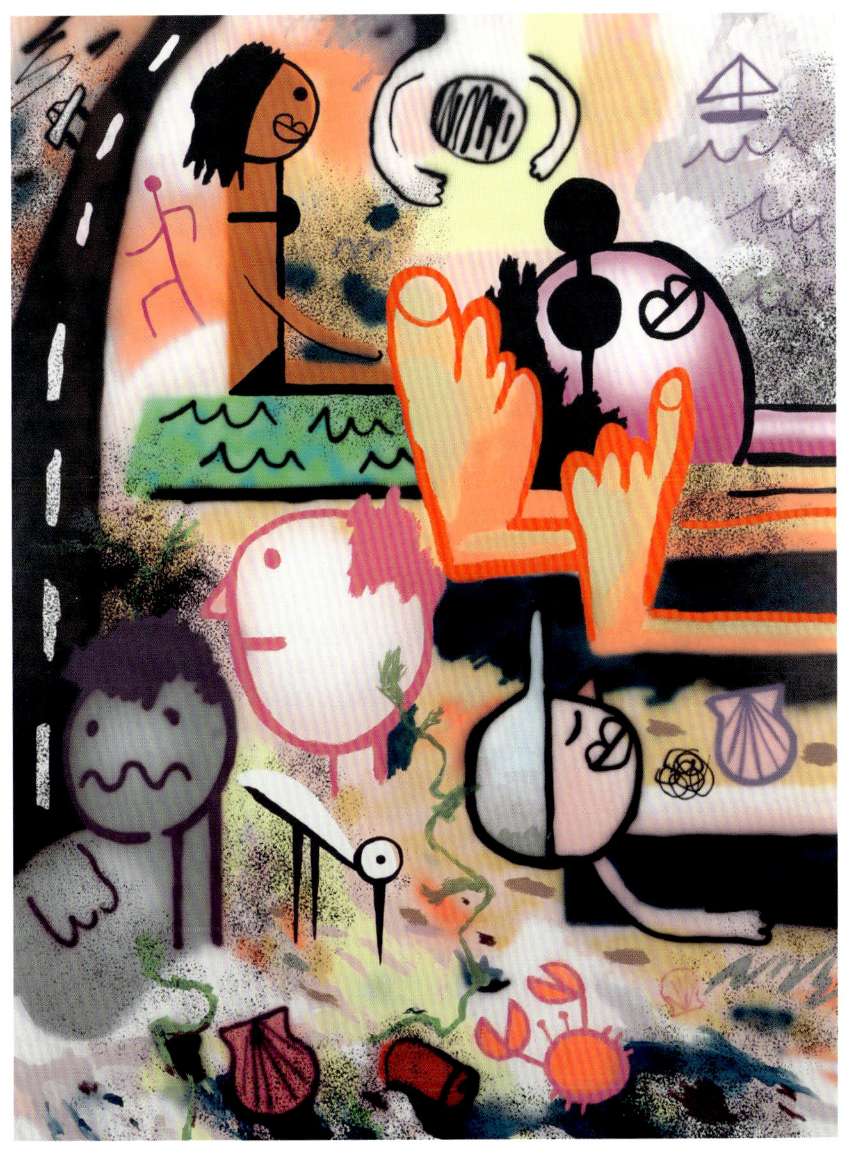

Joshua Nathanson, *Is it late yet?*, 2015 —Acrylic and oil stick on canvas, 84 × 61$\frac{1}{16}$ in. (213.4 × 155.1 cm)

The proposition of virtual assembly with fluent human interaction is also at the heart of Cécile B. Evans's practice. Consistently unsatisfied by the use of the term *virtual*, which the artist argues is mistakenly used for something that is not real or defined as mediated, Evans fashions layered artworks that interrogate the middle ground between the perceived physical and the virtual, manifesting her works as multi-user theater, television, and everyday performance. My first intense encounter with her works took place on the newly launched website for the Serpentine Gallery, based in Hyde Park in London, in 2014. The page loads, I click, and a friendly voice begins to speak to me. This is *AGNES* (2014), a virtual avatar, a bot that lived on this website and interacted with online visitors until 2019. On every appearance, her presence would surprise me, and I wondered if she was supervising or surveilling me. "The End is Near," she warned. It felt like Y2K all over again. She began to spurt answers to invisible questions. It was not clear if they were gleaned from voices in her head, people online, or elsewhere. The avatar's experience of what it was like to live in the cloud came to the fore over time. *AGNES* was potentially proposing a possible future for us all. Entrapped and ensnared, we could all become holograms, mere stand-ins for bodies on a website.

In 2016, Evans expanded these questions into the ambitious installation *Sprung a Leak* at Tate Liverpool. The automated play underpinning the work mystified and bewildered me at first. I did not understand where to direct my gaze or situate my body in the gallery. My brother, once a Silicon Valley tech nerd obsessed with automation, was equally uneasy. For nearly seventeen minutes, two humanoid robots and a robot dog, along with three human "users"—avatars that were tethered to poles on screens—moved in unsettling synchronicity. The absence of bodily flesh within this sphere intimated a world devoid of traditional forms of physicality. I wanted to contact the artist to ask if she knew something that I didn't know. We hadn't met except, perhaps, once on a budget airline on our way to somewhere to the Venice Biennale or perhaps in a protracted email chain.

When I visited my father in Glasgow in 2019, we stopped by the Tramway arts venue for a coffee. The man I call Baba proclaims not to understand art in any form and wanted to get in and out. But the installation in the adjacent gallery by Evans featuring *AMOS' WORLD* (2017–ongoing), a TV show set in a progressive social-housing estate inspired by Brutalist complexes caught his attention with its irresistibly plotted story. Baba identified with the irritable protagonist Amos, conceived as an amalgamation of the world's starchitects. Propositions about our lived future appeared and vanished before I could catch them. Perching himself on a gray, concretelike scaled model of Amos's building (which probably was not supposed to be touched), he turned to me and asked, "Why don't you make art like this?"

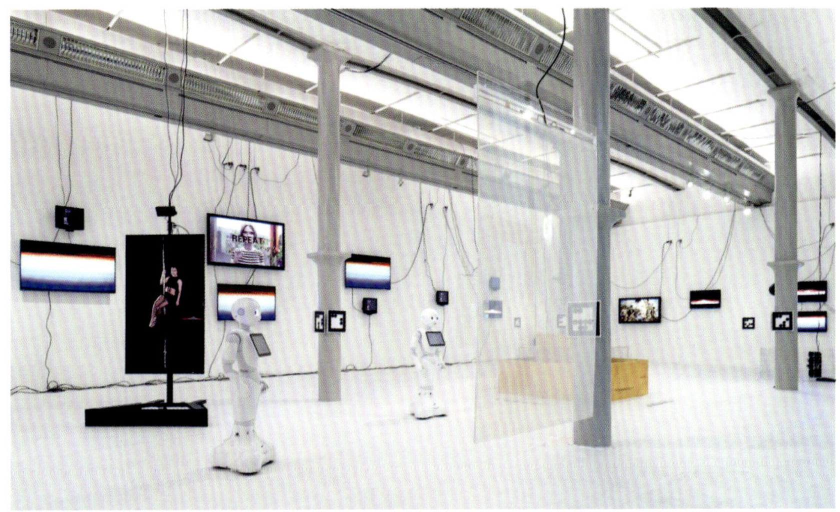

Cécile B. Evans, *Sprung a Leak*, 2016 __Multi-channel video, raspberry pis, cables, humanoid robots, robot dog, custom fountain, privacy shades, lamps, dog pen, bookshelf, assorted books, miscellaneous items, solar vitamin bottles, c.18 min. (looped). Installation view: Tate Liverpool, UK, 2016

Virtual Reality (VR)

VR is an acronym at the tip of everyone's tongue in the world of art and also increasingly in advertising, medical science, and retail spaces. "Is there any VR in your exhibition about the internet?" asked the fundraising team at the museum in Chicago where I worked. Every press article in the lead-up to the 2019 launch of Sharjah Biennial 14 spoke of my expertise in virtual reality, assuring the public that I had put some in the show. And yet, the most ambitious exhibition that I had organized in my career, and the most expansive treatise on the internet, *Electronic Superhighway (2016–1966)*, was entirely devoid of VR. It was not an oversight. Nor was it a cost issue. My position at the time was that if you can experience perceived reality, why would an audience want to experience a mere simulation of it on a pair of glasses?

As novel as it may seem, VR has been around for a long time. NASA began developing a headset in the late 1970s that was in the world by 1985.[10] Sega, the company that gave us Sonic the Hedgehog, created a headset in the early 1990s. Today, these virtual goggles are available at a significantly lower price point, and VR has become a mass-market commodity, perhaps most widely associated in the twenty-first century with the Oculus Rift. The latter began its life in a Kickstarter campaign in 2012. Two years later,

Facebook, Inc. (now known as Meta), purchased the company for two billion U.S. dollars—one of the corporation's largest acquisitions at the time, double what it paid to acquire Instagram, which it purchased in 2012.

VR is experienced through a headset and seeks to simulate an experience that is more enhanced than the real world (which may be real or imagined). Or at the least, it seeks to be a mirror of a world—perhaps of one that we cannot access. I have been putting on VR headsets for about twenty years. My initial critique was that it was little more than a way to experience cinema up close and personal, but not as crisp as a celluloid or digital projection, or even a domestic TV set. Enter the words: *immersive*, *mixed reality*, and *extended-reality VR*. These are forms of experience where the VR encourages the viewer to become embodied. Turn your head left, or right. Life is a video game, and the suggestion is that you've just not been playing it correctly.

Artists' excursions into the VR field proliferated in the second decade of the millennium, with improvements in graphics and enhanced technical stability encouraging VR technologies to be considered a pivotal medium. In 2019, curator Daniel Birnbaum left his post as director of Moderna Museet before the end of his tenure to head up Acute Art in London, an ambitious production house of VR for artists, which has commissioned works by the likes of Tomás Saraceno, KAWS, Olafur Eliasson, Ai Weiwei, and Marina Abramović, to name a few. But not every artist is afforded the luxury of such an opportunity: the cost of producing such material can still act as a barrier. In 2014, I met Jacolby Satterwhite, an artist and performer whose vision of the world had exploded beyond the limits of what the eyes could digest. We wandered through the museum corridors of the Whitney with a friend of his, whom I would later come to know as David Casavant, the twenty-something stylist and collector who leveraged social media to bring his rare archive of thousands of looks by Raf Simons and Helmut Lang into the mainstream. He had begun acquiring these garments as a teenager at sample sales and online and was now getting phone calls from Kanye West and Rihanna who wanted to borrow his wares.

Satterwhite had just completed his now-iconic *Reifying Desire* (2014), which was a conversation starter at that year's Whitney Biennial—the final biennial to take place in the museum's Breuer building. In 2016, I invited Satterwhite to participate in an exhibition I was cocurating, *Imitation of Life: Melodrama and Race in the 21st Century* at HOME in Manchester. I asked for a new commission. He proposed a work, which was then titled *En Plein Air: Music of Objective Romance*, a multipart opera that would transform the visual lexicon around queer gender representation, labor, and the expression of desire. At the time, Jacolby was rendering 3-D images using the complex software Autodesk Maya.

The work, played from the artist's computer, included compositions with contents that were gleaned from cassette tapes of his mother singing and her drawings rendered in digital form. These appeared alongside the artist embodying a multitude of characters on screen who produced orgiastic visions of a future universe—constellations of egomaniacal self-love, nimble and contorted bodily experience, oh, and did I mention, queer sex? And a lot of fashion. Users would also have the option to experience this up close and personal on a VR headset. The exhibition opening was upon us, and the artwork was almost ready, but Satterwhite's old-school computer suddenly stopped working. We had no choice but to fill the spot with an older work by the artist. We did not change the wall labels, nor did we identify this switch to the press. They seemingly didn't notice and still wrote about the work with mystical wonder.

In 2017, the project took off in earnest with the support of the New Museum and Rhizome as part of their *First Look* series, for which they presented a multitude of new artist VR commissions, from Jayson Musson to Porpentine Charity Heartscape. That same year, Satterwhite premiered *En Plein Air: Music of Objective Romance* at the San Francisco Museum of Modern Art, presenting an evening of Afrofuturism—a cultural aesthetic that incorporates various tropes of the African diasporic life. S&M chains led to a live performance; seated VR interventions led into a multiracial dystopia, where race and gender were perennially unresolved.

The New Museum has been a regular site of VR adventure. In 2015, Lauren Cornell and artist Ryan Trecartin cocurated and presented *Surround Audience*, the third iteration of the institution's cornerstone triennial. The day after the opening, lines of people gathered to experience, via Oculus, Daniel Steegmann Mangrané's *Phantom (Kingdom of all the animals and all the beasts is my name)* (2015), which led the visitor through a VR circular maze and the Brazilian Atlantic rain forest, which is quickly disappearing due to deforestation. When you put on the headset, a nauseating impact occurs within the body, the result of a tension between what is real and imagined. From the sense of discombobulation, you could infer the artwork's message to be that this rain forest should be experienced physically. Yet, in reality, this disappearing site should only be seen from a distance, bearing enough proximity to keep the forest alive.

The issue of life and its contingency was at the core of enfant terrible Jordan Wolfson's 2017 Whitney Biennial presentation, *Real Violence* (2017). Arguably the most controversial VR artwork released to the public to date, Wolfson's all-encompassing scene begins on a sunny day on a stretch of city sidewalk with what at first sounds like an overture—hushed voices singing the two Hebrew blessings recited during Hanukkah. These nondiegetic

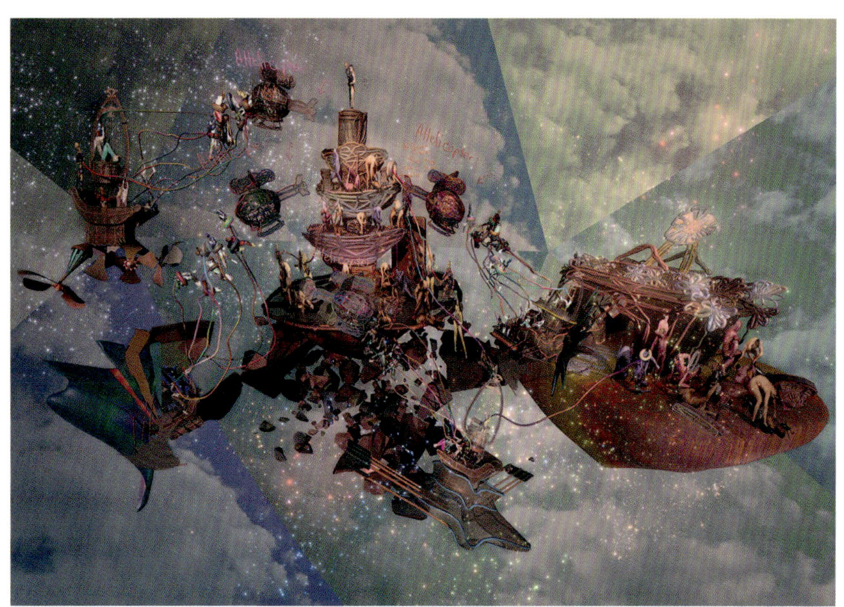

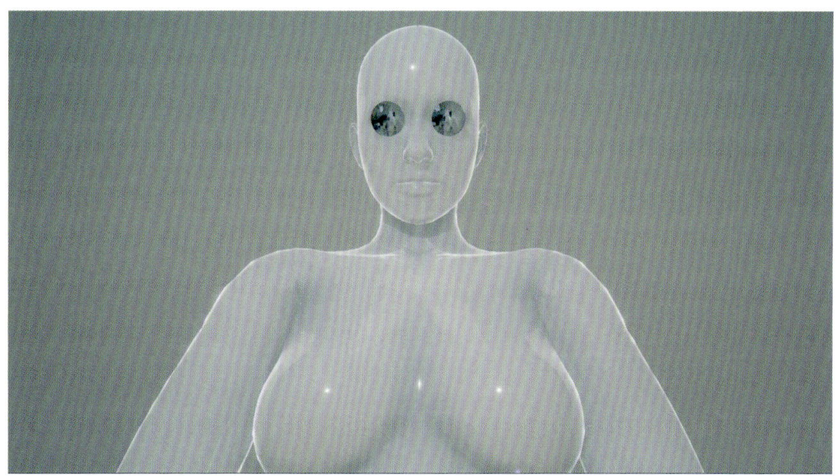

Jacolby Satterwhite, *En Plein Air: Vassalage I*, 2014
—C-print, 60 × 84 × 3 in. (152.4 × 213.4 × 7.6 cm)

Sidsel Meineche Hansen, *SECOND SEX WAR ZONE*, 2016
—Computer generated image

soliloquies persist as the viewer is confronted with the artist holding a baseball bat over a young man kneeling on the pavement, his captive, who he then graphically bludgeons to death. The act of assault, of murder, of street violence, of explicit and unbridled rage juxtaposed against Wolfson's chosen aural backdrop, raises multiple questions and concerns regarding violence against people of the Jewish faith. The artwork was so hyped for its explicit violence that my apprehension outweighed the visceral effects of seeing the act as it happened. At less than three minutes in length, the work disappeared in the blink of an eye. Fast-forward to 2021, when police brutality is replayed on social media and filtered through mainstream news media ad nauseam, and this work feels comparatively quotidian.

The audience at the time felt differently. During my first loop in the line leading to *Real Violence*, a man experiencing Wolfson's artwork in the station before me thrust off his headset and made as if he was about to throw up in a corner. After patiently waiting, I put on the set but was interrupted by two female voices screaming simultaneously. Despite the noise-canceling headphones, I could hear them both expressing how proud they were "not to have gone through with it." However, it was made clear to audience members at the Whitney by the docents that the violence took place in a studio, where Wolfson deployed an animatronic doll and edited the bashing into the filmed sequence during postproduction. The robotic doll, a source of constant return for the artist, is an apt metaphor for Wolfson, who presents a view of the world where we are unsure whether it will be man or machine holding the bat.

Taboo subjects are persistent themes for artists eager to explore the possibilities of VR. In 2016, at the headquarters of Gasworks in Vauxhall, London, I entered an exhibition by Sidsel Meineche Hansen entitled *SECOND SEX WAR* (2016). I had encountered Hansen's work previously in the same location years before when she was part of the collective Model Court (founded 2009). Back then, the focus was on war tribunals performed over Skype—the concept of a mediated legal system.

In 2016, wall reliefs, sculptures, and drawings explored concepts of pornography and feminist approaches to sex positivism that emerged in the 1980s, as well as the visual representation of pornography through various modes, including virtual reality.

The gallery's location near some of the world's most notorious gay male bathhouses, such as Chariots (which has now gone into liquidation), as well as gay male-centric bars and clubs, such as the Royal Vauxhall Tavern, the Eagle London, and the Cock Tavern, made the work feel all the more situated.

Augmented Reality (AR)

Some might perceive AR as little more than a functioning QR code, the gridded square that accompanied many museum wall labels in the first ten years of this millennium and which in many cases led to nowhere due to technical difficulties. Although AR (an extended reality software) is considered a subset of VR, this framework isn't necessarily all that useful. AR is not necessarily regarded as stationary viewing, but a real-world experience that is enhanced by adding a layer of technology to it. It almost always demands human interaction. The most common form of it might well be found on your phone. Facetune, an app that lets you edit your facial features for selfies, is one simple example. The Swedish conglomerate IKEA uses it in its phone app to help shoppers populate physical spaces with its furniture.

The creative possibilities of the form, however, did not become fully apparent to me until I met Jeremy Bailey in 2009. The artist and technologist, who often presents art through the fictional persona Famous New Media Artist Jeremy Bailey, was crafting emotional landscapes for video, performing through an Xbox Live Vision webcam in hotel rooms when we met. A year later, the Kinect for Xbox One was released as a way for gamers to use infrared to control their gaming software remotely. The motion-sensor function of the new device, used counterintuitively to its intended function, allowed for the artist to visualize 3-D animated objects, seemingly conjured out of thin air, adding a material layer to his body during live performances. These experiments formed the foundation for a multidimensional practice that involved reanimating historical artifacts with the traces of the evolving present.

In 2013, I introduced Bailey to Stephanie Pereira, who was then director of Kickstarter's cultural programs, who offered the artist advice on using the platform to launch his project *Important Portraits*. He and Stephanie explained to me that Kickstarter was not simply a crowdfunding site, per se, but offered artists a chance to create a gallery with guaranteed presales for the artist. Therefore, those who paid through the Kickstarter site could choose a historical painting from a selection offered by the artist and have the picture restaged for their own portrait using AR technologies, including the Kinect. *Important Portrait of Omar Kholeif and Frank Gallacher* (2013) depicts me with a plunging green neckline of animated crystals and oversize sparkling earrings in red alongside my partner, whose left shoulder is emblazoned with hexagonal metallic shapes. That I do not even recall the historical artwork that we chose to base our portrait on or what it is meant to evoke, beyond that it was from the seventeenth-century Vermeer era, is beside the point. Bailey's project used the two-way configuration of the Kickstarter campaign to foster a dialogue between the artist and collectors who became subjects. Their portraits are executed through divergent aesthetics enabled by using technological tools. In Bailey's case, this use was counter to their original purpose: the Kinect, in its initial iteration, was not intended as a creative tool for self-expression outside of the confines of Microsoft's Xbox gaming machine.

During the COVID-19 pandemic, Bailey and I worked together across great expanses—he in Toronto, I in Sharjah—to create a virtual community platform for "anxiety-fueled art and commentary." But the artist's concerns moved elsewhere. He felt a need to put our project on hold and founded YOUar, an e-commerce platform that facilitates the sale by artists of AR art directly to consumers. The site functions as both an incubator and a sales gallery. Editions of art include *Curvy Corten Steel* (2020), which features a rubber mat with a QR code that positions your digitally rendered image inside a giant Richard Serra sculpture, which you can broadcast onto a screen of your choice or keep within the palm of your hand.

The construct of AR and its relationship to the three-dimensional sphere varies, depending on the context. In 2012, Oliver Laric initiated a seemingly endless project, *Lincoln 3D Scans* (2012–ongoing), where he 3-D scanned hundreds of art objects from the Collection, the county museum and gallery in Lincolnshire, England, and published these online as animated rotating indexical objects. These can be downloaded, and the public is free to use them in any way that they choose. They could be used as visual appendages to the physical body, in a selfie, or perhaps in one's home. In 2014, at London's Whitechapel Gallery, they were put on display in a group show exploring public art collections from outside of the city. In theory, anything you aspire to do with them is possible.

Ian Cheng's self-playing video games proffer another form of augmentation. A prime case is his *Emissary* (2015–17) series, which I believe to be more alluring than anything that a corporate piece of software, entity, or self-run machine has produced in aesthetic terms thus far. In *Emissary Forks for You* (2016), his idea of a sage figure is a Shiba Inu, a breed of hunting dog from Japan, inspired by a 2013 dog meme that guided you around the gallery at the 2016 Liverpool Biennial. You were handed a Google Tango tablet that took you, by way of the dog, on an adventure through algorithmically programmed simulations. Your field of vision was constantly mediated from the empty space onto the screen, where the world was animated with lush flora and fauna. This wondrous incarnation of an ongoing project combined 3-D mapping, AI, and a little Pokémon Go, inviting you to reconsider the multidimensional textures that one can perpetually layer and animate through the tools proliferating in the AR sphere.

Some of the most affecting AR works have been those where the artists have been provided with customized technological resources. Painter Nina Chanel Abney's Acute Art commission, *Imaginary Friend* (2020) presents a hologram of a modern-day sagacious figure who interacts with and empowers people in difficult situations. Launched to coincide with the 57th anniversary of the March on Washington—the largest civil rights gathering of its time—Abney's AR intervention, which uses Washington, DC, as a backdrop, premiered at the same time as two hundred thousand Black Lives Matter protestors took to the streets in 2020 to continue the fight against racially fueled social injustice and police brutality.

Digital Divide

In principle, I can now connect with anyone, anywhere. My seven-year-old crush was the first person whom I emailed. I received a response. It did not lead to marriage, children, or white picket fences, but it initiated a conversation around community. Growing up in an isolated and remote place, I could begin to keep in contact and develop companionship with those whom I could have lost to the geographic expanse of the vastly distributed Earth. Caution is nonetheless necessary when dealing with this global conglomerate that is the internet. And the idea that it enables us to live in a borderless world is an illusion.

The concept of the digital divide—the social disparity that separates individuals with access to digital tools from those without, based on geography, economic status, class, and race, among other attendant factors—has been the subject of much public debate by social scientists since the emergence of the internet. Professor of Communication Science at the University of Twente, the Netherlands, Jan van Dijk has debated whether the prevalence of digital spaces has prevented certain groups from being able to acquire functions and skills that they would otherwise have been able to pursue.[11] The University of Oxford's research and data unit and Oxford Internet Surveys reported that in 2018, 55.8 percent of the world's population was online in some capacity.[12] Hootsuite, a social-media management firm, noted in 2020 that two million new users are joining the virtual sphere through the internet every day, estimating that upward of four billion people are somehow engaged with the internet through its attendant platforms.[13] Today, that number is estimated to be more than four billion and it will surely continue to rise as the internet has verifiably become the mass-communication medium of our time. With the Earth's population nearing eight billion people, that still leaves about half of the people in the world disconnected. Those are humans, therefore, forced outside the scope of a global conversation.

The shape of the internet's movement and development is often misunderstood in the public sphere. Sociologists spent the better half of the first two decades of the WWW's existence arguing that the internet was reenshrining the historic divisions between east and west, the colonizer and colonized. Despite fears of censorship and suppression restricting users, the majority of the world's internet traffic is now propelled by and from the east—with more than 2.3 billion people online in Asia, and more than 800 million in China alone.[14] India, which is perceived to be one of the poorest nations in the world based on individual income, economic distribution, and GDP per capita, has one of the world's largest internet populations, with more than 560 million folks online at the time of writing.[15] Since 2010, Africa, which in the 1990s was deemed one of the signature exemplars of the unequal nature of the world's new mass medium, has continually shifted. The advent of the smartphone, essentially a megacomputer in your pocket or at your fingertips, is largely credited for bringing more than 85 percent of Kenyans online.[16] Although these metrics will evolve and shift over time, these figures represent a historical example of how rapidly global internet penetration can develop, even in economies with large socioeconomic inequities or financial scarcity.

This reflection intimates that, unlike the appliances that came to embody the social status of a western baby boomer or Gen X life (i.e., the television, the refrigerator, the washing machine), the internet is a mass medium that has the potential to transcend economic, social, and political barriers. It is a vessel to get one through to the most necessary aspects of life. In a utopic sense, it could also suggest a unification of culture—a potential society that can cluster together around both social causes and entertainment, finding forms of shared artistic value across expanses. That being said, it would clearly be naive to believe that the internet, like any mass medium, may ever be used by the entire population.

Digital Freedoms

In 2021, the "leader of the free world" President Donald Trump was banned from the majority of the major Web 2.0 platforms, which until then had been the soapboxes on which he broadcasted his controversial views. Although there may be a delicious sense of hand-rubbing revenge for some individuals, in the act of silencing a person who used social media to excoriate or bully others, this action is worrisome, no matter how offensive his views might be to one's personal beliefs or politics. The very spaces that enabled him to become a self-anointed and appointed messiah of "truth" were now tearing him down, just as he was on his way out of office. Never mind that the CEOs and founders of those same tech companies were up until that point in constant court proceedings, being interrogated by members of Congress for allowing racist, misogynist, and homophobic hate groups to congregate and use their platforms in pursuit of social injustice. Perhaps this social-media shutdown could be perceived as a gesture that could quiet the new government and allow them to get on with their vertical takeovers until another set of fiscally loose politicians rolls in. That is one interpretation.

If citizens are hopeful that the internet can be used to change the world for the "greater good," (i.e., allowing certain freedoms of expression room to breathe), then the platforms we use do need to maintain a certain neutrality. Alerting authorities to potential hate groups or suspending clusters of activity where violence can be made manifest is different from deleting an entire human being's public identity, especially one whom you've allowed to exist on your platform previously without comment or censure. The mere fact that big tech is responsible for archiving and reshaping who and what we see, whether we like it or not, defeats the nature of certain civil liberties that are protected within governing legal documents, such as the U.S. Constitution, and specifically the First Amendment. If the counterargument is that these spaces are privatized through ownership, then anticompetition laws must prevent the five large tech companies from subsuming more companies, because otherwise there will be no space in the market for autonomous speech to exist without risk of being shut down. The trials and travails of whistleblowers, such as WikiLeaks and the generation that came out of it, including Chelsea Manning and Edward Snowden, highlight a divide fostered by constant surveillance from governments, public agencies, and social-media platforms themselves. Web 2.0 is teeming with every kind of human, yet only some are offered the microphone and the required amplification. Even fewer are handed the keys to the server room. Is it ethical for internet technologies, which are analogous to public spaces, to silence a person's virtual presence without that individual's consent?

Considering the ongoing admonition by western nations against internet censorship in countries such as China, it is hypocritical to engage in such an act oneself—to cut off the mouthpiece of someone who only weeks prior had held the keys to the free world and the codes to the nuclear arsenal. Living by such a double standard erodes public trust and, by proxy, leaves our mass medium subject to constant manipulation and tampering. By letting this go unchecked, the U.S. government has, to a degree, played right into the hands of the Silicon Valley billionaires. They hide one thing, and another slate gets tidied up a little, perhaps. By not reprimanding this act in a juridical sense, tech executives used this incident to look heroic. An ostensible pardon.

It was perhaps no surprise that following this, Zuckerberg's suite of companies formerly living under the umbrella of Facebook, rebranded themselves as Meta—a suggestion that it is they who comment on the commentary, it is they who create and shape the narrative, who decide the different angles of popular culture, and just how to point their arrow, or, indeed, grind their ax. This rebrand was part and parcel of Facebook's launch of Creative X, a glossy in-house digital agency. It was perceived as Facebook's way to give itself a facelift.

China, the United States's most squarely articulated rival among the five permanent UN Security Council members, in contrast, is consistently having its hand slapped for censoring online content. Tech companies, such as Alphabet Inc., the parent company of Google, have agreed to their search engines being used in what one can argue is a clipped or even censorious fashion in order to maintain good business relations within the Chinese market. Obfuscating or concealing the essence of language, however, can leave a society limp and isolated. This subject is explored in Miao Ying's 2007 artwork *Blind Spot*, where she annotated a 1,869-page Mandarin dictionary to indicate the more than 2,000 words that had been censored from search engines in China, which, by extension, reveals the types of language, some expected and some surprising, that the country was working to erase from the popular lexicon. The artist searched every dictionary entry on Google.cn, an undertaking that required extraordinary labor. Throughout the process, her service would continually be blocked—a result of searching what the forces that be deemed inappropriate. Miao argued that censorship had changed her person. She was a "user," not a citizen; nothing more or less.

The inverse of censorship—the overabundance of targeted marketing generated by using confidential user data gleaned from one's activities online—can equally function as a form of ongoing societal control and manipulation if gone unchecked. During the authoring of this book, my relationship with social media thickened, because the COVID-19 global lockdowns left me, like many others, in despair and hungering for any form of human interaction.

I developed a debilitating obsession whereby every few minutes, I felt an anxious obligation to check at least six different internet applications, which ranged from friendship apps, such as Bumble, as well as Instagram,

Snapchat, WhatsApp, and Gmail, among others. I would fall into chaotic disrepair, losing sense of space and time in this sphere, “liking” images that would later generate similar images, constantly returning to entice or sell me something. The goal equaled a buzz of instant gratification. If you are lonely and alone, expending beyond one’s means can become an addictive form of solace. An internet troll suddenly reappears on the home screen: your perfect match in life, your ideal overpriced underwear, a new housing development underway across the street—the necessary upgrade to your life, you are informed—a cure for your depression. Searches for physical therapy and the pursuit of home weight-loss programs lead to streams of torsos forwarded to me as advertisements—ones that I am presented with each time I desire to walk through that virtual corridor to see what I have actually intended to see. I don’t remember how many times I forgot what I had come into these virtual spaces to do. The lockdowns led to constant mailers for leisure and loungewear, which I acquired sight unseen—unreturnable and sometimes never to be delivered. In the end, I realized that the option of pressing delete and entering this world anonymously without the burden of being spoon-fed addictive and aspirational behavioral content was an option that I could simply not choose in my state of ongoing isolation.

Bearing some of these nuanced experiences, there remains a digital divide that exists, but its contours have changed and become even more specific to different social, political, and cultural contexts. That said, it would be misguided to see technology as antidemocratic. According to Statista, as economically affordable as TVs have now become, in 2021, only 1.72 billion people owned a TV set, less than half of those individuals who regularly use the internet.[17] Even in the most rural and deprived parts of Egypt, where I was born, I have been witness to both adults and teenagers haggling to spend time in internet cafés, in most cases, to connect with others using linked gaming platforms. Arguably the next form of the digital divide will emerge when we as human beings lose control of the technologies that we have invented, or when we allow the few who own them to control how we use them. If we submit to the notion that we cannot live without networked technologies, we are essentially surrendering and submitting ourselves entirely, losing a sense of our autonomy. To invoke the theories of Kate Crawford and Trevor Paglen on artificial intelligence, if machines accelerate and catch up with our knowledge, which is a known inevitability, how do we comprehend how these machines will discriminate for or against us? Will our class, race, and socioeconomic status isolate us further, because the computer says no?

Twitter Revolution

On December 17, 2010, a street vendor by the name of Mohamed Bouazizi sacrificed his life in an act of self-immolation in Ben Arous, Tunisia. News of the event—unanimously perceived as courageous activism against the exploitation wrought by Tunisia's autocratic government—rapidly sparked across the social-media platform Twitter before being picked up by western news media. It was a political turning point, ushering in what came to be known as the Arab Spring or, more appropriately, the Arab Uprisings of the early 2010s. The big fish in the game was Egypt. At the time of writing, the nation with the second-largest GDP in Africa, as well as the central node that links the continent to western Asia, is perceived by many to be the seat of what is commonly referred to as the Arab world. At the time of the uprisings, Egypt was one of the largest recipients of foreign aid from the United States, an ally to the western bloc of nations and with a growing GDP to boot. Yet, there was growing public dissent against the military dictatorship of Hosni Mubarak, Egypt's fourth president. Despite the perception that he had been publicly elected, Mubarak was a former vice president who entered office after the assassination of his predecessor Anwar Sadat. He remained in power for nearly thirty years and, with the constant monopoly of this office, few aspects of the nation's culture had changed since Egyptian independence from British colonial rule during the early 1950s. Unfair distribution of wealth, corrupt self-gain, sectarian division, racism, political violence, censorship, and voter suppression were but some of the public's grievances with the incumbent regime. Mobilization on a mass scale under Mubarak's reign was largely counteracted by the military; the countermovements, whether in peaceful protest or not, would be at the risk of severe persecution—political imprisonment for dissidence was common and continues to be the case to this day.

When the "Day of Revolt," January 25, 2011, came around, it seemed that the whole of Egypt was hurtling toward Tahrir Square (which translates to "Freedom Square"). It is notable that the mobilization of hundreds of thousands of human bodies seemingly occurred in an instant due to word of mouth sparked on social media. One of the terms bandied about at the time was the *Twitter revolution.* The concept, as articulated by semioticians, is that Twitter is an ecology that allows for the constant cross-embedding of information. This facilitates coordinated movement and an information cascade that has the potential to spring out of the bounds of the virtual sphere and into crevices of society where there may not even be internet access. One of the bonuses is Twitter's potential to draw public attention to a revolutionary event and the conversations, discussions, and dissidents who craft its formation become exalted voice boxes for the cause or struggle.

During the first eighteen days of the Egyptian Revolution of 2011, numerous cultural figures helped contribute to the cavalcade that was to come. Among them, my friend, the Egyptian-British actor and writer Khalid Abdalla, who at that point was best known as the star of the film *The Kite Runner* (2007), came into full view as a conduit for the young revolutionary guard. Along with a consortium of artists, filmmakers, designers, and community organizers, Abdalla cofounded Mosireen (meaning "we are determined"), an independent media collective that sought to unbuckle the truth beneath the Egyptian mainstream media's silence regarding the revolution, but, equally, of what was to ensue in the years to come. Quickly, the group's YouTube channel became the most-watched station by a nonprofit entity on the platform globally. Their activities mobilized social media to stage screenings, conversations, and think tanks on what the future of the country could look like, consistently drawing a cross section of society.

The fire in the belly of Egyptians moved like Zeus's thundering bolts through Yemen, Syria, and Bahrain, coming to a crescendo at the end of 2012. The ripple effects of this moment continue in civil wars and ongoing dictatorships. Certainly, this political fervor could not have simply been generated by the novel utopia engendered by the WWW and its attendant applications. The concept of the Tweeting revolution soon became attributed to every public revolt that occurred from Iran to Syria. Journalists intimated that social-media platforms were easily co-opted by PR groups and politicians spewing hate, instead of just having the capacity to mobilize everyday citizens together in pursuit of social change.[18] As to whether or not these Twitter revolutions were simply a cheap PR stunt or a generative and auspicious act inherent to the web is tricky to determine. Although it took significant digging to find, an analysis of Twitter's stock price between mid-2011 and early 2013 reveals that it approximately doubled during the utopic height of those perceived revolutions and the unsuccessful demise of those societies that ensued thereafter.[19] The height of global strife, in the end, filled the pockets of a few shareholders while the reality of the so-called Twitter revolution was that with weak ties and little space for intersectional dialogue, an outcome has yet to be resolved formally in almost any of these nations.

Of all the incidences that occurred during this period, there is one key moment that describes the spirited belief in the human right to the internet. On January 28, 2011, former Egyptian President Mubarak shut down internet facilities and cell phone networks across the whole country. This led to an explosion of people in the street in what was dubbed the Friday of anger. If Twitter was not available, would people simulate its effects?

Genuine political mobilization may still be an experience that is elicited from shared embodied experience.

Utilizing a similar thought process, two entrepreneurs with a background in journalism founded the online photo agency Demotix in 2008. The question that the platform posited was relatively simple: with the fastening of purse strings at the big news agencies, how could original photojournalism find a home? On their site, anyone who had published ten or more news articles, which was subjectively decided by the editors, could sign up for an account and upload images that were licensable at reasonable rates by news agencies across the world. You could be an artist, a layperson, or an engineer, as long as you met the quota and had something to reveal to the world that no one else did.

The platform proliferated with content relating to the Arab Spring, which existed outside of the regional news media blockade and the state-run, governed, or censored media. Demotix provided an alternative until a buyer came into the fold in the form of the Bill Gates–owned Corbis Images. The sale occurred in 2012, and four years later Corbis was sold to the Visual China Group, the third-largest provider of stock images in the world, and a company known for controversially removing what it deems to be "non-compliant images." This brings up one of the paradoxes of using web platforms for social causes: essentially a mainstream platform, such as Instagram or Twitter, provides a user pool that is so large that the threat of a person's disappearance is less probable than with a unique or boutique independent platform, where content may ultimately have to be subsumed into the agenda of a single conglomerate for the company to sustain itself. Despite a democratic wish for a globally equal share of information flow, for now it may be more strategic for one to choose to use platforms headquartered in western democracies where certain civil liberties, from LGBTQ+ rights to freedom of speech, are protected.

It is in these moments that the space of and for art can feel liberating. During the first eighteen days of the Egyptian Revolution, a young artist, a father of two young children, was killed by a sniper in Tahrir Square. His name was Ahmed Basiony (1978–2011). A little-known figure internationally, his work at the time sought to integrate open-source software with themes of embodiment. After his death, major global exhibitions, from the Venice Biennale to documenta (13), presented the artist's work alongside footage of himself and others protesting in Tahrir Square, which he had captured on his mobile phone and saved to his laptop. For a moment, Basiony became an emblem, his face occupying street banners, graffiti, and posters, not only across Cairo and Egypt but all over the world. The artist used freely available adaptive software in his practice, notably in his performance *30 Days of*

Running in the Place (2010). For thirty days, the artist ran for an hour outside the Cairo Opera House while hooked up to sensors that measured data, such as heart rate and blood flow. He then projected this information as semiabstract forms onto a visible screen. The artist's commitment to using publicly and freely accessible software functions as a kind of metaphor. If we are to use technology to disrupt the world, then the providers too must embody the freedom and openness of the activism that they purport to support.

Glitch

An awareness of the glitch, "a short-lived system error," first consciously entered my mind when playing my Sega Mega Drive, known as a Sega Genesis in North America, in my kidulthood years. Sonic, the iconic gaming avatar, would leap forward, only to scrawl across the TV set, caught between ground and air, for a seeming eternity. For one of my brothers, this caused enormous frustration. "So, have you tried switching it on and off again?" may be a line popularized in British TV's *The IT Crowd* (2006–13), but at the time, it was the prime example of tech support. In fact, for a glitch—technical, formal, or visual—to disappear, it is still the most probable solution. Take out the game cartridge, switch the machine off, remove it from power, and reboot. But the glitch does not have to disappear. In fact, imperfection is an innately human characteristic. Errors, it can be said, produce bountiful forms that are a by-product of an interaction between human and machine, or so one could posit.

When I began working as senior visiting curator at Cornerhouse in Manchester in 2010 at the behest of then artistic director Sarah Perks, I joined a consortium of other colleagues, and one of the projects I was assigned to realize as part of my new role was to remix the legendary hypertext artist Mark Amerika's ongoing project, *The Museum of Glitch Aesthetics* (2010–12 and ongoing). Like many at the time, I was introduced to the artist through the pages of *Time Magazine*, where he was named one of the one hundred innovators of the twenty-first century for his interactive browser-based novel *GRAMMATRON* (1997). A self-professed underground alt-kid in the spirit of Kathy Acker, taking cues from Stanley Kubrick and the early handheld cinema of Mike Figgis, the artist is a hybrid pulp novelist and tech aficionado. *GRAMMATRON* resulted from a project made during his master's program in creative writing at Brown University, Providence, Rhode Island, and spearheaded a movement in a genre field that was to become known as electronic literature, before the commercial popularization of Kindles and e-books as a form of literary consumption was widely accessible.

When I first sat down in the Cornerhouse café with Amerika, he had found himself soaked in the UK's unpredictable weather. His curly hair had morphed into the frizz of Dr. Emmett Brown's coif in *Back to the Future* (1985). His hurried speech—an expression of sensitive enthusiasm—mirrored the character that I had anticipated. At this point, Amerika had been working with the new digital technology festival Abandon Normal Devices, for which I also served as a cocurator, traveling around the country with his latest obsession—his mobile phone and its camera. Nearly a decade before artist Charlotte Prodger won the 2018 Turner Prize for a feature film that was filmed on her iPhone, Amerika had become immersed in the glitch as an aesthetic concept that emerged as an offshoot of aspirational technologies embedded in day-to-day devices. He was composing a museum, as he deemed it, of aesthetic glitches, with the hope that multiple practitioners would convene individually or separately to represent it in whatever fashion they felt reflected their perception and personality.

After two years of mining his archives, I gathered dozens of these videos, mostly of prosaic landscapes, and conceived of a show titled *The Museum of Glitch Aesthetics* in 2012, which stretched from Cornerhouse to the artist-run space Lionel Dobie in the Deansgate area of Manchester. Here, I took inspiration from the 1989 movie *Honey, I Shrunk the Kids*, lowering the ceilings and building a one-way movement system so that people would feel they were on a miniature stage set shrunk down to size. I presented the works on various kinds of phones, most of which had become obsolete, off-market relics, but which still offered a playback function for video. I homed in on specific glitches, seeking to accentuate what Amerika had deemed to be aesthetically charged by-products of so-called error. In other cases, I chose to balloon certain glitches to a comparatively large projected scale, creating a visual disparity with the minute devices that were lined up like an abandoned phone store display frozen in time.

A couple of months later, in fall 2012, I visited Halle in Germany for the Werkleitz Festival, where the results of our collaborative efforts, running what is now known as the European Media Art Platform (EMAP) between Europe and Mexico, were presented in an exhibition curated by Peter Zorn titled *.move forward*. I arrived late, and by the time I was checking in, artists were gathering in the lobby to head to the opening. I spritzed myself with a perfunctory scent and joined them. As we left, a young woman with long red hair hurtled forward and landed on the ground, her six-inch heels skidding on the invisible sleet. She jumped back up, as if on stilts, adamant that she was unscathed. It was Rosa Menkman, the artist and theorist, whose writings on the glitch, notably, *Glitch Moment/um* (2011) led me to understand that these technical errata were not only producing sensuous aesthetic possibilities but equally emblematized a politics for those marginalized or invisible within society. At the time, she was pursuing a PhD at Goldsmiths' College, University of London, in media and communication, while working against the exploitation of the glitch and for the expression of feminism. Her video works, such as *Xilitla* (2012), use 3-D animation to create a hallucinatory world where the viewer is constantly forced to question what the product of errata is and how a formally precise aesthetic choice is made and consumed.

The possibility to choose which of the internet's multifarious components to keep or lose has been one of its most ennobling characteristics. In 2020, Legacy Russell, an artist, activist, writer, and curator from New York, released *Glitch Feminism: A Manifesto.* An accumulation of years of research developed through staging events, exhibitions, performances, and writings, *Glitch Feminism* is often beguiling yet understated in its modest pocket size, given the expansiveness of the ideas that it touches upon. Fusing references from the resuscitated queer Black writer Audre Lorde to the deconstructive gaze found in visual essays and installations by Victoria Sin (now Sin Wai Kin), Russell reveals her manifesto through a mix of personal biography and carefully selected case studies, positing the glitch's potential as a tool to work against the detrimental impacts of gentrification, pinkwashing, white male dominance in the technical sphere, and the binary function of digital dualism. Through examples such as Sin's *Narrative Reflections on Looking* (2016–17) series, which explores how the iconography of women's identities is produced, and Tabita Rezaire's *Afro Cyber Resistance* (2014), which interrogates the unidirectional manner in which the Black African body is consumed online, Russell opens a space for one to consider how they look at bodies—bodies of color, gendered bodies, queer bodies, disabled bodies—where the concept of technological perfection, Photoshopped and manicured, takes precedence. *Glitch Feminism* invites one to decenter their gaze, and to consider one's complicity within the mechanisms of Web 2.0's image machine.

In a 2020 Artnet interview headlined, "I Say Tear it All Down," Russell challenged the assumption that IRL is better than a life lived online as outmoded at best. Instead, she uses a term that came into parlance in the 2010s: *AFK* (away from keyboard), driving a wedge into IRL's assumption that we have two separate selves: the online/virtual one and the embodied one. Russell argues that space and time are contoured, and likewise, the multiplicity of identities that one can hold and express are multiple. She invokes Lorde, poet Essex Hemphill, and revisionist readings of W. E. B. Du Bois's *The Souls of Black Folk* (1903), where he articulates the concept of double consciousness, the idea that Black people's consciousness is fragmented between how they are seen and treated within the Black community and

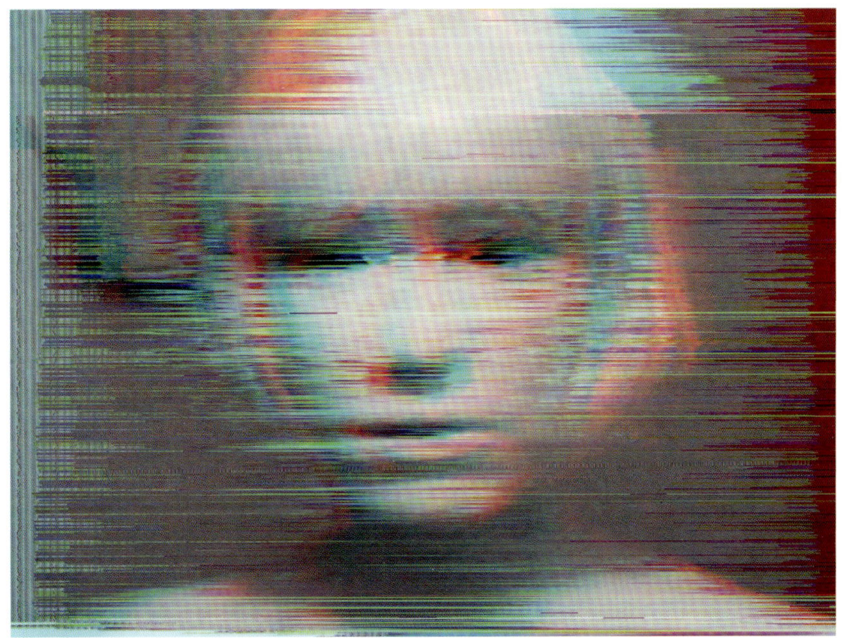

Rosa Menkman, *Vernacular of File Formats. Photoshop*, 2009–10
__Digital prints on Dibond

how they witness the manner in which white people encounter and see them. Today, manifestations of triple and multiple consciousnesses and beyond have evolved. One of the most pressing points in Du Bois's texts is that humans can embody multiple forms of being, affinity, and affiliation, which can lead to various methods of solidarity. Glitch does not propose how we reach a point of cultural understanding, but more appropriately how to conceive of spaces and identities where difference is not only celebrated but becomes enmeshed in a stream of lived experiences where one no longer exists in a binary us and them scenario. It is in imperfection, in the apertures between what is seen and withheld, that we find the exquisite features that make us who we are.

Living Media

Our Fickle World

When I began writing this book, fellow authors, editors, and publishers warned me that I would need uninterrupted time without online distraction to write about the internet. The irony was not lost on me. I spent three hours researching a suitable Wi-Fi blocker. Skimming through web-based applications and how-to videos on how to readjust your router did not phase me. What did was the paternalistic and finger-wagging forms of language that were used to describe the implementation of blocking. The first website that I landed upon encouraged one to, "Control your kids' internet access with the click of a button." The next to, "Take control of your Wi-Fi, take control of your life," as if the two were synonymous. These digital tools took me down a rabbit hole of sites offering to help find out who was "leeching" off of my Wi-Fi—and how to either block them or report them. Having spent significant time growing up in a country where the internet was and continues to be policed by faceless authorities, the thought of detaching myself from what could be perceived as an open platform sits at odds with my belief that the internet should be an accessible space for civil liberty.

I was reminded of visiting an installation with the artist Constant Dullaart, which I saw at the now-defunct Carroll/Fletcher, once a pioneering gallery in London of midcareer artists engaged with the internet. The installation I was most intrigued by was in the basement gallery. Dullaart ushered me down and presented me with *The Censored Internet* (2014). The blacked-out space was lined with the half-mast flags of the countries named by the UN as "enemies of the internet," as if awaiting the procession of a dignitary or a group of ambassadors. Constantly changing LED spot lighting altered the colors of the flags, creating constellations of erasure and visibility in the darkened space. The United Arab Emirates hung next to the United States and Saudi Arabia, moving backward to Great Britain and Iraq, among numerous others that have been culpable of blocking, tapping, and shielding data sets. This was not just a matter of identifying a surveillance state, but of giving a visual language to how we as individuals are controlled, and how accepting of it we are.

So, if I was going to take the "internet into my hands," to invoke the author Stephanie Bailey, who in 2014 discussed it as a form of material culture,[1] the disciplined act of negotiating my relationship with it had to fall on me. Otherwise, I would be supporting the notion that the internet is bad for us.

In 2012, the cultural critic Mark Deuze argued in his book *Media Life* that we are living within our media worlds.[2] Even before app-based culture had completely shifted how we live and engage, we were all clearly "cross-embedded" in our media, to quote the influential cultural critic Norman M. Klein.[3] Deuze posited that the way in which we communicate and experience the world is forever altered by the way our media continue to subsume us. The clearest example today would be our smartphones, which now integrate cameras with functionality that historically few would be able to afford. We walk around with the equivalent of what only thirty years ago would have been gargantuan computers in our pockets.

Giving a nod to Marshall McLuhan's historic motto "The medium is the message," we can now consider that we have each become a living form of media. An iPhone, for instance, becomes a tool for rehearsal, broadcast, and communication; everything from banking to creativity can be performed from a single object that ostensibly breaks down all the walls blocking us from the outside world. The DNA of a lived experience has been fused with an apparatus that will quickly be updated and upgraded, just as we have come to absorb its full functionality.

I started to think about the need for this book in the early weeks of the first global lockdown of the COVID-19 pandemic that subsumed the world in 2020, pushing people behind the shuttered doors of their homes and, in many places, behind the enforced legal borders of the nation-state. Physical mobility was deterred or deeply discouraged—at least in the countries that I have called home: the UAE, the United States, and the UK. The initial weeks of lockdown for many of the people I knew were seemingly euphoric, as recorded by screenshots of friends reconnecting on FaceTime, WhatsApp, or, surprisingly, a tech platform that I hadn't heard of called Zoom. Sherry Turkle's book from 2011, *Alone Together: Why We Expect More from Technology and Less from Each Other*, came to mind. When would this euphoria of increased time to connect and to share wear off?

As the death toll increased despite social-distancing measures, it became evident that the reality of the experience was shifting. Museums scrambled, in many cases haphazardly, to put exhibitions and other ancillary content online in an effort to maintain audiences and to test out mechanisms for income generation due to the sudden loss of ticket sales. Those smiling faces in the first weeks of lockdown were now posting diatribes about having to claim unemployment benefits and the impossibilities of finding work. The space of the digital was no longer one of connection but of spilling sorrow and disenfranchisement, which included the brutal realities of loss—the death of friends and loved ones—people for whom gathering for a physical memorial was not possible.

I would regularly communicate with artists, seeking their reflections and asking: "What are you making now?" My queries were often met with autoreplies. Had the artists of the internet gone offline, or was something else cooking that we did not yet know of? The visuals that presented themselves were reminiscent of wartime posters of resistance and survival: valiant hospital workers were occupying social-media screens and street posters. At London's Southbank Centre, the UK's largest mixed-media art center, Michael Armitage, Lydia Blakeley, Jeremy Deller, and Evan Ifekoya, among others, were invited to create portraits of "essential workers" in a campus-wide presentation, *Everyday Heroes* (2020).

In the meantime, Jeff Bezos, cofounder and then CEO of Amazon, enjoyed a surge in sales, with most reports suggesting that the pandemic had increased the company's profits by nearly 200 percent.[4] Despite media criticism of the exploitation of frontline workers, the undercutting of traditional retailers had already made it almost impossible to avoid using the service. I am not sure whether I should be ashamed, but a tally of the single-largest slice of my income in 2020 was no longer my rent, but products purchased via Amazon—books, toilet paper, sanitizer, face masks, toothpaste, hard drives, I hasten to say more.

The ripple effect of newfound market reliance on the internet has seen retail streets in cities small and large completely transformed; independent art and creative businesses, as well as commercial galleries from New York to London and Dubai were shuttered, and most have remained closed. The crown may have not simply been taken by Amazon, but the virtual-surfing culture also saw consumers of art and culture move to using Instagram, as well as online platforms, such as Artsy, the buzz-driven editions platform Avant Arte, and AucArt, or returning to eBay or even Etsy. The *Art Newspaper*, which maintained the most incisive coverage during this period, now has an entire column dedicated to the Facebook-owned platform Instagram, with features, for example, on how art advisors now use the space as a primary tool for the discovery of art and artists. Some of their headlines include: "Can Instagram bring the big auction houses into the digital age?"; "Who needs a gallery space? Meet the people creating Instagram-only exhibitions"; and "Curate-It Yourself: French museums take to social media to ask the public what they want to see in their galleries."

The pejorative comments of certain artists as well as Instagram's sponsored algorithms, which promote certain forms of content over others based on the possibility of financial return, serve as apt reminders that content producers are feeding a privately owned corporation with free content for those privileged enough to have solvent cash during a global pandemic to mine at the producer's expense. In October 2020, at an apex of public debate and interest in the reclusive Facebook founder Mark Zuckerberg, artist Jeremy Hutchison announced that he had been corresponding with the tech billionaire directly through Instagram Messenger and would speak with him on Instagram live on October 27 at 6:00 p.m. The media believed it, although it was a prank. The performance, as it were, was the media's gullibility, but equally their desire to "see" (ironically) the unfiltered Zuckerberg. Hutchison has now collated his "correspondence" along with myriad sculpturally rendered images of Zuckerberg, transforming them into a synth-pop music video. Whether this is an artful critique or simply feeding a hunger for information about a person who has had more biographies authored about him than most living people of his age is a question for the reader to answer.

Explode the Material: Haroon Mirza

Haroon Mirza and I sit in an Afghan restaurant in East London as lockdown restrictions ease in Great Britain at some point postpandemic 1.0. about fall 2021. We are recounting the first time we met. He professes that the curator Hans Ulrich Obrist had introduced us in Bangladesh and that I had not paid much attention to him. I correct him. We had met at the opening of curator Barbara London's final exhibition at MoMA, titled *Soundings: A Contemporary Score* in 2013. He clarifies that he was not present. That's the thing with hyperlinked memory, as Mirza reminds me then; with Google sitting in for our memory banks and so many of our encounters happening in the amorphous digital world, placing time becomes an increasingly warped process—one that makes history seem nebulous even with our online archives.

For much of his career, Haroon Mirza has operated under the collective umbrella hrm199 and, more recently, the alias of Waves Unlimited. His early independent work, which he shows me on his phone at the restaurant, involved two-dimensional images created for computer screens that he informs me he is considering putting online as digital editions. He would later grow to be subsumed by both the physical hardware of the computer and the elemental concepts of the internet. The internet's function as a generator of networked culture is fueled by energy, he reminds me, most often made manifest through electricity. The artist now refers to the latter as his primary medium.

Artworks produced by Mirza in the early 2000s sit without titles or descriptions on my phone within photo-messaging apps. Sent to me by him for years, they are continually uploaded and downloaded to different devices via the cloud. His earliest pieces from my records consisted of disassembled computer parts, sometimes resting against walls, resembling the readymades of Marcel Duchamp. Yet here, the tech company logos, the aesthetics of an integrated online culture, is weighted in its presence, activating multiple forms of knowing within this viewer.

Twenty years later, the field of the internet would become one of both collaboration and resistance for the artist. During the early days of the COVID-19 pandemic, Mirza and a group of collaborators, including musician Nik Void, colaunched a record label called OUTPUTS, which existed both online and in the physical sphere. It launched with the concept album *The Wave Epoch* (2021), a collaboration with musician Jack Jelfs and featuring GAIKA, a British artist known for his industrial dance-hall music. In the gallery, Mirza had become renowned for creating anechoic chambers that created a sense of the monastic, resisting all forms of cellular or connective interference. Now, he was using the internet to connect with listeners virtually during the pandemic.

The first artwork of Mirza's that captured my attention was titled *Adhân* (2008), referencing the Islamic call to prayer. The artist has noted what is sometimes referred to as the Islamic Golden Age, from between the eighth and fourteenth centuries, as a source for scientific research in his artwork. He points out the discovery of how to make glass from stone, as well as the evolution of optics to amplify, condense, and mutate visual forms of glass. The significant publication *Kitāb al-manāẓir* (The Book of Optics), written by Ibn al-Haytham, known more commonly today as Alhazen, laid down a systematic method for the creation of the camera obscura. This fostered a blueprint for some of the earliest pinhole cameras (with a simple aperture, no lens) and, in time, the advent of an entire field of photography and with it the visual thinking that we are familiar with today. Arabic numerals (which are what we use in the western world), frequency analysis, the mapping of sounds, and the revolutionary studies of geometry and astronomy all coalesce in Mirza's collaged multimedia videos, which invite the viewer to examine alternative historical narratives.

hrm199: An Evolving Collaboration, for a Moment in Time

Mirza's studio door bears the sign "hrm199"—the name of the collective identity that the artist sketched out in 2004. Having just emerged from a recent quarantine with the privileged security of being vaccinated, I relish going to hrm199 headquarters, a quiet haven for queer, socially engaged artists of color and their networks to speak without judgment and have discussions in the common area. Figures whom I have encountered there have included the fashion designer Osman Yousefzada; the previously mentioned electronic musician Nik Void; the minimalist sculptor and painter Rana Begum, along with her children; Shezad Dawood, who is now famous for his VR works; the video artist James Richards; and the architecture collective Assemble.

As you enter, tessellating forms rotate on glass: solar panels are being carefully choreographed into currents of charge that are sometimes analog, sometimes connected to invisible computers. Everything is hazy and discomfiting. Sitting in the backroom, Mirza pulls out a shruti box, an instrument that works on a system of bellows to create a droning backdrop for accompaniment. I assume this to be an invitation to jam in the classical sense of the word, so I conjure up my breath and begin murmuring sounds, which turn into lyrics, snippets of poems, and quotes. Eventually, I ask him to stop, not realizing that he has been filming me on his iPhone. I insist that he is forbidden from uploading the video to social media.

This was a period in which the atmosphere of hrm199 was one of evolving collaboration. Its members morphed and changed, swelling to as many as twenty-plus individuals who often communicated via networked technologies across the world throughout the year, but who always convened together, often at this HQ, which was then in Hackney Wick in London.

The many voices who have embodied hrm199 speak to the cornucopia of influences, forms, and processes deployed by Mirza over the years. In 2006, he was known for meticulously tuning microphones to everyday objects, such as buckets, to explore sonic resonance in his installations, including *Canon Remix* (2006) and *Lo-Tech Proposed* (2006). This work evolved into trash cans and secondhand radios. In 2011, two of the artist's signature media forms, pyramid-shaped foam and automated LED lighting surfaces, appeared in his installations, such as *Cross Section of a Revolution*, *Electric Vacuum*, and *Tent Life*. That summer, Mirza's global breakthrough came at the 54th Venice Biennale with *The National Apavilion of Then and Now*. The first of his major anechoic chamber works, the piece was a sensory-deprivation chamber where no light or sound can be reflected; there is no physical possibility of embodying the internet here. Once the person submits to the site, the body, the artist suggests, simulates the sensorial aspects of releasing dimethyltryptamine (DMT), a hallucinogenic drug found in plants that can reorientate one's perception of reality. The installation won Mirza the Silver Lion Award, one of the most prestigious prizes for a young artist. *The National Apavilion of Then and Now* is now in the collection of MoMA.

As I left Mirza's studio that afternoon, I found myself suddenly shaken by the kinetic murmur of one of his new solar-powered LED circuits. Resin shaped like eyes? A halo was rotating. Charred gold flakes descended the

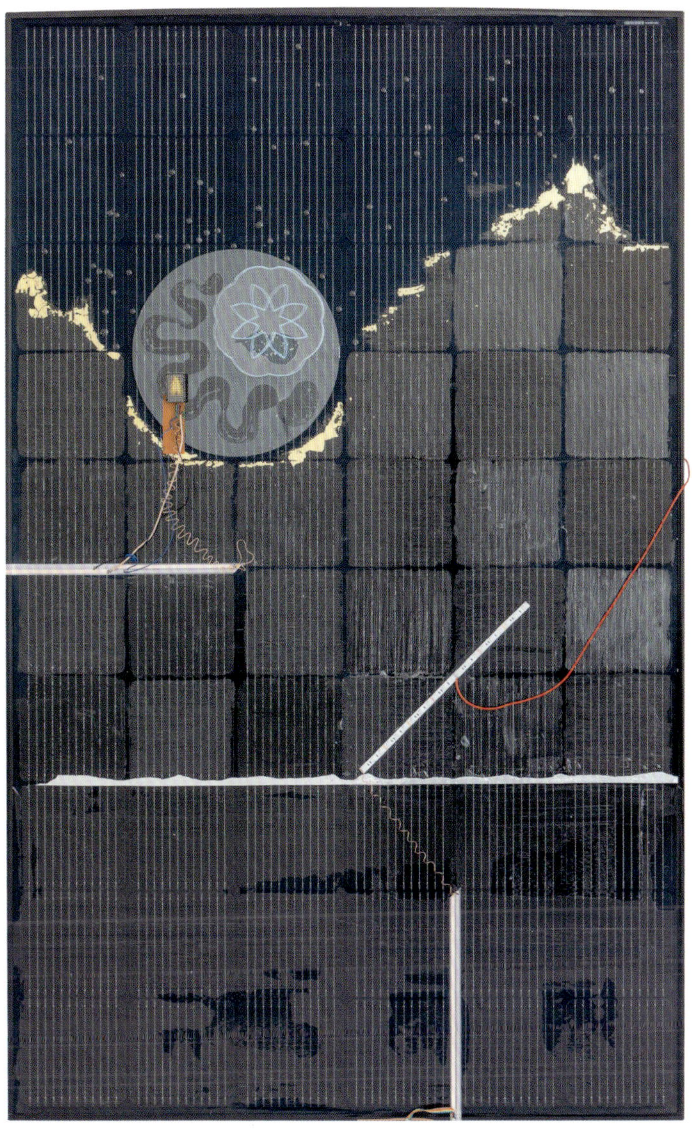

Haroon Mirza, *Genzken & Richter (Solar Powered LED Circuit Composition 41),* 2021 __RGB LED tape, electrical wire, copper tape, magnetic wire, LED Matrix, aluminum tape, gold leaf, glass, polyurethane resin, acrylic paint, polarized film, trinket, gel medium on photovoltaic panel, 64⅝ × 39⅜ × 3⅛ in. (164 × 100 × 8 cm)

expanse, a solar panel repurposed as a canvas forming networked actions before me. Incongruous beams of metal sparked, and precipitously a candle lit up. I asked him about the beguiling work. Mirza's response was, "It is called Genzken and Richter"—the names of one of the art world's most acrimoniously divorced couples. The trailing circuit continues—a broken relationship transformed into a networked form of media.

LARPing Through Life

I discovered live action role-playing (LARPing) when visiting my father in the midwestern United States. It was the late 1990s and LARPing was considered the apex of the geek maxim, so much so that I recoiled at the thought of pursuing it. I was mortified when my parent attempted to enroll me in the reenactment of an American Civil War event. We settled on a compromise of watching the action rather than participating. The role-playing was staged on a small set and seemed like little more than a hobby for aspiring actors. I assumed it would remain a pastime restricted to an esoteric group. How wrong I was.

In 2004, the artist Cao Fei produced the cinematic installation titled *COSplayers*. Set in her native city of Guangzhou, China, myriad *cosplayer* (costume player) youth are seen taking on the visual personas of video-game characters, from pixie princesses to magnanimous knights, in an attempt to transcend what Cao argued at the time was their disenchantment with their lived experience. She crafted a space where they could traverse the city at will, without the implicit judgment that awaited them when they returned home to transfer from their alter egos back into reality. Fast-forward to 2021 and statistics reveal that LARPing is the "hottest entertainment trend in China."[5]

In a study by media agency iiMedia, 84.9 percent of Chinese internet users who took the survey revealed themselves to have engaged in a LARPing game of some form.[6] LARPing now also exists online, contradictory as that might at first seem, and has involved narratives that are often inspired by TV programs. The most popular form of this game among young Chinese netizens, it is reported, often involves players seeking to collectively solve a murder mystery. Now a multibillion-dollar business, the proliferation of the form, with its specific dress, rules, and active presence, represents a fascinating blurring with the avatar culture deployed in virtual environments such as Second Life.[7] Within this juncture, any person can transpose themselves into a character chosen from a list, adopt the necessary instructions and rules, and sneak off the container that is the screen into another life.

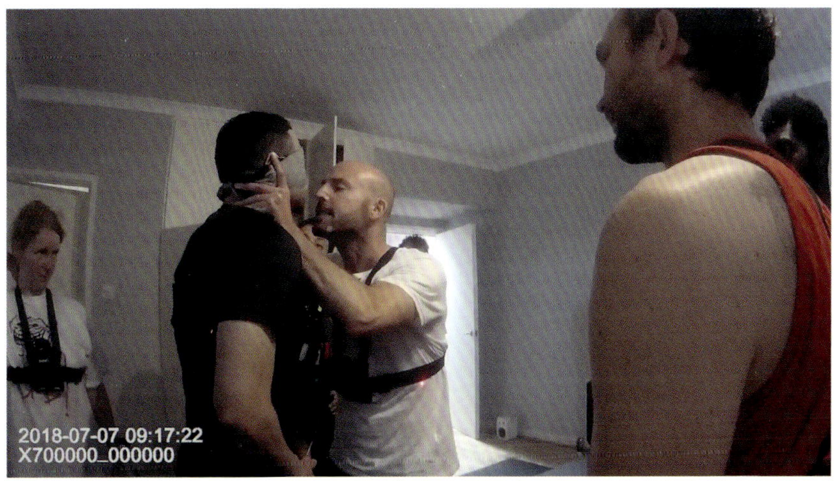

Ed Fornieles, *Cel*, 2019 __Two-channel video, 40 min. 21 sec.

An imaginative artwork to critically explore this phenomenon is Ed Fornieles's *Cel* (2019). In a staging of a LARPing event, the artist sought to interrogate the growth of toxic masculinity in mainstream society, especially among online hate groups led by what the artist calls individuals who "encourage fear, hatred, and mass repression" and have extensive online followings.[8] This phenomenon, it is intimated in the accompanying publication text, is as much the result of a culture of emasculating hazing found in college fraternity culture as it is connected to the different ideologies that underpin male anger. The ten participants in Fornieles's game took on the role of members of a fictional alt-right group who were on a quest for self-betterment. Over the course of what we are informed are three days, we see characters that are pinned down and waterboarded, reduced to infantile behavior and sometimes tears. Audiences witness these simulated acts—the threshold of real and unreal always unclear—across two large screens and through the attendant publication. *Cel* envisages how power is used and ideology constructed in multiple forms of roles across society. In particular, it examines how the culture of role-play can operate as a mechanism for developing an embodied context that emerges from the virtual realm, which might enable us to comprehend varying facets shaping contemporary identity. No longer a subculture, LARPing is now used for academic research purposes, to explore connections between geolocative technologies, interactive gaming methods, and the social strata of the players who engage with it. It has also been reported that high-school, college, and university educators use LARPing as a method for immersing their students in history. In 2018, the *Guardian* newspaper reported that communities had begun using LARPing to go back in time and experience specific historical ruptures—for example, facing the traumas of the AIDS pandemic and the lived experience of exiled refugees.[9] The physical act of role-play in this context seemingly creates an emotional link between the persona and the historical subject, cultivating connections that would otherwise not exist.

Anita Fontaine, who refers to herself as a "speculative future artist," creates LARP-like gaming environments using VR software—what I argue is an in-between or interstitial form of embodiment. During the COVID-19 pandemic, she created *Corona Paraíso Secreto VR* (2020), an immersive jungle and beach experience intended to submerge the viewer's senses and let them feel as if they were outdoors. In her *Bitmap Banshees* (2016), VR transports the viewer to the streets of Amsterdam—now a psychedelic sci-fi backwater. While riding a bike, viewers collect supernatural carrots to save themselves and the city—throwing them at the banshees that attempt to destroy them. As part of the Abandon Normal Devices Festival in 2021, Fontaine reimagined the experience of the touristic boat tour. When passengers boarded *The Blue Violet River* (2021), Liverpool's iconic waterfront became animated using AR forms. The skyline was overtaken by dancers, a living rainbow, and air balloons overhead crafted in the shapes of hands casting spells and wielding a protective meditative rulebook.

Reverse Embodiment: Screens Everywhere

With his landmark 1997 book *The History of Forgetting: Los Angeles and the Erasure of Memory*, Norman M. Klein earned global repute for his imaginative descriptions of the City of Angels. The author narrates the constant urban regeneration, decay, and reanimation of downtown Los Angeles, which through the Hollywood system, has become one of the most recognizable sites on the planet. But do we ever truly see it at all? A central node of pop culture that is both synonymous with mediated fantasy and vagrant poverty, Los Angeles is also an embodied metaphor for society's codependence on trends of global capital. As ethnic minority communities are funneled in and out of downtown to the east and south based on the desires of those more affluent, one can ask: who really lives here? Who belongs here? The makers of physical seem all but destined to vanish.

Toward the book's end, *cyberspace*—the term popularized by sci-fi author William Gibson—becomes imagined as a final vestige: the last suburb of Los Angeles, a city that is an endless studio lot, known for its strip malls, its incongruous architecture spanning Art Deco to haphazard Brutalism, edged by the illusory Pacific Ocean. The comparison is apt. Cyberspace assumes a world where one is teleported into an alternative space. It suggests that the internet is separate from reality—ostensibly the model on which the Hollywood system of stars and their movies was built, but equally the model for urban metropolises, such as Las Vegas, where make-believe constructed through animated billboards and brassy architecture offers an escape from the everyday.

In New York, Times Square functions as one of these sites of dense urban digitization. Its branded screens create a central nook for us to ring in the New Year or to ingest iconic acts of performance, whether in person or from the security of a television or mobile device. Times Square is one of the most televised places on Earth, among New York's top tourist attractions and most popular film locations. It is, therefore, no surprise that this site has been a historic point of departure for artistic intervention. In 1987 (and restaged in 2014), Alfredo Jaar was commissioned by the Public Art Fund to contribute to their ongoing program *Messages to the Public* (1982–90), a series of artist-created vignettes created for the Spectacolor board at Times Square, which altered how political art infiltrated mainstream culture. Jaar's *A Logo for America* sought to challenge ideas about the American identity. A map of the United States, animated with the scrolling words "This is not America" alternated with a map of both North and South America—a reiteration that the United States is not synonymous with America as well as a proposition against bias and a call for unity.

Since Jaar's project, the use of media screens as sites of intervention and dissemination has taken on many incarnations. In 2011, the Performa Biennial, founded by RoseLee Goldberg, commissioned Haroon Mirza, who worked in collaboration with the iconic artists Ed Atkins and James Richards, to take over Times Square. Occupying the site's epic Toshiba Vision screen and working with Times Square Arts, the trio presented *An Echo Button*, a presentation of video works, many of which were rendered from appropriated and animated sources associated with the mythology of Times Square as an epicenter of marketing. Presented here was a cornucopia of digital images and logos gathered from various sources, including the internet. Brands and simulations of the New Year's ball drop—remixed through filters and applets—alongside slogans about the unknown futurity that awaits us. Mirza referred to this work as a form of critique, disentangling the "echo chamber" that creates the circuitous media loop from which we are constantly spoon-fed the same messages that subliminally encourage us to adopt certain ways of looking and feeling.[10]

The internet is now the most ubiquitous mass medium to evolve since the advent of television or the printing press. But unlike any other mass medium, its necessity and permanence have evolved in such a fashion that many people, me included, do not have the faculties to decode its intent or purpose. A culture of constant update is a destabilizing prospect. Yet, by experiencing the interventions that artists have made in this space, I have developed a more fine-tuned awareness. I may still be a target for web advertising, but the eye has become more discerning and the senses more attuned as one considers how artists interrogate the visual lexicon of the emerging technologies that continue to evolve around us.

One of the primary facets of this awareness, which is still coming into focus, is the necessity for intimate forms of encounter through art, even if they are natively digital in their construction. One of the most joyous encounters that I have ever had at an art-school degree show was in 2013, when I went to the graduating cohort's presentation at the Royal Academy Schools (RA Schools) in London. It was a golden year for this prestigious three-year fine art program: Adham Faramawy revealed haptic patterns of technology through their precise use of software; Charlie Billingham presented paintings that straddled the Renaissance and Scooby-Doo; Prem Sahib animated queer subculture in a Tetris-like maze; and then there was Eddie Peake, whose work and person I had previously stumbled upon after seeing him perform a musical composition in a derelict basement in Dalston in East London.

The RA Schools, one of the oldest, most vaunted, and competitive independent art schools in history, was upturned when Peake transformed it into his neighborhood of Finsbury Park, North London. The artist invited an online radio station, Kool London, at the time a multicultural broadcaster based in North London in the diverse area where he grew up, to occupy this space with its own narrative. Peake's choreographies of the body transcended into installations and paintings that blend together poetry, appropriated language, and painstakingly composed compositions. This practice of delegation and collaboration was to come to the fore in two spectacular performances from Peake: *Endymion* (2013), commissioned by Performa 13, and its sequel *Head* (2016), which took place at Jeffrey Deitch's restored gallery on Wooster Street in New York, in the same building where *Endymion* was staged.

Coding Architecture

In 2010, I was invited to form part of the curatorial team of a global network called the Media Facades Festival. I was enthralled by the range of materials that revealed itself to me through the work of the consortium, which at the time was led by curator Susa Pop. My intervention was a curated program that took place across large-scale exterior sites in cities from the UK to Austria. It was titled, *I-dent: Identity and Media Contortion.* I wanted to interrogate how intimately our identities have been shaped by the language of advertising. Legendary artist Ryan Trecartin presented *Tommy Chat Just E-mailed Me* (2006), a psychedelic film staged within the imagined confines of an email chain. Takeshi Murata's propulsive soundtrack in *Monster Movie* (2005) sat next to the hushed silence of Peggy Ahwesh's uniquely engineered imaging technology in *Warm Objects* (2007), which sought to slow audiences down.

As I watched these narratives on public screens across the city of Liverpool and mediated across screens in Berlin, I was captivated by how intrusive some of their audience found them. A man passing by Liverpool's Bold Street made a complaint asserting, and I am paraphrasing, that he shouldn't have to be forced to "think" while navigating the streets in the city center on a weekend. That said, the tendency to produce works that engage with public fields of visuality continues.

Recently, I was made aware of Andrea Polli's *Particle Falls* (2015–20), a data visualization that runs on the facade of a museum, revealing the air quality in each city or site. Perhaps most spectacularly, during the 2012 London Olympics, I came face to face with Julius Popp's *Bit.Fall* (2012), a never-ending waterfall of words that would appear from thin air in the Olympic Park and descend to the ground. These floating words were gleaned through an algorithm fed to the website of the London *Times*, forming a connective tissue between what we see in a given moment and that which remains unseen or in the background.

3-D ME

The first video game that I ever played was Sonic the Hedgehog on a Sega Mega Drive. I recall being mesmerized by the plentiful colors and details—a world away from the Tetris block games that I had witnessed on mobile Nintendo devices. During the quest into adulthood, public discussion consistently seemed to revolve around computer graphics. The more real, which by proxy meant the more 3-D these facets became, the more real our narrative experiences would be. I quickly lost interest, seeing them as little more than marketing tools. Who wanted a video game to resemble drab reality?

My naivety at the time was to do with my limited conception of dimension, detail, graphics, and scale. The spaces that were being constructed

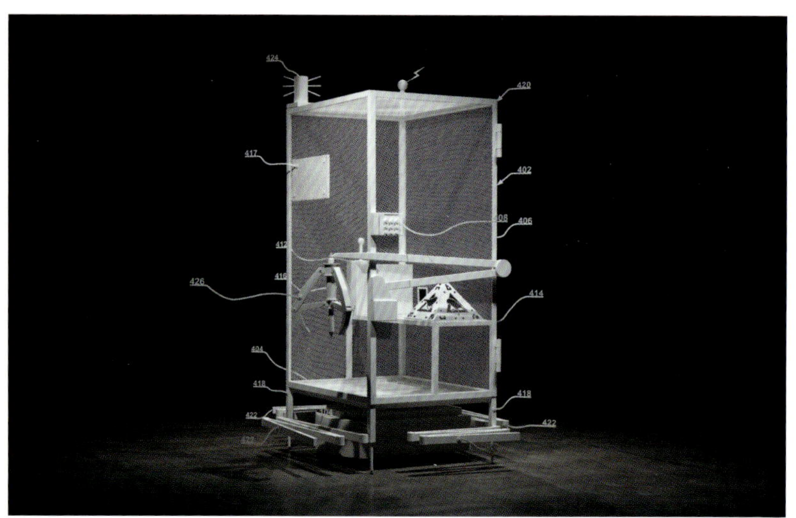

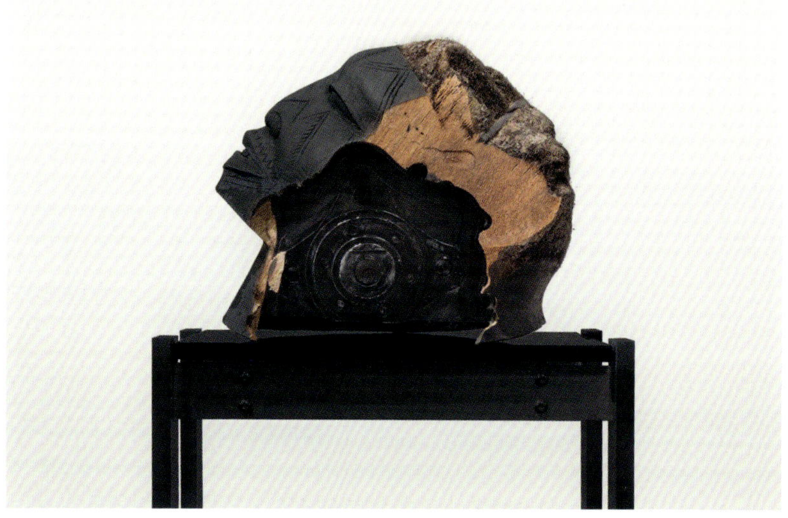

Simon Denny, *Amazon worker cage patent drawing as virtual King Island Brown Thornbill cage, (US 9,280,157 B2: "System and method for transporting personnel within an active workspace," 2016),* 2019 —Powder-coated metal, MDF, plastic, digital print on cardboard, iOS augmented-reality interface, 115 3/8 × 87 3/8 × 99 5/8 in. (293 × 222 × 253 cm)

Matthew Angelo Harrison, *Synthetic Lipiko no. 3,* 2018 —Wooden sculpture, polyurethane resin, anodized aluminum, acrylic, overall: 54 × 13 × 10 in. (137.2 × 33 × 25.4 cm) were not mere simulations, but context-specific fields of production that referenced the history of graphics and special effects. The final project by legendary filmmaker Harun Farocki (1944–2014) before his unexpected death was a four-part work entitled *Parallel I–IV* (2012–14), where he traced the history of computer-game graphics for about thirty years. Unlike special effects in cinema, Farocki argues, video gaming has its own situated visual language that belongs to and of the world that generates it. In this regard, cinema begins to resemble video games, not vice versa.

During the ubiquitous escalation of the technical sphere, many have become fascinated with the advent of 3-D-printing technologies, which can produce an object from either a simple or complex architectural drawing. Initially developed for rapid prototyping in research and development, they offered possibilities for creating "a world on site," helping to reduce the environmental costs of movement and waste. Like every successful technology, their accessibility enables them to proliferate. Now, for as relatively little as a couple of hundred dollars, anyone can access scalable versions of such devices, or as has become common, can send off for pictures of themselves to be made into synthetic 3-D dolls that can be used as cake toppers or door stoppers—more future landfill.

New Zealand–born artist Simon Denny has explored the propositional nature of 3-D technologies through his work. In summer 2019, he showed me images of the first rendition of his 3-D visualization of an *Amazon worker cage*—an artwork developed from a blueprint for a literal cage that would move Amazon workers within a highly automated workplace. Amazon executives probably acknowledged the all-too-real poignancy of the metaphor, and the plans were thwarted. But Denny produced a 3-D model with diagrammatic details, an augmented-reality interface, and a soundtrack.

As 3-D printing continues to evolve, 4-D printing, which adopts a similar formal approach to fabricating physical objects from computer drawings, is now in mass existence. The difference is that things printed in 4-D are not fixed but morph and contort over time, shape-shifting to the contours of their given environment. Detroit-born Matthew Angelo Harrison inverts these processes to their analog with his encapsulations of what he asserts are tribal sculptures. A cornerstone in Harrison's growing body of work is a series created under the umbrella of *Dark Povera* (2017–ongoing). Delving down to archaeological depths, he constructs African artifacts from myriad contexts, but instead of rendering them with silicone, he adopts wet clay as the material for his homemade 3-D printer—thereby returning the object to a semblance of tactility.

In 2010, I met Stephanie Pereira, a tech-focused arts executive who had cut her teeth at the Eyebeam Center, which at the time was still headquartered in a warehouse in Chelsea, New York. Pereira had recently taken up her new role as director of the art program at Kickstarter—a crowdfunding site—and, at the time, I was skeptical about what could emerge from our encounter. During our back and forth over herbal tea, however, my concept of the field of internet art was transformed. Perhaps a world could exist where artists were funded directly by their audiences via an online platform. What would transparency around pricing and the economy of art do for artists, whether they had major gallery representation or not?

From Kickstarter, Stephanie moved to NEW INC, the New Museum's arts and technology incubator for creative professionals, and subsequently to Rally, an organization that specializes in enabling creatives to effectively use cryptocurrencies to form myriad online communities. One of Pereira's volleys to me was the question of economy. "Culture shouldn't be free," was a motto she instilled within me. On a Zoom call between us in late 2021, Pereira noted, "If we want to continue to generate an inclusive space for all voices—especially minorities, including people of color and queer people—to flourish creatively, then everyone should be compensated appropriately." This belief has led to a tidal wave of both physical and online protest in the world of culture, where many museums and other nonprofits present themselves as status symbols in order to pay artists in exposure or cachet rather than money. In response, we saw the burgeoning popularity of collectives, such as Working Artists and the Greater Economy (W.A.G.E.), which was founded in 2008 as a coalition that lobbied for minimum payment for artists, initially in the United States, and offers fee calculators for artists, institutional certification for organizations with a history of and commitment to voluntarily paying artists to W.A.GE. standards, and surveys demonstrating the complex socioeconomic lives of artists. It was similar in many ways to Canadian Artists' Representation/ *Le Front des artistes canadiens* (CARFAC), set up in 1967 as a national lobbying voice for creative professionals that has produced a system of benchmarking and an industry standard for artists' remuneration.

"If you value something, you pay for it," said Pereira from her new HQ at Rally. "The realm of culture is filled with abundance . . . we just need to rally to shape and build it to its potential." Her proposal presupposes that "culture is a lifeblood"—a space that should never be free, or else it will be taken for granted, as one has witnessed in England, where the government proposed in 2021 to decimate the funding of all studies in the humanities,

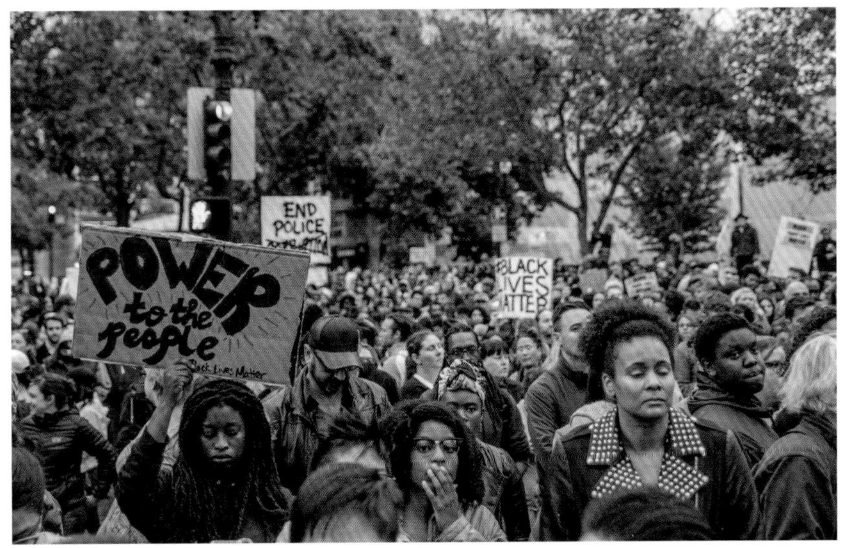

Black Lives Matter protest in Oakland, California, 2016

cutting the annual budget by 50 percent.[11] Political rhetoric about the necessity to reorientate toward science and technology seems naively negligent of the interdependence of these multiple worlds and the propensity for these creative forms to give voice to multiple publics previously unheard.

An online campaign by artists, academics, and students to express the necessity for arts and culture subjects in higher education was met with defensive rhetoric from UK politicians. On September 9, 2021, the secretary of state for education was telecast offering an out-of-touch presentation to senior university officials, arguing that universities are more interested in "canceling national heroes" than instilling public confidence in higher education.[12] Lubaina Himid, the first woman of color to win the nation's prestigious Turner Prize in 2017, who has been a professor of fine arts for more than thirty years, believes that this rhetoric works counterintuitively against the strides made to enable queer communities and British Black artists to begin to thrive, also citing the Black Lives Matter movement's recent global influence. "If you remove the arts," she told me, "you take away the hat that you're wearing, your shirt, your tie, your trousers—indeed, everything. . . . This plate, these glasses, food, the concept of leisure, experience is altered. . . . It makes absolutely no sense how politicians don't understand that creativity is one of the fundamental building blocks to everything."[13] Helen Cammock, a queer artist of color who in 2019 also won the Turner Prize, spent much of her life working simultaneously as a social worker until recently devoting herself full time to art. In 2021, she stated in the *Guardian* that the government is going to "walk us back sixty years"—restricting the pursuit of art to an isolated fragment of individuals who possess great wealth.[14] Can we find alternative models to shift this paradigm? A means to use the technological sphere to speak truth to power, perhaps. The story is still being written.

Queering History

The question of political and social polarization has been a topic in civil society for centuries, but the advent of socially engaged technologies has contoured the debate. Some attribute this to the popularity of Donald Trump on social media in the lead-up to his single-term election, while media outlets tend to focus on the period after 2019, when the Black Lives Matter movement coalesced to form a global network to speak out against police brutality and social injustice against African Americans. In tandem with these developments, the world has become witness to a more fluent dialogue around gender identity—*nonbinary*, with which I have always identified, did not mean anything in mainstream culture until the digital field allowed a generation to connect and claim fluidity of identity.

Much of this is steeped in the cyberfeminist movement, for which Donna Haraway informally became a spokesperson in the mid-1980s; it was also brought to wider attention through the popularization of the underground riot grrrl movement that emerged out of Olympia, Washington, in the early 1990s, in parallel with the global domination of grunge music. Here, no topic was off-limits, from rape and sexual abuse to patriarchy, the expectations of gender, and what was perceived as an inherent culture of racism. I recall this proliferation after the brutal violence by police against the African American man Rodney King in Los Angeles and the subsequent riots and protests in Los Angeles and across the country when the officers were acquitted on all but one charge.

The constellation of riot grrrl activity revolved around the punk band Bikini Kill and its founder Kathleen Hanna's anarchic voice, lyricism, and stage presence. Hanna is also a member of Le Tigre, an electronic rock band she cofounded with now-legendary transgender artist Sadie Benning and Johanna Fateman, who is now a contributing editor to *Artforum*. Activist politics have long existed in hybrid form—existing between the pop culture and the highbrow world of art. This is also evidenced through the popularization of queercore music, a genre that seeks to protest and document the difficulties facing the LGBTQ+ community. Intersex artist polymath Vaginal Davis found roots here, as well as English band Sister George, and perhaps most famously Green Day, whose lead singer Billie Joe Armstrong is bisexual.

In 2011, the influence of these movements swelled to a crescendo, becoming one of the most visually recognizable cultural phenomena of the social-media era, with the global appearance of Pussy Riot. Citing the aforementioned musical influences as inspiration for their colorful costumes and musical style, the variable members of this Russian feminist performance art collective performed on stages protesting the country's treatment of LGBTQ+ citizens in spontaneous guerrilla performances, including at such sites as the Cathedral of Christ the Savior—an Orthodox church just a few hundred yards away from the Kremlin.

The group was also astutely aware of the power of the internet to telecast their performances and the dissidence that ensued around their collective acts of protest. Infamously, members of the group were put on trial and jailed by the local government for their acts of hooliganism. Self-documented images of these experiences by members, including Maria Alyokhina and Nadezhda Tolokonnikova, led to a tornado of international attention—the support of human rights group Amnesty International, and, further down the line, the European Court of Human Rights. Two of the biggest-selling music artists of all time—Madonna and Paul McCartney—showed their solidarity. The press attention continued to burgeon, primarily around the legal trial of its members, spiraling into offshoot protests, dance, and street art. The fire that Pussy Riot sparked enabled the entry of their performances into museums, and the debate around their censorship raised the question, if it is human nature to oppress dissent, how can we conceive of living in any form of democratic civil society? The debate also caused extant tensions around issues of LGBTQ+ culture to rise to the surface.

Techno-Queer

As soon as I joined Facebook in 2007, I began receiving messages from critical friends, who warned me about social media and its dangers. I was told to be wary of what they called the *panopticon*—the all-seeing eye, their nickname for Facebook. My friends were primarily researchers, engineers, and computer scientists situated in academia, the same set who had also introduced me to the authors associated with a field known as accelerationism. Ranging from Mark Fisher and Sadie Plant to Alex Williams, they varied greatly in their approach, but at the base of it all

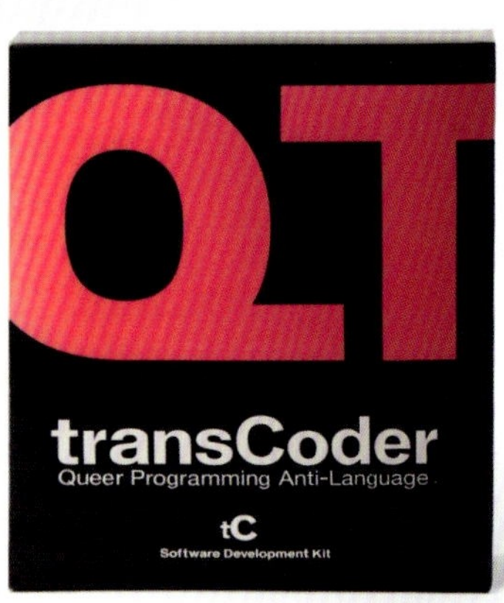

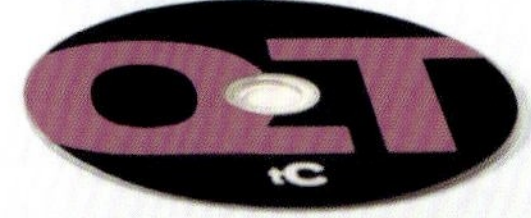

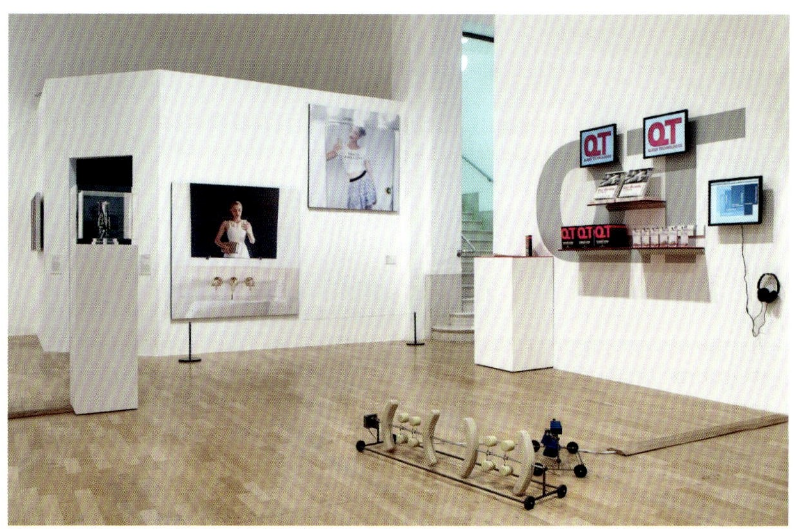

Zach Blas, *Queer Technologies: transCoder: Queer Programming Anti-Language*, 2008

Electronic Superhighway (2016–1966), 2016
—Installation view: Whitechapel Gallery, London, 2016

was a simmering unease with the political and economic frameworks around mass technology.

What was going to happen? One suggestion was that humans would be subsumed by capitalism and self-implode. At the time, Facebook's reputation for surveillance and data mining had not yet come to the fore. Instead, I found myself connecting with queer communities who were posting aspects of their lives that had at first seemed so distant from my own daily life. One of those early tendencies was to self-document your activities, moods, and feelings through captioned photographs. For a short-lived period, I found myself feeling comfortable documenting aspects of a queer life that, to this day, I hide from members of my family; in these digital pages, I felt, or believed, that I could choose my audiences, and so did many others.

This initial feeling of safety is commonly referenced by early users of Facebook, who were primarily college and university students. There was a sense that the space was fashioned for like-minded individuals, with whom one could choose to connect. With these frameworks also emerged new strategies for artistic documentation and presentation. In 2014, I was introduced to Zackary Drucker, one of the consulting producers on an Amazon Studios TV show called *Transparent* (2014–17), a comedy-drama that aimed to disentangle trans culture for a mass audience. Drucker, a trans woman artist, was also showing a project that she had completed with her now ex-partner, Rhys Ernst, at the Whitney Biennial in New York. Titled *Relationship* (2008–14), this body of work presents photographs accompanied by myriad annotations of the life of the duo as they both transitioned genders, Drucker from male to female, and Ernst from female to male. Despite the complex context in which they found themselves—both in a relationship, undergoing the complexities of various forms of treatment—the visual outcome reveals something altogether different. Instead of zooming in on the medicalized aspects of transition, *Relationship* emphasizes the quotidian: the intimate moments of holding one another amidst moments of pain and grief, loss, or desire. What I saw in these photographs, pinned to the wall akin to a Pinterest board, was a personified experience of gender fluidity. This was an intimacy, a narrative gaze that had emerged from Web 2.0, and I was all the happier for its existence, because it gave me the confidence to interrogate my own gender identity.

Through Zach Blas, I met Canadian-born Cassils in 2011 while I was temporarily stationed in an Airbnb in East Los Angeles. Cassils is an artist whose performative acts incorporate their own body as a material. After living in shoe-box spaces in metropolises, I was thrilled to have an outdoor space with a firepit, and I invited artists to join me at the grill. We soon realized that the carnivorous contingent was minimal and few knew how to cook on a BBQ, including me. As most of my friends got into their cars and went down to Los Feliz to find food on a Saturday night, Cassils and Blas stayed behind. In the intervening years, Cassils has come to international repute, becoming an image of an archetype while at the same time also deconstructing it.

One of the defining features of geolocative mobile telephony is online dating, which was pioneered in a smartphone application called Grindr. Since its invention, Grindr's user base has morphed in its visuality, which is reflected in the app's most recent series of advertisements: an endless sea of six-packs, torsos instead of faces, whiteness at the fore. The presentation of the gay male body as agile, nimble, and robust is a subject that has been tackled by theorists, such as José Esteban Muñoz, Judith Butler, and Lauren Berlant, as well as body-image sociologists and sexologists, including Thomas W. Laqueur and Ricky Varghese, who have collectively fostered a view that the construction of the overtly masculine white male body is a post-HIV and AIDS crisis form of resistance. The by-product of the culture of body obsession that it has generated is one of consistent online body shaming, which has now spread across platforms to all genders. It has also pushed the queer minority into individualized apps that are suited to so-called tribes, whether you are a cub, an otter, a bear, or so forth. Cassils's performative work thereby creates a specific ontological lens through which we can decode the contortion of the body, whether it is the confluence of health and mindfulness or the belief systems of how power is represented through the apparatus of the body itself.

Zach Blas, whom I met on a message board in the first ten years of the millennium when responding to a blog post, was an early conduit to debates around issues between queer sexuality and representation. He came to renown with a project devised as a collective called Queer Technologies (QT). Soon after completing study graduate study at the University of California, Los Angeles, and with the aid of a suite of collaborators, Blas constructed a faux Apple Genius Bar–style setup, "the disingenuous bar," presenting queer technologies from "gay bombs" to unique queer programming language.

These products, professionally packaged, were also "shop-dropped" with fake barcodes into stores, such as Radio Shack, where customers would attempt to purchase them, only to find that they did not exist in any form of official record. The invisibility of what is still perceived by many as a subculture—queer technology—was a critical line of inquiry that Blas was developing through his PhD at Duke University. "What is the aesthetic of queerness in the technosphere?" he regularly asked me. He has since inserted them into every kind of museum, gallery, and storefront.

In response to reports that the U.S. government was prepared to deploy facial-recognition software to discern features of queer or homosexual faces, he developed a project titled *Facial Weaponization Suite* (2012–14). As a form of resistance, the artist created this body of works, which are individually referred to as "fagfaces," by taking amalgamations of multiple queer faces and reconstructing them as 3-D-printed masks that were worn by performers in acts of protest. The artist's line of thought continued to evolve as a critique of how the internet homogenized queer identity.

In 2013, while working together on a residency in London, Blas presented me with "Contra-Internet Aesthetics," which I subsequently published in *You Are Here: Art After the Internet*—the first anthology on the freewheeling genre that had come to be known as post-internet art and its attendant movements and aesthetics. Attention around Blas exploded, and he won multiple awards that aided in the development of these ideas into an installation first presented at the Gasworks London gallery. At its core, *Contra-Internet* (2015–19) is a sci-fi film starring Cassils set in a not-so-distant future where the internet is used to manipulate collective human consciousness around the whims of an invisible state.

Being a queer, subaltern subject is a complex-enough construction to contend with today, but if one adds the intricacies of surveillance and the two-way mirror of an all-encompassing media, the picture becomes all the more brittle. The first time that my restlessness around this subject emerged was in 2014 while on a sponsored trip to Berlin. I was visiting Galerie Isabella Bortolozzi to see a new exhibition by my friend Wu Tsang, a queer, trans artist who was presenting an exhibition, *A day in the life of bliss* (2014). This multimedia sci-fi project, which also manifested as a web series in situ, was a discombobulating experience. Two large screens in the central gallery created a mirrored effect that seemed to suggest multiple ulterior hidden spaces. The images would flicker, appearing and disappearing, as the film's protagonist, Blis, streamed out onto the walls in myriad colors. Blis, a character performed by artist Boychild (Tosh Basco), exists in a world controlled by a social-media platform called PRSM, in essence, the panopticon. Through juxtapositions of street scenes of Blis in a derelict future-scape and a controlled interior-scape, the audience can bear witness to performative bodily gestures—expressions of anger and defiance with the world in which one has come to live.

Unlike popular television series, such as Charlie Brooker's sci-fi drama *Black Mirror*, the artists engaging with the technical apparatus of

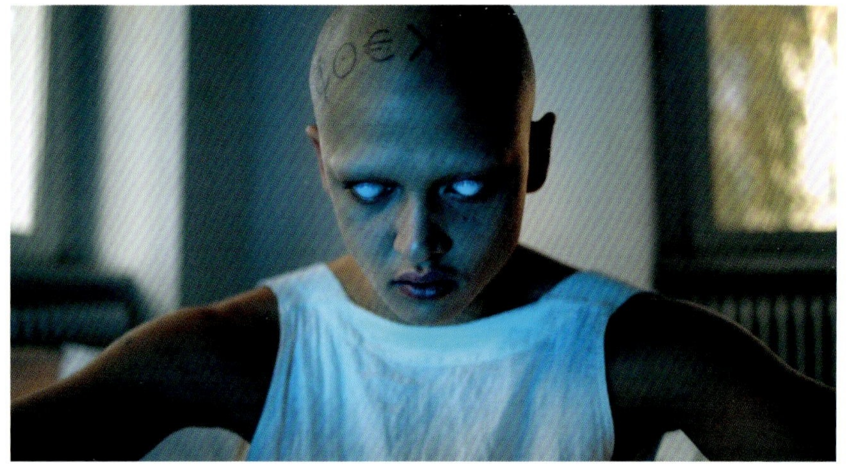

Wu Tsang, *A day in the life of bliss*, 2014 (still) —Two-channel HD video installation, surround sound, projection screens, mirror, two-way mirror, seating, dimensions variable, 20 min.

social media to express their identity are equally reflecting on what it means to be queer in the twenty-first century and, specifically, how the form that this takes is continually evolving, with the risk that if we do not pay attention, the contours of who we are may just slip out of our hands.

Race and Representation Online

When the words *data visualization* were first uttered to me, I thought of the complex diagrams in my economics classes that digitally segmented surveys of income. I did not interrogate what they meant. For a course on human rights, I began digging into library files and happened on W. E. B. Du Bois's data portraits of Black America, proposing to map out the "color line" of American racial representation and segregation, which was anthologized and published for the first time in their entirety in 2018. Du Bois forged the concept of double-consciousness in *The Souls of Black Folk* (1903), which explored the concept of being both American and Black. Slavery was outwardly abolished in the 13th Amendment in 1865, but to be a person of color in the United States means constant segregation and demands more than one gaze; an interior and exterior one, a lens through which one is continually forced to recodify to survive within the parameters of a white-led capitalist society.

It has been more than one hundred years since the publication of Du Bois's treatise, yet the concept of mapping race is as polarizing as ever.

Today, data visualization easily conjures the practice of gerrymandering—the often unfair redistricting by local governments to create political advantages for certain politicians and groups. This conjures images of *rigged elections*, a term that continually sprouts up in the mainstream media. I begin to interrogate who made this data, who owns it, and what has been concealed from public view? In a tweet on October 18, 2020, author and activist Mona Eltahawy revealed that the Egyptian government was arresting women for dancing and singing on the social-media application TikTok. She juxtaposed this information with a video of a parade of recent male graduates from the national police academy, who stood with bare chests in a government-sanctioned parade, put on display and celebrated for their "virility, masculinity, [and] strength" but also as a specific form of social-media power.[15] Who runs the world? Not girls, or whatever Beyoncé might say.

The way data is revealed to the public is constantly subject to manipulation. When I lived in Chicago, footage of the heinous murder of an innocent African American teenager called Laquan McDonald, by police, was held back from public view until the incumbent mayor of Chicago at the time, Rahm Emanuel, had completed his reelection campaign. Despite the outcry, Emanuel remained in power. On the surface, Emanuel was a genteel soul, and I saw him often at museum openings. During every interaction, he would return to the same question: "Tell me, what is your training?" The idea of training, of being coached to exercise and prepare, was not lost on me. These words were being uttered by a man who had spent a few weeks as a civilian volunteer assisting the Israeli Defense Forces during the 1991 Gulf War. But training also denotes status and class, affinity and validation—a privilege for the few. His brother, media mogul and Endeavor CEO Ariel Emanuel, whom I met at the New York edition of Frieze Art Fair, spoke to me with warmth as we studied a work by Arthur Jafa (discussed in more depth in the "The Shape of the Future" chapter) at the booth of the now-shuttered New York gallery, Gavin Brown's Enterprise. Despite his media portrayals, Ari seemed curious to understand the context of my gaze, regardless of pedigree or PhD.

But the world turns in an unusual fashion. Mine is a gaze from the outside. I lived my early years on a housing development in Glasgow before moving at the age of seven to South Central Los Angeles, before we stretched to the South Bay. Being the oldest of four, a specimen constructed from mixed-race parents, I was bred with a persistent narrative—a fear of authority. The pigment of my skin came out lighter than most in my unit—"rice pudding" as I was nicknamed. I assume this was the result of the Black men in my family marrying fairer-skinned women so they could "pass"—that is, ascend to positions and status in the western world that

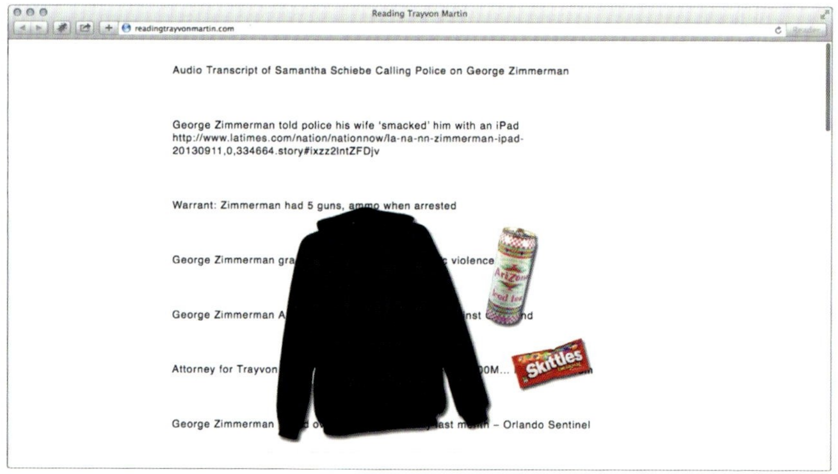

Martine Syms, *Reading Trayvon Martin*, 2012 —First Look: New Art Online series, New Museum, New York, 2012

they believed were withheld from them. When I returned to the United States as an adult, my sense that I was an imposter, as a therapist once diagnosed it, returned. I became fixated on graphs and charts, like the one the *Guardian* published titled "The Counted," the most comprehensive database of U.S. police killings. They ran the project in 2015 and 2016, and most of the dots sat squarely where I then lived in middle America.

The tendency to map and document police killings has spread across multiple platforms and websites, such as Mapping Police Violence, which at the time of writing reveals that in 2021, 705 people have been slain by police in the United States. In 2013, a decentralized social movement called Black Lives Matter emerged after the acquittal of George Zimmerman in the trial of the murder of seventeen-year-old African American Trayvon Martin. The hashtag, #BlackLivesMatter spread globally, fostering a network in solidarity with Black life that now has branches all over the world. The original impetus of the movement, which was, and in many respects still is, to reveal datasets that demonstrate the inequity of police violence against Black bodies, took on new life through the shape of social media. Internet-connected platforms became mechanisms to mobilize not just the African American and Black communities in various countries but every person able and willing to show solidarity.

Digging into the vortex of the web and proposing a new form of visuality is artist Martine Syms. I first encountered Syms's work online with a project called *Reading Trayvon Martin*, which she began in 2012. The web-based project began when Syms bookmarked a CNN online article about

Martin's last minutes. The teenager was brutally murdered in Florida and had become a subject of perpetual public interrogation. Syms's website, on the contrary, functioned as an internal archive or memory bank through bookmarked articles, essays, and digital artifacts relating to Martin's case. These are sources that we use to find and hear Black narratives of violence and dissent, the language that these spaces accumulate and spread, as well as how one negotiates the flurry of data that is created by such a context. Syms began making websites in a DIY fashion, but her interests extend more broadly into what she has referred to as image in our flesh—the life of the image.[16]

Her accumulated pictures of Black archives from a Detroit record store have been made manifest across walls and floors, such as in her installation *Boon* (2019), held at Secession in Vienna. If memory serves me correctly, I first exhibited Syms's work in the exhibition *Imitation of Life: Melodrama and Race in the 21st Century*, a three-year research project and exhibition presented at HOME in Manchester in 2016. My line of inquiry here was to utilize Douglas Sirk's iconic film *Imitation of Life* (1959) as a framework to interrogate the ideas of passing and code-switching in a time that the media had dubbed a "post-racial era" due to the election of President Barrack Obama. Syms's *A Pilot for a Show About Nowhere* (2015) is a masterpiece of video collage that sought to frame how poor Black bodies are presented or erased within the conventions of television.

During this time, new forms of creative practice emerged into public view. Claudia Rankine's book of lyric poetry *Citizen* (2014) used mixed forms, presenting hyperlinked conversations between images and text. Together, they narrate U.S. race relations during the Obama years. Here, one is witness to a juxtaposition between Hennessy Youngman (Jayson Musson) and Serena Williams, in image-prose that interrogates body and speech, as well as the expression of their ethnicity. The book became a global sensation, winning the National Book Critics Circle Award for Poetry and the Forward Poetry Prize, among other honors, and sold more than hree hundred thousand copies. Rankine was awarded a MacArthur Foundation "Genius" Award, which she used to fund a project titled the Racial Imaginary Institute—a collective endeavor to "capture the enduring truth of race."[17]

Citizen became an animate act of protest. In the second printing of the book, Rankine included the name of Michael Brown—an eighteen-year-old Black man who was fatally shot by a white police officer in Ferguson, Missouri, in 2014—in the book's in memoria end section, followed by hollow spaces standing for all the deaths assumed to come. The watershed moment for the Black Lives Matter movement, however, occurred on May 25, 2020, during the height of global lockdowns. Darnella Frazier,

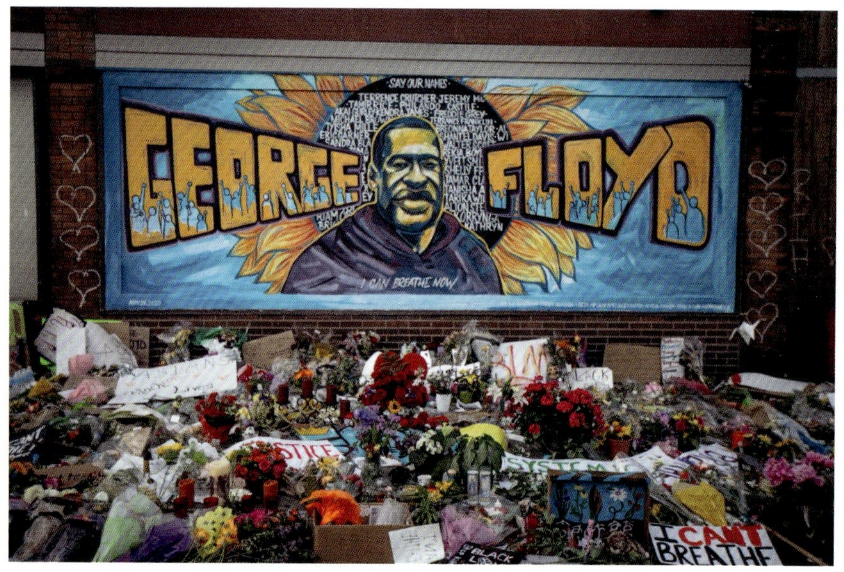

Memorial for George Floyd, Minneapolis, 2020

a teenager in Minneapolis, held her iPhone camera steady while Derek Chauvin, a police officer, pressed his knee into the neck of George Floyd, an African American man who for the nine minutes and twenty-nine seconds that he was held down by Chauvin, tried to howl for life. “I can’t breathe,” he gasped. In the last two minutes of being held down, he visibly had no pulse and was motionless, yet the police officer’s knee remained where it was, and in the frame of Frazier’s camera. Floyd had served as a religious mentor and worked as a truck driver and bouncer. Floyd lost his job due to the devastating economic ramifications of the global pandemic. He had allegedly tried to pass a fake twenty-dollar bill in a bodega. His punishment equated to death. Gone was a father. What distinguished this occasion from every other case of police brutality against Black bodies may have been the haphazardly shot but continuous nature of Frazier’s video—filmed by a then barely seventeen-year-old girl who chose to post the video on Facebook. She said, “I opened my phone and I started recording because I knew if I didn’t, no one would believe me.”[18] The pleading utterances by Floyd, “I can’t breathe” and “My stomach hurts”—pleas of vulnerability from a helpless voice that despite its unnerving tenor, were continually played by mainstream news media. Frazier’s testimony immediately debunked the accounts of the Minneapolis Police Department surrounding the course of events.

Regardless of the pandemic's social-distancing rules, Frazier's video became a rallying call for protest around the world. Human chains formed against barricades of police forces with shields. Portraits of Floyd were erected across buildings on city blocks with his last words, "I Can't Breathe," which became a mantra chanted by protestors. What may have initially seemed like an uncoordinated effort spread to the hands of the Black Lives Matter movement, who organized peaceful protests in more than two thousand cities and sixty countries. In the United States, various polls indicate that between fifteen and twenty-six million people engaged in protest against Floyd's death and police brutality.[19] These figures do not simply suggest but they attest to the fact that this is the largest coordinated protest around a single cause in the United States's history.

Online debate in every forum—from LinkedIn to Instagram—took the matter of race to the fore. Suddenly, museums, such as the Walker Art Center in Minneapolis, professed that they would not work with the city's police department, which encouraged similar abdications from working with local police units from other museums across the country. The increasing energy around the subject of racial equity encouraged museums and institutions of higher learning to release antiracism statements, propose new inclusive structures of working, and renew interest in exploring the legacies of ongoing Black oppression. Statues of slave traders from the United States to Great Britain were removed, sometimes in a coordinated fashion and sometimes in acts the authorities called vandalism.

Every act made a perfect picture. Every act was a broadcast. Every body emitted the light of a camera. This was an ideological war that brought back the word of solidarity into popular debate. By June 2020, in the United States, twenty-five protestors had died; fourteen thousand arrests were performed. By October 2020, the *Guardian* reported that nearly one thousand of the incidences of violence toward civilians during protests were enacted by police officers.[20] So imagine the other ramifications of an iPhone film documenting police brutality. Frazier's fearless act led to public harassment against her and interrogation. She understandably professed to feeling traumatized, a sense complicated further by the death of the teenage girl's uncle in a police car chase the following year.

What would have happened had this footage been handed over to the police? Would it have sat in a vault—protected and silenced, deemed to be unsafe and not to be seen? In June 2021, Chauvin was sentenced to twenty-two-and-a-half years in prison for murdering George Floyd; in March 2021, the city of Minneapolis settled a federal lawsuit with Floyd's family in what the family's attorney called the largest pretrial civil rights settlement ever. The dial has turned an inch, but there is still a long way for us all to run.

A Space for Mongrels?

In the mid-1990s, a group inspired by conversations at the Arts and Technology Center in London's Borough of Islington took shape. Afterward, artistic figures and theorists, including Graham Harwood, Matthew Fuller, Richard Pierre-Davis, and Matsuko Yokokoji, established a new organization/art collective called Mongrel. Another driving force was feedback from Black students both at the Arts and Technology Center and in the academic sphere where many of these individuals were teaching, including Goldsmiths College, asserting difficulties in gaining traction within the industry. In its initial incarnation, Mongrel produced browser-based artworks that sought to polemicize the identifying cultural tropes that define everyday humans. In 1996, Harwood, Mongrel released the first iteration of *Heritage Gold*, a piece of downloadable software that would allow you to alter your racial features using a standard Photoshop color palette. Your racialized skin could become Japanese, Black, or Caucasian, among a number of categorizations. By invoking concepts of heritage and intimating that there is a gold standard to which to aspire, the collective proposed a decoding of racial structures, which have been further explored by YoHA, Harwood and Yokokoji's reconfigured outfit. Since then, the duo has focused on labor exploitation in a culture where technology and its power structures form the central apparatus, exerting juridical control.

Artist damali ayo released *Rent-A-Negro.com* (2003), a website that advertised a business where anyone could "rent" a Black person for their personal entertainment and potential exploitation. The site would remain online until 2012. Ayo notes that her impetus was to encourage the public to "wake . . . up and see things in ways they had been willfully ignoring."[21]

Combatting erasure returns us to artist Martine Syms, who cofounded Dominica Publishing, an imprint based in Los Angeles that explores "Blackness as a topic." Now operating primarily online, one example release is Syms's 2020 book published by Primary Information titled *Shame Space*, in which images mashed up with diary entries are presented in a form intended to mimic the half-letter (A5)-size and golden edges of the Bible. Reclaiming the Bible as an object of Blackness is demonstrative of the artist's penchant for deconstructing narrative forms and stitching them together again, as Dominica does with its T-shirts featuring bleak aphoristic slogans, including, "To Hell with My Suffering," "Anxious Avoidant," and "Club Heart Break."

The impulse to use fashion, and clothing more generally, as a means for articulating and reenvisaging constructions of race is an idea at the core of

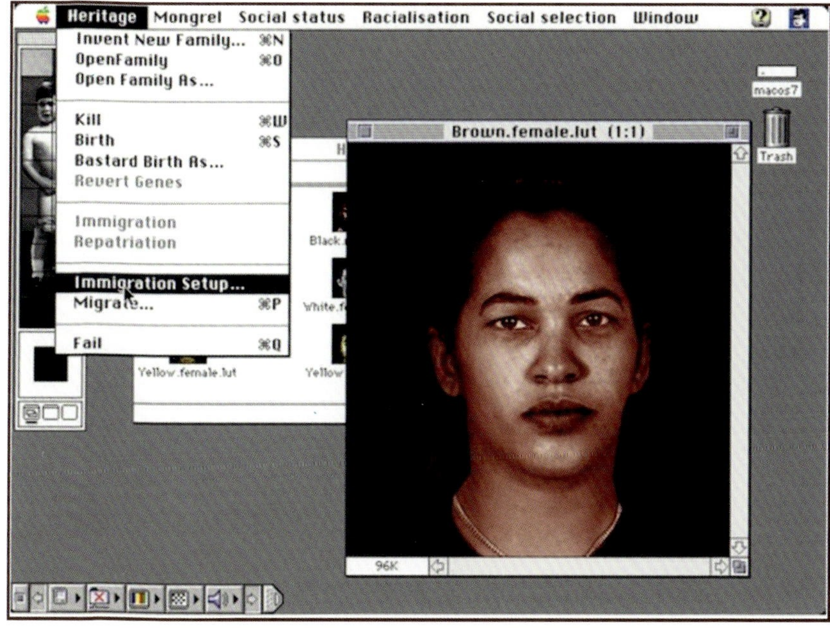

Harwood, Mongrel, *Heritage Gold*, 1996

the art fashion label CFGNY. Cofounded by Daniel Chew and Tin Nguyen in 2016 and later joined by Ten Izu and Kirsten Kilponen, CFGNY is a label that, as described on its website, seeks to explore the "intersection of fashion, race, identity, and sexuality." It embraces concepts of alienation as part of its visual lexicon, nodding to the fact that the two founders are self-taught designers who watched YouTube tutorials as part of their learning process. As they developed a small following, they began to solicit and coerce friends to offer lessons on pattern cutting. Nguyen had a background in sculpture, which anchored the clothing's form, while Chew's self-professed "childhood addiction to internet fashion forums" brought contemporary discourse into the mix.[22] I discovered the collective's work when they showed at 47 Canal, a gallery in New York's Lower East Side that represents some of the most significant artistic voices, from Anicka Yi to Josh Kline.

At first, I was uncertain what to make of CFGNY's seemingly genderless clothing until my partner, the fashion and costume designer Frank Gallacher, explained that the label was akin to a mutable series of set pieces. Recent examples include counterfeit North Face jackets found in Vietnam that have been completely deconstructed and reconstructed, the incorporation of family heirlooms from the designers' Asian heritage, and markers from the

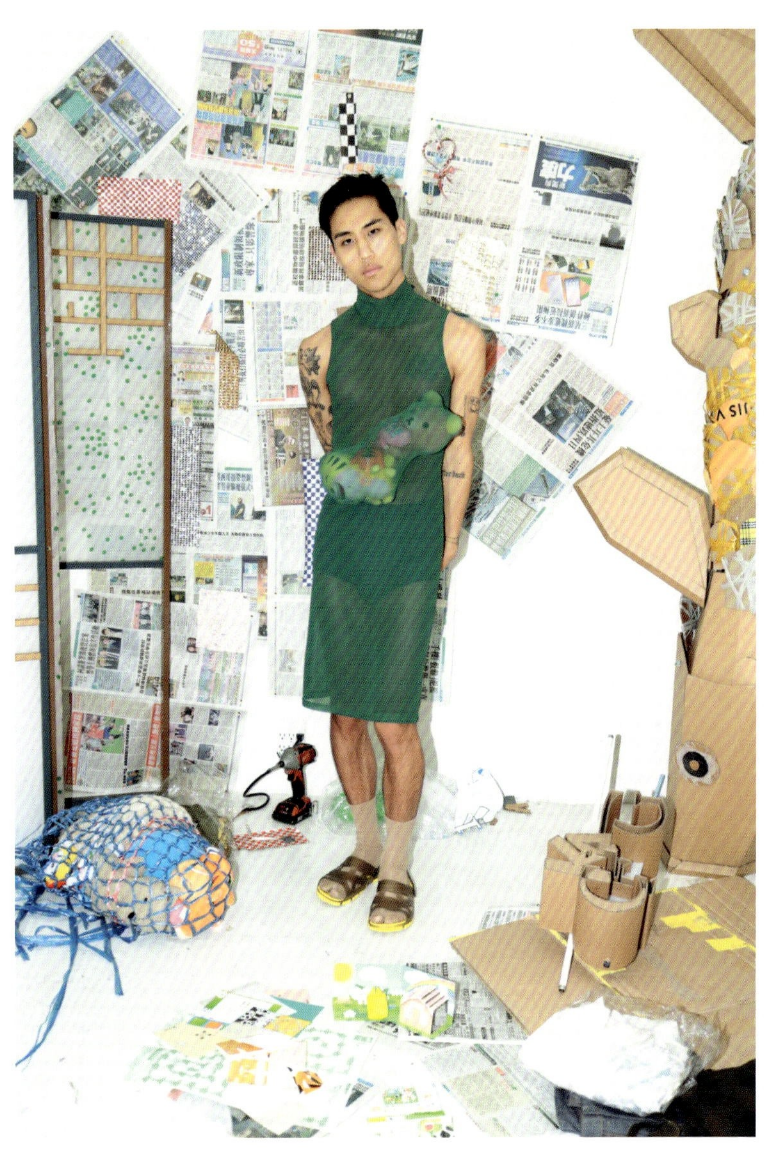

CFGNY, *Henry in Bump Dress*, 2018

world of Pokémon. Constantly fluctuating between the duality of the pair's identity, the label has recently grown to encompass a wider community of designers and patrons. Today, a bodice might be constructed from a bag found in an Asian American grocery store; the genteel male might don a blazer and a half-kilt, generating a sense of flow that mirrors the creative process itself. And as for the name, CFGNY stands for Concept Foreign Garments New York, or, per their Instagram bio, Cute Fucking Gay New York.

Black Futures

In 2017, while in a car with José Esparza Chong Cuy, my colleague at the Museum of Contemporary Art Chicago, making our way to Michigan, Chong Cuy insisted that we listen to a *New York Times* podcast called *Still Processing*. I thought that podcasts had died a decade earlier, but within five or so minutes, I was consumed by the teasing chitchat of the culture podcast. It was cohosted by *New York Times Magazine* writer Jenna Wortham and Wesley Morris, now the paper's critic at large and two-time winner of the Pulitzer Prize, both African American, who as we understand, are members of the queer community. The podcast was fizzing with an energy I had not heard in my recent lifetime. Here, Britney Spears's conservatorship and Cathy Park Hong's memoir of essays, *Minor Feelings* (2020)—a treatise on in betweenness—could be spoken of in the same breath; healing and clarity mixed in with Lil Nas X, the history of racial slurs, online dating, Whitney Houston, and Harry Styles. No subject was off-limits and none too trivial for discussion. Everything could be scrupulously examined from a critical gaze.

In 2020, Wortham, with collaborator Kimberly Drew, released *Black Futures*, an anthology of Black creative work. Drew, an African American woman and a member of the queer community, had grown in fame through her former position as the Metropolitan Museum of Art's manager of social media. A curator and author, she came to public renown through her social-media handle @museummammy, which led to a following so expansive that she was invited to take over the White House's Instagram account in 2016. At the same time, she maintained the Tumblr she founded, Black Contemporary Art, and continued her activism against racial inequity.

Working together, Drew and Wortham pieced together a collage of Black life that was as expansive as possible, asking the fundamental question: "What does it mean to be Black and alive right now?"[23] Memes and tweets sit with poetry, photo essays, and conversations from such figures as painter Nina Chanel Abney, technologically inclined thought-practitioner American Artist, academic Tina Campt, and best-selling authors Ta-Nehisi Coates and

Teju Cole, to name but a few examples. The spirit of the five-hundred-plus page volume was propulsive and encouraged cross-border thinking of Blackness, including members of the diasporic communities.

The same could be said, despite some polemical subtext, of seeing the first major Black Marvel superhero thrillingly take center stage in Ryan Coogler's *Black Panther* (2018)—the highest-grossing film by a Black film director, earning more than a billion dollars at the box office. Many complained that it was a derivative form of African and Black culture, but the influence that it bore phenomenally outweighed such gesticulating. The same year, Janelle Monáe, the art-pop sensation, continued to speak openly about her desire to bring back a technologically infused African sensibility into the collective imagination. The notion of the cyborg and the circulation of trends in the fashion industry feature as key motifs in her music videos and album art from this time, and not least, her music itself, with her album *Dirty Computer* (2018) an exemplar. Black sci-fi author Octavia E. Butler's surge in popularity, alongside the speculative Black bodies of Kenyan American artist Wangechi Mutu's works, speak to a sense of the possible.

The internet and its encompassing technologies continue to contort and mutate. In the field of racial politics, its influence has been undeniable. The essence of how bodies are portrayed and articulated in space is morphing. Not only do digital billboards include myriad racialized bodies, but ASOS, the UK's fourth-largest online clothing retailer and the largest geared toward the youth market, is designed to appeal to people of color through its choice of models—a marked shift from the original branding at its launch in the early millennium. When such shifts occur in the realm of commerce, audiences are forced to reorientate their gaze into a realm that is no longer othered but representative of society's broad spectrum.

Political Blackness?

In 2021, British Ghanian artist Larry Achiampong was nominated for Film London's Jarman Award, for among other works, a piece called *Beyond the Substrata* (2020). In this video, a series of performers in all-black body suits occupy an abandoned East London supermarket. The work, Achiampong has noted, is an appraisal of the limited sources for products in western supermarkets—a circuitous loop of supply and demand that relies on a handful of businesses, wiping out minority producers and the demand for their products. If one considers *Beyond the Substrata* a reflection on the hollow dereliction of a whitewashed material culture, then the campaign that also emerged online in 2020, #BAMEOver, speaks to the question of the white-controlled hegemony over language. BAME, an acronym used in Great Britain that stands for Black, Asian, and minority ethnic, is intended to essentially group together all ethnic minorities who are nonwhite.

In the 1980s and 1990s, concepts of language at the intersection of race in the UK were very different. In the early 1980s, collectives supporting the work of British Black artists, such as the BLK Art Group, formed in the Midlands. Meanwhile, a broader constellation of artists constituted the more informal British Black Art movement, which led to open dialogue and debate among artists from across a spectrum that included such figures as Eddie Chambers, Claudette Johnson, Lubaina Himid, and Keith Piper, to name just a few. In 1987, the minimalist sculptor Rasheed Araeen founded the leading journal of postcolonial art, *Third Text*. Also a curator, his *The Other Story* (1989) exhibition of Black artists opened two years later at the Hayward Gallery, London. What was distinctive about this form of "political blackness," to cite American artist and author Lorraine O'Grady's introduction to her collected writings,[24] is that, at the time, *Black* was often used as an inclusive term of solidarity for any person who was not white—or at least that is how that history was recited to me by my teacher Jean Fisher, who served as an editor for *Third Text* for many years.

#BAMEOver, however, a decentralized group of individuals, asked: "What do we want to be called?" We are still being lumped into a singular bundle of otherness, so how can we be seen, like any person or object, for what we are? "Call us by our name," they chanted in the echo chamber of the internet, mobilizing mainstream media attention through newspapers, broadcast debates, as well as through online petitions. Interestingly for me, as someone whose racial identity developed in parallel between the United States and the UK, the collective admonishes the use of a term that I have felt safe to use, *person of color*, noting that in Great Britain it could be seen as a racial slur. The group professes that we are bound by lived experience, not the color of our skin.[25]

Such affinities have consistently held sway in the world of art, linking individuals to cultures distant from them, something made even more possible through digital technologies. In the 2010s, the global art market experienced a sizable boom in attention, alongside the burgeoning interest in visual work by African American artists. In 2013, the 1–54 Contemporary African Art Fair—the world's leading event of its kind—launched in London before incorporating other cities, such as New York, Marrakech, and Paris. It became a site for tastemakers and newly formed galleries from across Africa to meet on equal ground since borders dividing many states of the continent can ironically be complex to traverse without a foreign (i.e., non-African)

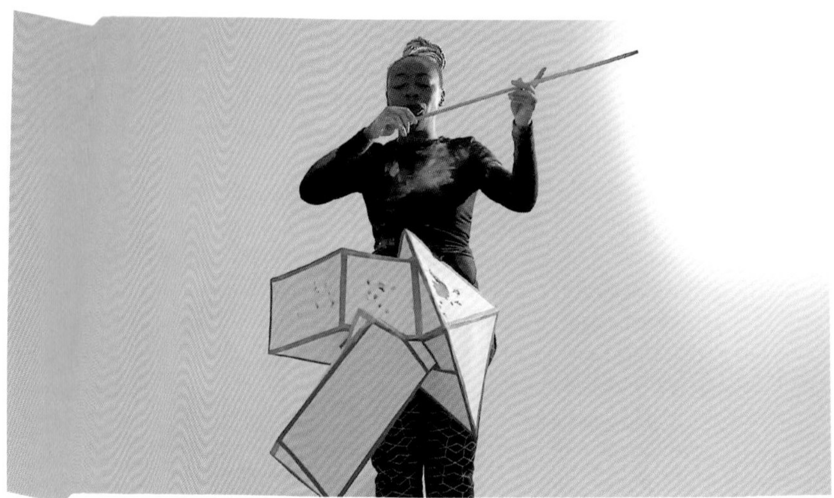

Otobong Nkanga, *Diaoptasia*, 2015 —9 min. 46 sec. Performance for BMW Tate Live: Performance Room, Tate Modern, London, November 26, 2015

passport. This experience became apparent to me only in graduate school, when I went to live in a remote village in Northeast Limpopo, South Africa. I would be required to demonstrate that I held what, back then, was an inordinate sum of money in my bank account to attain an initial visa, which I would be required to extend. At the time, I held an Egyptian passport and had yet to naturalize as a citizen of a western country. Once in situ, visiting neighboring countries, such as Botswana, Zimbabwe, and Mozambique, could be performed with relative ease, but the more I moved in an uncoordinated fashion, the more complex an endeavor it became.

The movement of bodies, especially within the mutable landscape of the African continent, is a defining feature in the art of Otobong Nkanga. At the 8th Berlin Biennale, the artist presented the installation *In Pursuit of Bling* (2014), which blistered and combusted the inner belly of the landscapes that I had come to know and inhabit. The mining of minerals is emblematized through a luminescent diptych—tapestries with threads that shimmer and shine like a pair of bright sneakers or the glistening mineral of mica found in objects from makeup to western spires and gypsum walls. Surrounding them were metal benches displaying texts, photographs, and minerals, including mica, malachite, and copper. Two videos showed Nkanga with shiny objects and walking through Berlin wearing a malachite crown. I immediately invited her to conceive an exhibition for the Museum of Contemporary Art, Chicago, where I was working at the

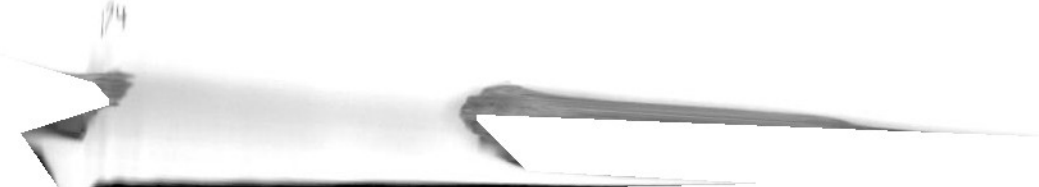

time. We've been collaborating on projects—exhibitions, commissions, vinyl records, and books—ever since. Her drawings paintings, installations, and performances delve into the physical experience of feeling in relation to concepts of "Mother Earth," that most vulnerable of vessels of and for human life.

In 2015, Nkanga transformed her signature breed of performance art for Tate Modern's online-only platform, Performance Room. She presented *Diaoptasia*, a performance for the camera that demanded live editing—something that I had not seen online in an art performance. The artist's body slid between images of barren landscapes situated in front of a green screen that came in and out of focus behind her. Her simple outfit was accentuated by a glistening crown, which she mined and stabbed, unfurling dust and glitter onto her body. For nearly ten minutes, her four-octave voice wove the viewer in and out of space and time, as the backdrop of scorched Earth in Namibia became a crystalline metaphor for the interchangeable destruction of body and land.

Vulnerability is a defining feature in the work of Simeon Barclay—a Black artist raised in Huddersfield, England, and currently based in nearby Leeds. Barclay encodes his emotions within the framework of the grand aspiration of British, or specifically northern English culture and heritage. In 2017, while on a trip from the United States, I wandered around the galleries of Tate Britain, London, and almost found myself falling into Barclay's solo exhibition *The Hero Wears Clay Shoes* (2017), my eyes fixated on the fuzz emanating from a blue box of neon light that wigwagged its finger at me. I quickly summoned from my telephone Barclay's minutely detailed description of the exhibition and his history. Interesting to me, given his seeming heterosexuality, was his fascination with *Vogue* magazine, which he had detailed in the online video accompanying the exhibition as a prime source of inspiration. *Vogue* was part of his paper route and collected while growing up.

Barclay's exhibition stayed with me but receded from the frontal cortex until, upon my return to my adopted home in London, his name began to resurface in my orbit. A retired property developer who volunteered with me for a charity invited me one afternoon to see an unusual storefront, where there was a group exhibition at a newly opened site for the Gateshead-based gallery and foundation, Workplace. Waiting for me on a strip of canal called Reliance Wharf were Barclay and artist-turned-gallerist Miles Thurlow, who was representing him though Workplace, which he cofounded. For more than four hours, Barclay and I talked like excitable teens who had just discovered intimacies and shared histories. We moved to a bar, where we were served unusual new-age mocktails, which we hoped that our onlookers would pay for.

The conversation moved from tailoring to appropriation, from the presentation of masculinity among Black male models and the iconography of Naomi Campbell. I pulled out my iPhone and scrolled through images of Black models and designers while reciting a private anecdote of meeting Virgil Abloh in Chicago—the first Black man to lead an imprint of French luxury fashion house, Louis Vuitton, and only the third in history to lead a French fashion house. I left an hour late for a dinner with a director from Michael Werner Gallery, London, whose brain I had hoped to pick about funding for my forthcoming exhibition in Sharjah.

Barclay invited me to engage him in a public conversation at his first solo exhibition at Thurlow's more centrally located outpost of Workplace in London. Titled *England's Lost Camelot* (2021), the exhibition explored the iconography and myths of nationhood and masculinity surrounding the gallant knight in British folklore. Strewn across the floor were red roses, alluding to the English rose, a symbol of a specifically British ideal of feminine beauty, race, class, and gender. The walls were lined with aluminum plates ensconced in steel frames that incorporated the artist's personal archive—magazine pages gleaned from his paper routes, diary entries, and cartoonish symbols of Black culture—that were expanded and abstracted into amorphous forms that resembled little JPEGs on the desktop of a laptop. Their titles *Clan in Da Front* (2021), *Chips on My Shoulders* (2021), and *King of Cowards* (2021) functioned as pointed poems that spoke to the artist's biography.

Elsewhere, a table mat from the artist's childhood, which featured Black iconographic figures, from Bob Marley to Martin Luther King Jr. and Malcolm X, was digitally rendered into a custom-made rug titled, *A Mystic Voyage (A pantheon of Omissions) for the centre piece of an imaginary drinking hole)* (2021). The image was also recrafted as a sign for an imaginary pub named the Monolith Arms, which was typically British apart from the figures depicted on it. In *Bird Cage* (2021), roses punctured a distressed replica of an amorous love scene between an archetypically virile Black man and a woman of color but of fairer skin.

Two of the most affecting pieces in this presentation were *I am down* and *Miss Jennifer* (both 2021). The first was a large double-image lenticular that, up close, looked as if it were using one of Cory Arcangel's Java applets to disguise a portrait of the artist. Although DIY, the digital silkscreen of illusion and cut and paste was clearly evident. As I pulled back from the image, a Black father reading the paper as his son (the artist) emerged. Two words fade in and out of focus: *peg* and *drift*. *Peg* was a word that I had not heard since my childhood in the 1980s, a slightly pejorative term that was used to describe someone who was small like a clothes peg (also known as a clothespin): a subject who sat in the interstices. Here, this othered outsider is constantly left drifting, attempting to find his place in the world.

In *Miss Jennifer*, Barclay layered a frame within a frame within another frame, digitally manipulating the cover of the aspirational *Country Life* magazine with the symbol of a red rose. It glistens radiantly out of the black background. It is the only oil-on-canvas work by the artist, and the choice of medium is an interesting symbol from an immigrant Black man whose family made their way from Carriacou in the Southeastern Caribbean Sea to Northern England. Oil, the most expensive of paints, has been exchanged by many contemporary artists for the versatility of acrylics, but others have avoided it because of the association it bears with the European Renaissance tradition and the obfuscating art history that it represents. When I interviewed Barclay outside of Workplace on London's Margaret Street in 2021, he told me, "Black migrants come to this country with the fixed idea, or aspiration that everything is attainable to you; all of the tropes of a glorified pop culture . . . until you realize it is absolutely not." When I asked him, "Was this exhibition an attempt to bare your soul?" He responded that he wasn't afraid to speak his truth anymore—a piercing reflection on the silencing act that has crumpled and buried the divergent stories of far too many artists for far too long.

— You and Me and Everyone We Know: Find Me in an Ocean of Images

Trust/Distrust

I am outside Bait Al Makrani, the heritage house in Sharjah, UAE, in 2019 with the British artist Heather Phillipson, who is squatting in the courtyard. Beads of sweat are running down our faces. The artist has responded to the specificity of the site—a pair of long lateral rooms straddling two enclosures made of brick, wood, and coral—by layering burned bread and digitally manipulated wallpaper onto the architecture. Here, there are three spatial orders: the hypersaturated realm of the two differing indoor spaces and the unalloyed quiet of the outside. Scorched earth and charred bread crumbs, multichannel sound, and luminous screens playing videos appropriated from the internet, which have been colored, laid over each other, and manipulated, provide the theatrical setting for her installation *Cyclone Palate Cleanser* (2019) —a meditation on illness and well-being. I became obsessed with Phillipson, because she had cracked the poetry world with subversive encoded language around perfectionism in the age of the internet. In addition, her oversize sculptural combines, which I'd seen in museums from Frankfurt to London and in such venues as the Frieze Art Fair, often sought to give form to characteristically digital features—constellations of emojis unspooled from the basement of the artist's browser and instant messaging applications.

One would not have imagined that a year later, Phillipson's reflections on sick interior spaces would feel so apt. It was near this site that I was to spend the first global lockdown during the COVID-19 pandemic. At this time, I returned to writing what artist Fiona Banner has referred to as my "picture poems"—single-sentence interventions, or short vignettes and lyrics that express severe emotional states: "I FEEL LIKE MY BRAIN IS FALLING OUT OF MY ARSEHOLE" or "CONSTANTLY SPEWING ANXIETY EVERYWHERE." The self-proclamation stemmed from my inability to communicate. People were constantly telling me that I should relax, because "You can't do anything about it." The sense of panic began to inflame a series of preexisting conditions that were near impossible to treat. At the time, I was completing the final page proofs of a book to accompany my show *Art in the Age of Anxiety*, which was yet to open. I found myself too anxious to think about it.

Mind Over Matter

In 2019, Aza Raskin, the developer of "the infinite scroll," speaking through the Center for Humane Technology, the organization he cofounded, drew out the addictive tendencies of technological gestures, drawing correlations between them and the rise in teenage depression.[1] At the time, various reports released on U.S. news revealed that since the proliferation of social media from 2005 to 2017, the moods and lives of young people had been affected in the United States, with a 52 percent rise in major depression among adolescents, and an even steeper rise among young adults of eighteen to twenty-five years of age.[2] Borderline personality disorder (BPD), a psychiatric condition defined by, among other aspects, the concept of emotional dysregulation, is deemed by the UK National Health Service as the most common and recognizable mood/personality disorder.[3] Parents might respond to these diagnostics by hurriedly hiding their offspring's smart devices, but in parallel with these worrying statistics, there has also been a more nuanced and open space online, through online therapy and forums, for the expression of one's psychological disturbances and, equally, of ways to comprehend and enable treatment, which are especially useful in parts of the world where discussions of mental health remain largely stigmatized.

When I was growing up, the term *highly sensitive people* was not part of any lexicon that I knew of. Many days were spent writing on a secondhand typewriter in silence and fear. I was called autistic, mute, withdrawn, ill, hysterical, and more, but never, highly sensitive. Highly sensitive people (HSP) is a category for individuals who lead complex inner lives and who may in some cases be more attuned to aspects of the world around them. This has been increasingly accepted in the western world, along with other forms of *neurodiversity*—a term used to encompass a variety of neurological states. Many organizations, from large tech companies to museums, now host neurodiversity acceptance month. Networked artists, such as Christine Borland, Brody Condon, and the late Harun Farocki, have explored the concepts of immersive states of being and consciousness, with Farocki specifically focused on networked gaming's relationship to post-traumatic stress disorder (PTSD), as evinced in his video series *Serious Games* (2009–10).

The orbit of the internet has certainly served as a propulsive sphere in the sharing of these stories, with organizations, such as the ADHD Foundation and the Brain Charity, posting videos, stories, and accounts on social media and respective websites. Artists and businesses have also used the virtual sphere to galvanize fiscal support for mental health funding and awareness. In March 2021, the World Health Organization helped mobilize renowned artists and a consortium of development agencies to use the auction house Christie's online platform to raise funds in what was dubbed the mirror pandemic.

Still, media engines from the BBC to the *Washington Post* have run articles arguing that technologies make us angrier, dumb, or more emotional. The reality, as social scientist Javier Serrano-Puche suggests,[4] is that emerging technologies, in particular, those on our smartphones, can function as triggers to deep-seated emotional traumas—as examined in the book edited by Sabine Roeser called *Emotions and Risky Technologies* (2010)—a facet also explored in Faroucki's films on gaming, immersion, and PTSD. Although it would seem as flippant to attribute our sadness to a chair as it would be to attribute it to our smartphone, if we include the context—everything around the chair, or in this case, the smartphone—we will probably be more successful at getting to the root.

Let us consider a context from a supposed present. You are about to go into a meeting where you will be making an important pitch. Your team wants this win, and a lot is at stake: reputation, the potential for promotion, as well as financial gain. While waiting in anxious anticipation, sweating in your blazer, the caretaker of your child tries to reach you. You ignore the call and are now consumed with worry. Your notifications are not entirely muted. You see that your online date for this weekend has made a crude, racially charged suggestion over WhatsApp. You are discomfited. You turn your phone on "do not disturb," but your ex-spouse manages to get through the call barrier to let you know that your son is in the hospital. You receive this info from a bot that spells out the voice mail in broken-up textual form. This elicits confusion. Feelings of abandonment abound about an ex, who has yet to sign the divorce papers. Your financial stakes and future are still on the line—something you did not want to be reminded of. You assume your son will be okay until the end of the meeting; you really hope so.

Artist Mahmoud Khaled has explored the intangible space of the phone as a site for negotiating conflict and emotion. In 2013, I commissioned the first iteration of *Do You Have Work Tomorrow* for the online magazine *Ibraaz*, where I was then the senior editor. Here, Khaled instrumentalized the context of the gay geolocative dating application Grindr as a setting through which to describe the context of illicit homosexual desire during the Egyptian Revolution of 2011. It simulated an imagined conversation between two men in a socially conservative country during the tumult and violence that took place between 2011 and 2013. In turn, the work presented the sense of longing and frustration activated by the smartphone's connective functions. The Grindr conversation was subsequently photographed and printed using analog techniques in a dark room. The result—a sprawling wall of unresolved wanting between two people—reminds us of how networked technologies can often delay the confrontation of an impossible situation.

If one considers the broad gamut of emotions that occur in this snapshot alone, it is evident that connectedness can also create forms of emotional exhaustion or instability. Since the second decade of the millennium, cellphones have become a corporeal appendage; they are embedded into the body, a microchip, ballooning into a computer with expansive power and range. However, this is not, as dystopian pundits might suggest, the outcome of corrupt AI but, instead, of ourselves.

What do we do? The eastern concept of mindfulness has now been sanctioned in the western world and has been referenced by many of the leading artists of our time, many of whom also use the internet as a tool or forum for their artwork. Most famously, the legendary Japanese artist Yayoi Kusama has openly discussed her depression and anxiety, living her life in a psychiatric unit in Japan. Her repetitive use of dots in her paintings and installations generates what the artist has noted in several public forums to be a therapeutic process. Of all her works, her popular *Infinity Mirror Rooms* series, such as *Infinity Mirror Room—Aftermath of the Obliteration of Eternity* (2009), reference the obliteration of the ego as invoked in the Buddhist tradition of the Bon Festival. The result creates a meditative trancelike state, intended to disconnect the individual not only from their self but also from the technological sphere. The irony is not lost on the museums and pundits who exhibit and review these works; sometimes viewing the work is limited to as short as a single minute for audience members. This stirred an international debate among critics, with some referring to these artworks as mechanisms to "reignite the selfie"—one of the defining aesthetic forms and digital assets to emerge in the age of the internet.[5]

Eastern philosophies have also affected the work of a younger generation of artists in the millennial age category. In the publication accompanying her exhibition at London's Serpentine North Gallery, the fashion-designer-artist Grace Wales Bonner mentioned that she wanted to bring meditation and spirituality to the galleries. A month earlier, the Serpentine Gallery's original venue, a ten-minute walk to the south, was taken over by "a collective healing offering" fashioned by the artist Tabita Rezaire. I had only known Rezaire for her intricate videos of appropriated and animated forms. Now it seemed that the speculative and soothing qualities of her installation work were being made manifest through a form of Kemetic yoga, an ancient Egyptian practice with links to the African science of yoga, and its potential to expand upon concepts of energy in the age of "the networked sciences."

The deployment of these spaces has increasingly become part of common parlance and social-media bragging.[6] Pursuing such activity is perceived as part of being upwardly mobile—a much better brag than of one's psychological woes. Now, many Fortune 500 companies, especially ones associated with lifestyle, offer meditation breaks for employees. Data Bridge Market Research presented findings in 2021 that reveal app-based meditation and mindfulness practices to have grown exponentially, with anticipation that the meditation market, largely fueled by digital aids, will grow to more than nine billion U.S. dollars by 2027.[7]

During the pandemic, some artists candidly spoke of their isolation online, while others told of their trips on psilocybin, among other psychedelics. My talks with artists who had become ill with COVID-19 revealed a recurring grievance: institutions failed to live up to their promise to support them, and the ones who carried on working with them expected more work for fewer resources and less capital. Phillipson—or H. P. as I refer to her affectionately—and I developed a habit of leaving each other twenty-minute-long voice messages, which we have attempted to whittle down over time. When I questioned her about working in this difficult time, she said, "Far too many of the people with whom we work assume that making art is about creating a product—that it's purely business. They seem to have forgotten that being an artist isn't merely a job; it's where you bank all of your emotional energies."[8] A multidisciplinary visual artist and poet, she is arguably now one of the UK's most recognizable and critically acclaimed young artists and yet chooses, for the time being, to operate independently of the commercial gallery system, relying primarily on making newly commissioned artworks to sustain her livelihood.

The Age of Emotion

With this context in mind, we must come to understand that we are living in an age of emotion, which can be defined through three features:

— **Chaos of Visuality**, i.e., an overabundance of images, without context.

— **Political Incoherence**, i.e., constant mistrust of government and fake news.

— **Resistance**, i.e., a willingness to admit the limits of being human.

The first two characteristics are what lead to mental instability and exhaustion, both perceived and genuine. They fuel the perceived need to constantly produce, while the politically incoherent context tells one not to produce at all. Resistance is also two-forked. Resistance can become an admission of boundaries. Some perceive it as a need to resist everything, which further fuels division and dereliction, anger, and angst, as well as a confluence of confusions. Technology's ubiquity is a funnel with two ends. We can choose to use it to progress the conversation or burn out sight unseen.

Rising temperatures have already affected the globe in devastating ways. Some people in the United States, myself among them, often reference the California wildfires—their potential to decimate homes and entire communities while wreaking billions of dollars in damages. In July and August 2021, more than two hundred wildfires burned 656 square miles (1,700 km^2) of forest around the Mediterranean region. At the time of writing in 2021, India's Simlipal National Park, Asia's second-largest biosphere reserve, has been on fire since February 11, with no clear end in sight. In June 2021, the taiga forests in Siberia burst into flames due to unprecedented heat, with reports of the first incidence of wildfire smoke making its way to the North Pole.

Meanwhile, as remote working has proliferated across the globe, the need for more stable, expedient broadband has increased. In 2016, Trevor Paglen produced a series of large-scale photographs of undersea internet cables, which are tapped and used for surveillance by government-run entities. Studies of the cables' impact on marine life are limited, but the growing internet infrastructure poses planetary impact and societal risks. The growing necessity for cloud computing and virtual telecasting has multiplied the number of data centers and data farms, which are often economic generators for local economies, which means that they are increasingly developing in economically challenged nations, such as the Philippines and India. They are increasingly conceived as megacampuses, such as China Mobile base in Hong Kong, measuring 7.7 million square feet (c.715,300 m^2), or Western UK's CWL1 near Cardiff, which occupies 1.49 million square feet (c.138,400 m^2). The energy use and potential carbon emissions produced by such vast entities are of great concern. With the surge in internet usage during the COVID-19 pandemic, political pundits argued that for such projects to continue to develop, the private companies opening them would need to become more socially responsible. The irony of such an ethical suggestion was evident when Amazon Web Services, the most successful and fastest-evolving cloud storage provider in the world, asserted that it would commit itself to climate neutrality. Project Earth—the skin that holds society within its fold—becomes a speculative notion of an increasingly uncertain future that is, in many respects, in the hands of a few wealthy corporate moguls.

In 2019, Julian Oliver collaborated with Tega Brain and Bengt Sjölén to devise *Asunder* using custom software and satellite imagery. A critical reflection on the scientific implementation of AI in examining the problems of the environment, the work interrogates what it would look like if we were to assume a neutral condition, where the needs of humans and the environment were nonhierarchically determined through a form of machine learning. As we scan from overhead images of Dubai's iconic Palm Island through to California's Silicon Valley, the absurdity of the solutions proposed by AI transpire into unlivable conditions, creating scenarios that could be as impossible as the results of climate change itself. The assumption that technology can save us all is shown to be a techno-utopian fantasy.

Eva & Franco Mattes have fueled debates around ecologies with their concepts of distributed labor, violence, and aesthetics that are developed online. The experience of these political subjects is altered in their work through an interplay of the uncanny and the sublime. The first time I ventured into the duo's Brooklyn studio in 2016, after having presented their work in exhibitions on several occasions, I was perplexed by the various forms of architecture oscillating in space. The duo was eager for me to experience an installation called *BEFNOED* (2014–ongoing), an acronym for "by everyone, for no one, every day." I lay beneath two large screens mounted over me like a pyramid and watched performative acts that ranged from the obscene to the surreal—someone with a fish strapped to his body, a South Asian man pouring water over his crotch in the front seat of a car, a person licking a car. A comment on the evolving nature of distributed labor pioneered by outlets, such as Amazon Mechanical Turk, *BEFNOED* is also a reflection on the varied economies that form online and the seeming absurdities that they foster, whether on a platform, such as OnlyFans, or in this case, through obscure interfaces. The artists provide instructions to the workers in the videos, who are hired through crowd-sourced platforms and are anonymous; they perform acts without knowing their purpose, and their images are dispersed across obscure networks, creating a media archaeology of services and platforms that exist outside of the western media loop. As a person of color, I could not help but notice the varied ethnic contexts from which the performers emerged.

Joana Hadjithomas and Khalil Joreige, an artistic and filmmaking duo, worked with me for years on a project about spamming and scamming. The pair collected spam and fraudulent emails for decades, curious about what it would mean to visualize and stage their anonymous authors—to give their skin its authentic pigment, their voice its presence, and their history the power to resonate. The result was a traveling exhibition called *I Must First Apologize* . . . and an accompanying book titled *The Rumors of the World* (2015). The exhibition began its journey in 2014 at Villa Arson, Nice, France, before traveling to HOME, the MIT List Visual Arts Center, and elsewhere. Through globular sculptural maps, 3-D renderings of the body, video portraits, and infinite scrolls, the duo revealed the world of spamming to be a kind of war between white privileged bodies and the Black and brown bodies of the developing world.

In 2013, before Instagram became the megasales pitch platform that it would eventually become for influencers, Constant Dullaart noted the potential social capital that social-media followers could provide for artists and curators. In a desire to foster a tongue-in-cheek social-equalizing exercise, the artist used his commission money from Paris's Jeu de Paume museum to acquire 2.5 million followers—one assumes they were mostly bots—and distributed them among a personal selection of art world accounts. Some friends were a touch bruised to find out that they were swirling in a constructed web of perceived importance, but most of the artists and curators kept mum on their feelings. After all, just as in day-to-day life, there is nothing less chic than discussing one's status.

In 2018, while in the Netherlands, I happened upon Upstream Gallery in Amsterdam. On view were a series of Dullaart's flags—a marvelous tessellation glistening against the painted white sheen of the building's ornate architecture. They were each composed of hundreds of SIM cards, which can be used to create fictional social-media accounts and are often purchased by aspirational influencers. His multiform paintings adopted military symbolism in their repeating phonetic graphic design. Collectively, the pieces in the show constituted what the interpretive text dubbed to be "an army against social-media affluence" and the fake standards used in validating journalistic news stories by relying on the constructed society of one's social-media following.

The corporate underpinnings of everyday technologies have long been a cause of concern, and parody, for the duo Young-Hae Chang Heavy Industries, based primarily in Seoul, South Korea. I met the pair with Kamal Ackarie—a mile-a-minute Duracell Bunny–artist and producer whom I met at Forma, a leading London-based commissioning agency for art that interfaces with art and technology. Young-Hae Chang and Marc Voge were showcasing a new work at the Sheffield Documentary Film Festival in the UK, which Ackarie had commissioned: *My Life as a Bloody Sheffield Butter Knife* (2014). I knew the artists for their playful text-based vignettes, but there was something much more aggressive here. Words—some of them poems, some slogans—pulsed with a vigorous sense of ire and instability. Seoul and Sheffield coalesced to reveal a narrative of immigration and the sense of in betweenness that it fosters within those who must traverse physical borders. Voge, a poet, may be responsible for interlacing the duo's stories with freewheeling references from Beckett to Borges. In the video animation *THE ART OF SLEEP* (2006), poetry is presented as a form of call-and-response, with the reader, juxtaposed against

(K0REAN F0R *MARRIED* *W0MAN*)

Young-Hae Chang Heavy Industries, *SAMSUNG (TANGO VERSION)*, 2009
—Digital video, 3 min. 52 sec.

a backbeat that resembles something pulled from a Foley sound-effects library; the viewer is left discomfited.

Unsettling you and me and everyone we know is a core characteristic of their work. Their online videos prod at everything from our intellectual capacities to our penchant for rampant consumerism. The three of us were standing in a tight elevator vestibule in London with Kamal Ackarie when one of them informed me in a serious tone of voice, "There is no God, but there is Samsung." My nervous laughter gave way to an hour of storytelling about corporate governance and its control of the imagination. Apparently, my Samsung TV was part of a network of complicity and circular ownership for a company that at the time of writing constituted the second-largest technology firm in the world by revenue. The pair's tango with Samsung, made manifest in numerous works, seeks to demystify the utopic potential of technology, baring its all-encompassing control of society.

The aesthetics of brand identity can also be found equally rooted in Pamela Rosenkranz's manifold explorations into the human pursuit of self-improvement. Entering a brightly lit New York gallery in the Lower East Side that belonged to Miguel Abreu, I came across a room full of FIJI Water bottles lined meticulously across the floor with various colored substances inside. It was 2009 and Rosenkranz had just launched her ongoing project *Firm Being* (2009–ongoing), an investigation into the various strategies that producers of mineral water use in their marketing to create an aspirational lifestyle brand for a white, middle-class consumer. The bottles were filled with silicone tinted to match the "white" skin tones found in makeup and film prosthetics. The result was a lampoon of the human quest for self-optimization. The plastic bottles themselves are metaphors for the sacrifices we are willing to make—even the existence of our planet—in favor of our own desires.

These various shades of whiteness have over the years become a point of fixation for Rosenkranz. At the 2015 Venice Biennale, the artist flooded the Swiss Pavilion with this silicone flesh in a riposte to her native Switzerland's status as a neutral territory. Adapting these color schematics into painting, light, and shadow, Rosenkranz has dialogued with the white-masculine dominance of such figures as the French artist Yves Klein (1928–1962), extrapolating his investigations into the monochrome with colors produced by running water. This work has evolved into biological explorations of the full spectrum of sensorial effects, from scent to aural dissonance. If art holds a mirror up to society, then Pamela Rosenkranz holds up the entire planetary sensorium to our skin, noses, and eyes.

Stop Looking at Me Like I'm the Future

In 1998, the Nobel Prize–winning author Toni Morrison was interviewed by Charlie Rose, who at the time was the host of a talk show with a cachet that came from asking celebrities, authors, actors, and politicians the difficult questions. Perhaps like many children who have attended English-speaking schools in various countries and cultures, my deepest written expressions came when I was given the chance to study Morrison and Maya Angelou—they were the only Black authors on my school's curriculum. However, it was not until this interview that I was able to make sense of the act and purpose of the work that I would come to do in my life. With precise eloquence, the author explained the monolithic culture of the white gaze and how consumption is geared toward an ethnocentrism that supposes that Black people must neglect their own culture or adopt hybrid roles that lead to their invisibility. One of the ideas discussed was the necessity of code-switching—the practice of alternating between two or more languages, forms of speech, or cultural understanding. In 2019, the *Harvard Business Review* published an article arguing that code-switching was a form of survival for ethnic-minority communities, because to ascend through the ranks alongside white peers, one must blend into the norms of society.[9] In 2012, a video of President Barack Obama went viral. It illustrated the different way Obama greeted a white assistant basketball coach and the Black NBA player Kevin Durant in a locker room. The immediate behavioral shift, with the sense of proximity and intimacy determined by race, put code-switching into the visual field of discussion.

Inversely, social media was rife with vehement criticism in relation to Kamala Harris's visual attestations to her Blackness. Joe Biden's running mate—now the highest-ranking woman of color in U.S. political history—was chastised for sporting, on the cover of *Vogue* magazine, the iconic Chuck Converse sneaker, named after the Black basketball player Chuck Taylor. The criticism was that her use of a popular, affordable basketball shoe as attire, on the campaign trail and in a fashion magazine while vice president-elect, was a prop to solidify her Blackness. Others criticized the move as a means to secure corporate allegiance with Converse and its parent company, Nike. Harris spent nearly five minutes "clearing this up" during U.S. morning television—her white husband jumping in to confirm that she had always worn Chucks for their comfort. The chatter on social media regarding her aesthetic veracity did not relent immediately.

In 2018, comedian Jordan Peele won an Oscar for best original screenplay for his box-office smash *Get Out*, a horror-comedy that critiqued Black assimilation into an evil white society. It is now the subject of its own online class about Black horror.[10] In 2018, comedian Boots Riley's feature film *Sorry to Bother You* received acclaim for its portrayal of a Black man who puts on a white voice to perform better in the workplace. The filmmaker dubbed his work of magical realism an exploration of the false consciousness that emerges from new capitalism.

In the digital realm, presenteeism—the illusion of always being at work despite illness or other personal circumstance—has become de rigueur. In 2016, the collective known as DIS (established 2010)—Lauren Boyle, Solomon Chase, Marco Roso, and David Toro—pooled together these shared societal anxieties in their inspired curatorial effort for the 9th Berlin Biennale, *The Present in Drag* (2016). I began noticing the group's hostile takeover through magazine advertisements and billboards of people of color and disability. A young misanthrope orders, "Stop looking at me like I'm the future"; a disabled woman in a wheelchair asks, "Why should fascists have fun?"; a Black mother with her child, face to camera, exclaims, "Why bring a child into this world? What a bourgeois question!"

The first video promotional video for the Berlin Biennial that I came across (devised by the group under the direction of artist Tilman Hornig) featured a perfectly toned male as if unspooled from a generic Grindr profile; he was wearing BDSM gear, dancing alone while texting. His correspondence appears on screen: "Imagine an institution in ruin"; "Imagine a radical Marxist theoretician cashing in a check for a speaking engagement"; "Now use them to diagnose our collective predicament." As one notices that his phone is a sheet of glass—a white mirror—he declares the end of the contemporary. *The Present in Drag* was a pointed critique of an art world that

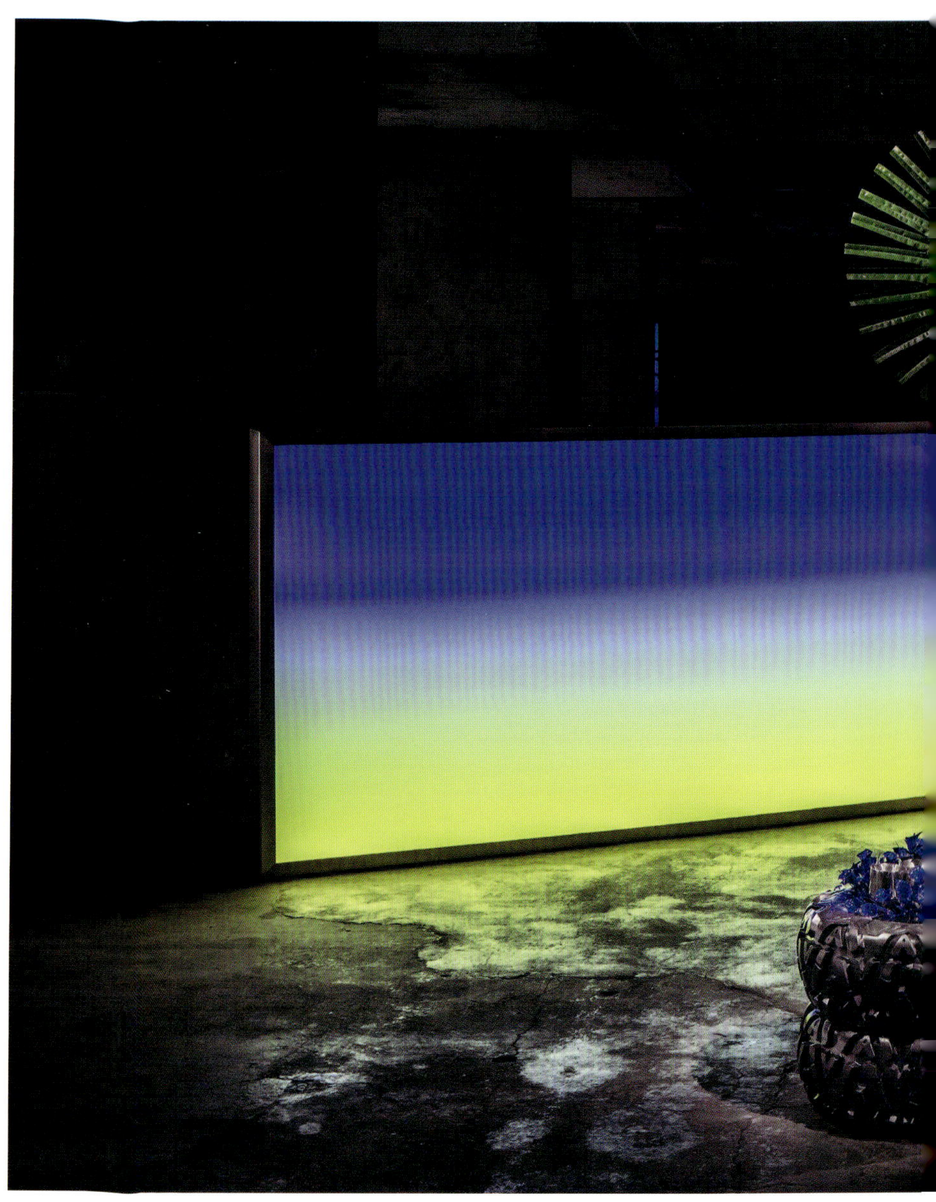

Guan Xiao, *Sunrise*, 2015 —Car tires, artificial plants, exhaust pipes, light box, installation: c.189 × 62¼ × 15¾ in. (c.480 × 158 × 40 cm); light box: c.59 × 157½ × 15¾ in. (c.150 × 400 × 40 cm); object in the back: c.47¼ × 29½ × 105⅞ in. (c.120 × 75 × 269 cm); object in the front: c.23⅝ × 23⅝ × 30¼ in. (c.60 × 60 × 77 cm); edition of 3 + 2 AP

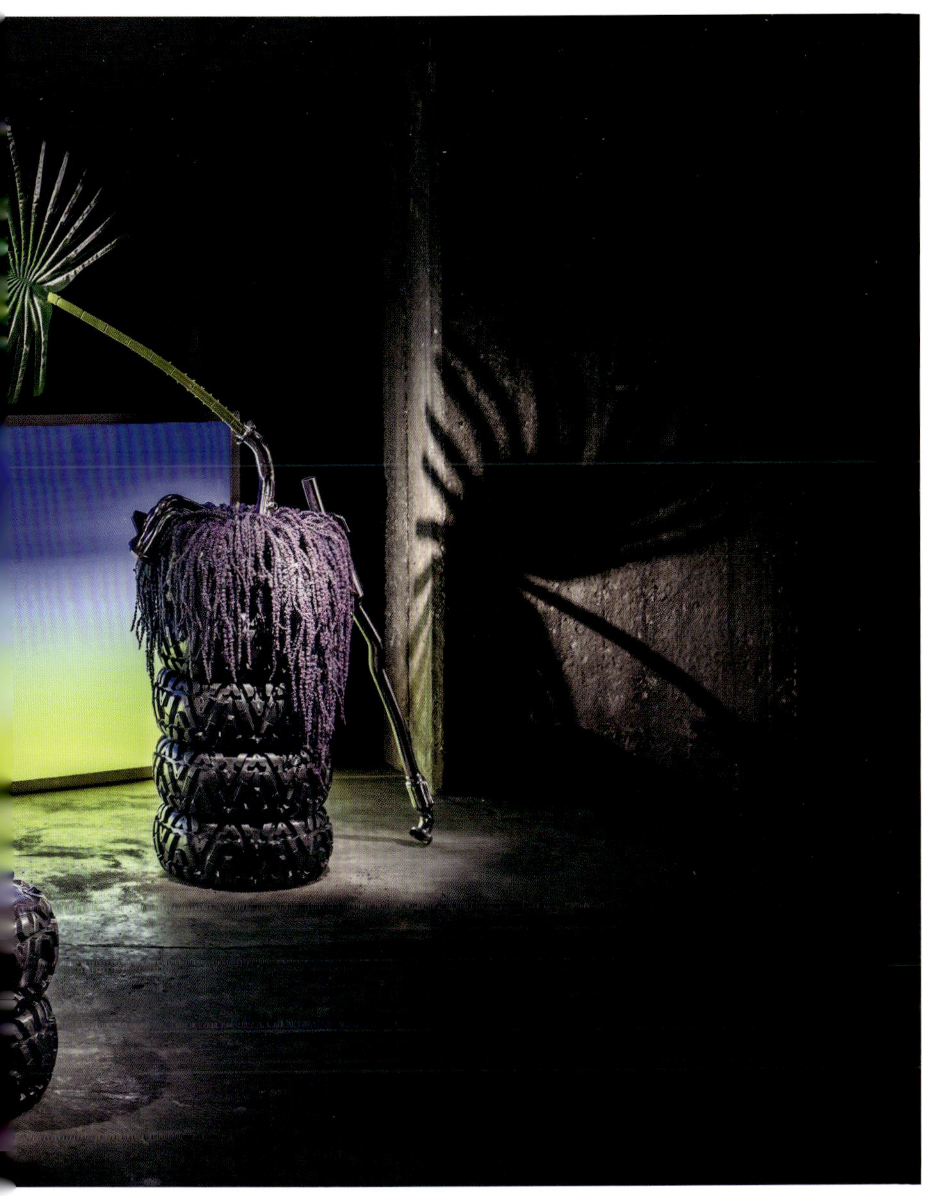

was increasingly fueled by consumerism and tokenism. “This is a format . . . where speaking and selling collapse,” reads one of the Biennial’s slogans.

The framing of the exhibition was an artwork in and of itself, but there was also a selection of artists’ work. Guan Xiao’s installations, such as *Sunrise* (2015), congealed assemblages from flat tires and fake flowers, reflecting her interest in unfolding “the endless global supply of products and images,” as noted in the installation’s accompanying text. Also on view was work by the collective åyr, which was founded in 2014 by Fabrizio Ballabio, Alessandro Bava, Luis Ortega Govela, and Octave Perrault, who conceived of a dematerialized wall, which they composed digitally. Studies of the Berlin Wall from the 1970s by Rem Koolhaas were the inspiration for a habitat influenced by the circular imagery of corporate architecture.

DISimages = Our Images

I met the four current members of the DIS collective in a dimly lit café in New York's Lower East Side sometime about 2013 or 2014. At that time, they were completing a residency at the New Museum’s art and technology incubator, NEW INC. This was the cheapest and most cheerful place that I could find close to their workspace. We had been mutual fans for several years. I would correspond with a generic DIS email address, never knowing with whom I was engaging unless one of the group’s members signed the email. I spent the first half hour of our conversation deciphering who was who, who had written to me about what, and who was dating whom until the natural shape of time took us on to the pressing issues of contemporary image culture. We bounced between the necessity for revised gender pronouns, being of mixed race, and of various other forms of inequity.

I was stupefied by the way the media had portrayed the collective—they were often described as apathetic, ironic, and unserious. They were anything but. The difference between them and me was that I was angry and helpless, but they had chosen to use the lexicon of contemporary visual culture to point a finger back at the invisible institutions of power that stimulate shaming around bodies, gender, and race. They encouraged me to make my way to MoMA, where they had a work in the exhibition *Ocean of Images: New Photography 2015.* As I entered the galleries, a rhythmic electronic beat led me to an integrated set of LED monitors screening the face of Conchita Wurst, an Austrian singer and drag performer who had become an internet sensation after winning the 2014 Eurovision Song Contest. An invisible wind machine flutters her flowing hair in stark juxtaposition to her bearded face. Camera lights blinker on the screen, but the star remains,

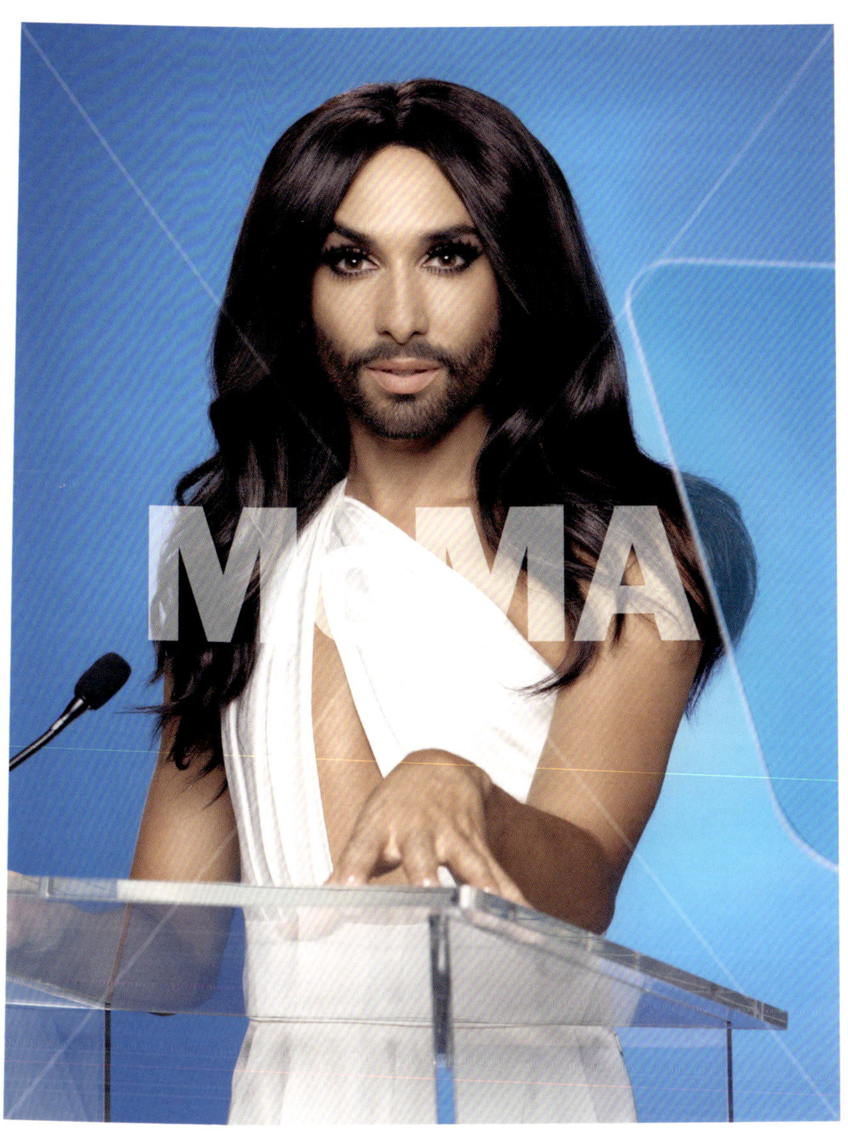

DIS, *Positive Ambiguity (beard, lectern, teleprompter, wind machine, confidence)*, 2015 —Single-channel HD video, 2 min. 45 sec.

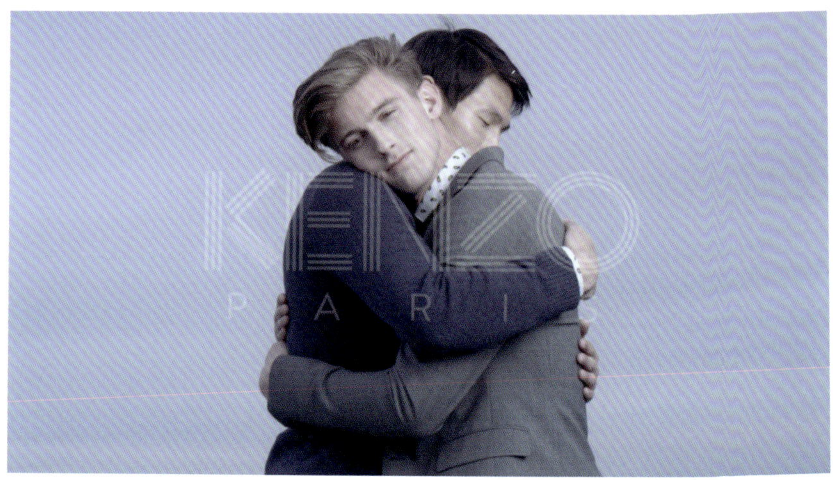

DIS, *Watermarked (KENZO)*, 2012 —Single-channel HD video, 1 min. 48 sec.

effortlessly rotating, singing in perfect tune. A reflection on the aesthetics of fame and the possibilities of transmuting traditionally heteronormative spaces, *Positive Ambiguity (beard, lectern, teleprompter, wind machine, confidence)* (2015), also sought to consider the corporate aesthetics of stock imagery. Using MoMA's logo in the center of the screen—the first time that it had ever been used as a watermark—DIS sought to interrogate the dichotomy of operating in spaces that offer certain forms of representation, but which also hold the possibility of flattening a given subject's agency.

The issues posed within this work had also featured in the collective's iconic series *DISimages*, which I first chanced upon in 2011. Setting up a photo library, they invited artists from every race, orientation, and gender to conceive of their own alternative stock image culture, arguing that stock images perpetuate stereotypes around identity. One of the pictures to gain the most traction included a watermark of the clothes label Kenzo logo across it. The group also presented this as a video work, *Watermarked (KENZO)* (2012), in which a perfectly manicured blond man with a blown-over hairdo embraces a pale Asian man, whose face is often eclipsed from view, in a prolonged dance of queer love and desire.

DIS operate in a multitude of zones and were once long-time publishers of an online magazine that gave voice to a generation of young artists. Today, the collective operates as curators and commissioners of an online art channel of new work and has ventured into retail, performance, and event-based culture, as well as all their interstices. "Image Life," as DIS refers to it, remains the driving impetus behind these endeavors. In 2016, London's Project Native Informant gallery was transformed by some of DIS's most pointed art on the life of the "post-internet image." A centerpiece was *Image Life (Related by Contour)* (2016), a wall-mounted digital print recalling a stock image and featuring a smiling, multiethnic family wearing what resembles contour makeup. A soundtrack composed by artist Lizzie Fitch plays as the print gradually splits in two, sliding apart to reveal a TV monitor, where the image of the mixed-race family is animated in slow motion, their teeth glistening white as their smiles broaden. An advertisement for multicultural success? Perhaps not, because the grins become grimaces before reversing into blank expressions.

The pictures composed by DIS have fostered a vocabulary for new forms of appropriation and reanimation that are devised through a collaborative spirit with a web of artists of their generation and beyond. Within the frame of DIS's world emerges the context for Katja Novitskova's large-scale 3-D cutouts of animal life in space; Guan Xiao's postapocalyptic speculations of an industrial future; and GCC's (established 2013) nationalistic aesthetic as pastiche. In parallel are Anne de Vries's experiments with the aesthetics of the mobile phone, the birth of hybrid art-brand agencies, such as K-HOLE (established 2011), as well as the collaborative spirit of fashion brands, such as Telfar and Hood By Air. The latter, which prides itself on its social conscience and its group ethic, has transformed BDSM into couture formal wear and streetwear. The intersection of these various poles of culture belongs to a community that materialized at the end of the first decade of the new millennium and into the second one—fostering solidarity of critical consciousness.

Can We Move Beyond These Walls?

When I first began my practice in the late 1990s, initially tinkering with making art and film, then staging exhibitions, the places I found art were in branded national museums or venues that were sanctioned by regional city councils. I had no concept of the potential for DIY spaces, commercial galleries, the public sphere, or private foundations to fill in the cultural gaps neglected by these nonprofits. From the late 1990s to the early years of the millennium, museums took center stage with the advent of what some pundits called the Bilbao effect. Referring to Frank Gehry's Guggenheim Museum in the Basque region of Spain, the term suggested that regional centers could become urban metropolises by erecting cultural centers with showy architectures designed by starchitects. The most successful of these have been franchises of existing brands, such as Centre Pompidou-Metz, France, and Louvre Abu Dhabi, UAE.

As in corporate culture, museums have grown with new extensions, restaurants, and merchandising opportunities to create a broader offer to sustain themselves. Tate Modern's extension, which opened in June 2016, is but one example. Enter a pandemic, shutter the doors, and suddenly without visitors, one is having to foot a much larger bill. SFMOMA, which opened its extension in May 2016, has spent the better part of 2021 in the headlines for slicing and dicing its many innovative programs and keeping most of its staff from returning to work full time (even when many smaller museums have bounced back post-COVID), with the institution's CEO eventually resigning. This continued propensity for growth, which one can see in such projects as the Guggenheim Abu Dhabi, UAE (scheduled to open in 2026), and the Box in Plymouth, England (opened in 2020), can be paralleled to any form of speculative hype, such as stock shares and prices, which are notoriously entrenched in the dot-com boom and crash of the late 1990s and early millennium. Where to from here?

Crossovers Involve Flip-Flops

When curator and art dealer Jeffrey Deitch took over as director and CEO at the Museum of Contemporary Art (MOCA), Los Angeles, one word stuck out to me from his various press interviews: nimble. When he was appointed in 2010, it was considered almost sacrilegious for an art dealer to head up a museum; the worlds were perceived as mutually exclusive, even though those of us who worked inside the belly of the beast were all too aware of the necessary support afforded to museums by commercial galleries, who contribute financially to their annual programs, sync curators up with collectors who lend works and sponsor exhibitions, and who often cohost the all-important opening dinners and galas. Deitch, with his penchant for both outsider and international art, felt like an exciting proposition to me. Would he break down the walls and expose what was hidden within the seams?

Deitch made no mistake that his signature imprimatur, a distinct brand of Pop tethered to networked and digital culture, would be present from the start. *Art in the Streets* (2011), an exhibition of graffiti and street art, was hailed as one of the most attended shows in the museum's history. Actor James Franco, who at the time was exploring performance art, filmed an episode of (or an intervention into) *General Hospital* at the museum's former outpost the Pacific Design Center in West Hollywood, California, with artist Kalup Linzy. This was followed by the U.S. premiere of *Any Ever* (2007–10) by enfant terrible of video art Ryan Trecartin, produced in collaboration

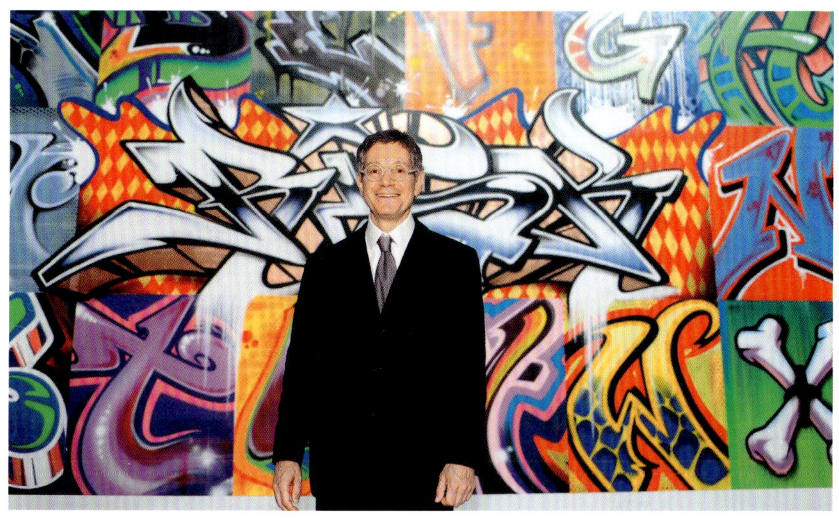

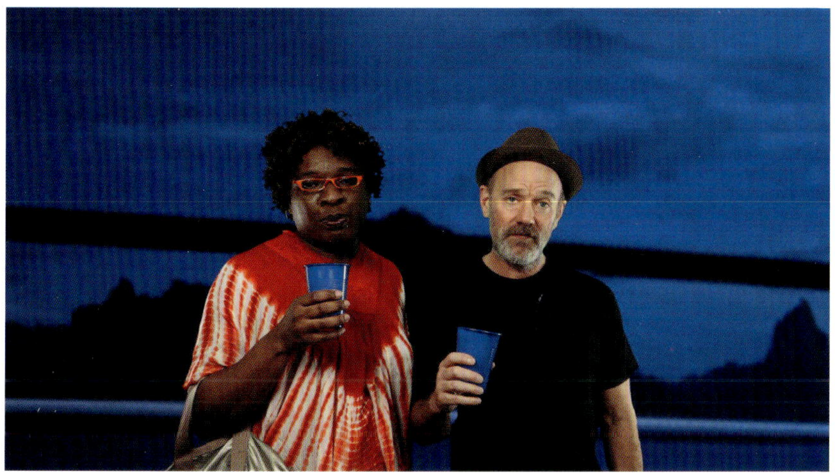

Jeffrey Deitch attends the Art in the Streets opening at MOCA, Los Angeles, 2011

Kalup Linzy, *Conversations Wit De Churen X: One Life To Heal*, 2013
__Video, 6 min. 54 sec.

with Lizzie Fitch and presented at the former MOCA venue at the Pacific Design Center. A major part of the installation was acquired by MOCA with support from Deitch himself. In 2012, MOCAtv, the first museum YouTube channel, launched. With its high-quality production values and insights, the ambitious platform set the pace for museums everywhere to realize that YouTube, as opposed to their own websites, was the quickest way to gain traction with broader audiences.

Since this time, we have seen the Los Angeles County Museum of Art (LACMA)—the largest museum on the West Coast of the United States—collaborate with Snapchat to commission augmented reality experiences for visitors. London's Tate Modern has collaborated with HTC on virtual reality, while museums from the Museum of Neon Art in Glendale, California, to the monolithic State Hermitage Museum in Saint Petersburg, Russia, have been using TikTok to disseminate campaigns and content. Since the end of Deitch's tenure at MOCA in 2013, seismic shifts have come into play through the emergence of platforms, including Avant Arte, which seeks to make high-quality art democratically available to all; DeviantArt, which claims to be one of the largest online communities for creatives; and African Digital Art, which has soared as an unparalleled digital archive.

In March 2021, artist and graphic designer Mike Winkelmann, known professionally as Beeple, broke a record at Christie's, selling something many of us had never heard of—a nonfungible token (NFT)—for a cryptocurrency amount equivalent at the time to sixty-nine million U.S. dollars. This digital asset, which we'll come back to in the "The Shape of the Future" chapter, fueled speculation and further innovation. Platforms, such as Foundation, Zora, and OpenSea, galvanized content from around the globe, while auction houses, such as Sotheby's, Christie's, and Phillips, continued to develop specialty expertise in this area.

In the same way that perhaps no one imagined social-media platforms, such as Instagram and Twitter, could be mobilized as primary political tools for Donald Trump's first election campaign or social justice as elucidated in the Black Lives Matter movement, one can also argue that museums and art institutions have been slow to embrace the possibilities of collaborating across and into the digital sphere, instrumentalizing its built-in audience as well as its myriad content creators. In a world where one can rent or try out artwork through the new online application Gertrude, we should get off the high horse and work through new proposals to secure the future of our shared culture.

If memes are a mode of communicating, if they are expressions of creativity that hold gravitas with audiences, they too must be archived for their historical significance. The NFT market has already evolved to fill in this space. Deitch's nimble model revealed that being responsive to current trends in your own distinctive fashion is a ticket to sustenance and renewal. One can invigorate the ideas of arts administrators, using the internet to speak of and to share a culture that bridges the gaps. Nimble programming can pay dividends and there are examples all around us. When large museums were closed during the pandemic, empty galleries or unconventional spaces could offer other functions, for example, shooting a movie. With the decrease in global tourism and the constant threat of travel being curtailed, could museums look to smaller institutions, such as the art societies of Germany known as kunstvereins, which rely on a membership model to fund and govern their running costs, as opposed to membership models geared toward the exclusivity of a seat in a soulless members' room?

Undoubtedly, digital programs can become core projects and programs as opposed to symbolic gestures, acts of transference, or stand-ins. If history has revealed anything about museums and their behavior, it is that they invest in technological infrastructure when it is a necessity for them, or if there is specific funding to do so. When this is gone, with it disappears all the effort that went into it, including, in many cases, the artworks that were commissioned for the digital sphere. But there is the potential to genuinely build community online. Community can be fostered in many fashions. I host online reading groups with members of my team—a simple gesture. In essence, we have lived in a shared culture since the advent of the second millennium. Cultural platforms exist to give voice not only to artists but to those who engage with them.

One of the first artworks to build community with a wide group of people that I was made aware of was Miranda July and Harrell Fletcher's *Learning to Love You More* (2002–9), a crowd-sourced project that directly engaged eight thousand contributors. On a simple website, users found themselves tasked with various assignments: "Take a photograph under your bed and post it"; "Record the sound that is keeping you awake and post it"; "Draw the news and post it." The act of sharing seemingly mundane tasks that encompass and traverse a global expanse of people became almost addictive to me. It formed an archive of the daily discomforts of collective life before Instagram even existed.

The formative era of internet art, often called *net.art*, was acutely attuned to dynamic interplay with the audience. An example is JODI (established 1994), a collective of Joan Heemskerk and Dirk Paesmans, who trained in Silicon Valley before venturing into coding and software development in the realm of visual art. As the group's biography professes, their most famous artwork is their website wwwwwwwww.jodi.org. The landing page features an elaborate array of green HTML code evoking an endless

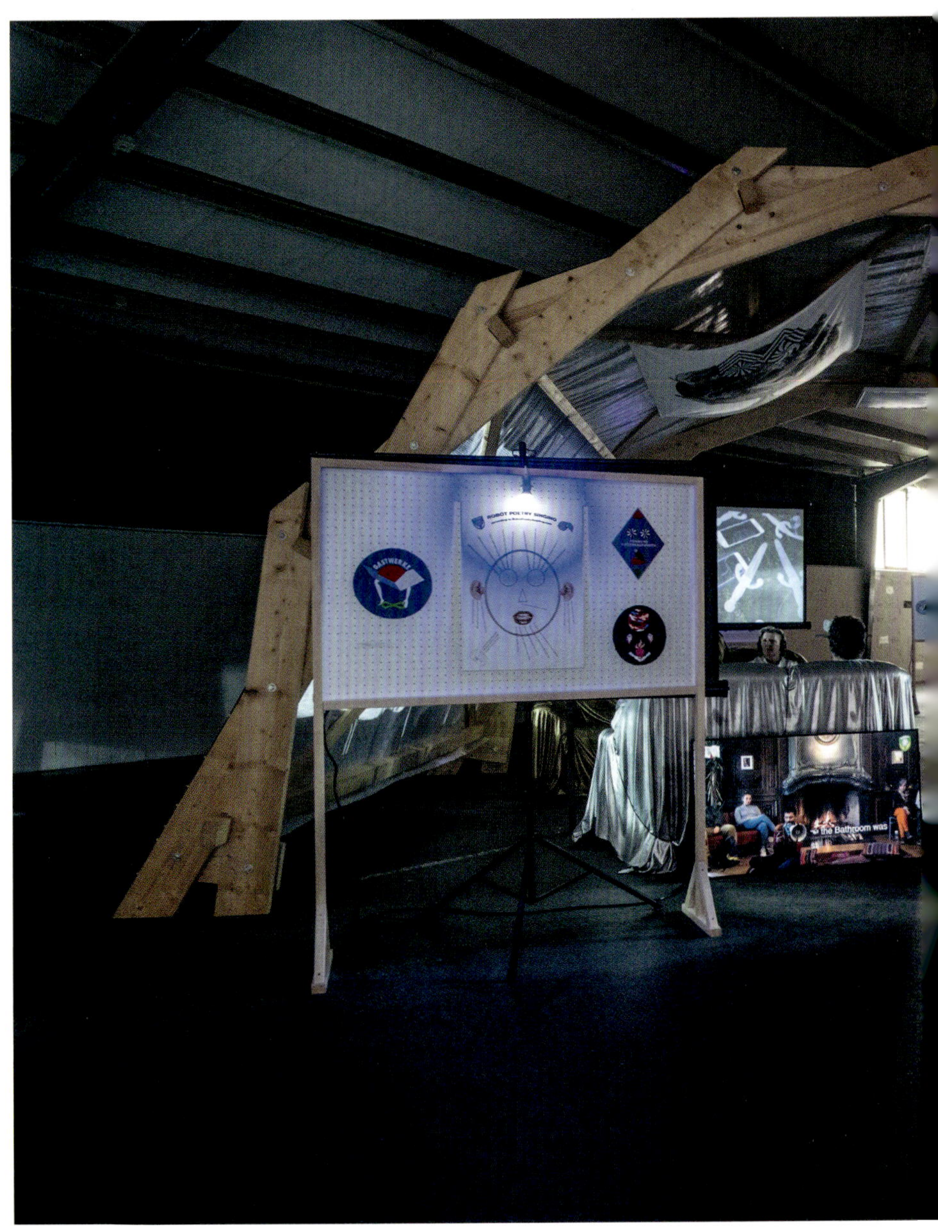

Angelo Plessas, *The Eternal Internet Brotherhood/Sisterhood 6*, 2017
__Multimedia installation. Installation view: documenta (14), Kassel, Germany, 2017

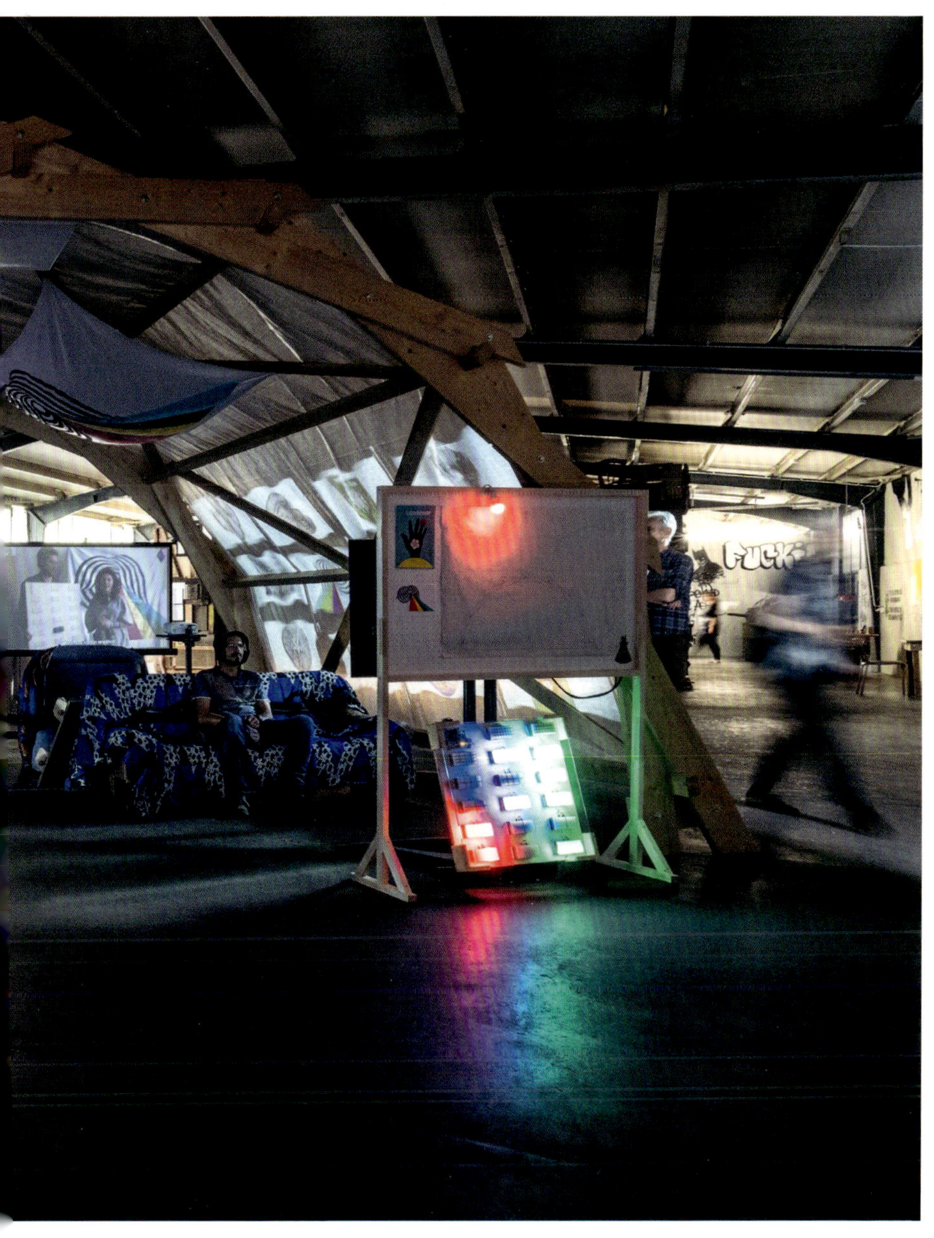

abstraction. Click the "view" function and render the "source" visible and it transpires that it is, in fact, the rough diagrammatic schema of an atomic bomb. It reveals the layered construction of coding: what can be concealed within it. But equally, it is a glaring reminder that the age of the internet is also the atomic age, one where nuclear power has been misused as an instrument of hard power relations between global cultures—the constant threat of obliteration poised right in front of us.

A pioneer of 1990s web-based art and various forms of installation art is Olia Lialina, whose work *My Boyfriend Came Back from the War* (1996) creates a user-generated film that is determined by the viewer's clicks. Angelo Plessas, in contrast, has sought to form a community online that transverses into physical encounters. In the performance project *Monument to Internet Hookups* (2009–ongoing), an open-ended triangular sculpture —one assumes, an homage to the LGBTQ+ use of the pink triangle symbol—takes a ride on a Pride float through Athens, celebrating online sexual encounters and hookups. Most monumental is Plessas's *The Eternal Internet Brotherhood/Sisterhood* (2012–17), a regular congregation of cultural practitioners in remote places, detached from connectivity. In these sites, conversations around post-technological life emerged over six different retreats. Islands, jungles, and the other meeting locations each became sites of interface, negotiating bordered territory, a metaphor that expresses the synchronicity between our lived and virtual selves.

Digital life enabled by the internet is not a futuristic fad. We are now discussing the greatest mass medium in all of history. The tightrope of life will seem even more narrow to those who choose not to diversify and react to the possibilities inherently embedded within the architecture of our present. If arts leaders embody a spirit of collaboration across fields and sectors, one could potentially build and fuel museum projects in the manner one would a start-up, creating generative accelerators that will be relevant to the future. An artwork that exemplifies this is RaFia Santana's *#PAYBLACKTIME* (2016–ongoing), a transference system set up by the artist that combined donations from "white money" to purchase meals for "Black and Brown folx across the North Americas." She has disseminated six thousand U.S. dollars in meals thus far, and those are just the efforts of one spirited human.

Heather Phillipson and COVID-19 Do Not Equate to the New Normal

As the months inched forward, giving an excruciating new definition to slow, I began working toward freedom. Airports started to resume their flights; I planned to make my breezy exit to London. I was delighted to see

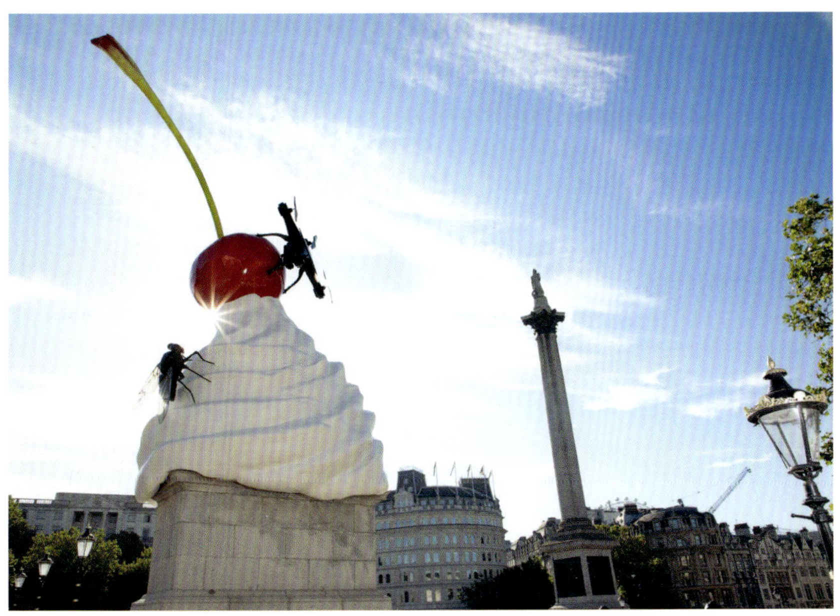

Heather Phillipson, *THE END*, 2016 _Installation view: Fourth Plinth, Trafalgar Square, London, 2020

on the BBC website that H. P.'s installation *THE END* (2016) was about to go up on the Fourth Plinth in Trafalgar Square—arguably the most significant and discernible place for public art in the world. It was July.

I recall seeing pictures of H. P. wearing a shimmering blue face mask with the mayor of London in an empty square—proud that an artist with whom I had worked and cherished was unveiling such an astounding sculpture and being honored, even if there was yet to be an audience. Her winning proposal, a saucy mound of whipped cream standing at thirty-one feet (9.4 m) with a delicious cherry on top, is the tallest Fourth Plinth sculpture to date. A sculpted fly scales the mound, while a drone has crashed into the cherry from out of nowhere, emitting a hissing sound. It acted as a constant surveillance device, producing an online livestream for individuals anywhere to keep an eye on a part of the world that was once referred to as the most surveilled place on Earth.[11]

I returned to London weeks after the unveiling. H. P. and I sat on opposing sofas, at least eight feet (2.4 m) apart. We did not hug or touch. We discussed *THE END*, but there was a hint of reticence in her voice. The work had been proposed to the Fourth Plinth Commissioning Group back in 2016. The surveillance aspect embodied by the drone was a metaphor for the panopticon of digital-image culture, but just as much, a nod to the heavily surveilled Trafalgar Square, which has been the site of political protests since the early 1960s. The sculpture was an object intended to survey the surveilling state apparatus itself, recalling the multitude of bodies that had occupied this site—a record of a record—meta! More than mere amusement fodder, it was meta all the time. But as Great Britain was just about to enter another lockdown, *THE END* took on an entirely different form and purpose. It became a document of emptiness, fear, illness, and of others and their illness, pointing us away from the seeming necessity of an overpopulated public sphere.

On first appearance, many works by H. P. may appear whimsical in form. They require a lot of looking and looking again (always a second take) until eventually one is filled with uncontrollable emotions. She uses fanciful aesthetics to invite the spectator into her inner world. Here, she can be found critically questioning how to live within the parameters of the present.

It was peak summer 2021, but being London, there was far from the necessary vitamin-inducing sunshine one might expect of the season. We hurriedly walked in circles around London Fields—our mutual meeting points for pacing, monologuing, and debriefing—to keep warm. I spent the first fifteen minutes blubbering lengthy explanations as to why I had not yet seen H. P.'s monumental new commission—one of the most esteemed in the UK, the Tate Britain Duveen Commission. The project had been delayed for over a year due, of course, to the pandemic, so the gestation period for H. P.'s ideas had become protracted and contorted into what we called a form of mutant time of forced reflection and illness.

H. P. has said that her experience of making art is "jamming together bits of stuff that [she's] hijacked from all over the place" with "no fixed starting point, only accumulation."[12] She expresses the mutability of objects in themselves as a defining characteristic in her artwork. Her sculptures, often produced with materials that have "lived a past life," bring with them multiple visual cues and meanings that reconfigure the way that people look at art. A used cardboard box becomes a site for a drawing and a poem. It may conjure a pocket-size poetry paperback or make you consider what was in the Amazon packaging that it was initially used for. Does the ashen bread on the walls of a gallery in Sharjah evoke the sensorial memory of burned toast, or does it leave you with the queasiness one feels when staring at a material that will soon fester and rot?

H. P. would not give me any clues in regards to what I should expect at Tate Britain. I ventured there the next day, somewhat dutifully—I had been avoiding the visit, because expansive venues with unknown numbers of people were spaces that I had been fearing to tread. This is why I and others have felt that the digital sphere is all the more enticing a universe. I arrived at Tate dehydrated and worn out after a doctor's appointment, where I was informed that my digital life was not compatible with my body's needs. A sedentary lifestyle was not acceptable for this diabetic: I required regular exercise, to eat more and better, and eventually find a means toward a rebalancing of certain hormones. This felt like an apt beginning. Scaling Tate Britain would be my prescribed exercise.

A visual overload of people smacked me in the face. I diverted into the bookstore, which was so silent I could hear the cashier breathing. Where were the usual customers hiding? Slowly, I inched to the entrance of the Duveen Galleries, a tubular expanse that engulfs you with its hollow echo and its irrefutable columns. I searched for the music in my ears but couldn't hear anything but an echo. H. P. is a polymath—a poet, composer, and music fiend who has said that she considers "her whole body as a set of ears." Consistently, our conversations lead to explorations of musical structure and composition, and she has analyzed the pitch and timbre of my voice. How the visitor will engage with and experience her immersive installations, and how to offer an affective space to feel and decode emotions, is of constant consideration in her work.

I veered past the dripping hand sanitizer stations and politely stood behind two wheelchair users who seemed mesmerized at the entrance to *RUPTURE NO 1: blowtorching the bitten peach* (2021). I listened to their hushed questions: "Is that an alien?" I swiftly moved behind the security guard, where I was confronted by a mélange of eyes disembodied from mutant creatures and reemboweled into new ones. I scurried across the length of the Duveen Galleries, passing a giant papier-mâché teddy bear anchored to the vaulted ceilings. Gas canisters dangled from the ceiling of a makeshift shed of corrugated iron. The sound of the canisters gently swooshing back and forth formed a tranquil orchestra that was serene but suggestive of entangled decay and estrangement. Images of protest—marches against inequity and hatred mutating into the violent outbreak that had occupied the headlines in that year—perched on the edges of my thoughts. Should we torch this prison, in the name of rock 'n' roll? Or does the toxic gas in this bunker suggest something more than gloominess, perhaps the impossibility of progress at a time of societal freefall?

Sheaths of painted sky lined the colossal walls, fashioning an illusory softness, a brittle reality that H. P. has called a "pre-post historic environment."[13] Unlike other work that I had seen by her, this one resisted the necessity for coherence. Its making, a result of the stop-start of the time in which we lived, had clearly fueled a bold antagonism. Instead of using this

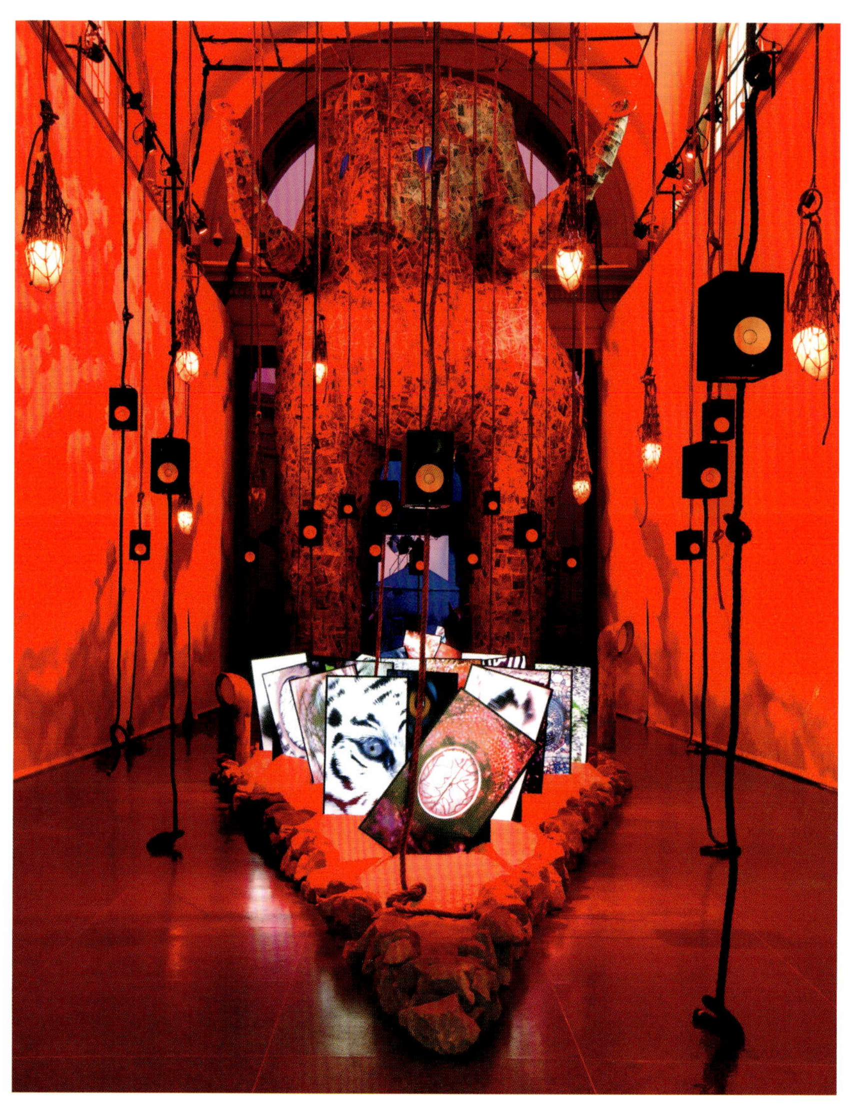

Heather Phillipson, *RUPTURE NO 1: blowtorching the bitten peach*, 2021
—Video and sculptural installation. Installation view: Duveen Galleries, Tate Britain, London, 2021

commission to present soft and tactile forms of colorful whimsy, H. P. had entrenched her installation with glistening sheaths of metallic paper that resembled residues of artworks, bodies, and other desires—presented here as if at their grave site. The lighting drenched me in purple-blues, magenta, and reddish pinks, but the tones were muted. This was not a space of ebullience or radiance but of constant exile from one's own body, which in my case was jolting with discomfort and melancholy. The buckled missiles sandwiched in buckets of concrete seemed to be stand-ins for the death of the human subject as much as they alluded to the accelerating forms of distributed warfare to come. The seductively concealed animation of a peach, projected behind the gallery's wall measuring three hundred feet (91.4 m), was an apt metaphor for the things we believe we should and could have. It is a ripe object of seduction removed from our hands without us even knowing it.

Heather Phillipson's installation at Tate Britain was the pinnacle of a form of internet art. The scoured objects sourced and conceived into an endless emotional storybook were developed using distinct techniques that mirror the infinite scroll of the World Wide Web and the searching troll who rummages through the contours of the crusty web. H. P.'s epic installation presented objects found in everyday life alongside others purchased online and accentuated by appropriated, edited, and looped video screens—animated eyes peered at us—a titular digital aesthetic wholly crafted out of the chaotic world where the real and virtual are intertwined.

To say that the predicaments of COVID-19 fostered a masterpiece would be to join in a game of media spin. Instead, personal trauma in all its forms has made many significant and moving artworks. Francisco Goya's (1746–1828) *The Disasters of War* (1810–20) is a series of such works, while Félix González-Torres used the distorted narrative around the AIDS pandemic to craft public acts of engagement that have outlived his person. Artwork can serve as a reminder of how the wounds of history sediment. In *RUPTURE NO 1: blowtorching the bitten peach,* we are able to see a world that has hardened. Underneath it, one assumes that the personal experiences of COVID-19 have left H. P. eager to plunge into a hard-bitten piece of existence and breathe new life into it. There was nothing normal here and, if anyone believes that the art world has concocted a new normal, then they are or most certainly were deluded.

Curated Desire, Curating Bodies: Everywhere, All the Time

Early February: "Be my Valentine," said the tall, pale Irishman. The svelte, strawberry blond went down on one knee in an act of chivalry. It was 2001, just over a year after the male dating site Gaydar had launched. The genteel fellow was the first and only person whom I would meet through the website. By February 14, shivering under thin threads, I waited for our next rendezvous outside London's Notting Hill underground station, circling between the subway exits for an hour. Finally, assuming that he'd been hit by a bus, I returned to my shared empty house midevening, the silence piercing, the absence of life suffocating me. I logged onto the site in search of reprieve. There he was. I asked, "What happened? I thought you were dead." "Who are you?" came the response.

The sense of intimacy—and alienation—that has emerged since the advent of online dating forums has been the subject of much discussion. From Tinder to Hinge, desire is now reduced to a checklist of predetermined factors, aspirational shopping lists of elusive amorous companions. On the other side of this are websites, such as Chatrandom, which became a point of obsession for the painter Celia Hempton. In her series, *Chat Random* (2014–ongoing), the artist logs onto the website, where she encounters anonymous strangers whom she seeks to engage as models for her portraits. Her online meetings—with men in search of physical connection, including trans women—wheel the artist around the contours of the globe. Through an informal invitation, Hempton initiates her process, painting the portrait of each subject on a canvas, often no larger than the size of a laptop screen. The result is a performative suite of works most often formed of gestural brushstrokes. Once the man in question clicks on the screen to the next person, the artist's process grinds to a halt. The finished work is an intimate snapshot into an unambiguous moment that could only be embodied in the act of engaging through a networked computer.

I first installed a suite of these paintings in *Electronic Superhighway (2016–1966)* at the Whitechapel Gallery, London. Clustered on a table, they began to resemble open windows on a computer screen. I chose to install them as if they were multiplying chat boxes, desirous conversations accumulating into an archive of wanton intimacies. These were experiences suspended in time, never to be completely realized. Despite the alienation of the mysterious platform Chatrandom, Hempton's paintings summon different emotions. They are studies of vulnerability, intimacy detailed by a stranger, and the abnormalities of bodies in places near and far.

The subject of online dating rooms and applications has occupied the visual field for nearly two decades. At the 2011 Venice Biennale, artist Frances Stark became the subject of much discussion for her video work, *My Best Thing* (2011). Here, sensual webcam conversations revolving around the subject of "cam sex" with Italian strangers were collected into an unassuming animation, embodying a conception of a virtual Adam and Eve. The topic of interactive romance has also been the subject of myriad fictive

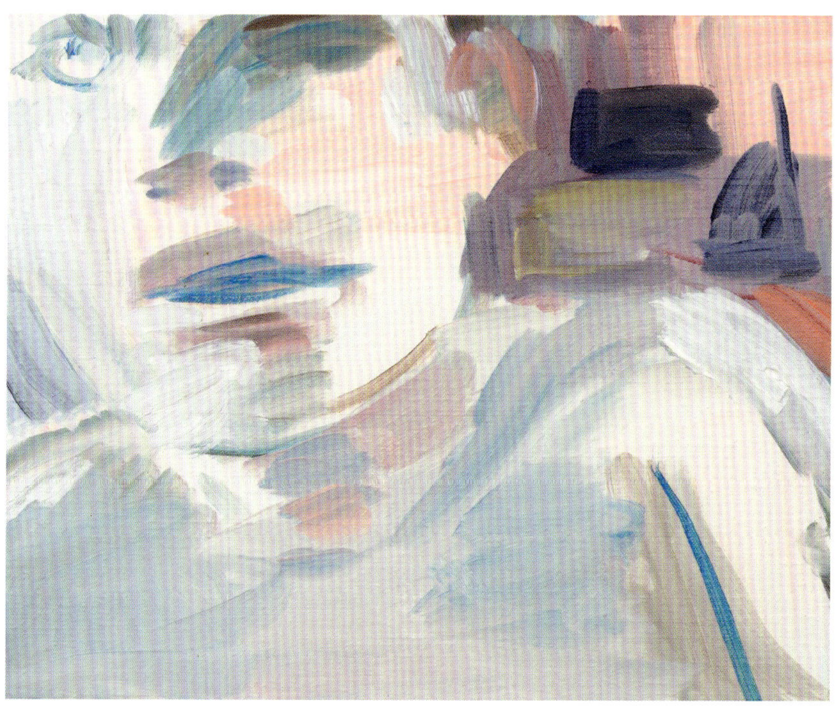

Celia Hempton, *Misha, Odessa, Ukraine, 8th July 2014,* 2014
—Oil on canvas, 9⅞ × 11¾ in. (25 × 30 cm)

interventions. In 2008, I came across Ann Hirsch's *Scandalishious* (2008–9), an eighteen-month performance on YouTube where the artist assumed the persona of Caroline, a self-aware college freshman whose sexualized dancing and video blogs attracted an interactive cohort who created responsive videos and commentary. The work revealed how satire could animate a world of minor celebrity—Andy Warhol's fifteen minutes of fame stretched out over months.

The most well-known example of such performative acts is Amalia Ulman's *Excellences & Perfections* (2014). A post on Instagram from April of that year began the project, in which Ulman took on the role of a fictional character with her own narrative. Her persona was consumed with a desire for physical augmentation and obsessed with extreme makeover culture. By the final post of the project on September 19, 2014, she had attracted 88,906 followers. Whether directly pointed against the Kim Kardashians of the world or not, the sardonic performance generated forms of feedback similar to those that might be directed at such a reality TV star. Aspirational messages from devoted followers gave way to abusive judgments, produced from nothing more than the selfies posted online. To answer the question posed by art historian W. J. T. Mitchell's book *What Do Pictures Want?* (2005), pictures want to be kissed. The image, as Ulman reveals, creates its own self-contained world, which summons and reveals the expectations of real-world society. Insecurity, chauvinism, and sexism are rife in the digital sphere, concealed behind the made-up names of internet users.

I was enthralled by how these female artists fashioned alternative routes that existed against the linear narratives of online dating and the manufactured image production that it engenders in the visual sphere. I exhibited these works, while also searching for male perspectives, whether cis male or otherwise. Braving the icy streets of Berlin in 2018, I met up with queer artist Andrew Holmquist. I was eager to catch up with him about the newfound life he had fashioned in Berlin, having moved there from Chicago. Speaking in angsty sound bites, the artist expressed a deep-seated frustration with the archetypal nature of gay male representation. We discussed the prototypes that had emerged from the male dating apps Grindr and Scruff—the tribal affinities, the sexualized notion of visual representation, which had to be made manifest through tiny square boxes on a smartphone. Holmquist's frustration was manifesting in his gestural, abstract action paintings. One of these forays was *Fuckboy* (2018), which featured an intertwined cornucopia of bodies, each holding a cellphone up in the inevitable and essential act of self-capture.

Three years later, Holmquist and I sit in his car waiting for my immigration appointment at a center in downtown Los Angeles, to which city he has relocated with his partner. He tells me that *Fuckboy* was about a kind of "new toxic masculinity," a form of longing constructed out of digital artifice. The accumulating bodies within his colorful canvas simultaneously represent a loss of the individual in favor of a construction of identity that is manicured to the contours of instantaneous capitalist desire. I pondered the artist's words as I sat spinning my wedding ring—an emblem of a relationship suspended between life and death.

On a studio visit with Laurie Simmons in Connecticut in 2017, I spent my idle time in the kitchen, gazing out over the green expanse. Her two studio managers darted about, fulfilling tasks. One of them, the artist Mary Simpson, sat down with me over a late lunch. She caught me in a melancholic mood, articulating incongruous emotions and making my piercing insecurities visible. Simpson had attended graduate school at Columbia University's prestigious painting program with my friend and neighbor, the Chicago artist Paul Heyer. This affinity brought the walls down. Swiftly,

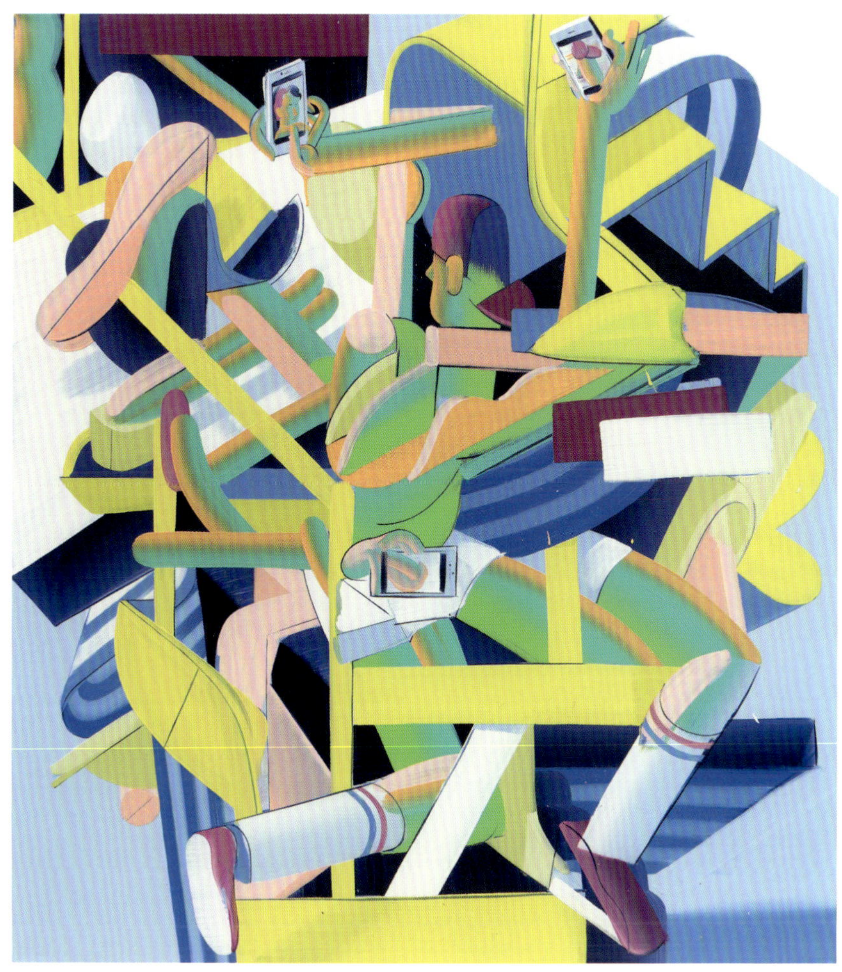

Andrew Holmquist, *Fuckboy*, 2018 __Oil on canvas, 59 × 51 in. (149.9 × 129.5 cm)

I found myself overpronouncing my words like never before: my attempts at transitioning, my fear of further alienation, of being rejected by a specific community, took center stage in our conversation. Simpson's art explores themes of separation from the self and other. Growing up in Alaska amidst a thorny familial situation and a queer father left her with probing questions of her own about how we see ourselves and the extent to which the mechanics of the digital have contorted our bodies so that we only manifest through the lens of others.

Upstairs, Simmons was preparing to run me through the works in her photography series, *How We See* (2015–ongoing), which had premiered at the Jewish Museum a couple of years earlier. Against saturated backdrops stand what the artist has dubbed doll girls—a reference to a look-alike syndrome generated by an idealized image culture, from the high-school portrait to the model headshot to the Facebook selfie. Their eyes are shut, but their lids are painted with phantasmagoric eyes so that they resemble cyborg figures in an alternative landscape removed from reality. I felt that this fabricated sense of identity was one of celebration and adulation, but it was also a satirical reflection on the performative musings in the vein of Ann Hirsch and Amalia Ulman.

As I stared at the life-size images, I became subsumed, disappearing into their worlds, only to stand back and catch my breath, realizing the illusion. Looking at these pictures extends beyond the subject and object to involve the viewer, who ascends into an almost psychedelic state of consciousness. Perhaps it is the fictional gaze constructed by such artists as Laurie Simmons—a gaze that is as adaptive as it is critical—that holds the potential to enable us to locate, not only our bodies but equally, our sense of self and that which it so deeply desires.

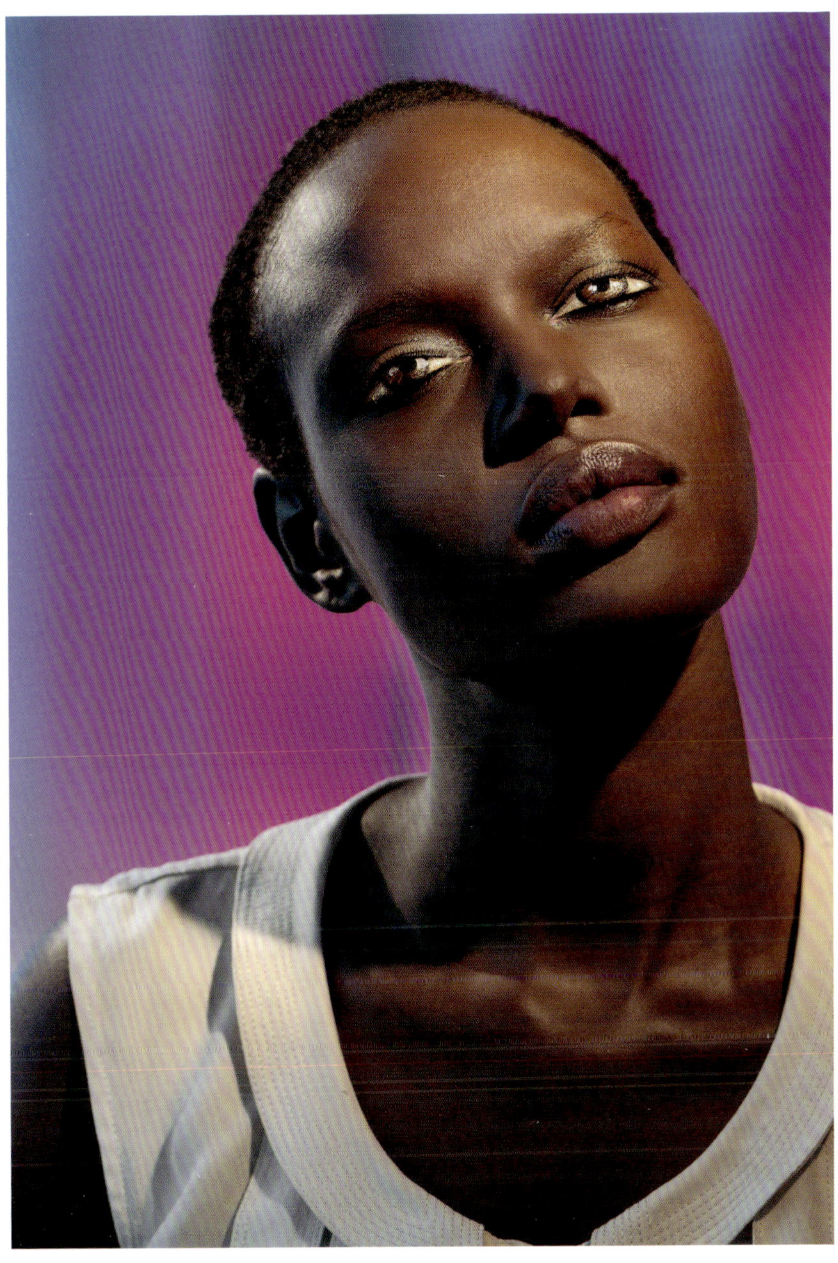

Laurie Simmons, *How We See/Ajak (Violet)*, 2015 _Pigment print, framed: 71⅛ × 49⅛ × 2 in. (180.7 × 124.8 × 5.1 cm)

The Possibilities of a Digital Culture

A Culture Jam

Over the last twenty years, both the mainstream media and more sophisticated solidarity movements, such as Decolonize This Place, W.A.G.E., and Strike MoMA, to name but three campaigns of different scale and makeup in New York, have sought to expose the conflicting interests of museum trustees, such as the former Whitney vice chairman Warren B. Kanders and his connections to weapons manufacturing. They have also attempted to secure remuneration standards for artists and cultural workers, arguing that merely exhibiting in a museum, offering free content in return for cultural capital, continues to create sites of exclusion.

Much of this activist focus has gained public momentum through internet forums and mass social-media platforms, including email news blasts, such as the art-focused electronic newsletter e-flux. The spaces one can use to explore the machinations of the contemporary museum allow for immediate responses as well as more detailed discussion. One form of protest is known as *culture jamming*: the tactic of using the language of consumerism against itself. Artworks by the likes of Barbara Kruger might first come to mind, but for my generation, more pervasive are such figures as the Yes Men, who in 1999 famously set up gwbush.com, a spoof website that made visible the duplicities in George W. Bush's presidential election campaign. Visit the site today and you might find an animated gif of the ex-leader of the free world picking his nose or videos interrogating his sobriety.

I also recall seeing a show at the Jeu de Paume in Paris in 2005, where Fluxus-inspired artist G. H. Hovagimyan collaborated with Peter Sinclair on an evolving project that began as *A SoapOpera for Laptops/iMacs* (1997–2005). The computers, which sat in a makeshift domestic setting, were connected to radio-controlled cars that became animated performers. At the time, I believed the four computers on chairs were a metaphor for the first four university computers to be connected to each other, which formed the basis of the internet as we know it. For *A SoapOpera for iMacs* (2005), more than anything, I was struck by the Apple brand of the iMac—its ascent in the world as a desired object to be consumed and owned by a generation of freethinking Gen Xers and early millennials. Did we believe that these devices presented a kind of embodiment—a notion of self, whether class or profession? For me, it proposed an apparatus that was an aesthetic form for creativity.

As we inched toward the second millennium, the concept that machines could fix humans felt even more real. When pop star Cher's single "Believe" became a worldwide hit in 1998, it made audible something we may previously have not noticed nor heard: a cyborg's voice. Auto-Tune,

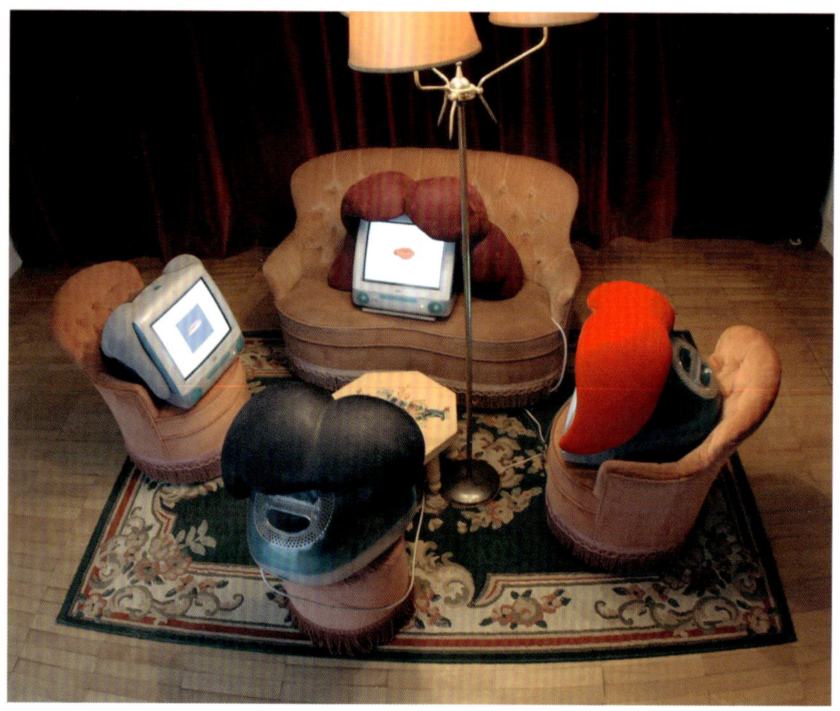

Peter Sinclair and G. H. Hovagimyan, *A SoapOpera for iMacs*, 2005
—Installation view: Burlesques Contemporains, Jeu de Paume, Paris, 2005

which was developed in 1997 to correct vocal pitch, was laid bare here as a recurring over-the-top motif in a cylindrical loop. Its potential to make the human voice sound like a vocoder has led to an explosion in popularity. Musicians have been ridiculed and acclaimed for deploying it, but its pervasive function is everywhere in the songs of T-Pain (who has been widely ridiculed for his overuse of the technique), Kanye West, Billie Eilish, and Bon Iver. As these tracks stream from mobile devices through Bluetooth speakers and are disseminated globally, a question looms: where does the human end and the machine begin?

Randomness

The artist and musician Brian Eno may perhaps be best known among techies for composing the Microsoft Windows 95 start-up sound. This somehow passed me by, as did his years as a successful musician with the British band Roxy Music. I became acquainted with his work while studying artist John Cage's popularization of the concept of aleatoric music—a form of composition where a part of the music is left to chance. Eno, who was a student of the pioneering Roy Ascott at Ipswich College of Art, emerged in the realm of art in the 1960s, becoming recognized for his *Permutational Drawings* in the same decade. These graphic scores reveal potentially infinite possibilities for nonlinear visual representation. At the time, Eno professed that they evolved from his interest in the concept and capacities of randomness—the causal act, which holds the potential to completely shift the form, meaning, or experience of a work of art.

These possibilities came to bear in a metaverse of the artist's own making titled *77 Million Paintings* (2006). Having introduced the term *generative music* into the popular lexicon, Eno was equally occupied with the realm of generative, algorithmically produced art. The work *77 Million Paintings* sought to explore the prospective variations that could be simulated by a piece of computer programming when the artist inputted 296 of his original image-based artworks. The result is a cornucopia of optical and chromatic references, which interrogate the seemingly arbitrary nature by and through which machines can interpret data and see the world. Concurrently, the work creates a framework for considering the genesis of concepts, such as machine vision, and how humans can choose to manipulate the delineations of such objects. If we are to consider the realm of the present as one of structured data, we must surely conclude that the output is dictated not by the computer but by whoever knows the evolving languages through which these machines speak.

Information

Can one exhibition of art change the arc of history? A show that arguably did just that was *Information*, held at MoMA in 1970. Curated by Kynaston McShine, once MoMA's chief curator of painting and sculpture, it has become a legend. This is substantiated by such works as John Giorno's *Dial-A-Poem* (1968), which invited people to call a phone number to listen to poetry and is claimed to have been of concern to the FBI. Hans Haacke's work *MoMA Poll* (1970), inquiring about the public's feelings regarding the museum's political connections, has been credited with altering the course of civic funding. Reflecting on the fiftieth anniversary of the exhibition, art historian Lucy Lippard attributes much of its historical weight to the venue itself.[1] As Paola Antonelli, the museum's senior curator of architecture and design noted, “when you do something at MoMA, the world watches.”[2] The exhibition, which many argue introduced conceptual art to the masses and paved the way for a form of artistic practice referred to as institutional critique, is perhaps more significant, articulated, and lauded now than it was when its doors were open.

Institutions are able to define or, indeed, defy the very histories upon which they were built. The way to achieve this is by deploying forms of cultural production that have evolved from new networks of thought and practice. Curators make crucial decisions about how audiences see the world. They can choose to submit to the nature of a present that is rapidly accelerating or to focus on a proposition or possibility enabled by artists. From a twenty-first-century vantage point, one could suggest to museum curators that despite the obsession with the new, artistic impulses and public references expand beyond the confines of what one might conceive as traditional artworks. For example, one could argue that archiving memes, data sets, and other reflective barometers of present history is a duty that museums should consider undertaking. Hierarchies of significance within this sphere are complicated due to the volume of such content, but it is for this implicit reason that multiple publics instill trust in major public and private institutions of art and culture. Indexing the fleeting and ephemeral aesthetic gestures, performances, and digital artifacts of the twenty-first century is a shared responsibility that can collectively be held for people to return to with the perspective of time and reflection.

Stories of Obsession with Lizzie Fitch and Ryan Trecartin

Obsessions can manifest as hauntings, insecurities, or probing interests. For many, myself included, these have increasingly become material. On Instagram’s search account function, I have recently begun to be presented with images of immaculately manicured feet. I am not sure if this has to do with the fact that I once posted information about where to acquire reasonably priced shoes, or because I have frequently grumbled of foot pain to my peers, or that my first ever job was selling shoes. Or, indeed, that I clicked on a single image and accidentally liked a picture of my friend’s feet in the frame of a picture.

Pedicured feet, protruding bulges, tight clothing, and seminude draped bodies of cis-gendered men from across the globe occupy the screen of my phone. The figures in question are supposedly everyday individuals—a dentist from Spain, a graduate student from one of the Nordic countries, and any number of other professions and locations. If you click on their accounts, the volume of their followers might suggest otherwise—some individuals have more than a million. Whether these followers are paid for influencers or bots or not is beyond importance. An idealized culture is presented as the preserve of personalities who supposedly exist outside the bounds of celebrity culture. Am I a fool? These tastemakers who exist online with their meticulously enlisted product placements advertise consumer goods and services from antiaging creams to weight-loss supplements. In many cases, these activities can earn them a robust living. The fact that I halted work on this chapter to receive my first pedicure should come as no surprise. The economy of desire fuels an economy of want and, in turn, action.

The early video works of Ryan Trecartin were developed with collaborator Lizzie Fitch. Both millennials, born in 1981, they met at art school in Providence, Rhode Island. Their first major collaboration was *A Family Finds Entertainment* (2004), a work scripted and directed by Trecartin for his thesis project that starred both artists. The result is a forty-plus-minute movie, as Trecartin refers to his video art pieces, that revolves around a party scene where the central character hides in a bathroom in a fit of panic, dealing with a jumble of distorted thoughts and trembling anxieties that are self-documented, perhaps on phones among other devices. The resonances with dissociative identity disorder (DID) or schizophrenia and its effects are not necessarily intentional but are by-products of a cultural examination of language and the layered ways in which humans consume information. Here, one is witness to the kaleidoscopic nature of phonology and communication, desire and aspiration, as it is funneled into the depths of our subconscious.

To parse out where Trecartin's authorship ends and Fitch's begins is a seemingly impossible task. *A Family Finds Entertainment*, like much of the art that emerged from the pair, is as the artists have expressed, deterministically nonhierarchical. Although most of the movies pre-2016 were "scripted, FX'd, and directed" by Trecartin, they also consistently involved a coterie of creative collaborators clustered in an orbit that the artists have argued seeks to flip the traditional director-actor relationship in favor of a fluid and responsive form of making art.[3] Following this project, the maxim, "video killed the radio star" was no longer antiquated. Fitch and Trecartin had resuscitated a field of practice they deemed to be sculptural theater—a form of expanded cinema where the quotidian and the hyperreal collide in virtuoso acts of dramaturgy.

Consumed with delirium at these videos, which I first encountered online on viewing platforms, such as UbuWeb and YouTube, where the artists consciously chose to release their work as it was produced in a shift away from traditional modes of installation-based video art.[4] At the time, I began a rampant chase to invite the duo to collaborate on a solo exhibition. I ventured to their various exhibition openings to track them down—from Rotterdam to New York to Berlin—but they were unattainable or absent. Both FACT's CEO Mike Stubbs and Cornerhouse's artistic director Sarah Perks had separately given me the green light to commission a two-city (Liverpool and Manchester) solo exhibition for the lead-up to the 2012 cultural program surrounding the London Olympic Games. This potentially meant more resources and more of everything to entice the artists. Although I had presented Trecartin's *Trill-ogy Comp* (2009) and featured their work in numerous group exhibitions that I had curated, my emails to the artists' then gallery, Elizabeth Dee in New York, went unanswered. I was to find out that a break was about to occur. The pair moved to Andrea Rosen Gallery, New York; Regen Projects, Los Angeles; and the European powerhouse gallery Sprüth Magers. Their prices soared. Not because of greed, as was explained to me by one dealer, but because the cost of their productions had become so expensive.

While celebrating my first Christmas with my betrothed in my former hometown of Los Angeles, I came across an online post by writer Kevin McGarry, one of the pair's biggest advocates and collaborators, which intimated that Fitch and Trecartin were now living in Los Angeles. Aram Moshayedi, at the time a curator at Roy and Edna Disney CalArts Theater (REDCAT) in LA, explained how to glean their coordinates. They were, in Los Angeles terms, a stone's throw away, occupying a large house in Los Feliz not far from where my family lived and where I picked up our favorite meatball subs. The duo's move to Los Angeles was part of a "need for more space" to fulfill ambitions, but it also signaled a broader, although seemingly temporary East Coast to West Coast shift among art practitioners. For an instant, LA was perceived as offering a cheaper and a more fulsome lifestyle than New York and its surrounding enclaves. Trecartin and Fitch were on the pulse again.

Approaching their home—blood coursing through my veins in palpable excitement—I felt like a stalker yet convinced myself that being an art historian is an act of stalking in and of itself. On the front porch, a man with strawberry blond hair sat behind a book and a pair of black sunglasses. He did not wince as I went for the doorbell. I would later learn that it was McGarry. Sergio, the artists' studio manager, opened the door as I expelled a hodgepodge of verbiage to justify my presence. It was Christmas. Trecartin could have been in Texas; Fitch in Indiana, perhaps? But Trecartin was home and unassumingly greeted me, welcoming me to peruse the house, a remnant in the Spanish Colonial style that was somewhere between a dilapidated film set and an old world LA fantasy.

I invited the artist to an "exhibition of magnificence" right on the spot, proffering scenarios that were outside the realm of reality or what I was authorized to sanction. A back and forth ensued with the studio for a year, but fitting into their schedule was impossible. I would invite them twice again: once to close Cornerhouse's old building on Manchester's Oxford Road and on another occasion to open a new venue, HOME, in the city's Northern Quarter. In the intervening years, I found myself on the guest list to celebrate their Venice Biennale installation and at a private dinner in London on the roof of Shoreditch House, always pitching, but to no avail. I put their work on the cover of my books, wrote about them, and advised informally on exhibition projects, but the buck stopped there. The world was shifting, and they could no longer maintain their residence. They downsized in LA before eventually settling in Athens, Ohio.

I don't think I have ever chased an artist with such vigor, either directly or through meanderingly coy requests sandwiched between brief conversational interludes at opening receptions and studio visits. Today, when I pitch their work for exhibition, my peers often present me with different barriers. Museum administrators inform me that the duo's scope is either too ambitious for them or that the "moment has come and gone." But I still believe that it has yet to come fully to bear. Early descriptions of their films by critics labeled them as frenetic, garish, and self-conscious. I found myself troubled by the encoded language. Was "frenetic" code for unwatchable? A screening of their films to a group of teenage art students in 2011 was met with uproarious applause. In calling them "self-conscious," certain art critics seemed unwilling to use the word postmodern or to call this work a genuine reflection of contemporary culture. When it was dubbed "garish," it stunk of an aversion and/or fear of the queer nuances that were embedded in the blended mishmash of language that encompassed internet speak and the tribal aphorisms of underrepresented communities.

Early on, Trecartin spoke of the videos as situating the viewer within a field of "identity tourism" and "personality shares"—a milieu where market research is undertaken by young people seeking to make extra dollars only to aid conglomerates with the necessary tools and language to help them spend those earned dollars. A turning point for Trecartin and Fitch was their exhibition at Kunst-Werke, Berlin, titled *Site Visit* (2014). A fortress of black La-Z-Boy armchairs, an aspirational preserve of the boomer generation, greeted my friends and me. I sat, my body contorting in the chair as I listened to innocuous sounds from the "thirty-channel sound installation," before descending into a six-channel movie that was above, in front of,

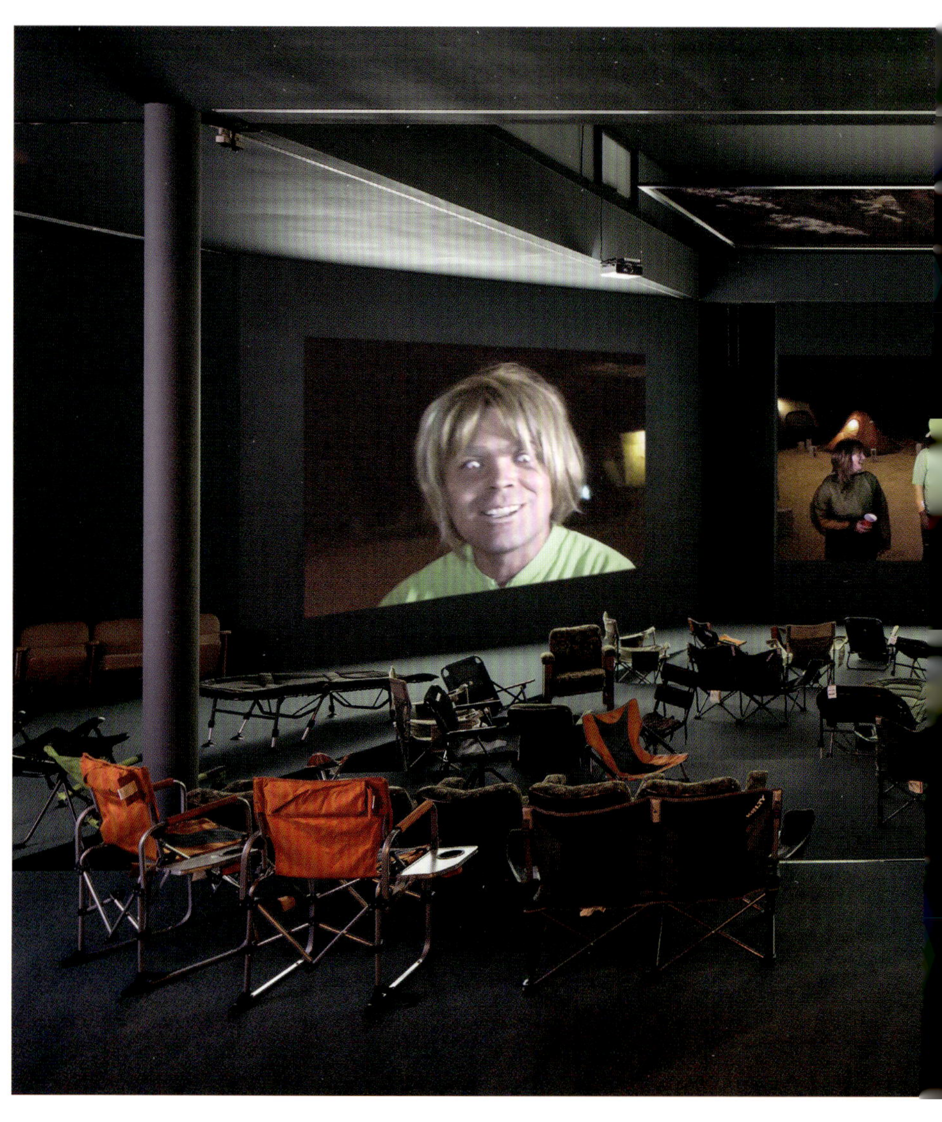

Lizzie Fitch and Ryan Trecartin, *Site Visit*, 2014 __Installation view: Kunst-Werke, Berlin, 2014–15

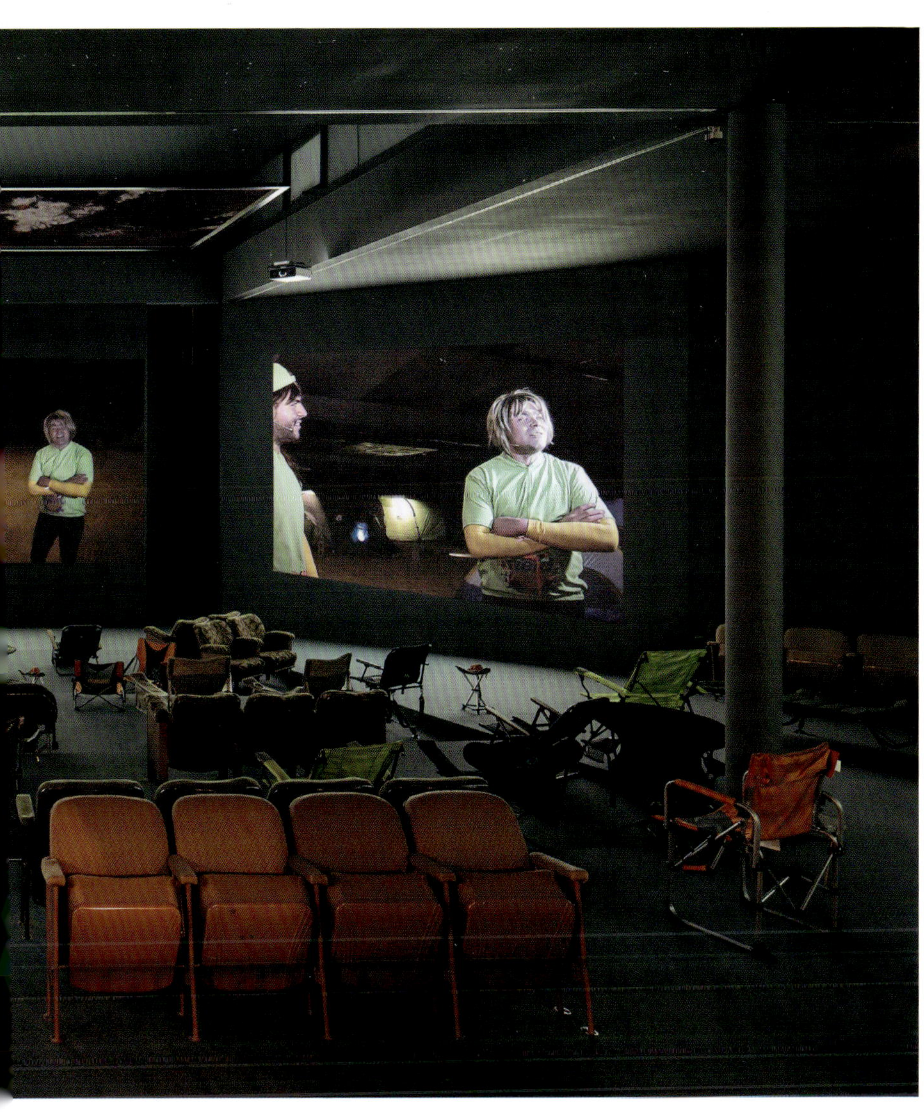

and beneath me. The makeup and costumes in the film might have borne the familiar aesthetic of Fitch and Trecartin, but the language and references were entirely different. A spoof of a spoof, this was a meta metaverse. The DIY sensation that was *The Blair Witch Project* (1999) and the *Scream* film franchise, which began in 1996, were the subjects of parody and framing. Presented here was an alluring narrative of how viewers choose to engage with and decode how they see the world.

The cinematic references from the 1990s would now be lost on much of the audience. Yet, it is this kernel—the commitment of archiving a recent present—that makes this work so resonant and profoundly emblematic. It is absurd that an aesthetic form so recent can diminish so quickly into remission, not even to be cited anymore. I was informed that the Kunst-Werke exhibition was an audience success but a commercial failure. It had cost an inordinate amount to produce, and it was intimated that it was near impossible for the galleries who had invested in the work's production to recoup their investment. To imagine the future is to take a risk that the present cannot yet handle—and then the dial turns again.

This Is the Future?

German artist and writer Hito Steyerl was an anomaly when she rose to international heights. She has been able to take densely theoretical interpretations of history that straddle a breadth of knowledge, from media theory to political philosophy, and translate them into art. Her interest in technology and the chains of power relations to finance have been elucidated in her installations and critical texts, bestowing her with cult status. By 2017, she had landed the top spot on *ArtReview* magazine's Power 100 annual list. Something was beginning to shift in the broader terrain, as though the firmament was seeking a savior, a voice of reason from amidst the shroud of images, to offer them a critical reflection of the future.

I witnessed Steyerl's work before she gained wider media attention. She was giving lectures as performances, or performances as lectures, the blurred lines forever at play. She produced documentary films that materialized as whodunnits; she was cited as a member of the essay documentary or essay film genealogy, in the spirit of fellow filmmakers, such as Alexander Kluge or, more aptly, Chris Marker, who in later life equally shared an interest in computer aesthetics. In between these works were mutating forms, such as *Red Alert* (2007), which I exhibited twice, including at the Whitechapel Gallery in *Electronic Superhighway (2016–1966)*. A triptych of red screens played on vertically installed, slender Apple computer monitors.

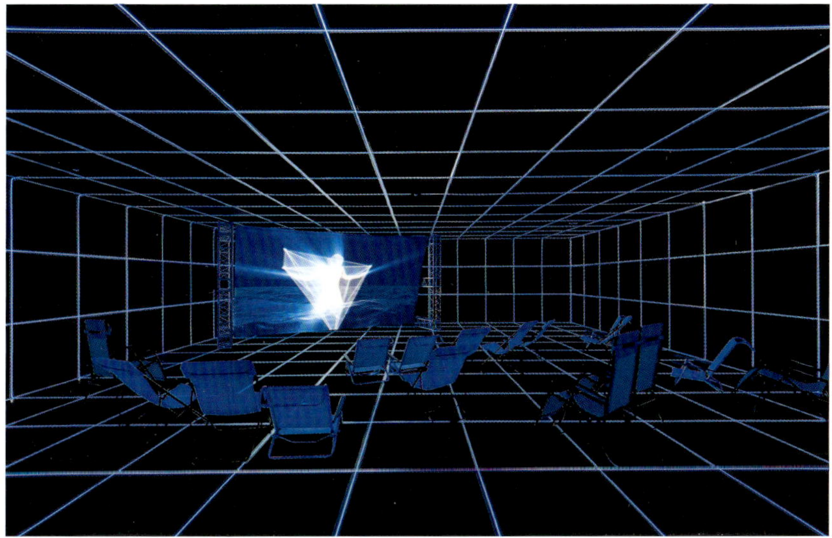

Hito Steyerl, *Factory of the Sun,* 2015 —Installation view: MOCA Grand Avenue, Los Angeles, 2016

A reference to the Russian artist Alexander Rodchenko (1891–1956) and the interrogation of painting, the work equally functioned as a jeer at language and government. Here, the use of color operated as symbolism—a metaphor for urgency and high-alert profiling in a post-9/11 world of fear propagated by such terms as the *war on terror*.

It was the 56th Venice Biennale in 2015 and the life had drained out of my face after endless days of touring people around the Cyprus Pavilion, which I had curated that year. Across the expanse and inside the bosom of the Biennale's main site for national pavilions known as the Giardini, there was the rampant chatter surrounding Steyerl's ambitious new installation in the German Pavilion. It was called *Factory of the Sun* (2015). As you entered a vestibule with a lowered ceiling, Tetris-like grids made of luminous vinyl led you to beach chairs, where you encountered Steyerl's latest treatise on the image. The video installation tells the tale of workers forced to create artificial sunshine. Who is it for? A huge finance conglomerate, a bank that needs them to radiate. Could this have been a foreshadowing of the global economy's fascination with patenting green technology? Or was the light a metaphor for the image itself?

I was to work with the Hammer Museum in Los Angeles and the San Jose Museum to acquire the final edition of this work, which had quickly entered other public and private collections. It had its U.S. premiere at

MOCA Grand Avenue, Los Angeles, in 2016. As I sat with the images before me, the trajectory in Steyerl's thinking became clearer. The cyclical play of pictures has long been a cornerstone of her arsenal and is perhaps most famously articulated in her significant essay "In Defense of the Poor Image" (2009).[5] Building on the lexicon that was once seen in Seth Price's artwork-as-essay *Dispersion* (2002–ongoing), the poor image for Steyerl takes on its own life. It holds its own autonomy and agency, devoid of the context of the original image. Low-resolution screen grabs and reproductions become disseminated, metamorphosing into phantoms of their former selves. Who owns the image? Who owns your person, your view of the world? It could be the author or someone else entirely; the copy is no longer a derogatory object or field of study but, instead, a site of decoding and reimagining.

Being Human

Our world of screens has been the subject of constant extrapolation and expansion by artists. Ken Okiishi, for example, has interrogated screen media, creating abstract acrylic paintings on mirrored flat screens. Siebren Versteeg has continually executed paintings in response to programmed codifications. These are often manifested on TV screens, consistently morphing into various input settings. The sensibilities expressed by artists working today extend beyond an assumption that screens are flat or two-dimensional media. Instead, they are perceived as a narrative space that expands beyond the confines of backlit projection into sentient conversation with the worlds that they inhabit.

An exemplary case of the spatial possibilities of screen technology is artist Christopher Kulendran Thomas's collaboration with curator Annika Kuhlmann titled *Being Human* (2019). Thomas first pitched the idea to me in a café in the East End of London, reasoning that it would be a physical rendering of a world after the end of human rights. I commissioned the artist with the support of the V-A-C Foundation for the collateral program of the 58th Venice Biennale in 2019. The work was restaged at the Schinkel Pavillon in Berlin later that year. The contours of his vision continually shifted as he and his collaborator made sense of AI technologies and how they could be used to elucidate the narrative arc of avatars they had created. Shot in the artist's familial home of Sri Lanka, the digital projection involved characters that were created by using machine-learning algorithms, which were responsive, self-improving manifestations of what was originally programmed—a form of AI. Wanting to explore the United Nations' role or lack thereof in Sri Lanka's recent conflict-laden history,

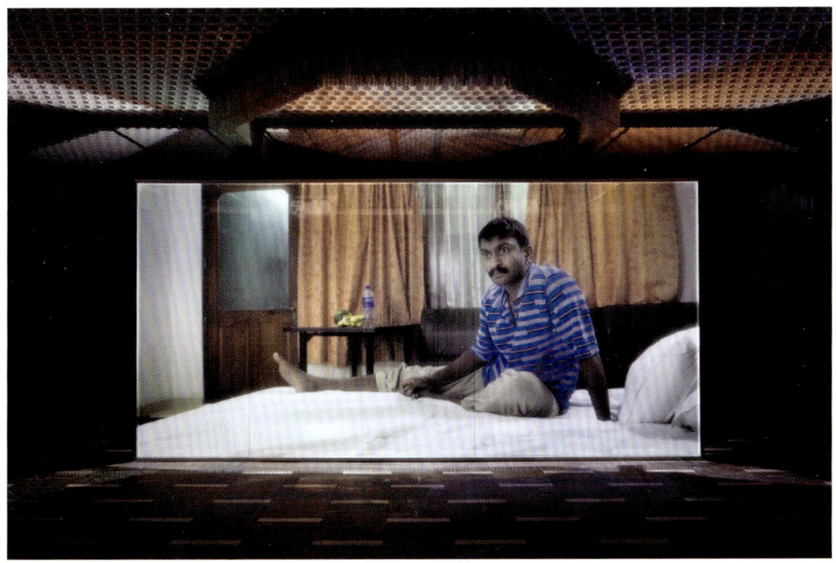

Christopher Kulendran Thomas, *Being Human*, 2019 —In collaboration with Annika Kuhlmann. HD projection on glass, aluminum, steel, featuring original works by Apali Unanda and Kingsley Gunatillake purchased from Saskia Fernando Gallery, Colombo. Installation view: Schinkel Pavilion, Berlin, 2019

Thomas used the art market as a lens through which to narrate his country's shifting socioeconomic landscape. Guided by the uneven compass of a post-conflict history, the artist focused on the quixotic relationship between conflict and emerging markets.

Thomas purchased sculptures and paintings by contemporary Sri Lankan artists from commercial galleries in Colombo, the country's capital city; these could be seen in the Palazzo, albeit only for a split second, if at all. In an effect like a Pepper's Ghost illusion, the works were installed behind a projection pane to conceal them from view. As the artist's film rolled, the projection screen occasionally came to a gentle halt, just for a split second between frames, intimating a hidden context behind the screen. In these odd and unsettling moments, a space behind the screen was illuminated, revealing a gallery of objects that were inaccessible to the viewer. As the light faded into darkness, the moving images resumed. Precipitously, one is made aware of the interpolation of the physical with the virtual. The haunting effects of the material on the light that emerges from within never escapes the mind's eye.

Elsewhere in the exhibition was a newly commissioned installation by Aleksandra Domanović. My introduction to Domanović happened about

2005 or 2006. At the time, she was involved in VVORK (pronounced "work"), an online blogging collective that sought to virtually document art for the virtual sphere. One of the first websites of its kind, VVORK, which unusually for such an endeavor, was operated and governed by artists, sought to interrogate the borders between the realm of the material and the screen. How could art be embodied? These questions continue to take shape in Domanović's visually striking *Votive* (2016–ongoing) series. In these, statues are 3-D printed from icons that are modeled on computers. The resulting sculptures invoke korai—ancient Greek monumental statues depicting female figures—and each holds an object in its robot arm. These cyborg-like limbs appear to be material visualizations of the dispossessed, giving life to hidden figures whose lives were marred, tainted, or ruined by the conservatism of a recent past. The apple that appears with one is perhaps a reference to Alan Turing, who killed himself with a cyanide-laden fruit after being persecuted for his sexuality.

At the turn of the millennium, Paul Pfeiffer, one of the progenitors of media explorations, had taken an inverse approach to the expression of the human body. He chose instead to remove figures from mass-media footage. In 2001, he presented *The Long Count (The Rumble in the Jungle)*, a video of Muhammed Ali and George Foreman fighting, bar the boxers themselves, who the artist digitally removed. Pfeiffer's tendency to reauthor and rearticulate history encourages the viewer to consider the formal and aesthetic histories of the digital image, a defining means by which artists have used the internet to extrapolate, recraft, and distribute digital video content. In *The Long Count*, the artist leaves the viewer with the artifice of the arena to stand in for the spectacle of the fight itself. When the Whitney opened in its new Renzo Piano building in New York's Meatpacking District, I came across a work in the inaugural collection exhibition *America Is Hard to See* (2015) that struck a nerve. Titled *Fragment of a Crucifixion (After Francis Bacon)* (1999), this thirty-second video projected from a minuscule self-mounted projector onto a small expanse of wall, which inversely submerged the viewer into the intimate details of human expression. Gleaning his material from a commercial video of a basketball player, elated after fulfilling a glorious slam dunk, the artist here removes everything else out of the frame, focusing on the player's ecstatic emotions. When looped repeatedly, such intimate details begin to take on new forms and meanings. Could one mistake his rapture for rage? The player becomes a fierce creature like the beasts struggling in the Francis Bacon (1909–1992) painting that is referenced in the work's title. As I stepped away from the image, I could not help but feel a sense of protectiveness for the person on the wall. Extrapolated from context, could his gestures be mistaken by police on the street for violence? Would he soon be a victim of brutality? Afterward, I still felt his ghostlike presence.

Artists throughout the ages have long sought to interrogate the presence of historic figures, but no more so than today. In 2015, I was stunned to enter a gallery to witness lifelike facial sculptures of the whistle-blower Chelsea Manning, who is most well-known for her involvement with WikiLeaks. The artwork, *Radical Love* (2015) by Heather Dewey-Hagborg, was composed of 3-D-printed sculptures developed from DNA samples collected from cheek swabs and nail clippings sent to the artist through snail mail by the then imprisoned activist. The figures were so convincing that one could almost feel a breath. When I queried Dewey-Hagborg regarding the title, she informed me that it was drawn from Manning's belief that contemporary political activism was not radical, but a product of a loving form of solidarity across diverse social strata. In these instances, art allows us to tread forward, just a little, giving us access to the glimmering apparitions of the present.

The Shape of the Future

De Je Veux

I am back where I first began when conceiving the idea of this book—a social history of the internet through art that would also be a social history of art told through the internet. I am typing a proposal on my laptop in a generic, global coffee chain while I wait for my comrade to get a haircut. It is in the basement of a megalopolis of adjoining concrete buildings that cohere into a nonspace inside a mall on the edge of Dubai. Or is it the edge of Sharjah? It could be anywhere, from Los Angeles to Hong Kong. The glistening lights of the all-encompassing digital billboards inside and outside of the mall recall an innately familiar feeling, imaginatively locating me in my past, a site of youth. The panes of interconnected glass continue to be under occupation by jumpy animations, cartoonish branding, and advertisements tethered to a bygone era. The Arabic music layered over these moving pictures creates a sonic reverie of a place that for many of us nomadic expats exists mainly in the site of the imagination. My youth was spent in the Gulf States during the 1990s. I went to international high schools in Saudi Arabia and now I live and work between Sharjah, a Gulf Emirate split across two coasts, the United Kingdom, an island in every sense of the word, and the empire of exceptionalism that is the United States.[1] Decoding images and their relationship to place has become an obsession of mine since I began working full time in my late teenage years.

The realm of culture in 1990s Saudi Arabia was limited in scope—there were no cinemas, theaters, or art galleries; all the music we listened to was bleeped out, and what little media by way of satellite television existed, was cleaned of its offensive content. When the World Wide Web became accessible, the same occurred, with firewalls blocking any website that was reported to a government authority. This meant that there were no images or explanations of sex or sexuality; Mariah Carey's neck was redacted on her cassette and CD artwork. There was most certainly not anything as dissident as queer culture. All the same, I gathered a small coterie of friends whose parents managed to gain them access to smuggled, uncensored movies and cassettes. We wore "No Fear" T-shirts and faded baggy jeans adorned with dangly metallic chains; our cracks hung out—just as the satellite TV stations instructed—those were not deemed worthy of censure. Fake Nike shoes purchased from market stalls bejeweled our feet. The sites we frequented in Saudi, including Heraa Mall in Jeddah, were blanketed with animated screens. The displays back then seemed just as big as today. They are now referred to as hulking screens, for their muscular backs and incongruous bases. Lithe and contoured now, they continue to spit out redundant jingles and advertising shtick in a lo-fi aesthetic.

This was our culture. It is our culture. It is how my generation came to make sense of the image and how it could move. The aesthetics can be likened to the artist and author Sophia Al-Maria's concept of "Gulf Futurism," except here, the future never arrives. Those screens continue looping decades later and what lives inside of them is all the same; content is less important than brand recognition.

Gulf Futurism intimates that western fantasies of the future already exist or have been made manifest in the Gulf states, a tendency that Al-Maria argues is reflected in the enveloping urbanization of cities, often in parallel with smart technologies. In her estimation, the case of the Gulf, in particular, the techno-desert sprawl most emblematic in Dubai, and later found in Doha, Qatar, and, more recently, the major cities of Saudi Arabia, such as Jeddah and Riyadh, are simply examples of the "eye of a great spreading storm."[2] The ideas surrounding this futurism have been elucidated in Al-Maria's artmaking such as in her epic sci-fi mall-drama, *Black Friday* (2016), voiced by *Jurassic Park*'s (1993) Sam Neill, as well as in music videos and performances with Fatima Al Qadiri, and public conversations with individuals such as Shumon Basar and Douglas Coupland. In 2012 Bruce Sterling wrote an article in *Wired* magazine highlighting the term as a "weird Arab-futurist ideology" and attributing its popularity to the aesthetics found in *Bidoun* magazine, a platform for Middle Eastern arts and culture and their diasporas.[3]

The sci-fi underpinnings inherent in Sterling's comment are perhaps a little misplaced. As far as I see it, we all live in and embody some form of a late-capitalist ideal that only a decade ago might have been considered surreal. What is specific about the place where I write from is that the digital aesthetic of the internet is seemingly less important than the gargantuan technological monuments, which invoke the megascreen of the jumbotron.

A Whoosh

A whooshing sound signifies that my book proposal has made its way from my computer, through cables across the ocean. I am back on the smooth asphalt ground outside the mall, waiting for surge pricing to end on the taxi app. Later, trying to get to sleep after hours spent in radiant light, the recesses of memory take over. Everything outside my window resembles my childhood, despite the twenty-year gap and the different geographic location, despite the seeming liberalization and accessibility to creative content; these cities where I roam still resemble an imaginary future. I continue to live in an architecture anchored in commerce, inflated through digital imagery—an orb that rarely secedes. The endless unbooked taxis still stop for no one. Now we have luxury Ubers at inflated prices. You receive a one-star review, no matter how obedient you have been on your ride. This feeling that we are in a place to which we will never arrive has been diagnosed by author Ahmad Makia as "the Pan-Arab Hangover."[4] Makia's research suggests that the potentially utopic ideal of an Arab cultural identity is out of touch and out of time. The pursuit of an Arab nationalism suggests a uniform cultural and political sphere among Arabic-speaking nations that does not reflect the fragmentary digital sphere of multiple and contradictory identities.

As I worked my way to this chapter, I reflected on the creative experiments I have used to denote the cultural shifts that have been enabled by and through the internet to consider how we have evolved, if at all, and more important, whether it even matters.

I Blame the Internet

Many artists have made a living from aestheticized sloganeering. David Shrigley has commoditized his artistic practice with mugs, coasters, dish towels, and notebooks bearing naively drawn words, such as: "It's All Your Fault"; "Stop Panicking"; or "Politicians Make Me Sick." I invited him to tattoo his musings onto real human beings as part of the Abandon Normal Devices Festival in 2011. Jeremy Deller is another artist to venture into this genre. In the art boutique House of Voltaire (of the arts organization Studio Voltaire) in Clapham, London, Deller has just reissued a handful of archival editions for sale. A shimmering blue sign by the Turner Prize–winning artist reads, "I Blame the Internet." The artwork—now sold out—evolves from an artistic practice where language can be used to erase, or perhaps, simply poke fun at, the wounds wrought upon society by different social and cultural conditions. In this regard, the internet is also to blame for the resuscitation of different forms of language. When Twitter launched and individuals were restricted to tweeting 140 characters, it generated a culture that saw users painstakingly composing slogans and haikulike prose. Abbreviations and acronyms native to the urban sphere of the internet also emerged, spreading from people's fingers and thumbs to commonly spoken parlance. The #Hashtag, perhaps most recognizably deployed on Instagram, in effect, is also a means to use language to connect with people, but also to popularize or trademark certain catchphrases. Cardi B's "Okurrr" has been attributed to making the musician and fashion mogul a household name.[5] It is now trademarked. Socialite Paris Hilton's catchphrase, "That's hot," was a famously debated patent, as was Taylor Swift's lyric, "this sick beat." In 2016, corporations began patenting the most used hashtags associated with their brands—#CokeCanPics and #SmileWithACoke belong to the Coca-Cola Company. In theory, you might not be the author of the language but can nab its IP—the bragging rights.

Contradictions Unfurling

The internet has often been seen as a kind of balm, as a way to find life's work-arounds. Can't work in the office? I, and probably you, now work from home 24/7 instead. Hunching over a computer for the better part of the last seventeen years, ingesting the stress of a world staring back at me, may be why my body began to decenter into spasmodic forms. But then again, the internet reveals all the potential causes of my ailments, such as the evolution of my Tourette's. In simple terms, it soothes me. The internet may have triggered fibromyalgia in me—ceaseless demands from every time zone require me at the device, but I also receive exercise videos from my doctor over email and can search for competitively priced prescription medication from online pharmacies for my comorbid conditions. The internet has led me, and many whom I know, into multiple states of dysmorphia—body and gender—but it has also offered me the resources to know where I do and do not have the right to process and negotiate these feelings and experiences. From my depression to my diabetes, I can only seem to find the resource and community to help me. It may well be that we are symbiotic, the internet and me, making each other, for better and worse, at the same time, all the time.

As artist Lawrence Abu Hamdan articulates in his ongoing treatise on what he refers to as the *Sonic Image*, we live in a world where sound, memory, and trauma are constantly leaking across seemingly invisible borders.[6] The edges are coming unstitched—that is, if they were ever properly sewn together at all. The interconnected galaxy of devices propels one into spheres where there is no division between work and life; play can be hollowed of its joy if your brain continues to circle that unanswered email, the news article, your company's stock price, and the unresolved budgetary issue on the Excel spreadsheet, all from which you will never be able to disconnect.

What's in a Meme? Welcome to the Meme Museum

We live in a multiverse that is also referred to as the *metaverse*. The metaverse, a term coined in Neal Stephenson's novel *Snow Crash* (1992), relates to a sense of a complete and self-contained virtual world. Unlike cyberspace, it is not conceived as an alternative to reality but as an augmentation of it; it is reality in and of itself. A defining feature of the world in which we live is a subset of the internet known as meme culture. A meme is an idea, behavior, or style that speeds through society via the internet, particularly through social media. One of the most offbeat trends to emerge from this sphere is the habit of planking—groups of people lying face down in incongruous and unusual settings. Often humorous, successful memes spread like wildfire. Images and people from popular culture, such as RuPaul or one of the Real Housewives of Atlanta, can be transformed into animated gifs. The most common form disseminated is a single picture of a person or event annotated with the words *epic fail*. These pictures are frequently of politicians, as well as animals—with cats being one of the most popular characters. As these visual markers have spread, they have sometimes become reclassified as artworks of cultural significance and sold at astronomical prices. Infamously, artists Eva & Franco Mattes transformed a LOLCat meme into a physical sculpture and attributed it to artist Maurizio Cattelan. It is called *Catt* (2010).

But who holds the keys to this world and is responsible for determining the cultural significance of these memes for both now and in the future? These digital files lack an obvious public home or landing spot, where they can be collected, archived, and interrogated for their cultural value, because the institutions historically charged with gathering and conserving culture deemed to be of importance are still focused on the material object. There is an undeniable demand for these works of art, which are often specific to cultural histories, to be collected and archived by museums and public archives as significant digital assets and cultural artifacts. In 2018, Vice Media published the article "Memes Have Finally Made It to the Museum," referring to the *Two Decades of Memes* exhibition at the Museum of the Moving Image in New York. In summer 2021, the world's first physical meme museum was reported to have opened in the K11 Art Foundation's Art Mall in Hong Kong. That said, the realities of whether these works are collected, conserved, and made publicly accessible in a properly contextualized fashion remain unclear. Much like the pitfalls that have faced browser-based artworks, resource scarcity will be an issue for these works, because they require a specialized skill set, including, for instance, intellectual property right law.

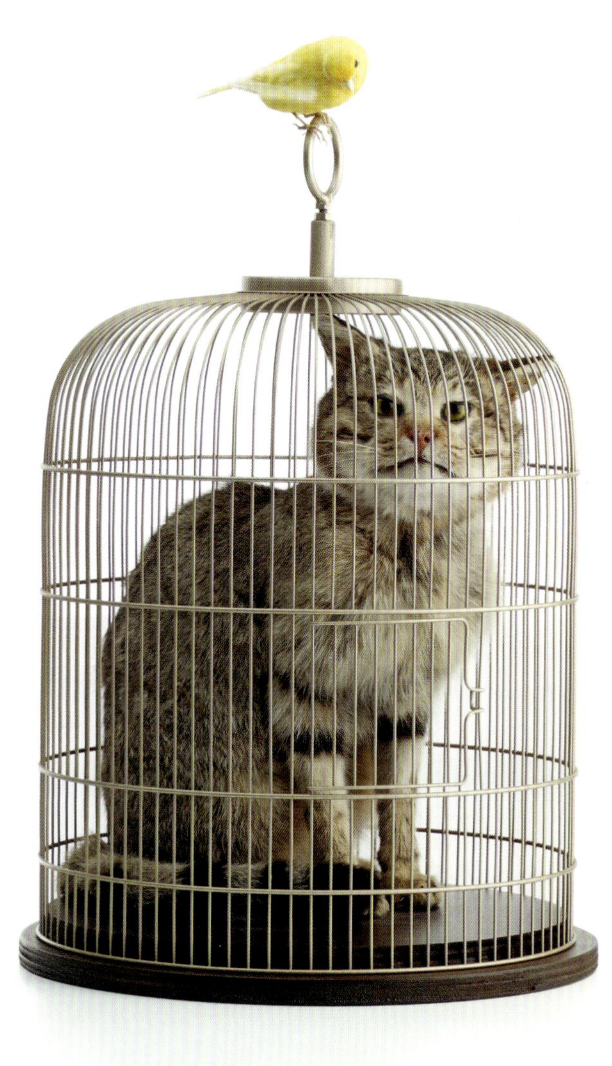

Eva & Franco Mattes, *Catt*, 2010 — Taxidermy cat and bird, cage, 21⅝ × 15¾ × 15¾ in. (55 × 40 × 40 cm)

Memes have also appeared in direct connection to the world of contemporary art at its most purely commercial: the art fair. In 2019, at Art Basel Miami, a booth by Perrotin gallery presented a work by trickster artist Maurizio Cattelan entitled *Comedian* (2019), which was simply a banana taped to a wall. Its sale at the fair for six figures spawned tremendous press buzz and before long, people lined up to see the banana in question, until someone ate it. On social media, cultural figures, such as actress Brooke Shields, and global food chains, such as Burger King, fashioned their own versions of, or responses to, the original artwork. Although the genesis of the event was staged in the real world, the life of the artwork came into being on social media, where even Damien Hirst, stalwart of the Young British Artists (YBAs), became obsessed with having his own banana-based artwork, offering to swap any of his multimillion-dollar artworks with Cattelan in return for the artist proof of the work. Publicly, at least, Cattelan said no.

The Price of Everything

In 2018, a public stir in the world of culture ensued following the release of a documentary with the blunt title *The Price of Everything*. Featuring many of the most noted art patrons and collectors in the United States, many of whom I had come to know through asking them to fund the institutions I represented over the years, it was hailed as an exposé of the art world's underlying impetus: money. Broadcast trade magazine *Variety* called it "enthralling." The standout "performance," as it was called, came from former Sotheby's vice president Amy Cappellazzo, who is pictured as a cutthroat agent and salesperson who collects art consignments as a cattle herder would accumulate well-bred livestock. Her thrills are gleaned from securing art deemed valuable by a series of invisible metrics. Viewers witness Cappellazzo's conversations with a smorgasbord of her loyal high-net-worth, clients such as the late art collector Stefan Edlis, a self-made man with a penchant for all things Pop. Doing her job entailed adjusting images in auction catalogs with the precision of an archivist and the savvy of an estate agent, the aim being to aid in inflating the price of, well, everything—including *Drown* (2012) by Los Angeles–based, Nigerian artist Njideka Akunyili Crosby, which ballooned to over one million U.S. dollars, well above its estimate of three hundred thousand U.S. dollars.[7]

Keeping art in the hands of the few has long been the preserve of an industry of for-profit labor who have worked in lockstep with curators—those underpaid nonprofit kinsfolk who broker taste with their Midas touch and focused gaze. Museums in the twenty-first century ostensibly operate as hybrid corporations but make profit only to reach net-zero; their curators lend their skill set to the for-profit sector in return for donations and corporate sponsorship. A seasoned institutional curator's Rolodex of contacts can be extremely hefty. Many will encompass artists and auctioneers, belligerent celebrity children and business moguls, fashion and furniture designers, noted authors, historians, social-media influencers, and their most immediate friends and colleagues. Because of my love of the internet, I have also enticed the interest of a small tech crowd—a set that has never fully ennobled itself within the art ecosystem.

In summer 2011, a chill, a pang, a thrill ensued following the arrival of a spate of new digital art platforms. The first invite that I received was to a website cofounded by entrepreneur and media mogul Wendi Deng Murdoch. She was supporting and investing in Artsy, an online marketplace for art founded by Carter Cleveland while he was a computer science student at Princeton University. Seeking to decorate his dorm room with art, the kid found that it wasn't so easy. Referencing Jeff Bezos as inspiration, he noted, following Artsy's launch, "Eventually we're going to become Amazon for the art world."[8] I could not have been more enthusiastic about the prospect. This would lead to heightened transparency around pricing and the market; it could cut out the middle person, and perhaps even offer the potential for underpaid culture workers, including curators and arts editors, to name two examples of those who work closely with art and artists, to find an affordable artwork. The result was anything but that.

Artists, for better or for worse, are entrenched in and by the system of the art world's secrecy. The volume of inventory available for sale dictates a scarcity model. Unless they've broken public auction records, artwork prices are most often withheld by commercial galleries to increase interest and demand. This perceived secrecy also enables art dealers to form long-term relationships with buyers directly, allowing them to invest in a client base that will grow sales and enhance their reputation. Mega-galleries, from Gagosian to David Zwirner, are notorious for cultivating high-profile collector bases, and even then, are often found implementing conditions on the sale of their most precious commodities.

For instance, in 2016, during painter Kerry James Marshall's landmark touring retrospective *Mastry*, the scant inventory of figurative paintings being sold on the primary market was only available for sale to private collectors who would be willing to promise the painting to a public museum. And why would that be? To limit the money someone could make by selling the work off at auction soon afterward, otherwise known as flipping? Or was it to do with the fact that association with prestigious museums enshrines the artist in history and helps their works maintain a certain price point? Both are true.

In 2015, I was invited to curate a special exhibition at the Armory Show—New York's flagship art fair—by Noah Horowitz, who since his directorship at the Armory has gone on to serve as director of the Americas for Art Basel and as a senior vice president at Sotheby's. A celebratory dinner was held to kickoff the Armory Week events at the Gramercy Park Hotel. I was strategically seated directly across from Carter Cleveland—Artsy being one of the fair's ongoing partners. I fizzed in anticipation. There were questions to be asked. I prodded Cleveland with queries that became more direct as the night gathered pace. What was the long-term growth model plan? When could we finally buy real art by simply dropping it into our Artsy shopping cart? Cleveland amiably tried to resist grimacing, but before long he was turning his head away, attempting not to squirm and trying to evade me. It had not been my intention to make him uncomfortable. I wanted Artsy to do well.

By the end of the dinner, I had discovered that Artsy was raising venture capital with a plan that seemed purely ideological. Its founders wanted it to be the first online showroom for buying and selling art. Being first outdid everything else. Second to that was a feature of the site titled the Art Genome Project, which attempted to break down art into constituent genes that could enable a more thoughtful appreciation of its distinct qualities. Or more strategically perhaps, it would enable a better tagging system for the cross-pollination of artworks levied to prospective buyers. But it never banked in on that potential and, eventually, the Art Genome Project seemed to be discontinued.

The way Artsy evolved in its operations, and its constantly reinvented business model, was to offer commercial galleries monthly subscriptions to list art for sale on their website. By collaborating with major art fairs and running editorial content in tandem, Artsy manages to sustain buzz and onboard new galleries, who form a large part of their core constituents, constantly. When a sale is made, Artsy takes 5 percent of the cut. For galleries, Artsy is a mere virtual showroom without all the added fuss. Each seller can choose what data to include. For example, many prestigious artists or galleries will not publish key information on their Artsy listing pages, such as the artwork's price. In the end, this makes much of Artsy just as opaque as any other gallery website, where one must be bold and make inquiries, hoping that they are worthy of being in the art club.

Over the years, I have engaged in numerous Artsy adventures. To get to the root of their operations, I attempted to purchase astronomically priced pieces of art, having it out in a relay with Artsy reps and gallery sales directors to better understand the serious expectations required of high-net-worth buyers. I have also contacted Artsy to update artist bios and remove incorrect gallery information. I even joined in some of their latest auctions, where the illusion of a work by a major name with a low reserve hooked me into constant browser refreshing, only to realize that I was looking through a store window into a world that was not my own.

My most fulfilling encounters on Artsy have been with galleries based in Africa—ones that list the odd piece here and there for an art fair and who magically appear to have a remnant of inventory. I have purchased artworks in the hundreds of dollars range from such countries as Namibia, Senegal, and South Africa. That said, those galleries could not use Artsy's online payment function, because their banks would not allow them to. In these instances, I had to navigate various convoluted processes and provide sheaths of paperwork to my bank to prove, for instance, that the artwork I purchased for 120 U.S. dollars was not a form of money laundering. When the artworks arrived, they sometimes differed from their visual representation and written description on Artsy. I could not be petulant or pedantic, because these brokers had already been subject to intense scrutiny and cross-examination by the western fiscal institutions whom I used to pay for the artworks. One assumes that these woes are not experienced by western galleries that use the platform.

My hope is for Artsy to become an equalizer in the field. This has yet to fully materialize, but perhaps the company's adaptability suggests it is here to stay. Like any start-up, Artsy, as far as public reports go, is unclear as to whether it has so far been able to turn over a sizable profit (at least certainly not with its original business model).[9] Instead, the company's website boasts and pronounces its significant metrics on its "about" page. At the time of writing, Artsy houses more than a billion works of art online, as well as an impressive segment of the art audience that would be the envy of many an art dealer or broker. The win for art, culture, and its publics, as it were, will be when platforms such as these can sustain multiple functions without the threat of erasure by the tumult located in the global trend market. These platforms serve as publicly curated archives and a historical record of art events, while also offering entry points for people to engage with and aid in sustaining an art economy on both the micro and macro level.

Window Shopping with Renders

I am obsessed with window shopping online: I hasten to find anyone who isn't in this day and age. Pick the poison that gobbles up the most of your time, from clothing to real estate one might never conceivably afford. I share a home with someone who spends all their spare time imagining a larger footprint on real-estate sites, such as Zillow and Zoopla. I also peruse things that I cannot have and should not want—for example, a reclaimed craftsman bed larger than our bedroom. But it's "one of a kind" and the price is almost "40 percent off." I ponder whether the makeshift living room and bedroom should be switched around. The internet makes us believe that we can have everything. Want this painting? Pay it off in multiple installments and spend nothing now; in the UK, Own Art offers interest-free loans to those buying art primarily to support public institutions. Or, if you prefer, you can "try before you buy," by borrowing it for a week, such as the rental plan called Gertrude. The e-commerce around art and other high-value goods scarce on the market is a fledgling field. This is a pity when you think of all the times that an artwork lived in storage as opposed to finding a loving home, because its value or perceived worth and how it is sold are often conflated with a person's status as a collector. Hence, there is a continuing growth in the world of editioned art, which is sold and distributed more widely and transparently.

This is how my own limited experience with acquiring art began with charity edition prints, which over time ballooned in price as nonprofit arts organizations realized the untapped economic potential of such products among an art-engaged audience eager to own works by well-known artists but unable to afford the unique original.

The most unusual platform for affordable editions is Sedition, which was cofounded by Harry Blain, an art dealer who had been involved in some major galleries in London, and Robert L. Norton, founder of Saatchi Online. Like every start-up hopes, the company launched with a bang. Famous big-name artists, including Tracey Emin, Damien Hirst, and Jenny Holzer, have used the site to release digital editions at affordable prices. For a couple of hundred dollars, you could own one of Emin's iconic text pieces normally rendered in actual neon light tubing, but here replicated in digital form in an edition of 250. You could exhibit it on a screen, project it in a darkened room at a party, or look at it on your phone while taking the tube. The point is that you own a work by these artists and you don't have to be rich to do so.

Reflecting on Sedition, which launched in 2011, around the same time as Artsy, one could argue that the form and manifestation of the art on the site may have precipitated the market economy around nonfungible tokens (NFTs)—unique digital assets sold and acquired through cryptocurrency. As I will come to discuss, NFTs have created a global furor and a multibillion-dollar market. Peculiarly, Sedition seems to remain in the background—a murmur, rarely spoken about.

Curious about the platform's relatively low profile in the field, I sought answers by accepting an invitation to be a contract consultant in 2013. As a guest curator for Sedition, I proposed a number of digital artist commissions native to the internet, which I then could curate into virtual shows and potentially see animated in a physical space, as the company had done with *The New Romantics* (2014) exhibition in collaboration with Eyebeam Art + Technology Center in New York. Thrilled to have this rare chance to experiment with online commissioning, I drew up a long list and began approaching artists almost instantly, but I was met with roadblocks. The first person I reached out to, an artist with whom I had worked on several occasions, insisted that their gallery would not allow them to participate unless they were directly involved with and managed every aspect of the process. Also, the fact that Sedition's cofounder was an established and well-known art dealer might have scared some artists off. As I went down my list, the negotiations became more animated and intriguing. One artist would only sign up if they could have full access to the site's back end. Another would only do it if their imagination could roam into the terrain of an unlimited budget, meaning an endless supply of engineering support. The answer in both cases was, of course, that these were impractical requests to manage. I, as is standard in the field, would not get paid anything unless I had secured a commission, which meant I eventually gave up. I certainly had no allegiance to the company beyond the aspiration to make art accessible through the internet.

The bifurcation of the internet, traditional art forms, and their markets somehow felt emblematized in this experience. An artist working natively to the platform and space will only want to produce and sell their artwork in the manner they choose, without any limits or restrictions. Those for whom this is a novel possibility, in contrast, expect a form of resource that is incredibly expensive; technical engineering support is a commodity that certainly does not come cheaply. Add in the trepidation around the exposure of one's art being offered online and not being deemed a critical or commercial success and whole swathes of enticing possibilities are erased.

The Illusion of Choice and the Birth of an NFT

Have you ever conceived of a brand new, original idea but, by the time you put it into action, you find that someone else has already thought of it? Everything is out there. Mark Twain famously said that there is "no such thing as a new idea." Instead, it is what we do with the packaging that matters. In the field of art, despite the hefty costs linked with its marketing, such concepts do not fly. Everything must be seeded with something original and authentic. Curators do not exist to simply care for art objects; they do not simply broker or accentuate taste, but they preserve and protect it, studying art in granular detail to appreciate its distinctive qualities. What makes the visual arts—once referred to as *high art*—so unique is that while curators and other trained professionals, such as conservators and appraisers, can identify an artist's influence and style, the vision of each artist is expected to bring something new into the world.

The commercialization of the internet has formed ideologues. Those who enter the field of networked technology with the aspiration of huge fiscal gain at a young age behave as if shrouded by a cloak of invincibility. That said, there are only a few youthful, ultrawealthy billionaires out there. They tend to be white and are perceived as unique talents or geniuses. There is only one Mark Zuckerberg, Steve Jobs, Jack Dorsey, and Evan Spiegel. Whether virtuoso figures or not, college dropouts or not, out of the billions who form the world's working population, only a couple of dozen folks have realized the Web 2.0 dream, which replaced the dot-com boom aspiration by targeting those individuals obsessively or not, who are engaged in share culture.

"If you're such a smart arse about all of this tech stuff, where's your castle?" quizzes an uncle—a self-professed, highly nonfunctioning entrepreneur. One of my younger brothers, who was at the time a sales director at Snapchat, says the same: "With what you know about art, tech, and culture, you should be retired by now. . . . You make bad choices." I've seen this MBA degree–holding graduate rebrand himself as a dropout, molding his indecision into carefully crafted cocktail party fodder. "Come work for me, and you'll be a winner. Unless you can't put that ego aside." The words fall out of his mouth as he sits on a home gym, bench pressing too many pounds, searching for himself in the mirror between sets.

I've decided not to take the bait. Instead, I've been quietly observing the scene surrounding a momentous event that swept the global imagination in spring 2021. Mike Winkelmann, a self-proclaimed digital artist known professionally as Beeple, had at the age of thirty-nine, sold an NFT called *EVERYDAYS: THE FIRST 5000 DAYS* (2021), at the international auction house Christie's for a cash equivalent of 69.3 million U.S. dollars. The price point gave him the third-highest sale achieved by a living artist at auction, inducting him into a hall of fame with some other notable white men, including Jeff Koons and David Hockney.[10] When news of the sale hit the press in March 2021, most of the art world, let alone the public, had never heard of an NFT, nor knew what it constituted. It continues to beguile and mystify even those who produce, sell, and collect them.

In the simplest sense, an NFT is a unit of data, part of a group of digital assets that, in some cases, are dubbed digital art, and it is primarily paid for using cryptocurrency. Cryptocurrency comes in almost as many forms as there are nations located across the globe, and it, akin to any currency, proportionately holds more value based on the trust instilled in the money by those who own and share it. Its value rises and falls much like any other currency.

Locked into a persistent form of digital utopianism, I initially held the belief that cryptocurrency, specifically Bitcoin, perceived to be the first cryptocurrency, would create a new social and political model of transparency.[11] The concept that currency could be governed by a community of users emerges from the fact that every cryptocurrency transaction is logged, i.e., recorded, on the blockchain. The blockchain is often referred to as an open ledger that allows transactions to be made publicly visible, as well as provides any set terms or conditions attached to a specific digital asset or token. For example, a digital artwork sold using cryptocurrency can be accompanied by an encoded and publicly visible smart contract, discussed later in this chapter.

The unique URL generated for a transaction is permanently stored there and thus traceable, which is believed to enshrine a sense of accountability within the user community. But my conviction that the blockchain was a democratic and honest fiscal community was fueled by a sprinkling of information gleaned from sales-pitch conversations with technologists and investors and the utopic potential intimated in Satoshi Nakamoto's white paper for blockchain.[12] The currency used to purchase Beeple's mind-boggling fetch at the market was a currency called Ethereum, typically referred to as Eth, and at the time of writing, the second strongest form of crypto globally after Bitcoin.

Some articles surrounding Beeple's *EVERYDAYS* were not preoccupied with the artwork's formal qualities or its hammer price but instead concentrated on the environmental impact of trading such a large sum of Ethereum for one work. Ethereum, or any currency that is not backed by silver or gold, such as fiat or cash money, must be fueled by something else. To verify transactions, cryptocurrencies require computers to solve complex problems to create proof of work (PoW). This process is energy intensive. In 2021, to take one example, Ethereum produced forty-seven million tons of carbon emissions, which was still reportedly more efficient than Bitcoin.[13]

Cofounded in about 2014 by Vitalik Buterin, when he was the ripe old age of twenty, Ethereum's use in the exchange of digital assets has helped maintain its overall perception as a reliable currency. The currency has its own applications for exchange, such as the MetaMask wallet, which can be accessed from a browser or smartphone. Up to the point of authoring this book, I had resisted the MetaMask wallet, until artist Simon Denny gifted me an NFT that could only be exchanged via an Ethereum wallet.

Ethereum generates the unique token of an NFT by encoding it with the command or request ERC-721. The ERC-721 creates a standard for users to exchange their currency for unique tokens, such as NFTs, accompanied by smart contracts, which can contain as much detail or instruction as the maker who mints the NFT demands. A digital asset—be it an artwork or a meme—cannot verifiably be sold or exchanged until it is minted. In other words, its status as unique has been made credible via publishing it to the blockchain. NFTs can be acquired or published in any cryptocurrency, but some digital assets can only be acquired using certain currencies. This has thus led to the rise of platforms for currency transactions, which is understood to lead to further energy consumption.

Sustaining cryptocurrency demands that currency holders do not continually seek to cash out for the most tenable currency or to transfer their coin into fiat cash. Otherwise, the same ramifications can occur as in any potential fiscal crash, such as a stock market collapse. The idea, perhaps, is to create and sustain a wholly independent economy atop a layer of traditional banking—one where a digital asset on the internet can be attributed value via other means.

Saving the Right to Brag

"The very first NFT vending machine in New York has just landed downtown," reads a February 2022 headline in *Time Out New York*; the deck continues, "We're not entirely sure what it is."[14] Later, I pick up the May/June 2022 of *Wired UK* at an airport. Its headlines profess to try and explain what tech industry pundits have dubbed *Web3*—a term associated with the rise of cryptocurrency, NFT sales, and the concept of the metaverse. But the articles here also allude to the cryptic nature of expressing the nature of the emerging field. The seemingly incongruous nature of this field has led skeptics of NFTs to write in mainstream media outlets from *Slate* to the *Guardian* that the very notion of owning an NFT is simply about possessing the bragging rights of ownership—of claiming something that they will never be able to hold in their hands or even to license. What is the future of the curator or, indeed, the artist, then, if asset management firms can curate sublicensed JPEGs and sell them for millions in currencies that most people do not own?

Like many things, it isn't that simple. At the time of writing, a new band of internet trolls is running rife online. Individuals are using the right-click button to download images of NFTs that were sold for large sums, and subsequently sharing them widely as a stick-it-to-them gesture. Funnily, the "right-click mentality," as one news outlet named it, was doing the owners a favor.[15] NFTs are modeled after any piece of art that one might buy. When you photograph a painting in a museum and post it on social media, you are promoting it and giving it currency, whether you mean to or not. Equally, when you acquire a physical painting, whether a Leonardo da Vinci, a Kevin McCoy, or a Beeple, you do not own the intellectual copyright to the work. That always rests with the artist, their estate, or a designated representative until seventy years after their death, according to most international IP laws. You can request permission to print a picture of an artwork, whether or not you own it, in a book or magazine by contacting the artist for a limited nonexclusive license, for which you may pay a small fee each time you reproduce the image; or you can contact organizations, such as the UK's Design and Artist Copyright Society (DACS), who will aid in this on behalf of their artist members. With smart contracts, some of these terms could change over time; for example, if copyright is conferred to the buyer, or even the physical object itself, the possibilities could self-execute after a set period. Nothing is off the table. The art world is often dubbed the last unregulated market—in every sense of the word—but it is for that reason that its brokers are not especially eager to change the way that it runs.

In 2021, speculative possibilities continued to run rife. Beeple's NFT, the accumulation of five thousand digital pictures the artist made—one every day for more than thirteen years—is not without merits. It functions much akin to a metaphorical archive for online surf culture. It could also be thought of as a kind of durational performance, a committed act of self-archiving in the digital age. The same can be said of Evan Roth's sculptural work *Internet Self Cache Portrait* (2012–ongoing) series, which I exhibited in *Electronic Superhighway (2016–1966)* in 2016. Here, Roth created portraits from stored data found on his web browsers. In situ, the seemingly random images disappeared into a constellation mirroring a three-dimensional landscape. Trevor Paglen's gesture of sending a curated selection of one hundred images of Earth into outer space in his *The Last Pictures* (2012) is equally suggestive of a form of reification—an archive of humanity.

Yet intriguingly, those artists, schooled in the fine arts and in possession of the required pedigree for the market—constituted by a confluence of museum exhibitions, reviews, monographic publications, commissions, as well as commercial gallery representation, do not aspire to the price points or levels of fame garnered by *EVERYDAYS*. Traditionally, most people who sell art at auction are collectors, or their heirs, turning their legacy into dollar signs, as opposed to artists themselves. Beeple, taking inspiration perhaps from one of the wealthiest artists alive, Damien Hirst (who in 2008 openly sold through an auction without work first being consigned to a gallery), may have just developed a new trend.

The Summer of Content

The two questions on everyone's lips as we moved into summer 2021, were why and how did Beeple do it? Although my career has almost exclusively been rooted in the nonprofit sphere, working for museums, universities, and public broadcasters, my inbox was flooded with requests for comment. As with anything perceived as completely new, I remained mum. Of course, NFTs were not entirely new. Artist Kevin McCoy minted the first NFT, *Quantum*, in 2014. McCoy sold it at Sotheby's in its "Natively Digital: A Curated NFT Sale" in 2021, after the Beeple extravaganza, for an equivalent of more than 1.4 million U.S. dollars—a gargantuan price tag at the time compared to any previous work by Kevin McCoy, who usually works collaboratively with Jennifer McCoy. I was suspicious about how the auction houses were now positioning themselves as curated spaces. Curated by whom? When a colleague attempted to set up a call with her self-proclaimed "dear friend," who was the CEO of Christie's, to speak about the possibilities of digital art, his ingratiating warmth dissipated as soon as I mentioned that I wanted to ask him a couple of questions about NFTs and one about Beeple. He made the excuse that it was a busy time of year and that, if I was interested, I could be connected with one of the NFT specialists based in New York. A band of specialists for a form of art that had only just been born. I was not so much intrigued as offended. The orbit of those individuals working on and through digital assets consisted of a small group of diligent and hardworking curators and conservators. Who were these unnamed individuals?

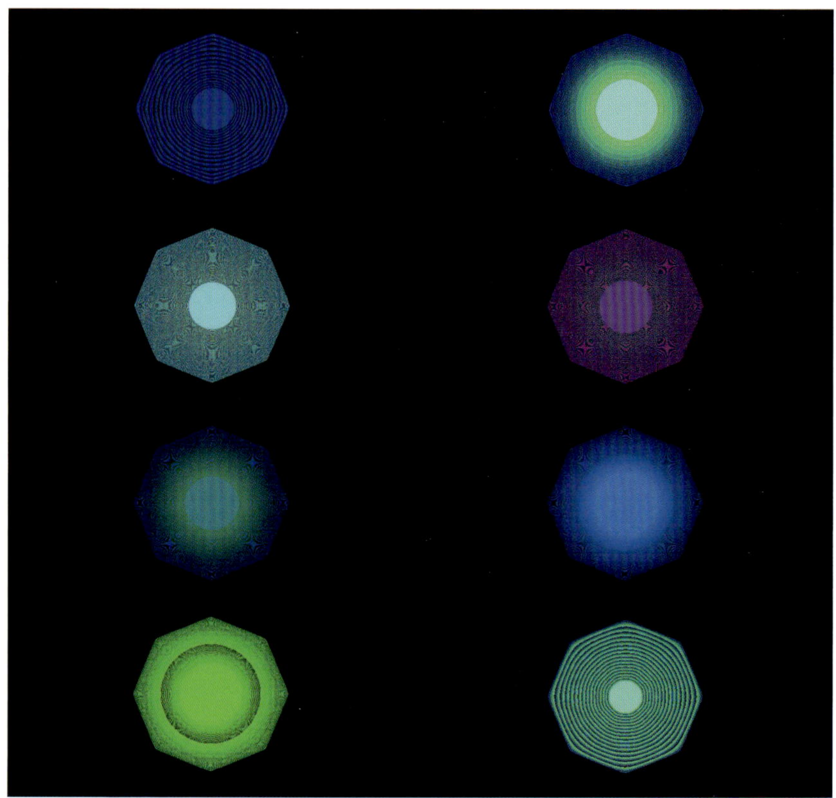

Kevin McCoy, *Quantum*, 2014 (multiple views) __Digital animation

Christie's, at the time, was resuscitating its aging brand, which had been eclipsed by other auction house brands, such as Phillips, who in the new millennium collaborated with nonprofits, for example the Design Museum and Whitechapel Gallery, on trendy exhibitions, including my own *Electronic Superhighway (2016-1966)*. When Phillips opened its doors to its new London headquarters on Berkeley Square, it became known for inviting prominent curators, such as former Venice Biennale artistic director Francesco Bonami, to curate exhibitions in their showroom. They also seemed to be the most forthcoming of the legacy auction houses to embrace the digital context.

The thing about the art world, as pioneering artist Barbara Kruger once noted, is that "the flavor of the month has quickly become the flavor of the minute."[16] Christie's—owned by François-Henri Pinault, actor

Salma Hayek's husband and the heir to Kering, which owns luxury fashion brands, such as Gucci and Balenciaga—was now seemingly cool and ahead of the curve, according to not only the upwardly mobile collectors of art I knew but even artists. All this thanks to the spotlight generated by one artist and a single sale that projected aspirational mythologies outside of the small bubble that comprises art's marching band. Pinault's auction house was now bragging that it was a "pioneer" of "new technologies," proclaiming expertise in the form of press releases and statements informing the public that Beeple is a "visionary."[17]

The museum suits—CEOs and directors of development and marketing—stuck their heads up from behind their weathered desks. The inquiries that they posed were not indecorous, but probing; this was art history, after all. Suggestions emerged that works by Old Masters or of potentially looted artifacts could be minted as NFTs to raise funds for conservation. Several organizations, such as the British Museum in London, the Albright-Knox Art Gallery in Buffalo, New York, and the Uffizi Gallery in Florence, jumped on the bandwagon and began minting NFTs, which the media dubbed as replicas.

When did the suits behind the coveted doors of asset management conglomerates, who sell watches, yachts, and luxury homes, determine taste, or what constitutes a worthy culture? It seems that the artist's self-assessment might be more discerning than that of the asset managers pushing his work. There is no dispute that Beeple's work is significant in the realm of culture. His specific brand of reflective political introspection is evident in his film *Manifest Destiny* (2019), a critique of U.S. capitalist impulses set to a soundtrack created by the rap duo Run the Jewels. His self-deprecating brand of humor might also suggest a steady head on his shoulders. But how can Mike Winkelmann, Beeple, produce art without forever being entangled in history as the progenitor of the NFT market and the popularization of blockchain technologies and currencies as a site for making money from art? Does he care? Time will tell.

What to Do with Your Coin

After several months, the global market for NFTs was reported to have ballooned to over three billion U.S. dollars in value; like all speculative markets, it would mushroom and collapse.[18] Some media outlets noted that NFTs were not yet sufficiently fulfilling their fiscal promise, while many others believed it was a fad that people should jump on quickly if they had the disposable coin to do so. In the space of months, tweets and memes were being auctioned off as NFTs. Tim Berners-Lee, the creator of the World Wide Web (WWW), sold the digital artifact of his original code document as an NFT. Elon Musk, Tesla's billionaire owner, toyed with the public's imagination, offering potential digital assets for sale, only to remove the prospect. A joke created for and among the ultrarich?

Everyone was asking me who has been acquiring these NFTs. While Beeple's sale of *EVERYDAYS* went to the crypto-entrepreneur Vignesh Sundaresan, I had spent the majority of my lockdown living next door to a retired banker, angel investor, and engineer whose pursuits had quickly funneled him into the NFT milieu. Although he did not have any direct involvement in the world of art, he would soon be making NFTs. I wondered to what extent this was a result of a certain form of privilege, or perhaps, technical know-how. He, like many, had purchased Ethereum and myriad currencies when they were being sold much more cheaply in their genesis. But he wanted to make good on his win and to fashion a collective space for other creatives to bloom.

This was not always to be in my experience. "Hefty transaction fees!" one friend hollered at me when asked why he was seeking to cash out a large sum of cryptocurrency. A scientist by training and profession, he invested in Bitcoin early, after having received them as a gift to get him started. I peered at him, perplexed that he could not see the economic chasm between us.

This friend had made nearly a million U.S. dollars at thirty-five years of age by acquiring coin early and moving it around, following what sounded like logical judgment. That said, with the antimoney laundering laws in the UK, the banks were making it exceedingly difficult for him to cash out so that he could acquire a property from a brokerage that only dealt with cash payments in pounds sterling. He tried withdrawing sums from Bitcoin ATMs and transferred funds to numerous bank accounts, many of which were being threatened with closure due to insufficient or total lack of documentation. Although numerous platforms enable such transfers, you lose a percentage, and the specifics will become messier as governments begin to comprehend that an entirely new currency that undergirds their own now exists. Not only could it destabilize the government-sanctioned and produced currency, but it also demands new structures of legislation to be quickly set up. The notion of taxation on such acquired wealth is nebulous. Up until that point, I was informed by several friends that they used their cryptocurrency simply to acquire their weekly dose of hashish or other drugs that are not legal where they lived or worked. Despite the openness of the blockchain, the unique identifying links can still be difficult to tether to specific individuals, due to the fact that an individual can set up many wallets and deploy middle managers to execute transactions on their behalf.

An ongoing concern among certain users in the cryptosphere is the potential fluctuation in the currency, which is evident in Christie's terms of sales for NFTs. A Christie's New York sale in 2021 was accompanied by a thirty-three-page document, where under clause 4 the buyer must accept that there are "risks associated with purchasing, holding and using NFTs."[19] Standing back and looking in, the entire scene could be perceived as vaudevillian. It was obvious that owners of crypto were returning to a specific intention—to create a self-sustaining universe that operates outside of the confines of the hierarchies of national clearing banks and their strictures. That said, art and aesthetic culture were also being put to auction as a form of social capital to give credence to this new world. In the months since Beeple's auction, many commercial entities intertwined with art, from galleries and auction sites, as well as real-estate brokerages and currency conversion sites emerged, all of them accepting only cryptocurrency. It is not worth speculating on their success or failure since, in the pop-up art world, relevance can be flash in the pan. What's cooking?

A New Business Venture?

Following the auction of *EVERYDAYS*, I have been approached by at least a dozen start-up ventures or collaboratives seeking my skill set for some kind of notional NFT platform that would beat all the rest. What did they want me to actually do? The answer is that they didn't really know. I could have been an advisor or a CEO, a consultant, an artistic director, or an all-around sage. In some instances, I was offered access to teams of engineers and market specialists to support whatever vision I had. It all sounded too good to be true, which it was. What would I get for all the time put into such an all-consuming position? Shares of a business in cryptocurrency were the pay. Shares that I could not cash out. Health insurance was covered by some, but how would it be paid for by those who did not provide it? Or rent for that matter?

It was at this point that I began to hear the terms *fiat* and *coin* mix in meetings, that is, real solvent cash money and a coin combo package. After listening to the humdrum of investors in virtual conference rooms, I would turn my gaze to them, and with my eyes, ask: "What 'skin' are *you* putting in the game?" Having begun my career in broadcast, focusing on documentary and nonfiction programming, I was attuned to the obsession with the new. One of my early side hustles was as a freelance scout researching talent on an early season of the UK edition of the talent show *The X Factor*. But discovery within this context had tangible contours. I was there to aid in finding a singer with unique vocal qualities, like a significant painting, or in some cases, everyday people whose delusions of grandeur extended beyond their lack of pitch, which helped shape action and drama as well as tear-jerking or hilarious scenes for tele tales. Could the thousands of uninitiated who now dub themselves NFT artists share a kinship with the reality TV contestant—the aspirational one who makes it through the meritocracy? I will not press this; we all deserve to rake it in, and we fashion our own compass. If you can appropriate an image from Instagram, Photoshop it, and annotate it with a sentence that makes people laugh, I see nothing wrong with someone paying to own the digital or even perpetual rights to such an image. The property created by the intellect is historically what funds certain forms of talent, especially within the music industry, where song catalogs can be sold for hundreds of millions of dollars.

The details of programming and legality for NFTs were to become of particular interest to start-up developers. I was invited to cultivate ideas around the aforementioned smart contracts, self-executing documents that automatically perform a promise encoded within. Although it may not necessarily be bound by law due to the lack of juridical precedent, one can insert any term to be fulfilled upon signature or sale. For instance, you could denote that a certain percentage of sales from an artwork must be donated back to the artist, their family, or their estate, which carries on in perpetuity if the artwork is resold. The same can be achieved with smart contracts and physical objects or artworks. However, it is this specific angle that many get excited about when first venturing into the NFT space. "Could NFTs end world hunger?" one venture capitalist asked me.

Now for an experiment—mint, sell, and buy an NFT with a random cryptocurrency. I knocked on the door of my favorite NFT autodidact—a self-styled artist and computer programmer, who maintains anonymity to the world, but whom I happened to have enticed into revealing their identity to me. We spent an afternoon developing a smart contract around an NFT of my own making. I proposed to sell a PDF of one of my most read and now out-of-print books as an NFT. The smart contract noted that the buyer could hold the NFT for a total of forty-eight hours before offering it back to the seller for the price they paid for it. I sold the NFT to my friend through an Algorand wallet, which he had set up for me and injected with some currency, because I had none and did not know how to get any. And just like that, after forty-eight hours, I was able to have the NFT sold back to me for the same amount of crypto that had been used to acquire it. Not all NFTs are encoded with a smart contract, which likewise constitutes considerable cost and labor to produce, but in the end, it was these encoded terms that made me consider tangential scenarios around intellectual property and digital assets going into the future. In short, it made me think. Whether or not we wake up to the grand delusion of it all is really of little consequence.

Stop and Start Again: An Interlude of Mourning

People stopped hugging from spring 2020 onward. Everyone might as well have said, “I don’t want your cooties.” In 2022, many still do not hug, and they may never again. We are living in an age of the transmissible, from pandemic to digital fad. I engage with people on Instagram, with individuals whom I have not spoken in years. The words “I miss you” and “I love you,” disingenuous or not, suture the absence of art or human encounter, or even the rabble-rousing caricature of a rogue president on the news 24/7. The world opens up for a brief moment before another variant appears. My first partner dies; we were twenty when we first danced. And then another one goes down. I switch off all my social-media applications. It is not so much an act of grief; it is my equivalent of wearing black—living in a constant shroud of shadow, much akin to the social-media blackout that took place after the death of George Floyd.

What Do You Want? The Future of the Curator after the Internet

I was online researching why the Canadian pop star Grimes had bracketed herself into the mythological label of *post-internet art*. As the person who compiled the first anthology on the subject, I wanted to decode the aesthetic and sonic links in her early art, music, and fashion. The internet sent me into a spluttering fury with its misogyny. Article after article referred to the artist and musician as Elon Musk’s “Baby Mama.” At the time of browsing, Musk had been all over the internet for accelerating in the billionaire game and was now the richest person in the world, ahead of Amazon’s cofounder and former CEO Jeff Bezos, who had also recently made headlines with his retirement and his shamanic-geekazoid journey into space and back.

If Grimes was the Baby Mama, then Musk was the Baby Daddy, but no one wrote this. The truth of the matter is that many journalists who write about business and technology are a specific kind of person—male, prejudiced, emitting chauvinism without shame. This sensibility continued to pour out through the continued sales of NFTs at the major auction houses. That summer was Sotheby's sale in partnership with Samsung, "Natively Digital: A Curated NFT Sale by Sotheby's" (2021), where Kevin McCoy's NFT was sold. As a whole, the auction results reenshrined entrenched hierarchies of the art world's bias toward an unambiguous group of artists. White men continued to dominate the auction, while some of the most talented artists working in the field of digital-based art, who happened to be women, people of color, or queer, among them Sara Ludy, LaJuné McMillian, and Ikaro Cavalcante, could be found on the bottom rung of the crypto-bidding spectrum.

Ordinarily, I would not be concerned with the price of anything. When I train junior staff in conservation care, for example, I teach them that any artwork is a distinct and sacred possession worthy of specific care. Whether the work cost a thousand or a million dollars, it should be handled and treated with the same attention. Why was I becoming obsessed with the cost of everything? The COVID-19 pandemic had stripped many of us of certain rights and benefits as civil servants. Others had lost their jobs. The least we could hope for was some form of redemptive justice in this newly formed space, which pundits were now speculating could destabilize the traditional gallery model in favor of allowing artists to sell directly to their client base. However, some sites, such as Pace Verso, an NFT platform set up by mega-gallery Pace, seemed to suggest otherwise.

My Feelings Are Not the Same As Your Feelings!

It was the eve of the tumultuous 2016 U.S. presidential election and, as a mixed-race immigrant living in Illinois without any sense of permanence, I was constantly fueled by anxiety. I was researching the works of artists, such as Ulysses Jenkins, whose *Mass of Images* (1978) and *Two-Zone Transfer* (1979) were some of the first artworks to explicitly consider notions of white supremacy, code-switching, and the dangerous illusion embedded within the concept of racial color blindness. My irate melancholy was exacerbated by the constant claim that politics is a public relations game and that my generation of Silicon Valley wannabes had made this happen. We had allegedly served up the agency to a singular personality, i.e., Donald Trump, to consume our Earth through all our media channels. Living in Chicago at the time, the stomping ground and home of the first Black U.S. president, Barrack Obama, offered some sense of solidarity. But Trump's torrent of verbal abuse and reprobate political maneuvering suffocated the hope that Obama had brought. Trump seemed hell-bent on decimating the ideological strides that Obama had made toward a United States where the president could be Jewish, Muslim, atheist, Black, white, or Latinx, and of any gender—binary or nonbinary.

My generation—the millennials, specifically, the first-gen of us who were born in the early 1980s—have also been accused of killing dinner dates at old-fashioned Applebee's, which parents worry will go out of business. But our alienation, wrought by the competitive marketplace, work-study, and the mountains of student debt, has led us to online dating as a distraction and to prevent squandering a buck or two on time wasters. We have been accused of spoiling movie culture with our obsession with personal screens, which are, of course, the cheaper option. We are told we are ruining work by demanding flexi-work hours. But even though we request more flexibility, we also work more and take fewer vacations, if any at all. We have things to pay off and everything costs more now than it ever did. We are a cynical mass who question everything from the use of fossil fuels and fracking to gender stereotypes in mainstream media. This means that everyone now has to buy electric and hybrid cars, or else they risk being canceled. Don't worry Pa, Cadillac now makes a hybrid Escalade! We also don't want your blood diamonds. Nor are we that keen on casinos, which tend to be owned by such figures as Trump. And yes, we frequently get divorced. We must learn to deal with it. All of these are but a minute summary of extensive studies and commentary by late-boomer and certain Gen X adults toward those who inherited their inflated burst-bubble economy. Millennials are also accused of desiring mobility—not wanting to settle down and breed, but to deploy their right to choose. But the truth of the matter is that we were born during a housing crisis that makes settling down unattainable. If real estate in the cities in which we work and to whose economies we contribute is so impossible to afford, then why live in them? Why sustain the roads, garbage removal, semi-inhabited libraries, and schools of those who are comparably wealthy?

In the tight grip of a slow-burning depressive spell, I was invited by my friend, a Chicago-based activist, doctor, and art collector by the name of Daniel S. Berger, to cocurate an exhibition as a form of relief. The show, *Broken Flag* (2016), was to be held in his modest gallery known as Iceberg Projects and was to open on the night of the election. We conceived it as a place to celebrate or mourn. The title was lent to us by the artist, author, and musician Patti Smith, with whom I had recently begun a brief dialogue about drawing, memory, and aspects of mythmaking.

The exhibition, in the end, became both an homage to the U.S. flag, with all its glitter and sparkle, as well as a site for its burial. The sadness of that November enveloped me like a shroud. Dr. Dan, as he is fondly referred to by many of Chicago's leading artists, is a unique specimen. A world-famous HIV/AIDS research specialist, he is a transplant from New York whose mother had escaped an Auschwitz concentration camp and whose father had served as Nazi-era slave labor. Dr. Dan has made some money but continues to live in the relatively humble Rogers Park neighborhood of Chicago. It was perhaps his family's precarious, traumatic history that informed his art collecting and philanthropy. He collects only LGBTQ+, African American, and outsider art that he discovers by venturing into exhibitions and studio visits. At the turn of the New Year, Dr. Dan had just returned from New York, where he had caught wind of Arthur Jafa's new film at Gavin Brown's Enterprise, which is now dissolved. He was fizzing. I recall words to the effect of, "The summer of our scorched earth is here, on screen, for the whole world to see."

He implored me to head to Brown's gallery in New York to watch the seven-or-so-minute video, which I declined to do. Within a week, it was announced that Jafa, whom at the time I had only known as the cinematographer on Julie Dash's landmark feature film, *Daughters of the Dust* (1991), would be making an in-person appearance at Northwestern University in Evanston—a suburb north of Chicago. I looked him up and recalled a series of works that I had seen earlier in 2016. Jafa was a polymath who had faced many a rejection in the neat confines of the art world. A collagist from a young age, he filled notebooks with cutouts, mastering shapes and forms with political fervor, transforming them into constellations as ambitious in their sprawl as the late German historian Aby Warburg's unfinished visual project, *Mnemosyne Atlas* (1924–29). A selection of Jafa's expressive notebook montages was presented in Los Angeles at the Hammer Museum's *Made in L.A.: a, the, though, only* (2016). The biennial exhibition was curated by Hamza Walker, a fellow Chicagoan who was a Renaissance Society curator at the time, and Aram Moshayedi, a Hammer Museum curator. Moshayedi, whose shows had become must-see adventures in the Los Angeles art scene, pushed the limits of exhibition making, fusing music and dance into gallery spaces and exploring subjects from ethnicity to architectural ruin. Jafa's work, presented in vitrines, displayed imaginative renderings of bodies in close-up, proximate but enclosed in folders. Never to be touched, it was a cinematic montage of endlessness.

On February 28, 2017, I hopped in a car with colleagues to travel from the Museum of Contemporary Art Chicago's downtown campus to see Jafa's presentation at the Block Museum at Northwestern University. I walked into the auditorium on that freezing evening, blowing cloudlike plumes into the air. In the theater's darkness, I experienced an unfathomable blaze that suffocated my breath for over seven minutes until I spat it all out in tears.

After seeing Jafa's film *Love Is The Message, The Message Is Death* (2016), the artist gave a public Q&A, but I could not even grasp his words, or manage to engage in the group discussion. The work had ruptured an inner galaxy of bottled-up pain that I could not articulate but only feel.

Jafa's work was a montage of appropriated and layered history. Appropriation—the art of borrowing, culling, layering, pasting, and collaging from primary and secondary sources into new composite pictures—is as magnificent a concept as the idea of contemporary art itself. We have borne witness to it from the conceptual master of the readymade, Marcel Duchamp, to Campbell's soup-can imagist Andy Warhol to Barbara Kruger's text paintings to Cindy Sherman's meticulous self-transformations into popular idols. The same can be alleged of every artist to emerge since the advent of networked technology, whose practices borrow from images to open-source code to hijacking mainstream distribution platforms. Since the 1980s and the era of ACT UP, many artistic forms have post-facto been situated within the western HIV/AIDS and Stonewall narrative. Appropriation art, after then, seemed to have reached its formal and resonant apex—a zenith of aesthetic and political action in one soup.

As the cross-embedded image has come to bear on our lives, it has also begun to feel as if something is missing. The art that preceded us seems aloof, too often expunged or inserted into the world for a specific purpose. Absent was a collage of emotion. Not simply any form of emotion, but the collective, unrelenting feeling of the present, expressed not through dispersal but through a visual world collected and pieced together. The answer to this came for me in *Love Is The Message, The Message Is Death*, arguably one of the most extraordinary artworks I've seen in recent memory. It is a work that is to be ingested, imbibed, and hurled back out into the world. It even offers moments of transcendence.

The backbone to this collage of sound and images from footage of moments of joy and pain in the Black American experience is a reverie of interpolated voices that builds to a natural crescendo. "Ultralight Beam," from Kanye West's 2016 album *The Life of Pablo*, is made central but unfamiliar. The programmed drums by Swizz Beatz have been slowed-down, thus forming a relay between flashes of communal abundance and pure violence. With each accelerating drum section, we draw out of love and into a bottomless pit of anguish. Choir maestro and singer Kirk Franklin is joined by a ten-piece choir, as well as musicians Chance the Rapper, El Debarge, The-Dream, West, and vocal samples taken from an Instagram video of Natalie and Samoria Green. Most familiar to this 1990s R & B fan is Kelly Price's immaculate phrasing, a vocalist whose tessitura sounds like an embittered wrestle with the congested throbbing pain that spindles out of catastrophe. How could we forget her relay with Faith Evans and Whitney Houston on "Heartbreak Hotel" (1998)? In Jafa's soundtrack, the sparing use of her voice makes the movement through breath and key change feel like a choreographed sermon.

But *Love Is The Message, The Message Is Death* is no sermon. It does not preach. The fact that it tells you what you might already know but have chosen to deny is what cuts. One could see this as an atlas of Black emotion in the Pan-African sense that its expression does not splinter but celebrates Black life until one is left understanding: this is why we code-switch—to survive. Self-loathing is on default. One catches themselves before they get caught. I was born Black and brown and grew up near Koreatown in Los Angeles. Gido, Mama, and Baba said I was blessed with a color "rice pudding" enough to marry an English rose. I would never tell them otherwise in 1994 in LA. Another person was living inside of me—one who is as queer as they were Muslim; a she as much as a he, who wanted to be equal parts the bombshell that was Norma Jeane, aka Marilyn Monroe, and boasting the gospel and accolades of Hattie McDaniel. But that person was told they needed to die to survive. And for the longest time, that person did.

That was until the rousing politics of a life transposed saw me being held at gunpoint by my kin, life as a constant stop and search, the toxicity inside seeping through. "We Are Not Aliens," says Martine Syms in *Love Is The Message, The Message Is Death*. I look at my ID card, an update to the one my father handed to this asylum seeker at the age of seven. She's right. It doesn't say "alien" anymore but "resident." I am a resident in my own home—never to be or belong, simply oscillating between which kind of American voice I want to put on today. I wouldn't know what constituted natural speech. Perhaps that is why I've lived with a form of tardive dyskinesia, myofascial Tourette's-like spasms, for the last number of years. I call it a speech impediment, but others might call it a condition of life.

Arthur Jafa has come to the fore in 2016 as one of the leading creative intellectuals on Black visual culture. As a mixed-race, queer, disabled person who grew up in the United States, his history is both a part of mine and not, since our traumas are personal, even if the oppression that we face today might be the same. Jafa has crystalline thinking about how we can be specific in the ways we annotate difference. He has often noted that the distinct qualities that define a communal Black culture or identity are equally those that withhold specific forms of development in how one sees oneself. His theories of "Black Visual Intonation" are complex and polemical.[20] He argues that contemporary Black visual culture lacks the nuance and mass cultural influence of popular Black music. Yet he links it to earlier forms of artistic practice, such as Picasso and Cubism, and how the inspiration for such art was derived from Black people, i.e., people like my grandfather who were living in Africa, not in the United States. So how does the interplay of history between the motherland and the colonization that was faced in those spaces relate to the lived experience of those who came to the United States as slaves and their descendants who continue to be entrenched in the practical structural inequity of that history?

In *Love Is The Message, The Message Is Death* police brutality is committed by those who are Black and white. Temporal order has collapsed: we could be in 1991 or 2010. Scenes with the Getty Images watermark convey the weight of an image culture managed and owned by conglomerates tethered to white aristocracy. Jafa is filling in the gaps to narrate not what has simply been lost but what has been withheld. It is no surprise, then, that authors, such as Saidiya Hartman, with her concept of critical fabulation, opened the door for writers, artists, and historians to piece together the felt imagination of the past—the loose threads that weigh us down with their ambiguity.[21] By acknowledging the feelings that dictate the direction of the lens—that ontological view of history—we allow others to step forward and join us in a critical unpicking of our difference, building nuanced, not flattened waves of solidarity against the constant oppression. In *Love Is The Message, The Message Is Death* we witness the beginning of a form of art making that has the potential to change the pace of society.

I have watched those seven-plus minutes more than one hundred times, and there has never been an instance when I have not felt something. The triggers change. Whether it's the teenager in that yellow bikini unassumingly bathing, only to be abruptly thrown to the ground, or the young boy up against the wall. That boy, whose daddy, like mine, taught him how the world would look at him, is being prepped, not for Ivy League education but for inevitable cruelty and police brutality. His tears are not acceptable. But we see them; I see them, and the cognitive processing that ensues. Then it all comes crashing down, and there is James Brown in a death drop. A charred soul resuscitated. Millions will watch. A movement will balloon. Art is not necessarily intended to change the world, but it can be a flash point—a chorale, a cry toward that journey. *Love Is The Message, The Message Is Death* is one of those rare songs of freedom to emerge in the age of the internet.

The Prophecy: Are We Looking Outward Yet?

An NFT drop: that's what they call coordinated NFT sales in batches on digital art online auction platforms, such as Nifty Gateway. It's a little like a hen laying eggs. An NFT drops at Art Basel Miami Beach! "I need to give you urgent feedback from my conversations with Pace!" screams an art advisor into my voice mail, music in the background. Nifty Gateway, we trust you for sales. Nifty Gateway, you are being sued. Nifty Gateway, we trust you again.

Sustaining our collective future is imperative but, equally, histories of the present need to be authored, or else we lose ourselves to history. The Otolith Group (Kodwo Eshun and Anjalika Sagar), whose incisive video works cut through the paradoxical context created by technology and its after effects, has made me consider this. In *The Radiant* (2012), the Anthropocene—the current geological age in which human activity is the dominant influence, an epoch of our own making and inevitable decay—is explored through the lens of nuclear history. Filmed in the aftermath of Japan's devastating March 2011 Tōhoku earthquake and tsunami, *The Radiant* considers how a damaged nuclear power plant and post-traumatic stress materialize as a kind of energy field. Here, a burdened history can be unspooled into visual abstraction. *Anathema* (2011) correspondingly engages with the phenomenology of technology. Examining the molecular relationship between crystals and the human touch on LCD touch screens, such as smartphones, The Otolith Group suggests that our gestures—the sense of touch itself—have become fetishistic commodities in the dream machine of late capitalism. Remember the patenting of tactile gestures by corporations? The visual splendor that radiates off the screen is equally soothing and unsettling, a revelation of the optical sorcery in which we have all become conduits.

Sitting at a screen after many sleepless nights, I consider this work and the hundreds discussed here. I am left with probing questions that we should seek to answer together, in galleries, street rallies, and community gatherings; in symposia and chatrooms; and through picture sharing, comment fields, and beyond. The internet, to invoke the architect Buckminster Fuller, can be envisaged as Dymaxion—a portmanteau of dynamic, maximum, and tension. If we imagine it as one of Fuller's cellular geodesic domes, what would it contain? The potential to promote or erase atomic culture? Can it enliven the possibility of peace on Earth? Or has it, indeed, become Earth? Will it swallow us whole, allowing us to live within its cables and escape the adverse environmental impact that its continued proliferation generates? Or, if we attain *net zero,* a term used to create a relative maxim for carbon emissions, will we reverse time? If this book is to make one teachable point, it is that the world after the advent of the WWW, and the internet that came before, does not exist in binaries. We are not digital natives versus digital immigrants. We do not simply make decisions as the result of preprogrammed algorithms. Instead, we have the capacity, as artist Cory Arcangel reminded me during a 2021 virtual tour of recent online artworks, to learn the way the algorithm functions and scramble it into disarray. We can twiddle with the aspirations of its programmers, crafting our own desires and counterintuitively pursuing technology, if not to control it, then at the least to collectively take ownership of it and begin to make sense of its contours.

The web is a generative and generous space. It was given to the people of the world by its founder for free. He did it to share and gather knowledge, as well as to develop mutual relationships of support and interest. Likewise, Wikipedia, which since its inception is regularly ranked as one of the top ten most-visited websites in the world, is governed by a nonprofit foundation. Its founder, Jimmy Wales, is not on any billionaire list, nor have he or his employees sought to profiteer or exploit our data to gain traction for Wikipedia. Instead, Wikipedia and the Wikimedia Foundation have crafted sets of enhanced community guidelines and trained everyday people in marathon sessions to engage communities to share their special knowledge on any subject. It encourages authors and editors to pursue original research and to generate information that opens doors to new ideas. All the website's finances are derived from reader donations, donors the board cultivates, and through the sale of Wikipedia-specific merchandise. In the same vein, UbuWeb—Kenneth Goldsmith's cache of avant-garde material—was uploaded for free in the poet's own time; he would pay to sustain and maintain it. Rhizome's Artbase and Net Art Anthology are treasure troves of net-based art that exist freely to the public, as is the work of many of the progenitors of web-based art who primarily emerged in the early 1990s.

How does one put a full stop, a period, on a story without an end?

Is the Earth a Scorched Cable?

My House Is My Museum

I am subletting in London from a friend, who has afforded me the respite of discounted rent so that I can complete this book. I wish I were home, although the concept of home no longer exists for me, as I constantly relocate based on the necessities of what is perceived as my chosen career. It is nearing the middle of 2022; I begin reading the first pages of Jonathan Crary's "Scorched Earth," an essay that takes on the biggest culprit that has led to our "time of emergency"—digital culture itself.[1] In these pages, the noted cultural historian who so poignantly and critically dissected the ocular experience of a 24/7 society is on a mission to thwart common human misconceptions about the age in which we live. Among these is the concept that the internet is something that can be taken into our hands, or indeed that can change hands, as certain digital utopians might intimate.[2] Instead, a cornucopia of deceit and betrayal is sketched out—from the concept that human beings hold the power to become the entrepreneurs of their own cultural capital to the disastrous mediated culture that has led to an energy-guzzling visual culture that fuels the internet. The latter, he argues, has led to "financialization of social existence, mass impoverishment, ecocide, and military terror."[3]

My takeaway from the book was that all culture exists to be subsumed. I was reminded of the journey of the Big Five tech companies and their mass consolidation, which mirrors many other industrial complexes, such as the Big Five publishing houses, the Big Five talent agencies, and the Big Five film studios, to name but a few cursory examples. Despite the internet's expression of itself as a transparent field of and for visual culture—i.e., seemingly impossible to distort, because it is an active agent in its making—the mirage of history persists. The continued amalgamation of tech culture is illustrative of a universe where aesthetics and ownership, access, and license are decided on by the few. Commitments to net neutrality—for example, service providers not blocking certain content access—quickly becomes a notion that can be reversed and dependent on individual companies and their financial interests.

Earth itself as a living thing, but also as a concept, is now charred physically and metaphorically.

I escaped my apartment that afternoon and made my way across London to the Mosaic Rooms, an exhibition space near Earl's Court, where I was to be reacquainted with the artist Mahmoud Khaled for the first time in many years. On view was Khaled's newly commissioned exhibition *Fantasies on a Found Phone, Dedicated to a Man Who Lost It* (2022). Outside the venue, a converted Victorian home, my image appears in a blue mirror.

This theme continued inside with introductory text panels glistening and reflecting my gaze. Here, the artist had converted the exhibition site into an imagined house museum for an avatar whom he had never met—the owner of a lost iPhone found by Khaled. The artist constructed this potentially fictional character based on images from the unlocked phone.

The exhibition was a dwelling for an imagined presence: an individual whom the artist deemed must have been interested in the decorative arts and who was experiencing anxiety and insomnia. Visitors entered a mostly empty room with little else besides red velvet curtains lining the walls and an elongated sofa invoking Sigmund Freud's daybed, which in black leather, expressed a BDSM aesthetic. Downstairs, a slowly rotating office bed, reminiscent of Hugh Hefner's in the 1960s, was accompanied by a calming sonic reverie. Elsewhere, the programmed sound of a bot, a stand-in for Siri or Alexa, provided instructions for an absent person to help them sleep—a surveilling app for comfort.

Within this staged house museum, something came into focus. A sense of safety arrived. The domesticity of the converted home, reconceived by Khaled once again as a domestic site, this time for an individual who was evidently queer and, potentially lost in their life, felt nurturing and kind, even generous. Perhaps, what the internet has taught us, I proffered to Khaled, is that the claim to a home is not merely a privilege but a right. In the end, it is the site where we make and unmake our identities, even more so than through the mediated platforms of Web 2.0 and beyond.

Architectures of the Future-Present

The 5:30 a.m. check-in calls with the team this morning in Sharjah lead to endless to-do lists upon my return. I am about to go on allocated vacation. A self-made liquid breakfast and a new day begins. In my hamster wheel, I exceed my daily word count authoring this book, purposefully typing as if I were a concert pianist. The reverb of my iPhone's generic ringtone punctures the air. Time to go home to Los Angeles to perform my biometrics and finally begin a path to citizenship. I've had a green card since I was a kid. COVID-19 reminded me that I needed an exit to home when the world was in free fall.

The interview was in five days and halfway across the globe. Meanwhile, in London, the world was gearing up for the cultural phenomenon known as Frieze Week, when the Frieze Art Fair comes to town. How this tentacular, global brand evolved from its genesis as a modest magazine with a Damien Hirst butterfly on its cover in 1991 is impressive. The majority of Frieze's value share, it is understood, was acquired by Endeavor Group Holdings, which was formerly known as William Morris Endeavor Entertainment, one of the largest entertainment agencies, spearheaded by Ari Emanuel. Emanuel chose to consolidate an existing brand, unlike other major talent agencies, such as United Talent Agency (UTA), which set up its own fine art division. Perhaps he was all too aware of the power of a brand and its attendant audience in this hypersaturated digital age of overflowing content.

I paid for my flight to Los Angeles using the balance of my PayPal Credit, with my bank account and credit card sucked dry by the first of the month when the bills go out. My many nights in Marriott hotels over the years offered me enough points for two free nights at the iconic Westin Bonaventure Hotel—a four-star icon of postmodern architecture, which appears in the opening scenes of producer Michael Deeley and director Ridley Scott's sci-fi movie *Blade Runner* (1982). In that film, a metallic flying car floats above a bulbous orb as it comes into frame, a shimmering structure that was used to represent the future—the year 2019. I came here to LA to write my ending, after the future. Seventeen hours of travel later, I made my way up in the rickety elevator, with its ashen gold detailing, to the twenty-ninth floor. I examined the Earth from the elevator window. In my sleepless state, I felt it descend beneath me with a pang of panic. How could this weathered-looking vestibule accommodate the hundreds of guests in the age of social distancing? Who would have the skill to upgrade this neolithic vessel from 1976?

In my insignificant room near the top floor, I peered out the window at the death drop below. Any sense of LA's endless possibilities, so often mythologized in Tinseltown, was absent. Examining the skyline, I did not have the sense that I was Tom Cruise in *Vanilla Sky* (2001). The air conditioner woke from its stupor, cranking uncontrollably in a symphonic spree. The empty refrigerator, which had not been defrosted, exploded out of its makeshift cabinet, spewing water and ice into the tight space. The ghosts in the machine, coming to life.

Encased in one of the hotel's shimmering towers, I felt as if I could not leave. I ventured to read an e-book that I had downloaded earlier by Fredric Jameson, published in 1991, where he refers to the Bonaventure's hyperspace as an enclosed city within a city, where every path winds up inward.[4] This is how the future was imagined—an intentionally confusing layout intended to lead to impulsive behavior, akin to Victor Gruen's theory of the shopping mall.[5] The reflective spires and the dark labyrinthian corridors with their low-slung ceilings enmesh the visitor. Evidently, the architect John C. Portman Jr. had been envisaging this self-contained city within

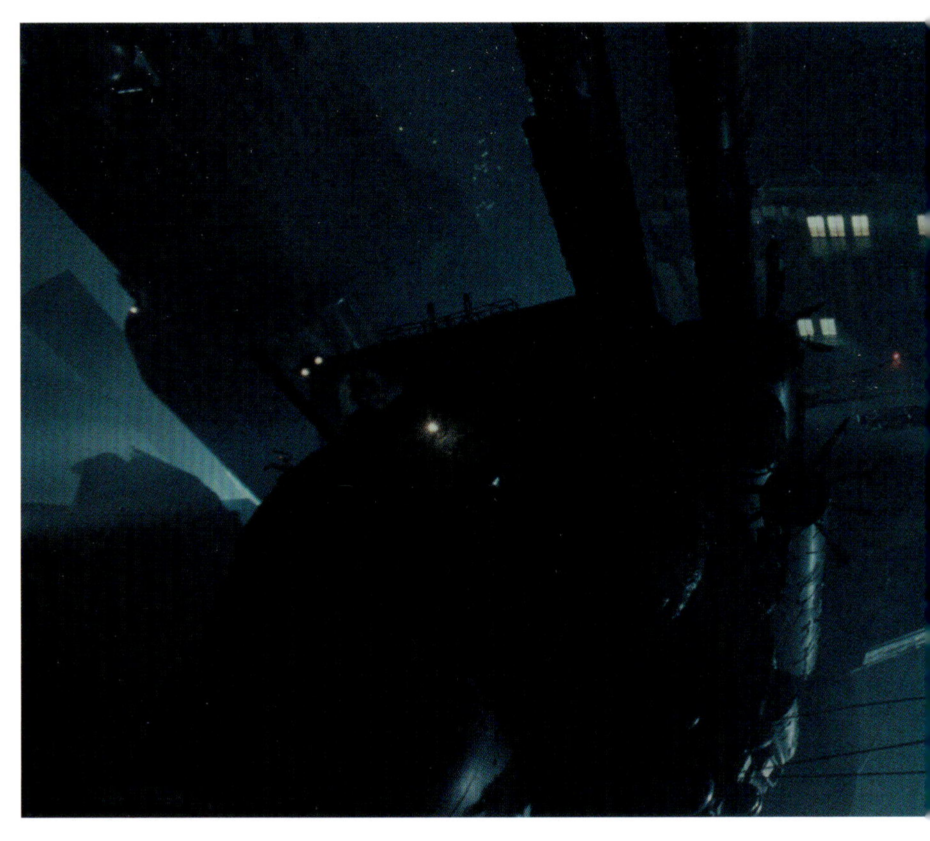

Ridley Scott, *Blade Runner*, 1982

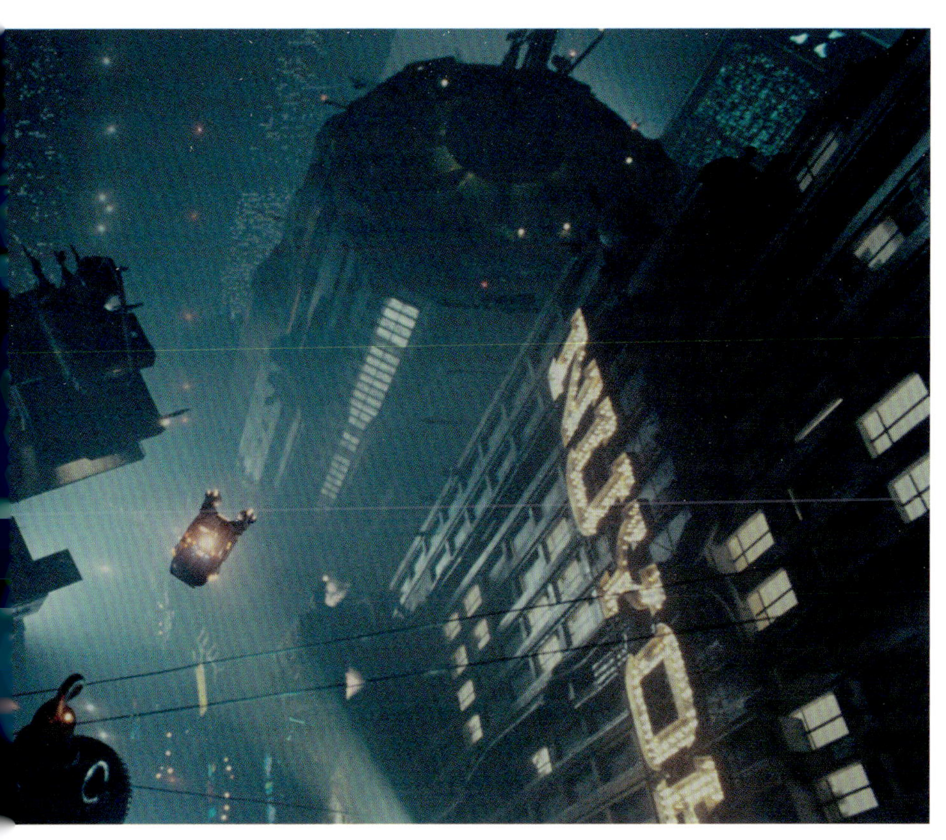

a city as a cellular metaphor for the various passages of the internet: web browsers, apps, services, spaces within spaces, with no exit.

The Bonaventure building, a Tower of Babel splintered from reality by endless car parking on each side, may not have lived up to its cinematic fantasies, but it still cataloged a distinctly digital history. Yet unlike a digital space, which exists today and can be erased tomorrow, it is a landmark piece of architecture, even if its condition and services are seriously underwhelming. In 2011, architect and historian Todd Reisz informed me colloquially, while we were both editors of *Portal 9*, a journal of urbanism and the city, that landmarks cannot be destroyed anymore, because human beings have begun to comprehend their residual value. They must be repurposed. I interrogated why we must maintain these relics. Because we have come to a point in history, Reisz eluded, where, unlike so many other forms, architecture can be iconographic beyond its function. The answer is embedded within the weight of history.

The public housing work of Le Corbusier, for example, was and remains controversial, but he is still considered a pioneer of Modern architecture. The legendary architect Ludwig Mies van der Rohe, whose buildings demarcate the cities of Chicago, New York, and Toronto, was tormented by his peers when in later life he began combining divergent styles in a single project. Lina Bo Bardi, perhaps one of the most renowned and referenced female architects today—a Brazilian born in Italy—was overlooked during most of her life for being an outsider and a woman. Had humankind decimated their ventures, of which a formidable majority were deemed unworthy at the time, the value of learning from the past would be lost. But with the perpetual archive of the internet could this concept evolve? Error! The internet is fueled by energy, and who is to say that it will be around in thirty years. What happens to the world then will demand that a new form of collective imagination emerge.

From Route to Route

At the age of ten, living in South LA, my aspirations for mobility were huge. I couldn't have cared less about the aesthetics of the motor vehicles themselves, but I wanted to get to the ocean, alone and fast. In 2005, I failed my driving test for the third time—the same year that artist Guthrie Lonergan released *Lonely Los Angeles*. Using the free software, MapQuest, this piece of browser-based art revealed endless, flowing roads and unnavigable expanses of LA's cityscape. The flat graphic renderings suggested geography that was poorly imagined or not intended to be traversed by everyone, and

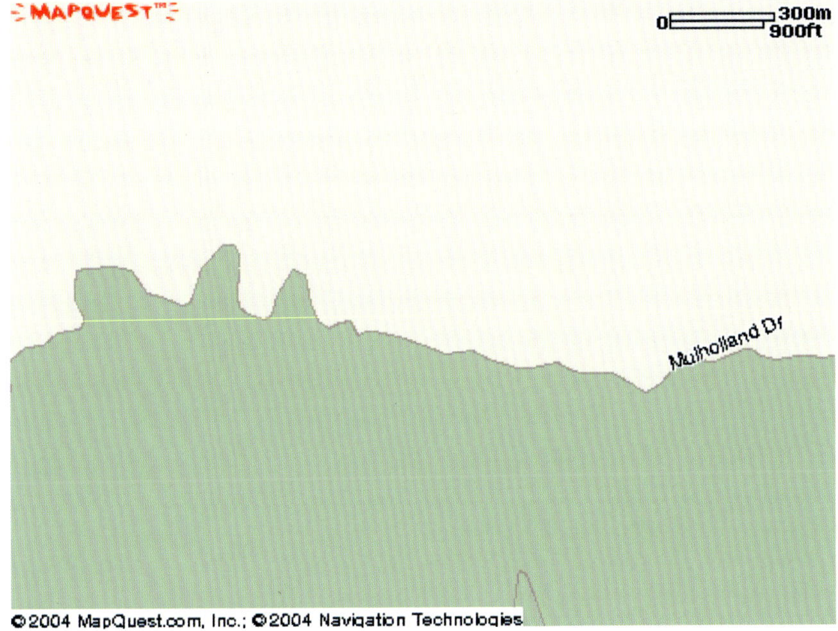

Guthrie Lonergan, *Lonely Los Angeles*, 2005 __Website

in parts, by anyone. The internet as a space, as much as a thing, whether justly or not, has fueled a wider cultural belief that the world is entirely traversable and controllable.

The concept of a world that could be tailored to one's desires may have been publicly born in 2017, when Mohammed bin Salman, the Crown Prince of Saudi Arabia, announced NEOM—a mammoth cross-border city that is entirely powered by renewable energy sources. Operating with an independent set of progressive laws, NEOM is a smart city built around the concept of human mobility through the continued study of emerging and networked technologies. NEOM boldly professes to be an "accelerator for human progress," and its developers are purported by the sales website to be "changing the future of water, entertainment and leisure," cultivating a responsive site that aims to be so livable that it will not matter what nation or state you exist within. Part of the Prince's "Vision 2030," which is anchored around ideals of a future multicultural society, NEOM's future itself might become its residents' primary obsession. With opportunities for its occupants to invest in its energy, financial services, manufacturing, and media, to name but a few examples, citizens can govern through capital. NEOM may well become the first city, as one architectural consultant who asked to remain anonymous, put it, "to be auctioned off as an IPO on the global stock market." So far, this model trumps any of the "future cities or countries" that we've seen on film, from *The Fifth Element* (1997) to *Minority Report* (2002) to the Wakanda of the Black Panther books and movies, or even contemporary futuristic metropolises, such as Dubai. The city's principles suggest that humans may want to see and experience the world through the stretchable parameters of technology. The question will remain whether such a costly venture that relies on the scarcity of energy and knowledge of technology can truly emerge to nourish and sustain the unexpected whims of the human mind and its desires.

The Future of the Brain

One of the responsive cultural phenomena to emerge in the wake of techno-futurism has been the "Eat, Pray, Love" business and belief system (a nod to the runaway success of Elizabeth Gilbert's memoir), which uses eastern philosophies to encourage a slowing down and disconnecting. It is a structure believed to be beneficial to collective well-being. If we must adopt strategies thousands of years old to maintain the motherboard that is the brain, why are we so obsessed with the future of technology or speculative forms of sci-fi literature, cinema, and broadcast content? The reason may be that the internet's evolution must be considered, not as paradoxically separate from historical imaginings of the future but in connection to it. The future is here, and it must be weighed against a system of checks and balances.

Knowledge is the subject of a constant chasm. Who sets the global agenda, and why, is an imperative line of questioning that attends to all fields of culture. The future of the brain must evolve, not as a form of nostalgia or a cinematic future but as an integrated process. In the beginning of the millennium, scientists have further developed research into the concept of neuroplasticity, where the brain can consistently change itself throughout its lifetime, evolving new neural networks. The fields of neuroscience, psychology, and psychiatry, while codependent, have developed almost completely independently of each other. Can the field of culture, with its consistent inter- and cross-disciplinary development, set a precedent for imagining how other fields of life evolve?

In 2018, I took my art-skeptic parents to an exhibition in London at the Serpentine Gallery of the artist Pierre Huyghe titled *UUmwelt*. Bluebottle flies buzzed and crawled around LED screens showing videos that

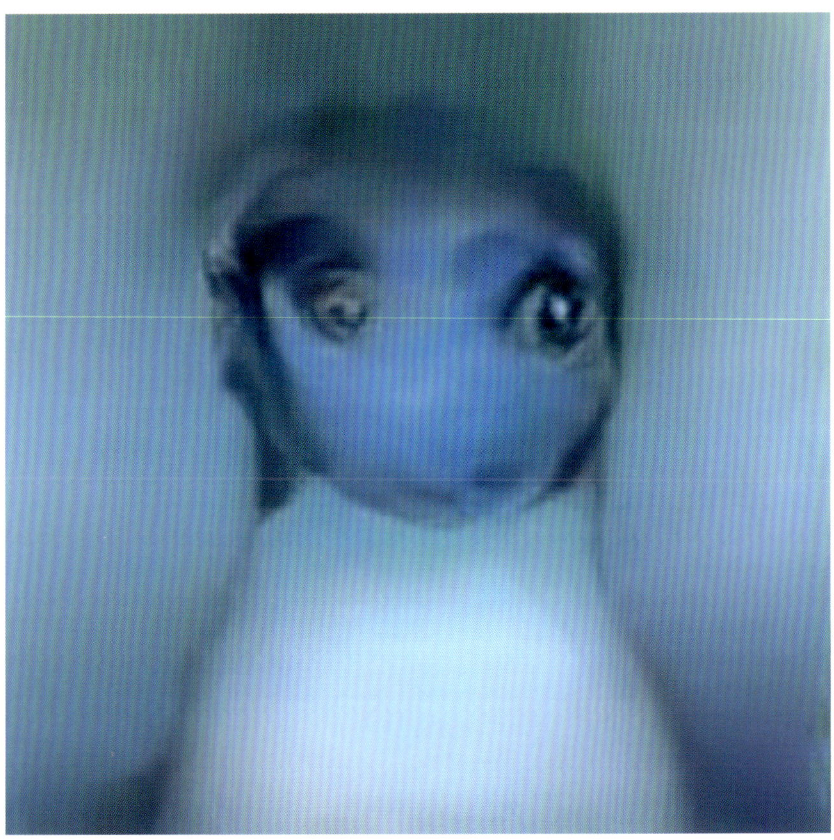

Pierre Huyghe, *Of Ideal*, 2019–ongoing __Still

would go on to inform the series *Of Ideal* (2019–ongoing). In these disturbing images, constantly morphing between barely recognizable biomorphic forms, the artist sought to capture the thought processes of waking subjects. He encouraged them to look at pictures or conjure mental images. Meanwhile, their brain patterns were run through complex scanners involving a process called magnetic resonance imaging (MRI). Subsequently, a computer visualization, an artificial neural network, reconstructed what was imagined by the subject, producing haunting pictures that shifted with viewer interaction. The result showed how machines see the neurons in our brains formulate images. How do these compare to images of real life? The insects in the gallery, creating a self-breeding, contained environment, constituted an unsettling nod to nature in relation to the machine.

My parents were disturbed. My mother, a healer of the mind, professed that she suffered from nightmares for days afterward. Her Facebook suddenly became animated with images she had taken in the gallery on her antiquated phone—a technical process I had not known she could perform. It seems as if today's art is a living continuum that can forge new conversations across generations like never before.

Scorched Cables

I texted the editor at Phaidon. The pages of the book will finally be with you in the morning, I announced. The words did not pass across the ocean, but became circular bubbles, forever loading. I opened Facebook to send her a personal message. An error page materialized. Were we undergoing a cyberattack? I peered out my window at the local roadworks. I wondered if the cables that lay beneath, in the upturned ground of rubble, prone to the blazing sun, had become scorched to such a point that the internet itself had burned to a pulp.

It transpired that Facebook was under threat. A whistleblower by the name of Frances Haugen had taken to the airwaves, professing in a 2001 interview with *60 Minutes* that "the version of Facebook that exists today is tearing our societies apart and causing ethnic violence around the world." Had Facebook taken its servers offline just as ImageNet had dumped the six thousand dubious images in its database after the revelations made by artist Trevor Paglen and AI specialist Kate Crawford? Was an act of cleansing and accountability about to take shape?

In the year that it took to author this book, server crashes of such major platforms had impeded my progress numerous times. The temporary collapse of data and telecommunication systems is now part of the everyday. Is this what they mean by the new normal?

I drift back to the monumental scene in *Blade Runner*, the oft-cited "tears in the rain" monologue that accompanies the death of Nexus 6 replicant, Roy Batty—a leader, a genius, an aspirational cyborg. Their words ring in my ear like a resonant song, "I've seen things you people wouldn't believe. Attack ships on fire on the shoulder of Orion. I've watched C-beams glitter in the dark near the Tannhäuser Gate. All those moments will be lost in time, like tears in rain. Time to die." If there is one thing that I've learned from these journeys, it is that we will all, like Batty, see different things, but it is through the power of our uniquely formed expression that we can hold those moments so that they are never lost to time or erased from collective memory. It's time for you to take the world into your hands.

The Future Hurts

In an effort to speak of contemporary culture that is underscored by the internet, I have tried to strip back codified language—the binary code of zeros and ones. I have not wished to sit behind the mask of academic credentials but to speak to a slice of truth, and specific histories, from the perspective of a present that seems to be constantly accelerating.

As much a reference book, this is a biography of a nascent history, for the seasoned early adopter, as well as the first timer. Each, I hope, has approached its pages from a different perspective. I have sought to capture a world that has been upturned by the internet. Together, we have walked a trenchant path from the 1980s to the present, where one is witness to a more inclusive view of cultural history.

Culture, as the author Jay David Bolter once noted, exists in a plenitude, where interleaving facets of the arts merge and collapse, hierarchies of the elite can be eroded, and no single art is greater than another.[6] Individuals need not be alienated by language that withholds meaning, nor should we think of art's audience in a fragmented fashion nor reduce their agency to simple algorithmic comprehension. Art's power exists in its ability to elicit emotions that may otherwise have been left unturned and to pose questions about society at large through contradictory perspectives, which can simultaneously clarify and frustrate.

We Are the Metaverse: A Parting Verse

Air Conditioning (2022), a work that I commissioned by the Turner Prize–winning artist Lawrence Abu Hamdan, was the subject of this June morning's news cycle in 2022. It is the preview day of the 12th Berlin Biennale, an arts festival in Germany that includes Abu Hamdan's installation—a sprawling visualization measuring 180 feet (54.8 m) of what the artist has referred to as the "atmospheric violence" that took place in Lebanese skies between 2007 and 2021.[1] This morning, the project, and the launch of the accompanying website www.airpressure.info, caught the *Guardian's* attention.[2]

In *Air Conditioning*, enveloping, thickening plumes of ash inflect bulbous clouds across a single painterly visualization that tightly lines the walls of the gallery. The work, developed in collaboration with the collective Cream Projects, London, comprises documents from the United Nations Digital Library that detail the number of unlawful entries by F35 planes, drones, and unmanned aerial vehicles (UAV) into Lebanon's airspace. The artist charted these incidences through a special-effects engine called Houdini, software that was also used in the making of Disney's *Frozen 2* (2019). In a supplementary film and website, Abu Hamdan reveals that these aerial encroachments pose severe health risks to the local populace below. These accompanying platforms play with the codification of digital imagery, which is simultaneously innocuous and violent.

In the gallery setting, the composite picture takes on art-historical resonances. The cloud paintings of J. M. W. Turner as well as Walter De Maria come to mind, as do the curved galleries at the Musée de l'Orangerie, Paris, that house the iconic *Water Lilies* (c.1914–26) by Claude Monet (1840–1926).[3] Rarely has the cloud felt like such an apt exploration of the wires and cables that make up the physical apparatus of the internet. By transmuting the data held on servers into the soothing and familiar aesthetic found within museums for centuries, *Air Conditioning* bestows the onlooker with multiple sensorial encounters. And just like the internet, its enjoyment brings to light various forms of human complicity.

Human responsibility for the internet is and will continue to be pivotal for societies to coexist. Within the scope of this book, the way the internet underscores art, and, inversely, the means that art accentuates the possibilities of the internet, is vital. By mapping out the field of art and culture since 1989, when the concept of the World Wide Web emerged, I have explored how the internet has fundamentally shifted almost every aspect of art making and its exhibition. The acceleration of networked computational technology has engendered a nervous class of citizens: 24/7 work and life. In response, artists have expanded the function and stories narrated by networked tools, holding the black mirror up to its manufacturers and users alike.

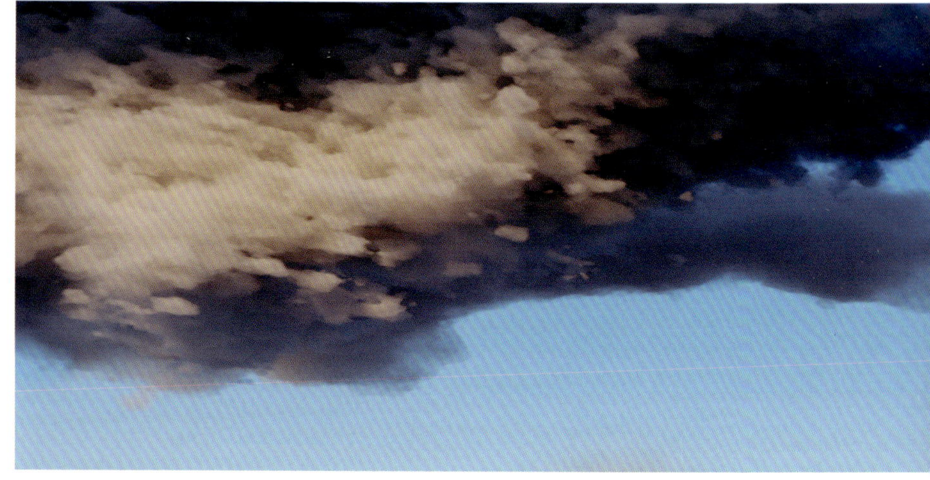

Lawrence Abu Hamdan, *Air Conditioning*, 2022 (detail) —Color inkjet print, 2 ft. 11 7/16 in. × 179 ft. 9½ in. (0.9 × 54.8 m)

Pioneering anarchists in the field of art, since the 1980s, have deployed technology creatively, unpicking programming languages and employing web browsers and phone-based applications to tell stories that otherwise might have escaped the pages of the official record or history. With the dot-com boom, its collapse, and the subsequent surge in social-media usage, artists have transformed the seemingly intangible realm of the internet into a form of living media, using images of power and corporate technology to socialize and mobilize around political causes. Culture jamming in the early 2000s would later open doors for minority representation, resuscitating hidden visual cultures, and promoting resistance to meet and supersede swelling waves of mass hate.

The seeds for these forms of artistic expression did not mature in a vacuum. The initial experiments with networked technology in the late 1960s enabled artists engaged with various forms of media, from Nam June Paik to Lynn Hershman Leeson, to speculatively map and propose techniques for imagining the very nature of the internet's existence. At every juncture onward—from the aestheticization of political storytelling in browser-based art through to the commodification of meme culture through the sale of NFTs—visual artists have generated forums for critical reflection through compelling, encompassing, agitating, thrilling, and affecting visual art.

The, at times, insular world of art is now confronted with a necessity to enact change. Augmented and virtual reality, as well as 3-D modeling,

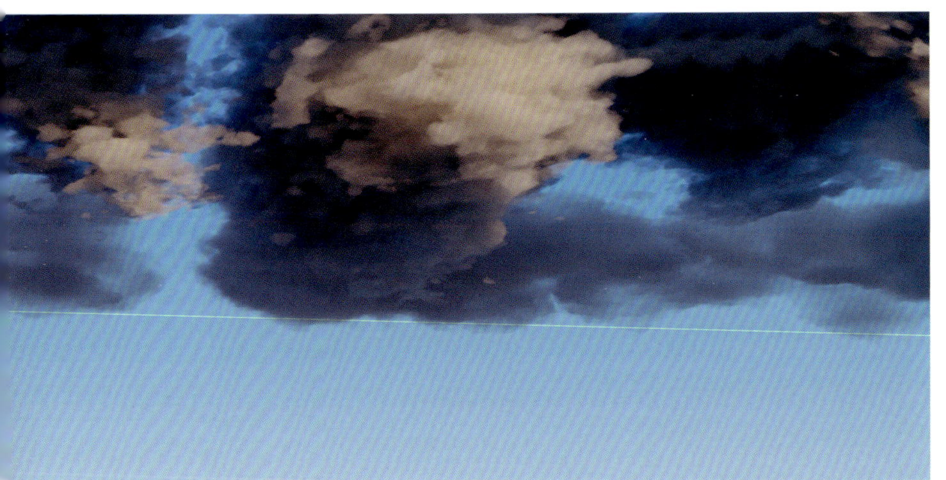

have generated a mediated means of experiencing art that some people prefer. The climate emergency might suggest this to be a more sustainable way of displaying art than shipping artworks all across the globe. Even so, the gargantuan energy-guzzling toll of complex networked technology cannot be underestimated. The initial buzz around the market potential of NFTs, and the subsequent collapse in interest and reward for them, may be seen as a similar undoing. But with every downfall, there emerges the potential to decode networked technology's expanded promise—what it really can do.

I was reminded of this by speaking with Simon Denny, whose exhibition *Blockchain Future States* (2016) first connoted the opportunities of cryptocurrency to me; he was also the first to introduce me to the model of the decentralized autonomous organization (DAO)—a subject for another book.[4] Denny proposed expanded methods of approaching cryptocurrency in ways that ravenous venture capitalists were then too narrow-sighted to comprehend: namely, that NFTs offer a variety of functions beyond the instrumentalization of art for capital gain. One can just as easily mint their toothbrush and toilet paper, a used condom, a piece of code, an idea, a dream, or their last will and testament. By doing so, one is officially archiving these assets in the digital world where they are traceable, sharable, and linkable. Through smart contracts and ancillary distribution mechanisms, these sources equally become remixed, innovated forms, hopefully evolving to become more technically stable and carbon neutral.

Standing at the edge of the metaverse, we find ourselves looking at an epoch, potentially anchored by a dormant term that has come back into view. The term *metaverse* and its popularization by the company formerly known as Facebook, Inc., has many believing that we are on the precipice of something new,[5] a perpetual obsession in the age of curated, contemporary culture.[6]

Orbiting this world, it is easy to see an emerging center of confusion. Once again, users are responding to what is perceived as a new world order, without the necessary vocabulary and context to do so. As discussed in the "Will This Destroy Us?" chapter, Lawrence Abu Hamdan asserted that language is an evolving technology, and I believe that the application of language evolves to the specific context of the individual using it. It is worth thinking of *metaverse* in relation to its Latin roots. *Meta* speaks to being "with," "across," or "after" events that occur in space and time. The metaverse, in its myriad manifestations, is also a site or space for transcending. In this regard, the metaverse is a world that surpasses the confines of a 3-D headset; it is something that is not only "self-referential" but also, as the word suggests, in a constant state of metamorphosis—like the nature of life itself.[7]

The metaverse for me, as I believe it could be for you, is as illustrative of the experience of diving into the more than fifty thousand memories and screenshots on a phone, as it is an immersion into the sculptural renderings of Lauren Halsey's *We the ones (blackngold)* (2016),[8] a work of colored synthetic hair and timber, an image lodged in my brain since I saw it.[9] I also see the immersion and augmentation of the metaverse as a field of cultural production that can be traced back to a world before the World Wide Web. Andy Warhol's studio, the Factory, a hangout for artists and a self-contained group of aspirational figures, could be interpreted as a total and complete world of social interaction. Likewise, the panoptical ecology fashioned in the evocations of drugs, lust, and rock 'n' roll in *CC5/Hendrix-War* (1973) by Hélio Oiticica (1937–1980) evoke a total sensorium as the visitor descends into the tranquil swing of the installation's hammocks. Keith Haring's multi-paneled Pop Shop in New York in the 1980s and 1990s is also my metaverse, as are Yayoi Kusama's *Infinity Mirror Rooms* series or the late Virgil Abloh's "inverted commas," which became the signature motif of his art project turned fashion label Off-White. All of these evoke or conjure an augmented, total, and social space of experience. The difference between these renderings of the metaverse and those produced by a software engine is that they are part and parcel of a culture, conceived and imagined by artists, as opposed to programmers employed by a corporation or their tech billionaire owners.

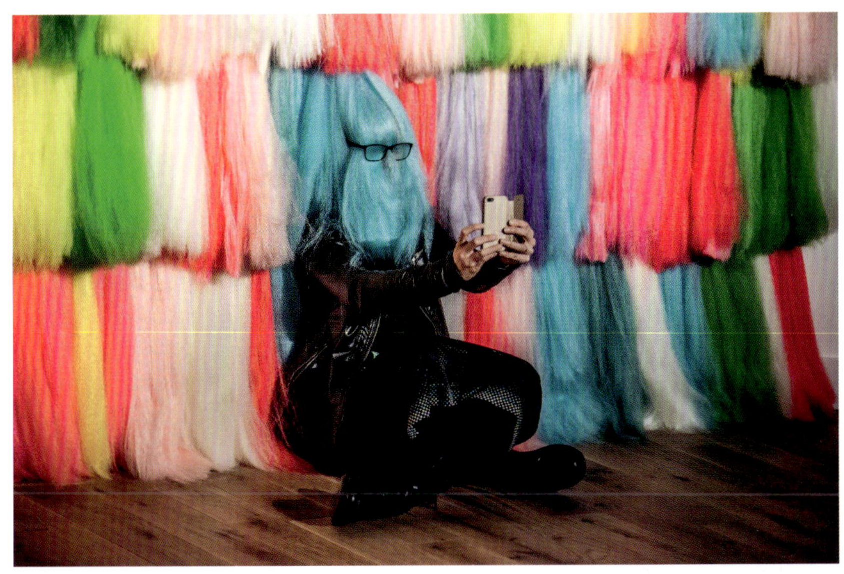

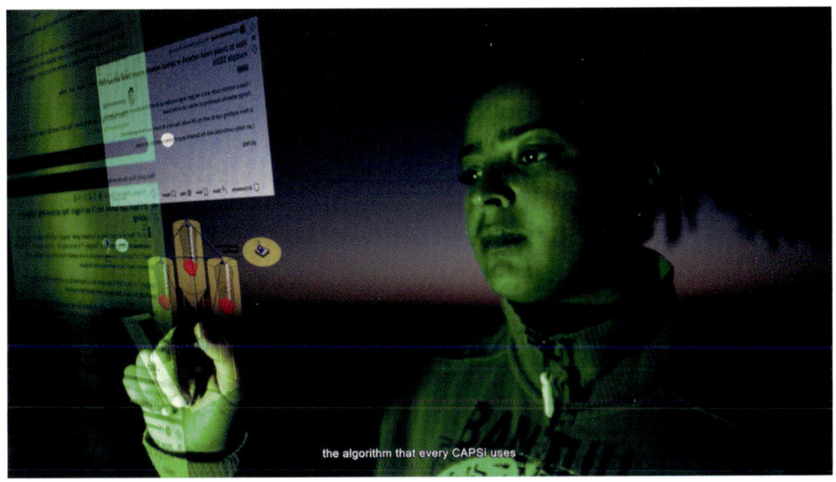

Lauren Halsey, *We the ones (blackngold)*, 2016 —Synthetic hair, timber
Installation view: Imitation of Life: Melodrama and Race in the 21st Century, HOME, Manchester, UK, 2016

Meriem Bennani, *Life on the CAPS*, 2022 —Video, sound, 34 min.

Of all the propositions by artists, one of the most transcendental evocations of a metaverse is Meriem Bennani's film *Life on the CAPS* (2022). CAPS is a fictional island set in the Atlantic. In an age where Dr. Who–style teleportation has replaced air travel, and people are held captive on CAPS for having teleported illegally, perhaps because their ethnic, social, and economic makeup does not entitle them to this method of travel. Through live and animated scenes, the detention center is reimagined as an artist colony where communal gatherings turn into righteous protest songs with choreographed clapping and dancing, a transgenerational, intercultural song of joy and solidarity. Can humankind unspool the puppeteer's strings, forming meta metaverses that are shaped and contoured entirely to their own desire and choosing? I say you/me/we must at least try!

—That's my mic drop.

Notes

Prelude: Time Is Just a Memory

1 Gabriel García Márquez's historic multigenerational family story, *One Hundred Years of Solitude* (Buenos Aires: Sudamericana Press, 1967), has been attributed with helping authors narrate linear stories with zigzags in time. Flashbacks are regularly deployed to offer texture and meaning, shifting the way contemporary narrative is evoked and articulated. See Gene H. Bell-Villada, ed., *Gabriel García Márquez's One Hundred Years of Solitude: A Casebook* (New York: Oxford University Press, 2002).

Beginnings: From Here to There to Everywhere

1 See Bruno Latour, *We Have Never Been Modern*, trans. Catherine Porter (Cambridge, MA: Harvard University Press, 1993), 151. Bruno Latour, one of the leading philosophers of science and technology, in his treatise *We Have Never Been Modern*, argued that the suggestive concept of progress associated with modernity is a matter of individual belief. Over the years, Latour has developed this argument to suggest that the digital realm fosters divides based on ideological notions, interminably linked to the nature of who and how we have access to different technologies.

2 One of the defining texts that has influenced the way that we see and engage with images, including art online, is Walter Benjamin's *The Work of Art in the Age of Mechanical Reproduction* (or *Reproducibility* as it was initially named) in 1935. These concepts were further elaborated by John Berger in 1972's BBC television program and attendant publication *Ways of Seeing*. One of the primary questions raised is: does the aura of the physical art object lose its influence when reproduced? If so, what does this say about the evolving potential of technology in relation to art?

3 *Storying* is a term found in Kevin Young's award-winning book *The Grey Album: On the Blackness of Blackness* (Minneapolis, MN: Graywolf Press, 2012). Here, Young argues that, for Black authors and creators, storying is a form of improvisational narrative that takes into consideration the necessity of encoding certain meanings.

4 Pundits and commenters alike will be aware that the introduction of net art into 1997's documenta X was critiqued for its unimaginative display and the technical difficulties that plagued the artists featured in the exhibition. By some, it was seen as a lost opportunity and, by others, as a destructive and detrimental act against the artists working within the field.

1989: The Year That Changed the World

1 That giant Panasonic TV on wheels resembled a living animal. I gave it a name that I can no longer recall. I grew to treasure it. It was to be the gateway that protected me from the polar worlds of violence on the street and my family's conservatism. Media as I had come to understand it from a young age became a site of promise and endless revelation.

2 See Guy Debord, *The Society of the Spectacle* (Detroit: Black & Red, 1970).

3 Omar Kholeif, "Performing the Self: On the Blurring of Fact and Fiction in the Age of YouTube," *Art Monthly* 343 (February 2011): 9–12.

4 This reading is often disputed and dubbed by some a western or even colonial construct.

5 See Tim Berners-Lee, *Weaving the Web: The Original Design and Ultimate Destiny of the World Wide Web* (New York: Harper Collins, 2008).

6 "How the Hillsborough disaster unfolded," *BBC News*, April 26, 2016, www.bbc.co.uk/news/uk-19545126. The game was rescheduled, and Liverpool won the FA cup that year.

7 Disco Demolition Night was a Major League Baseball promotion that occurred July 12, 1979, at Comiskey Park in Chicago. The event ended in a riot, during which a crate filled with disco records was blown up. This historic moment, which followed the release of the Bee Gees original film soundtrack for *Saturday Night Fever*, was seen as a hateful attack by many at the time on an inclusive culture of "camp" that was associated with the underground queer scene of the time.

8 For further reading, see Christian Sorace, Ivan Franceschini, and Nicholas Loubere, eds., *Afterlives of Chinese Communism: Political Concepts from Mao to Xi* (Acton, Australia: ANU Press; London: Verso Books, 2019).

9 See Jean Fisher, "The Other Story and Past Imperfect," *Tate Papers* no. 12 (Autumn 2009), www.tate.org.uk/research/publications/tate-papers/no-12/the-other-story-and-the-past-imperfect. See also Jean Fisher, "Fictional Histories Magiciens de la Terre," *Artforum International* (September 1989), www.artforum.com/print/reviews/198907/magiciens-de-la-terre-in-paris-34359.

10 The Facebook Cambridge Analytica scandal in 2015 was a notorious act of social and political obstruction on social media. More than fifty million Facebook users had their private data shared with a market research firm that was targeting voters to support the election of Donald Trump.

11 There are numerous biographies on Moore, the most exhaustive being Arnold Thackray, David C. Brock, and Rachel Jones, *Moore's Law:*

The Life of Gordon Moore, Silicon Valley's Quiet Revolutionary (New York: Basic Books, 2015).

12 David Priestland, *The Red Flag* (London: Penguin, 2010) makes a compelling case for the relationship between communism and globalization.

13 Amazon Web Services (AWS) is one of the most unique digital phenomena but is rarely discussed critically. The subsidiary of Amazon, the world's largest retailer, offers on-demand cloud computing platforms to major corporations on a metered pay-as-you-go basis. It is now the dominant virtual storage option on the market with the quickest growth spurt of any such organization and with more market share than Microsoft or Google. The concept that makes AWS attractive is the initial affordable outlay. Those using the services do not need to pay a hefty up-front sum to store their data. Data retrieval, on the other hand, much like in a real-life archive, is where the cost kicks in for the customer, consumer, or company. There are numerous concerns here, with market monopoly being one. Do we all want our data with one organization, which also reaps our metrics through the activity from its sales platform, Amazon.com? To what extent and at what expense would AWS grow? Digital commodities are not intangible or invisible. A digital photo needs to be stored just like a real one, and just because you cannot see it, doesn't mean that someone isn't plowing through land to build data centers to house it.

14 Lynn Hershman Leeson, emails with author, summer 2020.

15 Lynn Hershman Leeson, excerpts from memoir in progress emailed to the author, fall 2020 and spring 2021.

16 Laura Mulvey is a noted film historian whose most historic text was first published as "Visual Pleasure and Narrative Cinema," *Screen 16*, no. 3 (Autumn 1975), 6–18. In this essay, Mulvey argues that the camera lens in traditional Hollywood cinema can be seen as a tool for female subjugation. She invokes psychoanalysis, including the theories of Jacques Lacan to argue that fearing castration from the female, the male figure has no choice but to destroy the female subject. Subject to much debate by her peers and revision by the author, the text laid the foundation for many key thinkers of our time, such as John Berger, to consider how artists and audiences see the world.

17 Lynn Hershman Leeson, gleaned from email correspondence with the author, spring 2021.

18 Dean Wilson, "Predictive policing management: a brief history of patrol automation," Sussex Research Online, 2020, sro.sussex.ac.uk/id/eprint/90743/3/DWAUTOMATIC%20POLICING%20FINAL%201.pdf.

19 Jori Finkel, "When Bots and Antibodies Are Art Materials," *New York Times*, June 18, 2021, www.nytimes.com/2021/06/18/t-magazine/lynn-hershman-leeson-art.html.

20 "ORLAN & THE ORLANOÏDE: Artistic, electronic & verbal Strip-tease," ORLAN, www.orlan.eu/wp-content/uploads/2018/04/ORLAN-THE-ORLANOI%CC%88DE.pdf.

21 "Domestic Tension: Wafaa Bilal," Net Art Anthology, Rhizome, anthology.rhizome.org/domestic-tension.

22 "Artist Forced to Remove Head Camera Implant," *BBC*, February 11, 2011, www.bbc.co.uk/news/entertainment-arts-12429353.

23 Wafaa Bilal, conversation with the author, spring 2016.

Will This Destroy Us?

1 See Lawrence Abu Hamdan, *[inaudible]: A Politics of Listening in 4 Acts* (Berlin: Sternberg Press, 2016).

2 Alli Shultes, "'Racist' AI Art Warns Against Bad Training Data," *BBC*, September 17, 2019, www.bbc.co.uk/news/technology-49726652. Also see Julia Carrie Wong, "The Viral Selfie App ImageNet Roulette Seemed Fun – Until it Called Me A Racist Slur," *Guardian*, September 18, 2019, www.theguardian.com/technology/2019/sep/17/imagenet-roulette-asian-racist-slur-selfie.

3 One aggregator of Meta's statistics, which will fluctuate, may be seen at Jason Wise, "Meta Platforms Inc Statistics 2022: Revenue, Users, Acquisitions & Shares," *Earthweb*, June 13, 2022, earthweb.com/meta-statistics.

4 See Joana Hadjithomas and Khalil Joreige, "I Must First Apologize: A Visual Essay," in *The Rumors of the World: Re-thinking Trust in the Age of the Internet*, ed. Omar Kholeif (Berlin: Sternberg Press, 2015).

5 Hennessy Youngman, "ART THOUGHTZ: Relational Aesthetics," March 15, 2011, video, 5:27, www.youtube.com/watch?v=7yea4qSJMx-4&t=1s.

6 Hennessy Youngman, "ART THOUGHTZ: On Beauty," May 2, 2011, video, 5:10, www.youtube.com/watch?v=xkSG9wrFPCQ.

7 Hennessy Youngman, "ART THOUGHTZ: Damien Hirst," January 10, 2012, video, 3:37, www.youtube.com/watch?v=5y_8DWg5W0w.

8 See Claire Bishop, "Digital Divide: Contemporary Art and New Media," *Artforum*, September 2012, www.artforum.com/print/201207/digital-divide-contemporary-art-and-new-media-31944. Also see Geert Lovink, "New Media Arts at a Crossroads," *Diagonal Thoughts*, May 4, 2007, www.diagonalthoughts.com/?p=204;

Domenico Quaranta, *Beyond New Media Art* (Brescia: Link Editions, 2013). Available at www.ocopy.net/wp-content/uploads/2016/04/quaranta-domenico_beyond-new-media-art.pdf; and Zach Blas, "Contra-Internet Aesthetics," in *You Are Here: Art After the Internet*, ed. Omar Kholeif (Manchester: Cornerhouse; London: Space, 2014).

9 Omar Kholeif, "Performing the Self: On the Blurring of Fact and Fiction in the Age of YouTube," *Art Monthly* 343 (February 2011): 9–12. In this article, I sought to popularize the term *performing the self*, pointing to how a new generation of artists used manufactured semblances of identity gleaned from the internet to torque cultural stereotypes. Here, I argued that the interpersonal nature of video-sharing websites creates platforms that help everyday individual artists to manufacture different forms of identity. The new internet-based digital platforms, I noted, have made the performance and documentation of the self a nearly ubiquitous mode of artistic practice.

Time Machine: Pioneering Anarchists

1 Katie Robinson and Charlotte Chilton, "Our Favorite Pictures of Celebrities Partying at Studio 54," *Town & Country*, October 26, 2020, www.townandcountrymag.com/the-scene/parties/g9570917/studio-54-pictures-celebrities.

2 Angela Watercutter, "Why *The Andy Warhol Diaries* Recreated the Artist's Voice With AI," *Wired*, March 9, 2022, www.wired.com/story/andy-warhol-diaries-artificial-intelligence-voice.

3 Cory Arcangel informs me that the project named *The Warhol Files* was in many senses an art project of his own. He was already thinking through the concepts of what he described as obsolescence and the readymade. He worked with numerous organizations throughout this process including the Carnegie Mellon University Computer Club. The final technical report by the Computer Club sent to me by Arcangel revealed that together they had unearthed the following by Warhol:

- Eleven signed works (including any composed of just a signature)
- Two unsigned works clearly in Warhol's style
- One work possibly by Warhol but not attributable
- Twelve unmodified video frame captures
- Three modified video frame captures
- Two animation files possibly by Warhol but not attributable

4 Cory Arcangel, conversation with the author on Zoom, May 25, 2021.

5 Cory Arcangel, gleaned from email exchanges with the author, June 10–18, 2021.

6 Roy Ascott, "Planetary Technoetics: Art, Technology and Consciousness," *Leonardo* 37, no. 2 (2004): 111–16, www.jstor.org/stable/1577468.

7 Louis Columbus, "Artificial Intelligence Will Enable 38% Profit Gains By 2035," *Forbes*, June 22, 2017, www.forbes.com/sites/louiscolumbus/2017/06/22/artificial-intelligence-will-enable-38-profit-gains-by-2035/?sh=7140c3341969.

8 For further speculations on AI and 2030, please see Peter Stone et al., "Artificial Intelligence and Life in 2030," One Hundred Year Study on Artificial Intelligence: Report of the 2015–2016 Study Panel, Stanford University, Stanford, CA, September 2016, ai100.stanford.edu/sites/g/files/sbiybj18871/files/media/file/ai100report10032016fnl_singles.pdf.

9 Michael S. Bernstein et al., "ESR: Ethics and Society Review of Artificial Intelligence Research," arXiv, June 22, 2021, arxiv.org/abs/2106.11521.

10 Consider consulting Aliza Vigderman and Gabe Turner, "The Data Big Tech Companies Have On You," Security.org, March 23, 2022, www.security.org/resources/data-tech-companies-have.

11 See Arthur I. Miller, "Ian Goodfellow's Generative Adversarial Networks: AI Learns to Imagine," in *The Artist in the Machine: The World of AI-Powered Creativity* (Cambridge, MA: MIT Press, 2019), 87–98. See also Ian Goodfellow et al., "Attacking Machine Learning with Adversarial Examples," OpenAI, February 24, 2017, openai.com/blog/adversarial-example-research.

12 Aimee Dawson, "Auctions, pledges and DMs: creative ways to buy and sell art on Instagram," *Art Newspaper*, November 20, 2020, www.theartnewspaper.com/2020/11/20/auctions-pledges-and-dms-creative-ways-to-buy-and-sell-art-on-instagram. See also the monthly blog Aimee Dawson, "Insta' gratification," *Art Newspaper*, www.theartnewspaper.com/series/insta-gratification.

13 Ian Bogost, "The AI-Art Gold Rush is Here," *Atlantic*, March 6, 2019, www.theatlantic.com/technology/archive/2019/03/ai-created-art-invades-chelsea-gallery-scene/584134.

14 Trevor Paglen, conversation with the author, January 2022.

The Rise of the Digital

1 The Art of With Project was commissioned by Sarah Perks, former artistic director of Cornerhouse and HOME, Manchester. As part of this program, Perks invited curator Michael Connor to write "A Manual for the 21st Century Gatekeeper" (2009). A conversation

between the duo regarding some of these concepts is available: Michael Connor and Sarah Perks, "A Manual for the 21st Century Gatekeeper," filmed December 14, 2009, video, 8:29, www.youtube.com/watch?v=PyR-jdwKiC1U.

2 Jay Mollica, email to author, summer 2020.

3 Jay Mollica, email to author, fall 2020.

4 After these initial interviews were conducted, many of the platforms initiated by Mollica at SFMOMA, including its online publication *Open Space*, were halted due to a lack of funding that was attributed to declining box-office returns caused by the COVID-19 pandemic.

5 Christiane Paul, "From Archives to Collections: Digital Art in/out of Institutions," filmed December 4, 2015, at MUMOK, Vienna, video, 60:00, www.youtube.com/watch?v=283LtZN-my5M. See also Christiane Paul, *Digital Art* (London: Thames; New York: Hudson, 2015).

6 Levin Haegele, conversation with the author, December 9, 2020.

7 Levin Haegele, conversation with the author, June 20, 2021.

8 Erika Balsom, "Against the Novelty of New Media: The Resuscitation of the Authentic," in *You Are Here: Art After the Internet*, ed. Omar Kholeif (Manchester: Cornerstone; London: SPACE, 2014).

9 Rory Greener, "Second Life Storefront User Traffic Jumps 35 Percent in 2021," XR Today, January 12, 2022, www.xrtoday.com/virtual-reality/second-life-user-traffic-jumps-35-percent-in-2021.

10 See Benny Kirk, "NASA VIEW Headset Defined VR Decades Before Oculus, Probably Can't Play Half-Life: Alyx," autoevolution, December 30, 2021, www.autoevolution.com/news/nasa-view-headset-defined-vr-decades-before-oculus-probably-can-t-play-half-life-alyx-177844.html.

11 See Jan A. G. M. van Dijk, "Closing the Digital Divide," www.un.org/development/desa/dspd/wp-content/uploads/sites/22/2020/07/Closing-the-Digital-Divide-by-Jan-A.G.M-van-Dijk-.pdf. See also Jan A. G. M. van Dijk, *The Deepening Divide: Inequality in the Information Society* (Thousand Oaks, CA: Sage Publications. 2005).

12 As figures are constantly changing, readers may find the most recent reports and statistics published by the Oxford Internet Institute at oxis.oii.ox.ac.uk.

13 Hootsuite operates a membership-based system and, since the time of writing, figures have fluctuated between 1.3 million and 2 million, according to regular check-ins on the platform and estimations.

14 See "Asia Home to Half of the World's Internet Users," DataCenter News, April 1, 2020, datacenternews.asia/story/asia-home-to-half-of-the-world-s-internet-users. This information is regularly updated and subject to change. Some of the most detailed results can be found on subscription-based services, such as Statista, which have up-to-date metrics.

15 Sandhya Keelery, "Internet Usage in India - Statistics & Facts," Statista, August 2, 2011, www.statista.com/topics/2157/internet-usage-in-india.

16 Jonathan W. Rose, "How Mobile Money Supercharged Kenya's Sports Betting Addiction," MIT Technology Review, April 14, 2022, www.technologyreview.com/2022/04/14/1049239/kenya-sports-betting-mobile-money.

17 Julia Stoll, "Number of TV households worldwide from 2010 to 2026," Statista, May 11, 2022, www.statista.com/statistics/268695/number-of-tv-households-worldwide.

18 See Richard Seymour, "We are witnessing the end of the 'Twitter Revolution,'" *New Statesman*, November 27, 2019, www.newstatesman.com/science-tech/2019/11/we-are-witnessing-the-end-of-the-twitter-revolution.

19 All public companies have their share prices publicly indexed, however, anything dating back more than a decade will require physical archival access to stock exchange records or a subscription-based service. One can take a cursory glance at "Twitter - Stock Price History | TWTR," Macrotrends, accessed May 24, 2022, www.macrotrends.net/stocks/charts/TWTR/twitter/stock-price-history.

Living Media

1 See Stephanie Bailey, "Our Space: Take the Net in Your Hands," in Y*ou Are Here: Art After the Internet*, ed. Omar Kholeif (Manchester: Cornerstone; London: SPACE, 2014).

2 See Mark Deuze, *Media Life* (Hoboken, New Jersey: Wiley, 2012).

3 See Norman M. Klein, "Cross-Embedded Media: A Brief Historical Introduction," in *Vision, Memory and Media*, eds. Andreas Brøgger and Omar Kholeif (Liverpool: Liverpool University Press, 2010).

4 Bruce Takefman, "Amazon Profits Increased Nearly 200% Since Start of Covid-19 Pandemic," ResearchFDI, January 6, 2021, researchfdi.com/amazon-covid-19-pandemic-profits.

5 See, for instance, "How LARPing Became the Hottest Entertainment Trend in China," *Celebrity Land!*, March 10, 2021, https://celebrity.land/en/how-larping-became-the-hottest-entertainment-trend-in-china.

6 Siyuan Meng, "What Is LARPing? And Why Do Chinese Youth Love to LARP?" *RADII*, May 20, 2021, radiichina.com/larp-china.

7 Jiayi Mao, "Chinese Gen Z's new obsession: Murder Mystery Games," *Vogue Business*, July 14, 2021, www.voguebusiness.com/consumers/chinese-gen-zs-new-obsession-murder-mystery-games.
8 As discussed at "*Cel*: A Screening and Conversation with Artist Ed Fornieles," (screening and conversation, New Museum, New York, December 12, 2019).
9 Tash Reith-Banks, "Beyond Dungeons and Dragons: can role play save the world?" *Guardian*, March 26, 2018, www.theguardian.com/world/2018/mar/26/can-live-action-role-play-larp-save-the-world.
10 See Jenny Cusack, "An Echo Button: Haroon Mirza," *Dazed*, November 7, 2011, www.dazeddigital.com/artsandculture/article/11934/1/an-echo-button-haroon-mirza.
11 See Sally Weale, "Funding Cuts to Go Ahead for University Arts Courses in England Despite Opposition," *Guardian*, July 20, 2021, www.theguardian.com/education/2021/jul/20/funding-cuts-to-go-ahead-for-university-arts-courses-in-england-despite-opposition.
12 See Richard Adams, "Universities in England Favour Cancel Culture Over Quality, Says Williamson," *Guardian*, September 9, 2021, www.theguardian.com/education/2021/sep/09/universities-in-england-favour-cancel-culture-over-quality-says-williamson.
13 Lubaina Himid, conversation with the author, July 30, 2021.
14 Lanre Bakare, "Cuts to Art Subjects Funding 'Walk Us Back 60 Years', Says Artist Helen Cammock," *Guardian*, July 28, 2021, www.theguardian.com/artanddesign/2021/jul/28/cuts-to-art-subjects-funding-walk-us-back-60-years-says-artist-helen-cammock.
15 Mona Eltahawy (@monaeltahawy), "The more they undress, the more #Egyptian men are celebrated for virility, masculinity, strength," Twitter, October 18, 2020, twitter.com/monaeltahawy/status/1317904267311808514.
16 See Martine Syms in Conversation with Beatrix Ruf, "The Image is Now Part of My Flesh," *Mousse*, April 1, 2019, bridgetdonahue-media-w2.s3-us-west-2.amazonaws.com/files/38PdG4TqRjeRp1gBU4wIPg.pdf.
17 For more information, visit www.theracialimaginary.org.
18 Joanna Stern, "They Used Smartphone Cameras to Record Police Brutality—and Change History," *Wall Street Journal*, June 13, 2020, www.wsj.com/articles/they-used-smartphone-cameras-to-record-police-brutalityand-change-history-11592020827.
19 Larry Buchanan, Quoctrung Bui, and Jugal K. Patel, "Black Lives Matter May Be the Largest Movement in U.S. History," *New York Times*, July 3, 2020, www.nytimes.com/interactive/2020/07/03/us/george-floyd-protests-crowd-size.html.
20 Tobi Thomas, Adam Gabbatt, and Caelainn Barr, "Nearly 1,000 Instances of Police Brutality Recorded in US Anti-Racism Protests," *Guardian*, October 29, 2020, www.theguardian.com/us-news/2020/oct/29/us-police-brutality-protest.
21 "Rent-A-Negro: damali ayo," Net Art Anthology, Rhizome, anthology.rhizome.org/rent-a-negro.
22 Monica Kim, "A New Art-Fashion Label Is Exploring Asian-American Identity," *Vogue*, May 24, 2018, www.vogue.com/article/cfgny-new-york-art-fashion-label-tin-nguyen-daniel-chew.
23 Mary Retta, "'What Does It Mean to Be Black and Alive Right Now?'" *Nation*, February 17, 2021, www.thenation.com/article/culture/jenna-wortham-kimberly-drew-interview.
24 Lorraine O'Grady, *Writing in Space, 1973–2019* (Durham, NC: Duke University Press, 2019), xvii.
25 "#BAMEOver—A Statement for the UK," docs.google.com/document/d/e/2PACX-1vQk-g5IIoeAqMjMF6VW-eIEtEUEgK3GLudW-1meE2DILbJPZYPiP0dO3Qwx6YVxBFx-OhI1KEp5swpok80/pub.

— You and Me and Everyone We Know: Find Me in an Ocean of Images

1 Io Dodds, "'We Lost Control of Our Creations': The Silicon Valley Heretic on a Mission to Make Big Tech Repent," *Telegraph*, May 10, 2019, www.telegraph.co.uk/technology/2019/05/10/lost-control-creations-silicon-valley-heretic-mission-make-big. See also Tom Knowles, "I'm So Sorry, Says Inventor of Endless Online Scrolling," *Times*, April 27, 2019, www.thetimes.co.uk/article/i-m-so-sorry-says-inventor-of-endless-online-scrolling-9lrv59mdk and Hilary Andersson, "Social Media Apps are 'Deliberately' Addictive to Users," *BBC*, July 4, 2019, www.bbc.com/news/technology 11610959.
2 "Mental Health Issues Increased Significantly in Young Adults Over Last Decade," American Psychological Association, March 14, 2019, www.apa.org/news/press/releases/2019/03/mental-health-adults.
3 "Overview—Borderline Personality Disorder," National Health Service, July 17, 2019, www.nhs.uk/mental-health/conditions/borderline-personality-disorder/overview.
4 Javier Serrano-Puche, "Emotions in the Use of Technology: An Analysis of the Research on Mobile Phones," ResearchGate, January 2015, www.researchgate.net/publication/292160311_Emotions_in_the_use_of_technology_An_analysis_of_the_research_on_mobile_phones.

See also Javier Serrano-Puche, "Emotions and Digital Technologies: Mapping the Field of Research in Media Studies," MEDIA@LSE *Working Paper Series* 33 (2015), hdl.handle.net/10171/39702.

5 Janelle Zara, "Yayoi Kusama's Infinity Mirrors Reignites Art's Selfie Debate," *Guardian*, November 9, 2017, www.theguardian.com/artanddesign/2017/nov/09/yayoi-kusama-infinity-mirrors-art-the-broad-los-angeles.

6 There are numerous debates that conflate social media and meditation or speculate that individuals pursue such practices simply to brag about them on Web 2.0. For instance, see Sarah Saccomanno, "A Meditation on Social Media," *Medium*, April 18, 2019, sarah-saccomanno.medium.com/a-meditation-on-social-media-37df9da2cbd9.

7 "Global Meditation Market Huge Growth Opportunity between 2020–2027," Pharmiweb, July 1, 2020, www.pharmiweb.com/press-release/2020-07-01/global-meditation-market-huge-growth-opportunity-between-2020-2027-inner-explorer-committee-for-chi. Other reports suggest the number will be closer to five billion U.S. dollars, depending on the long-lasting impact of meditation-based techniques after the COVID-19 pandemic.

8 Heather Phillipson, conversation with the author, August 17, 2021.

9 Courtney L. McCluney et al., "The Costs of Code-Switching," *Harvard Business Review*, November 15, 2019, hbr.org/2019/11/the-costs-of-codeswitching.

10 The webinar is based on a University of California, Los Angeles, college course. See more at Shannon Liao, "*Get Out* Now has its Own Online Class about Black Horror," *The Verge*, January 27, 2018, www.theverge.com/2018/1/27/16938664/get-out-jordan-peele-ucla-seminar-online-course.

11 One used to be able to access the livestream at web102.secure-secure.co.uk/theend.today. However, the stream has moved offline since the sculpture's two-year tenure on the Fourth Plinth came to an end. The result of the thousands of hours of surveillance footage of the square is something the artist will have to debate along with the implicit legalities this will entail.

12 Heather Phillipson, "'I Have no Fixed Starting Point, Only Accumulation,'" Tate, July 16, 2021, video, 4:14, www.youtube.com/watch?v=bJ652L7XLf0.

13 "Tate Britain Commission Heather Phillipson Rupture No 1: blowtorching the bitten peach," Tate, www.tate.org.uk/whats-on/tate-britain/heather-phillipson.

— The Possibilities of a Digital Culture

1 Lawrence Weiner et al., "50 Years Later, A Contemporary Art Exhibition Still Courts Controversy," *MoMA Magazine*, January 28, 2020, www.moma.org/magazine/articles/225.

2 Ibid.

3 I first heard Trecartin discuss some of these tropes as part of a conversation organized by Rhizome: "Nowadays: A Conversation and Screening with Ryan Trecartin," (screening and conversation, New Museum, December 13, 2007). He and Fitch would later discuss these details with me in conversations at their former home in Los Feliz, California, in 2011 and 2012, as well as in numerous public arenas.

4 Media reports at the time of the film's release regularly attributed the social-media platform Friendster as the site where the art world first saw *A Family Finds Entertainment*, which was included in the 2006 Whitney Biennial.

5 Hito Steyerl, "In Defense of the Poor Image," *e-flux Journal* 10, November 2009, www.e-flux.com/journal/10/61362/in-defense-of-the-poor-image.

— The Shape of the Future

1 Wary of my carbon footprint, I do not tend to move outside of these three continental routes, not that I could afford to, anyway. Still, there is no real excuse beyond feeling. I work in one place, my partner in another, and our immediate family elsewhere. Some experience, intimacy, and sense of being present for your kin cannot entirely be felt virtually, at least not to the same intensity for some, just yet.

2 Sophia Al-Maria, *Sad Sack* (London: Bookworks, 2018), 72.

3 Bruce Sterling, "Gulf Futurism," *Wired*, November 11, 2012, www.wired.com/2012/11/gulf-futurism.

4 The Pan-Arab Hangover is an ongoing research project by Ahmad Makia that has been made manifest in multiple forums, including in the now-dormant culture magazine the *State*, coedited by Rahel Aima. Some of his ideas are outlined in his constantly updated essay "The Arabist," a version of which is published in Fawz Kabra, *No to the Invasion: Breakdowns and Side-Effects* (Annandale-on-Hudson: Center for Curatorial Studies, Bard College, 2017).

5 Katherine Gillespie, "Paper's A to Z of Celebrity Catchphrases," *Paper*, March 28, 2019, www.papermag.com/a-z-celebrity-catchphrases-2632507742.html?rebelltitem=107 - rebelltitem107.

6 Lawrence Abu Hamdan, "The Sonic Image," *Infrasonica*, April 2021, infrasonica.org/en/audiblematter/thesonicimage.

7 It is worth noting that Cappellazzo stated in an interview that she didn't necessarily feel that the film was representative of the time the crew spent filming with her. See Colleen Hochberger, "'Art Has Always Been a Global Asset Class': Amy Cappellazzo on HBO's Exposé About Art and Wealth," *Artspace*, November 14, 2018, www.artspace.com/magazine/interviews_features/qa/amy-cappellazzo-on-the-price-of-everything-55764.

8 Natalie Robehmed, "Why Artsy Is Succeeding In Putting The Art World Online," *Forbes*, September 6, 2013, www.forbes.com/sites/natalierobehmed/2013/09/06/why-artsy-is-succeeding-in-putting-the-art-world-online/?sh=1e49a1f21894.

9 This is based on an analysis of Artsy's constantly changing business model, documentation of their various funding round cycles (and their logic), miscellaneous press articles released over several years, and observations of high turnover in key senior level and executive positions. For more, one could begin with Tim Schneider, "The Gray Market: How to Make Sense of Artsy's Latest Funding Round (and Other Insights)," *Artnet*, July 24, 2017, news.artnet.com/market/the-gray-market-broad-kusama-artsy-nea-1030751.

10 Scott Reyburn, "JPG File Sells for $69 Million, as 'NFT Mania' Gathers Pace," *New York Times*, March 11, 2021, www.nytimes.com/2021/03/11/arts/design/nft-auction-christies-beeple.html.

11 The first cryptocurrency is often debated, as is the first minted NFT. Artist Sarah Meyohas, for example, has argued that her own currency BitchCoin launched five months before Ethereum and represents the first token of art on the blockchain.

12 Bitcoin came to prominence in the wake of the 2008 financial crisis with the publication of a white paper by Satoshi Nakamoto, the perceived pseudonym of an individual or group of individuals who developed Bitcoin, including its original technical references and implementation instructions. An expanded volume, *The White Paper* (London: Ignota Books, 2019), which was edited by artist and technologist Ben Vickers, the former chief technology officer of Serpentine Galleries, London, also includes an exploratory essay by artist and author James Bridle, and an annotated theoretical journey by researcher and historian Jaya Klara Brekke. Together, they decode the political ideas proposed in the original white paper and the global movement of decentralization. Fueled by ideologies of encryption, the authors argue that the currency held the potential for reimagining the hierarchy of social and political order through the technical means through which this currency is deployed.

13 Monika Ghosh, "Can Ethereum's Proof-of-Stake Transition Save the Planet?" *Forkast. News*, March 31, 2022, forkast.news/ethereum-save-with-proof-of-stake.

14 Anna Rahmanan, "The Very First NFT Vending Machine in New York Has Just Landed Downtown," *Time Out New York*, February 18, 2022, www.timeout.com/newyork/news/the-very-first-nft-vending-machine-in-new-york-has-just-landed-downtown-021822.

15 Matthew Gault, "This Powerful Right-Click Artwork Is Made of 10,000 NFTs," *Vice*, November 12, 2021, www.vice.com/en/article/3abnwv/this-powerful-right-click-artwork-is-made-of-10000-nfts.

16 Barbara Kruger's now-famous quote in full: "The art world has always been an unrelenting taste machine, but now flavors of the month have morphed into flavors of the minute. Again, all a reflection of a wider cultural condition. I mean, the art world is slow compared with the music and movie businesses." I first came to know of this quote through a talk I attended by School of the Art Institute of Chicago professor James Elkins in 2019. Online, it is attributed to Kruger repeatedly through websites that aggregate quotes by individuals, but no direct originating moment is articulated.

17 "Christie's Surpasses $100 Million in NFT Sales," *Christie's*, September 28, 2021, www.christies.com/about-us/press-archive/details?-PressReleaseID=10210. See also, "Beeple's Opus," *Christie's*, www.christies.com/features/monumental-collage-by-beeple-is-first-purely-digital-artwork-nft-to-come-to-auction-11510-7.aspx.

18 See Ben Munster, "Has the NFT Bubble Finally Burst? Not Yet, New Data Suggests," *Art Newspaper*, June 6, 2022, www.theartnewspaper.com/2022/06/06/has-the-nft-art-bubble-finally-burst-not-yet-new-data-suggests.

19 At the moment, the document may be downloaded, but the link will go offline in due course. "New York Conditions of Sale Buying at Christie's," *Christie's*, www.christies.com/media-library/pdf/conditions-of-sale/new-york-conditions-of-sale.pdf.

20 See "Arthur Jafa: Visualizing a Continuum of Black Visual-Culture Image Production," *Afrovisualism*, June 2, 2019, afrovisualism.medium.com/arthur-jafa-visualizing-a-continuum-of-black-visual-cultural-image-production-e9d38ef44de0. I was first introduced to these ideas in Arthur Jafa's work in his essay "My Black Death," in *Everything but the Burden: What White People are Taking from*

Black Culture, ed. Greg Tate (New York: Crown Publishing, 2003).

21 This term first appeared in Saidiya Hartman's 2007 landmark text "Venus in Two Acts," *Small Axe*, 26 (2008): 1–14. The author's award-winning book *Wayward Lives, Beautiful Experiments* (New York: W.W. Norton & Company, 2019) used the technique of creative semi-nonfiction to fill in the interstices, the gaps of history, with a fluid imagination about the potential lives of young Black women and queer individuals. These were frequently people whose stories could not be narrated due to missing records, erasure often determined by race and class.

— Is the Earth a Scorched Cable?

1 See Jonathan Crary, *Scorched Earth: Beyond the Digital Age to a Post-Capitalist World* (London: Verso, 2022).

2 Ibid., 4.

3 Ibid.

4 Frederic Jameson, *Postmodernism, or, The Cultural Logic of Late Capitalism* (Durham, NC: Duke University Press, 1991), 39–119.

5 The Gruen Transfer, also known as the Gruen Effect, is the concept of when one enters a mall and becomes disoriented and unaware of their original intentions. The individual is subjected to the possibly manipulative effects of the architect. Finding solace or comfort in pursuing capital, the act of purchasing, becomes a suturing resolve.

6 See Jay David Bolter, *The Digital Plenitude: The Decline of Elite Culture and the Rise of Digital Media* (Cambridge, MA: MIT Press, 2019).

— We Are the Metaverse: A Parting Verse

1 Lawrence Abu Hamdan and Skye Arundhati Thomas, "One Long Crime," May 5, 2022, www.art-agenda.com/criticism/465965/one-long-crime.

2 See Martin Chulov, "Huge Scale and Impact of Israeli Incursions Over Lebanon's Skies Revealed," *Guardian*, June 9, 2022, www.theguardian.com/world/2022/jun/09/huge-scale-and-impact-of-israeli-incursions-over-lebanon-skies-revealed-research-overflights.

3 These references were also gleaned from conversations with the artist while developing the project with him between June 2021 and March 2022.

4 For more, see Simon Denny, "Blockchain Future States," *e-flux Architecture*, www.e-flux.com/architecture/superhumanity/68703/blockchain-future-states.

5 Many individuals, including the artists whom I work with, have begun to accidentally conflate cyberspace, which was conceived as a kind of metaphor for the World Wide Web, specifically as a world apart from reality, with metaverse, which contrarily intimates a world together.

6 It is peculiar that NFTs, which are unique sets of digits, i.e., URLs on the blockchain, are most often used to mint two-dimensional digital assets and yet are widely described in the media and common parlance as a by-product of the metaverse. This is seemingly incongruous, because the metaverse is currently articulated as a self-contained three-dimensional, and/or spatialized virtual world, formally augmenting reality.

7 The popularization of *meta* in the broader lexicon emerged in the late 1980s, following the publication of Noam Cohen's essay "Meta-Musings" in the *New Republic*. It was at this time that Gen Xers schooled in postmodern thought, a self-reflexive field of discourse, transformed it from a prefix to an adjective: "that's so *meta*!" Millennials arguably turned the self-reflexive quality into self-referential forms of discourse. Accordingly, one cannot help but feel cynical when witnessing corporate forces professing *meta* to be an entirely new and distinctive prefix, phrase, or portmanteau.

8 This image was taken at the exhibition entitled *Imitation of Life: Melodrama and Race in the 21st Century* cocurated by yours truly and Professor Sarah Perks.

9 I also believe that the culture of the community center, a form of caring safety net in an enclosed social setting, is indicative of a kind of metaverse. An example can be made of Summaeverythang, a venture that artist Lauren Halsey codeveloped during the COVID-19 lockdown that delivers organic produce from Southern Californian farms to homes in South Central Los Angeles. In the end, such spaces function as sites of social immersion and activation.

Index

Page numbers in *italics* indicate figures.

Picture credits

We would like to thank all those who gave their permission to reproduce the listed material. Every reasonable effort has been made to acknowledge the ownership of copyright for photographs included in this volume. Any errors that may have occurred are inadvertent and will be corrected in subsequent editions provided notification is sent in writing to the publisher. Abbreviations are t: top, b: bottom.

6: Courtesy the artist. 15: iStock/Getty Images Plus. 21: Historical/Getty Images. 24b: Robert Wallis/Getty Images. 24t: ullstein bild/Getty Images. 31: Smithsonian American Art Museum, Washington, DC/Art Resource, NY/© Nam June Paik Estate. 33: Courtesy the Computer History Museum. 39: Courtesy Bridget Donahue Gallery, New York City, and Claudia Altman-Siegel Gallery, San Francisco. Collection Donald Hess. 40: Courtesy Bridget Donahue Gallery, New York City, and Claudia Altman-Siegel Gallery, San Francisco. Collection Whitney Museum of American Art, New York, and Fine Arts Museums of San Francisco. 42: ORLAN Studio. 43: Héctor Adalid. 45: Courtesy the artist. 50: © Trevor Paglen. Courtesy the artist. 52: Photo: Danko Stjepanovic/Sharjah Art Foundation. 56b: © Cao Fei 2022. Courtesy Vitamin Creative Space and Sprüth Magers. 56t: Courtesy the artist and mor charpentier. Photo: Roberto Chamoro. 58: Photo: Danko Stjepanovic. Collection Sharjah Art Foundation. 65: Courtesy the artist. 67: Courtesy the artist and Salon 94, New York. 73: Tayfun Coskun/Anadolu Agency via Getty Images. 83b, 83t: © 2022 The Andy Warhol Foundation for the Visual Arts, Inc./Licensed by DACS, London. 84b: Photo: Elliot Kaufman. Courtesy: Arcangel Surfware. 84t: Courtesy the artist. © Cory Arcangel. 87: © Roy Ascott. 89: Courtesy the artist. Photo: Danko Stjepanovic. 95: Courtesy the artist. 97: Courtesy the artist. 99: Courtesy the artist. 103: Courtesy the artist and Nevada Museum of Art. 105: Courtesy the artist and Michael Lett, Auckland. Photo: Nick Ash. 108b, 108t: © Pipilotti Rist. Courtesy the artist, Hauser & Wirth, and Luhring Augustine/FACT Liverpool. 110: Solomon R. Guggenheim Museum, New York. 113: Jennifer Ringley. 117: Courtesy Various Small Fires. Collection Museum of Contemporary Art Chicago. 119: Courtesy the artist. 122b: Werkflow. 2016. Courtesy the artist and Rodeo, London/Piraeus. 122t: © Jacolby Satterwhite. Courtesy the artist; Mitchell-Innes & Nash, New York; and Morán Morán, Los Angeles. 137: Courtesy the artist. Collection Stedelijk Museum Amsterdam. 145: Courtesy max goelitz. © the artist. Photo: Dirk Tacke. Private collection, Munich. 147: © Ed Fornieles 2022. Courtesy the artist and Carlos/Ishikawa, London. 152b: Courtesy the artist and Jessica Silverman, San Francisco. 152t: Photo: Jesse Hunniford/MONA. Courtesy the artist; Altman Siegel, San Francisco; and Petzel, New York. 155: Sean Hodrick/Alamy Stock Photo. 158b: Photo: Stephen White. Courtesy Whitechapel Gallery Archive. 158t: Courtesy the artist. 162: Courtesy the artist and Galerie Isabella Bortolozzi, Berlin. 164: © Martine Syms. 166: Jason Armond/Getty Images. 169: Courtesy the artist. 170: Courtesy the artist. Photo: Kirsten Kilponen. 174: Courtesy the artist and Tate Modern. 187: Courtesy the artist. 190–91: Courtesy the artist. Kraupa-Tuskany Zeidler, Berlin. 193, 194: Courtesy the artist and Project Native Informant, London. 197b: Courtesy the artist. 197t: Stefanie Keenan/Getty Images. 200–201: Courtesy the artist. Photo: Mathias Voelzke. 203: Commissioned by the GLA. Photo: James O Jenkins. Courtesy the artist. © Heather Phillipson. All rights reserved, DACS 2022. 206: Photo: Tate. Courtesy the artist. © Heather Phillipson. All rights reserved, DACS 2022. 209: Courtesy the artist and Southard Reid. 211: Courtesy the artist and Carrie Secrist Gallery. Photo: Anna Olthoff. 213: Courtesy the artist and Salon 94, New York. © Laurie Simmons. 216: Photo: G. H. Hovagimyan. 222–23: Courtesy Sprüth Magers and Regen Projects, Los Angeles. © Lizzie Fitch/Ryan Trecartin 2022. Photo: Timo Ohler. 225: Courtesy the Museum of Contemporary Art, Los Angeles. Photo: Justin Lubliner and Carter Seddon. 227: Image: Andrea Rossetti. 236: Courtesy the artist. 248: Courtesy the artist. 266–67: Ladd Company/Warner Bros/Kobal/Shutterstock. 269: Courtesy the artist. 271: Courtesy the artist, TARO NASU, Marian Goodman Gallery, and Hauser and Wirth. © Kamitani Lab/Kyoto. 276–77: Visualization by Cream Projects. Commissioned by Sharjah Art Foundation. Courtesy the artist. 279b: Courtesy the artist. 279t: Photo: Chris Payne. 295: Craig Blankenhorn/HBO/Darren Star Prods/Kobal/Shutterstock.

Acknowledgments

The "lonely writer syndrome" is an often-mythologized state of existence. But writing this book of critical reflection over the last year and a half has been a lifeline during one of the loneliest periods, not just in my life, but in many of our lives. This was made more complicated by the white lab coats of the medical-industrial complex who have exposed illnesses that have at times made me both terrified and ashamed to live within the confines of my own body. For arguing the case for this "crestfallen" individual's perspective, I must first and foremost thank Rebecca Morrill, the commissioning editor, who brought this project to Phaidon, and whose critical feedback has helped focus and enliven this story. Maia Murphy, senior editor at Phaidon, has been a diligent and patient force who I can only hope to work with again. Melissa Larner helped finesse and refine this prose—thank you. Editing is not a thankless job—it is ever more important amidst the stream of RSS feeds. Our value exists in the care that we show one another, and in the decisive risks that we take. I am proud to be able to say that we worked together.

I am indebted to the artists, curators, and arts administrators who have over the last seventeen years, opened their lives, hearts, and brilliant minds to me. Many are referenced in these pages, and there are more to whom I am grateful.

There are certain people who have known me throughout the years and who have remained loyal and supportive of my work, even if we were not always able to be together. I am especially grateful to Khalid Abdalla, Lawrence Abu Hamdan, Hoor Al Qasimi, Jeremy Bailey, Fiona Banner, Zachary Cahill, Carla Chammas, Michaela Crimmin, Maya El Khalil, Jean Fisher, Joana Hadjithomas, Malu Halasa, Alison Hearst, Celia Hempton, Paul Heyer, Ryan Inouye, Amrita Jhaveri, Khalil Joreige, Mahmoud Khaled, Chris McCormack, Terence McCormack, Haroon Mirza, W. J. T. Mitchell, Otobong Nkanga, Trevor Paglen, Heather Phillipson, Eddie Peake, Sarah Perks, Harry Samuel Pilkington, Khalil Rabah, Sunny Rahbar, Todd Reisz, Judi Roaman, Candy Stobbs, Helen Weaver, and Sultan Sooud Al Qassemi.

To my newfound family with artPost21—Ana Nicolaescu and Sebastian Tiew of Cream Projects, and Aron Morel, in particular, I thank you for encouraging me to find my voice again. Lubaina Himid, I am indebted to you for your support on many levels. You have offered newfound perspectives on both my life and work. To the team that I work with most closely at Sharjah Art Foundation daily, Souraya Kreidieh, John Labib, and Reem Sawan, thank you for believing in me and for sustaining me.

A special shout out to Cat Villiers who phoned me every morning to make sure that I was writing, and to James Viggers, who forced me out of my shell, to breathe in that toxic air from time to time. Special props to João Mota for translating these ideas into the bold document that you hold in your hand. Cheers to Keith Fox for thinking strategically about the book's place within Phaidon's catalog and to Deborah Aaronson for being accommodating with the publication's schedule and oversight, of course.

This book is dedicated to my family, all of whom are adopted, the people who found me. Frank, for being a loving partner; Sofia, for always being the calming sibling when I need one; Blake Karim, for sharing a body with me; Hrair and Eline, for making a home for me. And to our children, to whom this book is dedicated.

About the Author

Dr. Omar Kholeif is an author, curator, broadcaster, and the avatar of Dr. O—a polymath who lives in the metaverse. A leading commentator on art and digital culture, Kholeif is the author of dozens of books, curator of over sixty exhibitions, and founder of www.artpost21.com, which supports art and social justice in the age of the "meta" metaverse. They are the Director of Collections and Senior Curator at Sharjah Art Foundation, UAE.

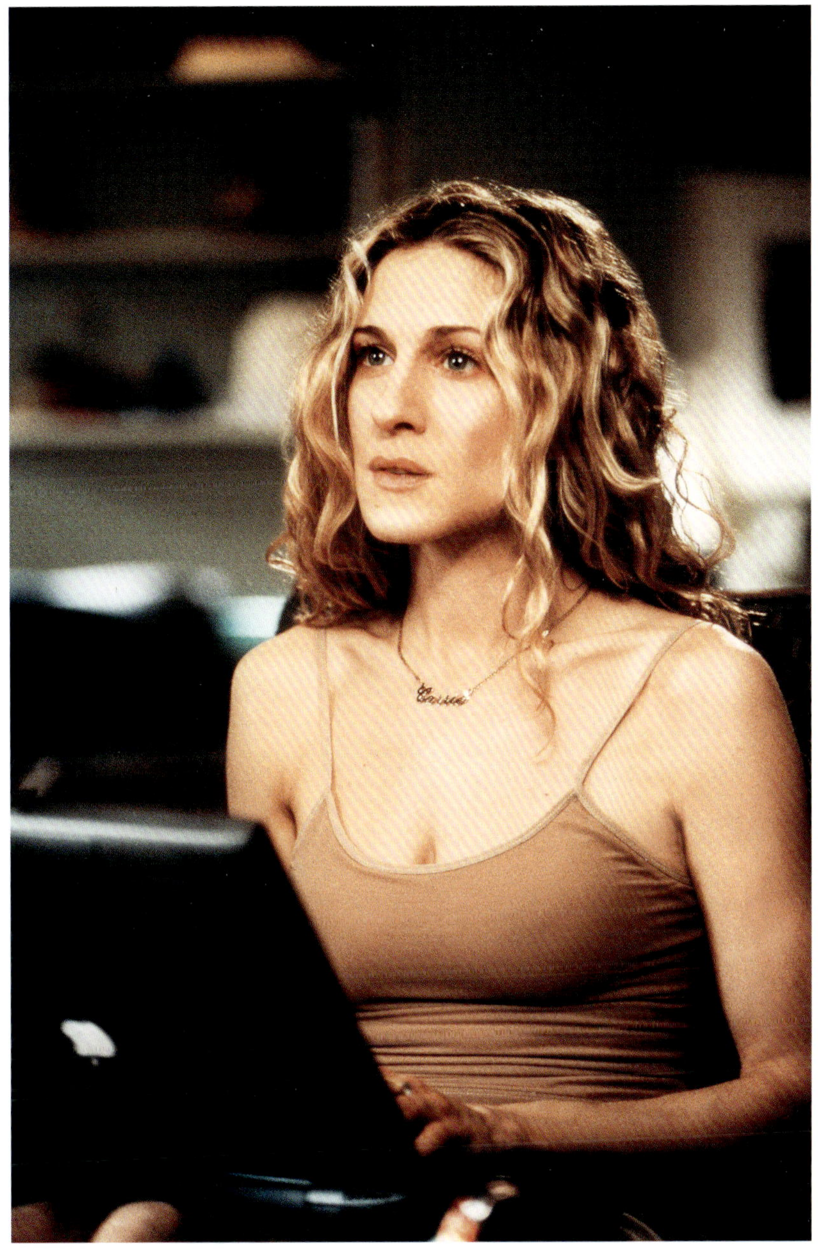

Sarah Jessica Parker as Carrie Bradshaw in
Sex and The City, 1998–2004

Publisher's Acknowledgments

The publisher would like to extend special thanks to Deborah Aaronson, Theresa Bebbington, Sarah Bell, James Brown, Keith Fox, Christopher Lacy, Melissa Larner, Catherine Meagher, Kendra H. Millis, Violeta Mitrova, João Mota, Elizabeth O'Rourke, Bav Shah, and Jonathan Whale for their many contributions to the book.

Phaidon Press Limited
2 Cooperage Yard
London E15 2QR

Phaidon Press Inc.
65 Bleecker Street
New York, NY 10012

phaidon.com

First published 2023

ISBN 978 1 83866 407 7

A CIP catalogue record for this book is available from the British Library and the Library of Congress.

Commissioning Editor__Rebecca Morrill
Project Editor__Maia Murphy
Production Controller__Rebecca Price
Design__João Mota
Typesetting__Cantina

Printed in Italy